Revolution
and Intervention
in Central America

The determinant factor has been the reorganization of the insurgent forces in Central America . . . and their ability to operate in the midst of counterinsurgency. In fact, they have turned the exploitative and repressive nature of the regime into a legitimation of their struggle in the eyes of the people and the world.

Ruy Mauro Marini
"The Nicaraguan Revolution and the Central American Revolutionary Process"

CONTEMPORARY MARXISM SERIES

Revolution and Intervention in Central America

Edited by
MARLENE DIXON and SUSANNE JONAS

SYNTHESIS PUBLICATIONS
San Francisco

CONTEMPORARY MARXISM SERIES

Series Editor: Marlene Dixon
Volume Editors: Marlene Dixon and Susanne Jonas

Editorial Assistance: John Horton, Elizabeth Sutherland Martínez, Ed McCaughan, Olga Talamante

Translations by: Peter Baird, Chile Resource Center and Clearing House, Suzie Dod, Tessa Koning Martínez, Ed McCaughan, Gerardo Ramos, Rini Templeton.

Translation Assistance: Pat McCloskey, Manuel Moreno, Oscar and Rebecca Schwaner.

Cover graphic: Mourners under attack at the funeral mass in San Salvador for Archbishop Romero, who was assassinated on March 24, 1980. Many were killed or wounded. The photographer's name has been withheld by request.

The Contemporary Marxism Series consists of book editions of *Contemporary Marxism*, a journal of the Institute for the Study of Militarism and Economic Crisis, San Francisco. This volume, now expanded and updated, includes material from *Contemporary Marxism* No. 3, 1981.

Excerpts from "The Iron Triangle: The Honduran Connection" by Philip E. Wheaton are reprinted by permission of Philip E. Wheaton and EPICA.

"The New Cold War and the Nicaraguan Revolution" is a revised version of an article from *Nicaragua in Revolution*, edited by Thomas W. Walker, published by Praeger Publishers in November 1981, and printed here by permission of the publishers.

Synthesis Publications, 2703 Folsom St., San Francisco, California 94110.

Library of Congress Cataloging in Publication Data
Main entry under title:
Revolution and intervention in Central America.

    (Contemporary Marxism series)
    Includes bibliographical references and index.
    1. Central America—Politics and government—1979- —Addresses, essays, lectures. 2. Central America—Foreign relations—United States—Addresses, essays, lectures. 3. United States—Foreign relations—Central America—Addresses, essays, lectures. 4. Revolutions—Central America—Addresses, essays, lectures. I. Dixon, Marlene, 1936- II. Jonas, Susanne Leilani. III. Series.
F1439.5.R48   1983   972.8'052   83-5068
ISBN 0-89935-029-1 (cloth); ISBN 0-89935-027-5 (paper)

Contents

Documents from Guatemala

Guerrilla Army of the Poor (EGP)

PART 2   U.S. STRATEGIES FOR COUNTERREVOLUTION

Foreword

This volume of the *Contemporary Marxism* series is a child of
anguish: the anguish of the tormented and brutalized peoples of Central
America, and most especially, and tragically, the insurgent peoples of El
Salvador and Guatemala. It is also a child of the anguish that we, as
citizens of this damned imperium, feel as acts of the most savage
barbarity are justified by the obscene lie that "freedom" and "democracy" are the holy causes of American corporate capitalism; as the U.S.
government seeks to destabilize and destroy the revolution in Nicaragua
which has transformed that society and brought new hope to humanity
around the world. There are not words to express the rage and outrage
that we feel. So we must call upon every person of conscience in this
country to unite and to fight against the continuation and escalation of
the butchery, torture and aggression which have become the unashamed
policy of the Reagan Administration. Above all the American people
must demand a policy of nonintervention. Let there never be another
Vietnam!

There were those Liberals in the United States who thought that a
Republican Administration would be more moderate in foreign policy
than the Democrats. The Liberals were wrong, they did not perceive
that the forces of reaction in the United States were growing with
malignant intelligence, that the collapse and impotence of the Democrats
and of New Deal liberalism put no brake, no restraint, upon what is
transparently a government of the right wing of the domestic corporate
ruling class. Yet, it does not rule alone, that is also clear. In the United
States we have at last a government that is direct rule by capital,
a United Front of capital no longer hampered by the populism of a
failing Democratic Party.

So it has come to pass that the outward face of the United States,
the face of the imperialists, the face of CIA, Special Forces, the face of
transnational capital, that face has now turned inward to confront the
masses of the people of the United States. It is the *implosion* of Empire,
it is the very beginning of an era in which the people of the United
States will begin to see the democratic veils stripped away from the face
of American power, they will begin to experience what has been the
fate of the colony. It seems to me that the people of the United States
have fulfilled a prophecy: First they came for the communists, but I
was not a communist so I did not protest; then they came for the Jews,

but I was not a Jew so I did not protest; then they came for the Catholics, but I was not a Catholic so I did not protest; and then they came for me, and there was no one left to protest.

Thus, when the Editors of the journal *Contemporary Marxism* sent out a call for an "emergency issue" (the origin of this book), it was not only the emergencies in El Salvador and Nicaragua or the terror in Guatemala that demanded a response. It was also the emergency within the United States, as the present government moves ever more swiftly to policies of domestic as well as international repression; of domestic war against labor as well as international war against workers' movements; of the destruction of domestic civil liberties as well as those in Central America. In this period in our history (as it was in the 1960's and the Vietnam War) every protest, every act of resistance against war and imperialism abroad is simultaneously a protest and an act of resistance against the domestic expression of repression and reaction. The United States since World War II has been Janus-headed: one dark, violent, brutal and murderous face to the world; one smiling, liberal, just, generous and white beaming over the millions at home. It was the spoils of Empire that allowed the white liberal face of paternalism to shine down on us. Now, transnational power is no longer nationally dependent, it no longer needs industrial peace at home, it can no longer indulge the working classes of its old home base. And so it turns against its once favored children its true face, its real nature, and implodes upon us. How long before we are forced to accept in our millions this changed circumstance? If too long, then it will be too late.

It is our hope that this book will contribute to the moving of our own people to understanding that no nation is an island, no nation stands alone; if you ask for whom the bell tolls, it tolls for thee. Every blow struck within this country to defend the rights of the peoples of the world, and most especially our brothers and sisters in the forefront of the struggle in Central America, is a blow struck for ourselves. We are one world, and one people, one humanity, as never before.

Marlene Dixon
July 1983

An Overview:
50 Years of Revolution and
Intervention in Central America

Susanne Jonas

For most Americans, Nicaragua, El Salvador, Guatemala were unfamiliar names, and the struggles of many decades in Central America were almost unknown until the victory of the Nicaraguan Frente Sandinista de Liberación Nacional in July 1979. Since that time, the revolution in Nicaragua and the revolutionary movements in El Salvador and Guatemala have become front-page news. In fact, however, revolutionary struggles in Central America, and U.S. interventions to stop these, date back to the 1930's.

We present here a preliminary effort to recast the history of the last 50 years of class struggle between the U.S. ruling class and the people of Central America (principally Guatemala, Nicaragua and El Salvador). Our objective is to analyze the most significant conjunctures in this struggle—but, beyond that, to understand Central American political movements and U.S. policies in relation to the great *structural* transformations in the capitalist world-economy and in the world balance of forces. Thus, we shall attempt to take into account the following general considerations:

1) Anti-imperialist struggle is always conditioned by continuing class struggle, within Central America and within the United States. A class analysis necessarily goes beyond simple anti-imperialist formulations and raises deeper questions for the workers' movement in the U.S. as well as in Central America.

2) U.S. actions in Central America are always conditioned by the world balance of power between the capitalist West and the socialist bloc, by its manifestations in Cold War or detente, and by the rise and decline of U.S. hegemony.

3) Underlying particular changes in the U.S. and Central America is a substructure of movements, disruptions and adjustments in the international or *transnational* capitalist economy. Over the past 50 years

we have witnessed profound shifts in that substructure. For one thing, the worldwide capitalist crisis is giving rise to a restructured international division of labor. Of equal significance, the world is itself becoming more transnational: capital has become more transnational in its operations; and the arena of struggle between capital and the exploited has been globalized.

4) As a consequence of the above, it is no longer possible to view Central America simply in terms of U.S. "national interests"; transnational capital is able to operate independently, although in coordination with the U.S. government.

5) As another consequence, U.S. policies toward Central America at a given moment cannot be reduced to simple voluntary desires on the part of one or another Administration. The great shifts in U.S. policy have been, by and large, *bipartisan* expressions of a ruling class response to changing conditions. To be sure, there are different fractions of the U.S. ruling class whose particular interests differ in particular situations; but *over time*, U.S. policies reflect *class interests* of the U.S. ruling class as a whole.

6) Because of the changes in the world economy, the interrelation between the workers' movement in the U.S. and the struggles in Central America is not simply a question of moral support by the former for the latter, but is grounded in objective historical and economic factors.

I. Sandino, Somoza and the U.S. Marines

Since the era of the Monroe Doctrine and increasingly toward the end of the 19th century, the U.S. government and U.S. capitalist interests had regarded Central America as the "backyard" of the United States—a place to be exploited economically and in which the U.S. government had the right to intervene politically and even to send military forces. U.S. intervention during the first part of the 20th century was a matter of defending "U.S. interests," i.e., the property and profits of U.S. corporations and banks. The early 20th century also saw the establishment of clear U.S. hegemony in the region, as previously significant European interests were forced out, particularly after World War I.

The clearest example of old-style U.S. intervention occurred in Nicaragua. In 1909 the U.S. government dealt with a challenge to U.S. banking interests by establishing a pro-U.S. regime and appointing representatives to collect and retain customs revenues—in effect putting the Nicaraguan economy into receivership. "Internal disturbances" were suppressed by a 2700-man Marine force, which remained in Nicaragua from 1912 to 1925.

Barely two years after their withdrawal, the U.S. Marines were sent back to Nicaragua, and remained there to put down an uprising led by Augusto César Sandino. Many U.S. analysts have referred to this guerrilla uprising and the U.S. efforts to smash it as the "first Vietnam" of the U.S., the first major counterinsurgency effort in Latin America. The uprising led by Sandino was first and foremost nationalist and anti-imperialist in character; although not a communist, Sandino clearly understood the class content of the struggle—as reflected in the organization of his popular army and its base among workers and peasants. Moreover, although the goals were not explicitly socialist, the U.S. was intervening to preserve, and Sandino was fighting to overthrow, the rule of the Nicaraguan oligarchy, class rule.

The U.S. government was unable to win this war, politically or militarily, through its direct military intervention, and also faced serious opposition to the war from within the United States and internationally. The U.S. working class and its political organizations, led by the Communist Party, far from seeing this as any defense of legitimate U.S. interests, voiced strong opposition to direct U.S. military intervention. Simultaneously they were demanding that the U.S. government take action to resolve the problems of unemployment and depression at home. It is significant that New Deal President Franklin Delano Roosevelt, while attempting to find patchwork reforms to the problems of capitalism in order to maintain industrial peace and mute the class struggle within the U.S., essentially continued the foreign policy of his Republican predecessors in Central America, intervening to stamp out revolutionary movements there.

Once the winning of an outright U.S. military victory in Nicaragua became impossible, U.S. strategy focused on the training and building of a Nicaraguan occupation force—the National Guard. By maintaining control over the National Guard, the U.S. would be able to play indirectly an interventionist role it could not play directly. In addition the U.S. directly chose Anastasio Somoza to run the National Guard; thus the Somoza dictatorship was born as an instrument of U.S. counterinsurgency, ruling Nicaragua from the 1930's until the victory of the Frente Sandinista in 1979. It was Somoza who arranged the assassination of Sandino in 1934, and his National Guard that "pacified" the popular movement; it was the U.S. government which kept both in power for the next 45 years.

This sordid episode in the history of the Americas raises an obvious question: how could the great reformer of capitalism within the U.S., President Roosevelt, be responsible for creating the Somoza dictatorship in Nicaragua? (Indeed, Roosevelt is well known to have said of Somoza, "He may be a son of a bitch, but he's our son of a bitch.") Somoza's Nicaragua came under direct U.S. control: this arrangement was as close as the U.S. has come to 19th century-style colonialism.

This was an era of national U.S. imperialism on the ascent (despite the world capitalist crisis and Depression), no longer seriously challenged by competing European interests in Central America, and not yet challenged by a socialist bloc. (The Soviet Union and the Comintern supported Third World movements such as that of Sandino in Nicaragua, but such support was always secondary to the primary goal of assuring the survival of socialism in the Soviet Union— which at that time, in the 1930's, faced the threat of rising fascism in Europe.) Roosevelt was later willing to form a wartime alliance with the Soviet Union, but Central America remained the preserve of U.S. imperialism, politically, militarily and economically. In a sense, the Pax Americana that produced the Somoza dictatorship in Nicaragua was as much a part of the New Deal for U.S. capitalism as Keynesian "solutions" within the United States.

II. Guatemala, 1954: "The Democracy Which Gave Way"

The years of ferment and revolutionary struggle in the early 1930's—in El Salvador as well as Nicaragua—were followed by the reconsolidation of military dictatorships throughout the Central American region. The next serious challenge to the status quo and to U.S. hegemony came in Guatemala in 1944, at the close of World War II, when a reformist movement overthrew the ruling military dictatorship. Under the two governments of the "Guatemalan Revolution" from 1944 to 1954 (Juan José Arévalo, 1945-50; Jacobo Arbenz, 1951-54), Guatemala began a profound national capitalist transformation. The Guatemalan Revolution was not communist, or even socialist, but progressive, nationalist and bourgeois democratic in nature. Its aims were to permit the development of a modern capitalist economy based on land reform, and to challenge U.S. economic domination openly.

Under the Arévalo government, the Guatemalan people got their first taste of democratic freedoms and social welfare programs. Most important for a population that had never before been protected by labor laws was the right to organize in labor unions and to strike. After 1951, President Arbenz, a progressive army officer, took measures to modernize the economy and to break the stranglehold of the huge U.S. monopolies with investments in Guatemala. Most important, in 1952, the Arbenz government passed an agrarian reform law, under which large estates of unused land were expropriated (and paid for) and redistributed to 100,000 peasant families within two years. The purpose of the law—a capitalist measure—was not to destroy individual ownership, but to distribute the land to *more* individual owners. Nevertheless, the big landowners opposed it violently—not only because it restricted their privileges, but also because it was administered by committees run largely by the peasants themselves.

The climax of the growing confrontation between the Arbenz government and U.S. interests came with the expropriation of some of the land owned by the United Fruit Company, the largest landowner in Guatemala, which had large areas of unused land. Actually, ever since Arévalo and Arbenz came to power, monopolistic corporate interests in the U.S. had mounted a propaganda campaign, accusing them of having "Communist tendencies." The nationalization of some of United Fruit Company's lands was the last straw. United Fruit mobilized all its friends in the State Department and the CIA (e.g., the Dulles brothers), and in Congress and the U.S. press to demand action. And the CIA and the State Department began to act. Their excuse for intervening in 1954 was that Guatemala had received a shipment of arms from Czechoslovakia; but in fact, Washington officials had been plotting against Arbenz since late 1952.

The CIA had trained a group of right-wing Guatemalan exiles living in other Central American countries, led by Col. Carlos Castillo Armas, to "invade" Guatemala, so that it would look like a civil war among Guatemalans. Meanwhile, the CIA prepared the Guatemalan population through psychological warfare (secret radio broadcasts, etc.), and attempted to get key Guatemalan army officers to go along with the invasion. The CIA also prepared to back up the ground invasion through aerial bombing of Guatemala City, to force Arbenz to resign. And finally, in March 1954, in the Organization of American States, the State Department (by threatening to cut off economic aid) pressured the Latin American governments to pass an anticommunist resolution directed against Guatemala; subsequently, Washington maneuvered to deny Guatemala its rights in the United Nations.

When it was put into effect in June 1954, the plan worked. Castillo Armas' small "invasion army" never fought a battle, but the bombing of Guatemala City was more effective. And the efforts of the U.S. to turn Guatemalan army officers against Arbenz also paid off: at the crucial moment, Arbenz's top advisers deserted him, convincing him to resign. Another strong ally was the Church in Guatemala, which helped whip up the anticommunist furor. Meanwhile, all over the country, workers and peasants who had benefited from the Revolution clamored for arms to defend the Arbenz government; but Arbenz and his military advisers did not arm them. Without arms, the resistance by worker and peasant militias failed.

Once Arbenz had been overthrown, the government of CIA protégé Castillo Armas, supported by the U.S., moved immediately to reverse the progress made during 10 years of the Revolution. It began with a suspension of all constitutional guarantees and a sweeping witch hunt against political and labor leaders. Thousands of workers and peasants were jailed, tortured, exiled or killed. The political parties supporting Arbenz were dissolved, and the labor unions were disbanded. Teachers were fired, books were burned. All of the progressive laws of the Revolutionary era—the land reform, the nationalistic laws regulating foreign investors, the labor code—were wiped off the books. All of the land distributed to the peasants under Arbenz was returned to its former owners. The doors of the country were opened wide to

U.S. private investors. Although anticommunists refer to the 1954 intervention as the "Liberation," in fact it has brought nothing but misery and repression to the Guatemalan people.

Why was the U.S. unable to tolerate the national capitalist policies of the Revolution? There were several reasons, both economic and ideological. First, the national capitalist Arbenz government regulated existing U.S. interests there and threatened future prospects for maintaining the area as a "safe" preserve for U.S. investments. In the postwar era of expansion, U.S. investors could not afford to rely on an unpredictable national bourgeoisie led by a nationalist like Arbenz. Having rid Guatemala of rival European interests during World War II, and having consolidated Guatemala within its sphere as a market for capital and commodity exports and a source of raw materials, the U.S. was not about to let go easily—particularly since the expanding monopolistic corporations like United Fruit Co. were well represented in Washington. Behind "anticommunism" as the motivation, then, lay opposition to *any* regime which might make trouble for U.S. capital.

Second, and related, U.S. private investors and the U.S. government became concerned over the increasing radicalization of the Guatemalan Revolution under Arbenz. Throughout these 10 years, the Revolution was principally directed by the Guatemalan national bourgeoisie and petty bourgeoisie, in alliance with sectors of the working class and peasants. Particularly after the land reform of 1952, the working class and peasants became more important in this alliance, and the degree of mass mobilization and worker organization increased greatly. In land invasions, for example, the peasants began to take initiatives, without waiting for permission from the government. From the point of view of the U.S. government, the situation could well get "out of control." Third, the Arbenz government refused to submit blindly to the dictates of Washington in foreign policy—an unpardonable sin in the 1950's, at the height of the Cold War.

Finally, and no less important, the U.S. was afraid that the Guatemalan Revolution would spread. Clearly, the McCarthyite visions of the Kremlin using Guatemala as a "base" spreading communism in the hemisphere were paranoid and unfounded. But at a less obvious level, the Guatemalan Revolution *was* serving as an example to progressive and democratic forces in other Latin American countries.

Faced with a real challenge to its hegemony in the Western Hemisphere, the U.S. government made Guatemala a test case for its Cold War strategy of containing liberation movements and a model for reversing the process of social revolution in Latin America. With its 1944-1954 Revolution, Guatemala provoked the first modern U.S. intervention in Latin America, the first achieved *without* sending the Marines.

The immediate success of the operation in Guatemala was not lost on U.S. policymakers, when faced with subsequent challenges. For the Bay of Pigs invasion against Cuba in 1961, the CIA even called on many of the same officials who had planned and carried out the Guatemala operation. And 19 years later, in 1973, U.S. planning for the coup against Allende in Chile followed the Guatemala model in many respects (e.g., mobilizing middle class anticommunism, cultivating key officers in the armed forces to turn against the progressive government, etc.).

The U.S. intervention in Guatemala represented a united policy, a consensus, of the U.S. ruling class as a whole. Serious planning for an intervention was begun by top advisers in the Truman Administration; the final execution was carried out by the Eisenhower Administration. In the words of Truman adviser Adolf Berle, "The U.S. cannot tolerate a Kremlin-controlled communist government in this hemisphere." This was the attitude taken by the entire ruling class. The only disagreements were *tactical*—how to overthrow Arbenz, and whom to bring in as his replacement.

Ultimately the U.S. intervention in Guatemala can only be understood in the larger framework of the Cold War; it was the first application in Latin America of a Cold War policy which had its initial expression in Greece. The Cold War had roots both inside the United States and abroad. In a nutshell, it meant that, in the period following World War II, the U.S. ruling class was consolidating its power and U.S. capital was expanding worldwide on an unprecedented scale, seeking hegemony over the capitalist world-economy. The Cold War was *not* a result of Soviet ambitions for world power (the Soviets had all they could manage just to survive and rebuild after the devastation of World War II), but the result of ascendant U.S. imperialism.

The workers' movements both in the U.S. and abroad were a clear threat to this expansion, and therefore had to be brought under control. These threats were very real. Within the U.S., workers unleashed the biggest strike wave in U.S. history—4.6 million workers were out on strike in 1946 alone. The Communist Party was a very real threat, having tens of thousands of members, and the general respect of the population for the wartime role of the Soviet people and the communist anti-fascist resistance, and for the vast gains for the American working class that the CPUSA had been so critical in winning during the Great Depression.

Abroad, the U.S. was faced with workers' movements in many countries of Europe, Africa, Asia and Latin America, fighting to win their liberation, self-determination, democratic rights and control over their own governments. Many were fighting for socialism, and in most countries the most militant fighters were communists. These movements gained strength and support from the very existence of the Soviet Union. The U.S. government regarded the Soviet Union as its strategic enemy for this reason, and because the Soviet Union was the only nation that opposed U.S. expansion and military domination.

To combat these interrelated threats, the U.S. ruling class launched its Cold War policies in a six-month period in 1947:

—March 1947: the Truman Doctrine, to justify U.S. intervention in Greece;

—March 1947: the Federal Employee Loyalty Program, subjecting millions of U.S. citizens to loyalty-security checks;

—June 1947: the Marshall Plan, sending massive economic "aid" to the Western European capitalist countries (whose economies had been devastated by World War II) to protect U.S. investments and to "stop Communism" there;

—June 1947: the Taft-Hartley Act, designed to destroy the U.S. labor movement as an independent force, and to give employers a new club to be used against workers and unions;

—Also in 1947: the National Security Act, laying the bases for creation of the CIA.

Abroad, the 1947 intervention in Greece set the precedent for future interventions. The U.S. poured hundreds of millions of dollars into Greece to crush a revolutionary uprising militarily—leaving 50,000 people dead. The "Truman Doctrine" provided the justification, stating that "it must be the policy of the U.S. to support free peoples who are resisting attempted subjugation by armed minorities." The experience in Greece showed that with sufficient U.S. funds, even the most oppressive right-wing regimes could be legitimated and used to smash revolutionary movements in the name of anticommunism. This became the basis for every Cold War U.S. intervention since that time, including Vietnam.

In addition, the Truman Doctrine carried with it the threat of world war—including the use of the U.S. nuclear arsenal—and the determination of the U.S. to maintain hegemony over the Soviet Union. Thus, with the "Truman Doctrine," Truman and the U.S. ruling class rejected any possibility of continuing the World War II detente with the Soviet Union, as established by Roosevelt—just as domestically, they destroyed the progressive aspects of Roosevelt's New Deal. The hegemony of corporate interests was to be absolute.

Guatemala represented the application of the logic of the Truman Doctrine to Latin America,* reconfirmed by the success of the 1953 operation against Mossadegh in Iran. Thus, the U.S. intervention in Guatemala was part of the worldwide Cold War strategy of the U.S.

If we are to be concerned with the history of the class struggle involving the United States and Central America, however, we cannot leave this chapter in U.S. Cold War history without asking some difficult

---

* It is no coincidence that when the Eisenhower Administration was preparing to intervene in Guatemala, it assigned as the new U.S. Ambassador John Peurifoy—the man who had been sent to Greece in 1950 to "clean up" the situation after the U.S. intervention, and to make Greece "safe for democracy."

questions: 1) Why was the Guatemalan Revolution so vulnerable to U.S. intervention? 2) Why was there so little outcry from the working class and progressive movements in the United States? 3) Why was there virtually no opposition to the U.S. intervention from the socialist world?

1) Why was the Guatemalan Revolution so vulnerable to U.S. intervention? The obvious reason was the overwhelming power the U.S. brought to bear against it. More fundamentally, however, the Revolution was incomplete, and the U.S. and the Guatemalan right were able to take advantage of its internal weaknesses.

To reverse a heritage of more than 400 years of dependent capitalism and underdevelopment within 10 years—particularly during 10 years of active worldwide expansion by U.S. capital—was, to be sure, a monumental task. Nevertheless, Cuba, faced with similar obstacles, learning from the Guatemalan experience, came much closer to breaking the heritage of underdevelopment in the first 10 years of its Revolution. The Guatemalan Revolutionary governments made no break from the economy of mono-export (coffee alone was 80% of all exports in 1952) nor from the economic grip of the U.S. in regard to trade. They failed to alter Guatemala's fundamental relation to the capitalist world market and to the U.S. because their goal was not to eliminate but to modernize capitalist structures; and in a country where underdevelopment was the legacy of 400 years of integration into the international capitalist system, capitalism was *necessarily* dependent.

These shortcomings were related to the class base of the Revolution. The "modern" bourgeoisie created by the Revolution—the new cotton, banking and industrial bourgeoisie—was more concerned with its own economic advance than with national development.

Similarly, a sizable portion of the urban petty bourgeoisie—initial supporters of the Revolution—eventually collaborated with or acquiesced in its destruction. Their alienation from the revolutionary process was not, as is often said, because Arbenz "betrayed" it, but because they never wanted a real revolution to begin with. Having made a break with the old bourgeoisie in 1944, these groups needed popular support to come to power, and thus allied themselves with the workers and other popular sectors. Nevertheless, as a class, their primary interest lay in consolidating their own power and in promoting their own careers through the Revolution. They were ambivalent about any alliance which might give the workers and peasants an independent power base. After the peasants began taking initiatives, they became skeptical of the agrarian reform; the proposal to arm the people also frightened them, particularly the military. Thus, with the fall of the Revolution, although an important minority of the petty bourgeoisie had been radicalized by contact with the masses and continued to struggle after 1954, the majority were easily incorporated into the Counterrevolution.

Arbenz's own vacillation and precipitous resignation in the face of the U.S.-organized invasion—and his ultimate reliance on his military colleagues rather than on the people—epitomized the incapacity of an entire *class* to lead the struggle against underdevelopment and imperialism. The U.S. and the Guatemalan right were able to take advantage of this internal contradiction.

A final weakness of the Guatemalan Revolution was the insufficient development of the popular forces. Without question, the Revolution brought real gains to the proletariat and peasants. Under Arbenz the labor and peasant movements even achieved a certain measure of influence. But the union leadership was largely petty bourgeois, and the principal political parties (with the exception of the PGT, the Communist Party) were not working class parties. Given the near absence of worker organization prior to 1944, 10 years were insufficient to permit the development of popular and working class organizations strong enough to withstand the unified attack by the Guatemalan right and the U.S.

Despite these weaknesses, and despite the failure to incorporate certain sectors of the population (e.g., Indians, women), the experience of the Revolution did leave a permanent mark on the Guatemalan consciousness. The climate of reform from 1944 to 1954 permitted a mass mobilization whose legacy has become clear in the rapid intensification of the class struggle since 1954, and the stark polarization between revolutionary and counterrevolutionary forces. Moreover, the experience of the Guatemalan Revolution was important to others in Latin America. A few years later, the Cuban revolutionaries were determined not to permit "another Guatemala" in Cuba. Che Guevara, who had come to Guatemala during the Revolution and was there during the overthrow of Arbenz, paid tribute to the lessons learned from Guatemala:

> . . . We should also like to express our gratitude to [Arbenz] and to the democracy which gave way, for the example they gave us and for the accurate estimate they enabled us to make of the weaknesses which that government was unable to overcome.

2) Why was there no significant protest from within the United States against the blatant U.S. intervention in Guatemala? It is too simple to conclude from lack of protest that the majority of Americans actively supported the intervention. In fact, there is ample evidence from public opinion polls that the American people after World War II did not want militarism, Cold War or any war with the Soviet Union. Popular opposition to postwar U.S. interventions abroad, dating back to the Truman intervention in Greece, was eventually silenced only by the fiercest, most manipulative propaganda campaign waged by Truman and his successors. The so-called "Cold War consensus" within the U.S.

was achieved only by a concerted effort on the part of the U.S. ruling class, to push the Big Lie that communism was the same as fascism — and to stifle foreign policy critics as well as working class organizations in domestic affairs. Essential to this effort were the powerful lobby groups such as the Committee on the Present Danger (supposedly outside, but actually linked to, the government) which literally bombarded the public and Congress in order to create the climate of support for the Cold War.* In the case of Guatemala, a carefully orchestrated pro-intervention campaign in the major media and Congress was waged by lobbyists ranging from United Fruit Co. public relations operatives to Cold War "liberals" with financial and political ties to the CIA.

Furthermore, the lack of a sizable protest movement against U.S. Cold War foreign policies by 1954 was the result of the emasculation or destruction of the organizations of the U.S. working class: the unions and the Communist Party. In regard to the unions, the Taft-Hartley Act consolidated the process begun under the New Deal of placing the unions under class collaborationist leadership. While the New Deal tamed the labor movement, the postwar offensive by capital utterly destroyed any independent power of rank-and-file democracy within the unions through an anticommunist purge of the most militant leaders and members, and through Taft-Hartley's union-smashing provisions. The result was the coronation of class collaborationist, anti-democratic, ideologically anticommunist official leadership. In the name of (*but without the consent of*) the rank-and-file, this leadership collaborated with the U.S. bourgeoisie and its CIA in subverting militant labor movements in Europe, Latin America and many other parts of the world after 1947. In the case of the Guatemalan Revolution, the AFL leadership went on record as supporting ("rejoicing in") the overthrow of Arbenz, and the CIO publicly attacked "Communism" in Guatemala. Labor rank-and-file had no means by which to counter the official anticommunism of the leadership; and this contributed to general public acquiescence in the intervention.

Given this situation with labor, the only organization that would have been capable of mounting a real opposition was the Communist Party. But the CPUSA was greatly weakened, as a direct result of the anticommunist campaigns and purges undertaken by Truman and the "liberals" of the late 1940's. These "liberal" Red-hunters expressed virtually nothing but support for the intervention in Guatemala. The Communist Party, in turn, was by 1954 too preoccupied with defending itself and its cadre from institutionalized McCarthyism to launch any real anti-interventionist movement — although the CPUSA did oppose

* On these crucial points, see Lawrence Wittner, *Cold War America* (New York, Praeger, 1974), Athan Theoharis, *Seeds of Repression* (Chicago, Quadrangle, 1951), and Jerry Sanders, "Shaping the Cold War Consensus" *Berkeley Journal of Sociology* XXV (1980).

the Guatemala intervention in its publications, etc. Thus, significant domestic opposition to the U.S. intervention in Guatemala was precluded by the anticommunist campaigns generally called McCarthyism (which really originated with Truman, with the support of "liberals" as far "left" as Americans for Democratic Action)—precluded, that is, by the ruling class offensive which had in effect destroyed working class organizations within the U.S.

5) Why was there virtually no opposition to the U.S. intervention in Guatemala from the socialist world? This intervention occurred at the height of the Cold War between the U.S. and the Soviet Union. The world at that time was bipolar, divided into two great camps. In addition, this was the era of unchallenged U.S. hegemony in the Western capitalist world. The Soviet Union and its allies basically accepted the fact that Central America was part of the sphere of U.S. domination. Given the fact that the Soviet Union has since World War II seen its national interests in terms of detente, the preservation of peace and the avoidance of a war with the U.S., Guatemala was not strategic enough to the Soviet Union to risk a major confrontation with the U.S. at a time when there were risks of war in other areas. These considerations gave the U.S. virtual freedom of action to smash the Guatemalan Revolution.

III. A "Reformist" Option—The Central American Common Market

Once having intervened in Guatemala, the U.S. government had to make its counterrevolution "work." This meant pouring in massive amounts of U.S. aid in order to stabilize the return to the old order in Guatemala, and in order to make Guatemala a "showcase for democracy." It also meant that the U.S. was committed to a continuing and long-range intervention in Guatemalan political life in order to keep down popular movements and shore up a pro-U.S. bourgeoisie in power.

By the end of the 1950's it became clear that simply overwhelming Guatemala with U.S. economic aid and political control would not work. After the initial shock of the "Liberation" wore off, and Guatemalan political life began to return to normal, political unrest increased, particularly among students and workers, and paved the way for the rise of an armed guerrilla movement by 1962.

Nor was Guatemala the only trouble spot. In neighboring El Salvador, a long-standing "overpopulation" and unemployment problem was becoming a clear threat to stability. It was this same problem which had led to class-based insurgency in El Salvador in the early 1930's, when the world capitalist crisis intensified unemployment and misery. The fledgling Salvadorean Communist Party, founded in 1930, had organized and led a mobilization of workers and peasants which culminated in the uprising of January 1932. Even with the arrest of Farabundo

Martí, who had led the mobilization, thousands of peasants and farm workers marched, virtually unarmed, on the cities and occupied government offices. The revolt was brutally crushed by the army, with casualties initially of 4,000, and in the massacre that followed, of 30,000 — 4% of the entire population. Given this history in El Salvador and the worsening of social conditions since the 1930's, it is not surprising that by the late 1950's U.S. officials were worried about instability in the region.

A final factor was the Cuban Revolution in 1959 — an object lesson to Washington of the effects of not addressing the problems of an underdeveloped country ruled by a dictatorship on behalf of U.S. corporate interests. Moreover, the victory of the Cuban Revolution provided an example to all of Latin America that the people could take history into their own hands and alter an intolerable situation.

For these reasons, among others, U.S. officials recognized the need for a structurally different approach in Central America, and in Latin America generally. Toward the end of the Eisenhower Administration and with the advent of the Kennedy Administration, U.S. policy toward Latin America underwent a basic alteration. The most concrete expression of this shift, which began as early as 1958, was the Alliance for Progress, formally adopted in 1961. The bases of the Alliance for Progress strategy were the following:

1) U.S. policymakers realized that, in order to prevent more revolutions like the Cuban Revolution, some basic reforms would have to be made — reforms designed to alleviate the extreme misery of the majority of the Latin American people and to redistribute income. Thus, initially, Alliance for Progress rhetoric supported structural (redistributive) tax and land reforms.

Modifying its monolithic Cold War policies of the 1950's, the U.S. also recognized that the main challenge to U.S. interests in Latin America came not from "International Communism" but from class struggle within Latin America, the "internal Communist threat." This threat was seen as particularly serious in Central America, the gateway to the Panama Canal. As ultimate insurance against revolutions, the U.S. embarked simultaneously on a systematic counterinsurgency campaign; in fact, the counterinsurgency "stick" was seen as the logical and necessary complement to the "carrot" of Alliance for Progress reforms.

2) There was also an economic consideration: the U.S. commitment to maintaining Latin America as a preserve for investment by giant U.S.-based transnational corporations.* These corporations were interested in making new investments in Latin America, *not* in extractive

---

* We use the term "transnational corporations" to refer to the process by which, after World War II, the largest monopoly corporations have over time restructured their domestic and overseas operations to become increasingly independent of any one national economy or government. Increasingly they are governed from the

mining and agriculture, which used Latin America as a base for export operations, but in manufacturing enterprises aimed at the consumer markets *in* the Latin American countries. To assure their own further expansion, then, at least in theory, these corporations required reforms which would raise living standards and turn Latin America's impoverished millions into consumers of their products. Increased private investment was also supposed to be the principal means of creating new jobs. Finally, the stabilizing influence of reforms was supposed to make Latin America a more "attractive" arena for corporate investors.

In practice, the U.S. did not and could not live up to its supposed commitment to structural reforms because it was unwilling to abandon its alliance with the Latin American bourgeoisie. To the extent that the U.S. government changed allies in Latin America, it merely shifted from the traditional landowning bourgeoisie to a newer industrial bourgeoisie which functioned as a kind of junior partner to the transnational corporations. The primary goal was "economic growth"; income redistribution would come as a secondary "trickle-down" effect. As we shall see, this approach (which derived its academic justification from "developmentalist" and "modernization" theories) created a fundamental contradiction with the reformist rhetoric of the Alliance for Progress.

For Central America these general shifts took a special form. After their unsuccessful attempt to prop up the Guatemalan economy in 1954-57, U.S. officials recognized that the economy could not continue to depend totally on coffee exports; the obvious alternative approach was to encourage "import-substituting industrialization." But industrialization could not be carried out in a market as small as Guatemala's, particularly since most Guatemalans were too poor to consume manufactured goods; the only solution was to combine Guatemala's market with those of the other Central American countries in a Central American Common Market.

Moreover, domestic reforms in Central America were not sufficient to create investment opportunities worthwhile to transnational corporations; it was necessary, in addition, to combine the national markets of the Central American countries. In fact, ultimately economic integration became the most practicable strategy because it permitted expansion of the market *without* really necessitating far-reaching social reforms in each country.

Moreover, the Central American governments were too weak to control unrest and class conflict individually. By the early 1960's U.S. officials were particularly worried about social pressures in Guatemala and El Salvador which would make those countries susceptible to

point of view of the corporate entity, not of any one nation. This is in distinction to (and a further development of) "multinational corporations," whose overseas profits are repatriated to the home base office, but which remain tied to the national economy and government of the home country (in this case, the U.S.).

"Communist influence" (i.e., susceptible to destabilization caused by exploitation by foreign capital). It was hoped that the regional framework could function as a safety valve for the existing system and could postpone at least the most dangerous manifestations of the basic socioeconomic problems.

In theory, then, the U.S. was committed to pursuing a relatively reformist strategy in Central America, compatible with corporate economic interests. But as soon as Washington began to put the strategy into practice, the contradictions emerged. These contradictions crystallized around a years-long rivalry with the United Nations Economic Commission for Latin America (CEPAL), which had been working closely with some groups of Central American businessmen on proposals for regional integration since the 1950's.

Beyond the competition for power and influence lay a profound philosophical/political dispute between the U.S. government and CEPAL. U.S. officials, who espoused free enterprise and free trade as absolute principles, regarded CEPAL's tenet that investment decisions should be based on planning as overly "statist," tending toward "socialism," hence dangerous. U.S. policy also reflected an aversion to the economic nationalism and protectionism (anti-free trade) inherent within CEPAL's formula for import-substitution.

Thus, from 1960 to the late 1960's, the U.S. subordinated the reformist component of its Central American integration strategy to the imposition of the U.S. integration model. Washington was able to accomplish this through the sheer weight of its financial resources, offering the Central American governments large aid loans on U.S. terms. These terms added up to absolute free trade, unrestricted operation of the "free market," and absolute freedom for foreign corporations investing in Central America.

The result of this approach was the total collapse of the Central American Common Market (CACM) institutionally in 1969. To summarize briefly: During the formative years of the CACM from 1960 to 1963, the U.S. exerted direct control, by penetrating the principal CACM institutions, and by intervening strategically in key decisions. In addition, the U.S. subsequently built a coalition with the most privileged sectors of the local bourgeoisie, which would promote U.S. interests, making overt U.S. intervention unnecessary.

Specifically, the U.S. threw its weight against a CEPAL-sponsored scheme to regulate large-scale industrial investment and achieve "balanced development" in Central America, on the grounds that *any* regulation was an interference in the freedom of a foreign corporation to make its investment decisions (where to locate, etc.). The result was a gross imbalance in industrial development among the Central American countries, putting the Guatemalan and Salvadorean bourgeoisies at a permanent advantage over those of the other countries.

Long-simmering resentments about this imbalance exploded in the so-called "soccer war" of 1969 between Honduras and El Salvador (sparked by Honduras' refusal to permit the Salvadorean ruling class to continue "solving" its unemployment and land concentration problems through massive migration of unemployed, landless Salvadoreans into Honduras). Honduras took the occasion of the war to insist on a restructuring of the CACM; the governments of El Salvador and Guatemala, indirectly supported by the U.S. government, refused to yield anything. At the end of 1970, Honduras formally abrogated all regional agreements, in effect withdrawing from the CACM. As the leader of a coalition of the most privileged foreign and local interests in Central America, the U.S. bore primary responsibility for the collapse of this 10-year experiment.

The contradictions in the U.S. strategy become concrete if we briefly recapitulate the two principal U.S. objectives: first, to promote the interests of foreign corporate investors in Central America; and second, to stabilize the potentially explosive situation in the region. With regard to the first, the strategy of dependent industrialization, which made the CACM a virtual playground of the foreign corporations, was contradictory. Because they were dependent—because they were controlled by foreign corporations and adapted to imported, capital-intensive technology—industrialization and integration did not alleviate urban unemployment. Meanwhile, the lack of an agrarian reform created increasing impoverishment in the countryside. Those social classes which were to have been incorporated within the national market remained marginal. This limited the expansion of the domestic market, which was necessary for increased foreign investment in Central America.

The contradictions in the second U.S. objective are even clearer. Somehow, the U.S. hoped to stabilize the socioeconomic system in Central America, but without really making the necessary reforms. Thus, the class structure of Central America remained that of dependent capitalism. The only significant shift in class structure during the 1960's was the incorporation of new groups of industrialists into the ruling class, allied with foreign capital. The function of the Central American state, and of the intergovernmental integration institutions, meanwhile, was reduced to the creation of the favorable conditions for private enterprise. Socioeconomic conditions within each country for the majority of the population worsened.* This, in turn, sharpened social tensions and the "threat" of internal revolution. In fact, it was during

---

* While the population grew at a rate of 3.2% a year and higher in cities, urban unemployment and underemployment rose, and industrial employment *declined* as a percent of total employment. The gaps in income distribution widened steadily. The "benefits" from integration all went to the industrialists; meanwhile, the costs of integration (e.g., the regressive sales taxes, to compensate for the governments' increasing fiscal problems) were borne by the working class and poor.

the 1960's that the guerrilla movements were growing, particularly in Guatemala and Nicaragua.

Finally, the U.S. could not have achieved the stabilization of Central America, precisely because it was in contradiction with the protection of international capital investing in the region. If the U.S. had been less concerned about protecting the absolute freedom of foreign investors, it could have accepted a degree of planning; this would have permitted greater balance and a more stable CACM, and more effective stopgap reforms within each country. In short, the commitment of U.S. policymakers to allowing international capital to operate freely and maximize profits crippled the U.S. effort at regional pacification. This was the essential contradiction of U.S. strategy for Central American integration.

IV. The Strategy of Austerity Capitalism

During the 1960's, U.S. government strategy and the strategy of international capital in Central America was oriented toward regional economic integration. At least in its original conception, the CACM was supposed to be reformist: it was designed to increase and rationalize industrial production *for the Central American market*, which presupposed a growing consumer market. This, in turn, required an improvement in the living standards of the majority of the population, and fuller incorporation of the working class into the economy.

But by the late 1960's and early 1970's, the bankruptcy of this model was clear. Neither the U.S. government nor international capital— nor the local Central American bourgeoisie—were willing to make any of the reforms which would have been needed to make the working classes of Central America into a decent-sized consumer market. On the contrary, international capital, together with the U.S. government, had directly undermined and sabotaged the few reformist structures of the CACM, in order to allow maximum corporate profits.

In the late 1960's, international capital, together with the U.S. government, coldly and deliberately devised a strategy for Central America which was *based on the assumption that no reforms would be made*—no land reform, no tax reform, no redistribution of wealth, and no industrial production for a Central American consumer market. In short, the new strategy was based on the assumption that the Central American working class (both rural and urban) would be kept at a bare subsistence level. Thus it was blatantly an *anti-reformist* strategy, a strategy of *enforced austerity*. This strategy remains in effect today.

The fact that this was a strategy of the U.S. government becomes clear from an examination of U.S. aid loans, which were no longer oriented toward fomenting industrial production for the Central American market, but instead toward stimulating exports from Central America. This strategy served the interests of a sector of foreign (primarily U.S.) capital, which saw in Central America an opportunity to use the resource of cheap labor to make overnight profits. These foreign capitalists, together with their local partners, turned the Central American economies into producers of "nontraditional" agricultural exports (i.e., other than coffee, bananas, sugar), cattle, tourism (including casinos), extractive mining. They also promoted a new kind of industry: runaway shops producing for export to other markets.

The new strategy was not *simply* a plan or plot for making higher profits without reforms in Central America. It was also a response by international capital to the crisis throughout the capitalist world which began in the late 1960's. This crisis in worldwide capital accumulation is manifested primarily as a crisis in the national economies of the advanced capitalist countries. This crisis is associated with and affected by (though it does not solely consist in) the post-Vietnam relative decline of U.S. imperialism — the end of post-World War II U.S. hegemony over the other core capitalist powers.

The current general crisis of capital accumulation became evident toward the end of the 1960's, when the long postwar boom began to falter — that is, when the rate of profit in the major industrialized countries began to decline, and profitable investment opportunities using existing technology began to shrink. These tendencies gave rise to a full-fledged recession by 1973-75 — the most serious since the Great Depression of the 1930's. This crisis is the result of forces which have been at work for more than 25 years and is, in part, the outgrowth of the very measures devised to "save" world capitalism in the 1930's.

First in the peripheral countries under Western capitalist domination, and later in the U.S. and the other core capitalist countries, this crisis signalled a shift from what we may heuristically call "prosperity capitalism" to "austerity capitalism." In the periphery, austerity capitalism has meant an intensification of the previous exploitation by foreign capital; this has resulted in declining real standards of living for the masses; rising unemployment, often reaching 30 to 40% of the labor force; increased poverty, malnutrition and even starvation.

In the traditional industrial or core countries, the change from prosperity to austerity capitalism is more dramatic. During the expansion period, the U.S. ruling class (notably from 1945 to the mid-1960's) could afford to make concessions to U.S. labor, consolidating the power of a class collaborationist union leadership and quite literally buying labor peace. This is no longer possible in an era of capitalist crisis and contraction manifested, for example, in growing unemployment, more bankruptcies and mergers, cutbacks in production and overcapacity, a declining rate of investment, and the combination of stagnation and inflation known as "stagflation." The ruling class can no longer afford to "buy off" the U.S. working class, and resorts to more openly exploitative and regressive practices. A most obvious example is the policy of deliberately engineering *higher* unemployment to lower wages and maintain profit levels — the reverse of New Deal policies of alleviating unemployment.

In a period of general crisis of accumulation—in order to solve its problems—capital must make many adjustments and modifications. We refer to this process of adjustment as the restructuring of the international division of labor, in this case a transformation of the previously existing post-World War II international division of labor. The classical division of labor could be best expressed in the image of town/country (industry/ agriculture). Specifically, this implies a "division of labor" between industrialized (core) countries producing capital and consumer goods, and underdeveloped (peripheral and semi-peripheral) countries incorporated into the capitalist world-economy as suppliers of raw materials and agricultural goods.

If the classical division of labor laid out by Marx is expressed in the town/country dichotomy, the emerging division of labor is between those processes which are heavily labor-intensive, which can be subdivided and reduced to the most simple and Taylorized processes (which can be performed by an unskilled, undervalued labor force), and those which cannot be thus reduced, which are capital-intensive, which require more skill and training.

The most visible expression of this shift is the relocation of industry (runaway shops) from the industrialized "core" countries, to take advantage of an almost limitless reservoir of cheap labor in the peripheral countries. The "new industry" in Third World countries produces almost exclusively for the world market.

The ultimate extremes of runaway operations are free trade zones—enclaves in which the local government offers special incentives so that foreign corporations will locate there that part of their production which requires large amounts of cheap, unorganized labor. The companies import raw materials duty-free into the host country, "transform" them there in labor-intensive assembly operations, and then re-export them for sale on the world market. The local government provides special installations, privileges and subsidies, principally tariff and tax exemptions and unlimited profit remittances.

Since production at these facilities is almost exclusively for the world market, and totally geared to the operating needs of the parent corporation based in the U.S. (or Germany or Japan), these operations make almost no contribution to the local economy. Nevertheless, because the international bourgeoisie has pushed this strategy, and because right-wing governments in peripheral nations understand that this is their only possible way to provide some jobs, to control unrest and hence to maintain themselves in power, these governments are fiercely competing with each other, each scrambling to offer the lowest possible wages and the most giveaway incentives to foreign corporations.

The political counterpart of this strategy is repression—Third World fascism. The free zones themselves have their own repressive laws (e.g., prohibition of labor disputes), and are often cut off from the rest of the country by barbed wire or concrete walls. More generally, at the national level, it requires a high degree of control and repression to maintain and attract foreign capital to these enclaves.

In the periphery and semi-periphery, whole societies are taking on the character of cheap labor havens. This pattern is not limited to runaway industrial production; the same effects come from reorganization of the economy to revolve around new forms of export agriculture, extractive mining, etc. The key is that the producers in these countries are not intended to be the consumers of what they produce (in contrast to the import-substituting industrialization model), and are decreasingly consumers at all.

These phenomena can be seen most clearly today in El Salvador, where the contradictions are very close to the surface. A population of 4.2 million people is squeezed into 8,000 square miles—meaning 525 persons per square mile (and much higher in the capital). The population is growing at almost 4% a year. One percent of the population owns 40% of the country's usable land while 41% of the families own no land at all; 45% of the population is unemployed or underemployed. And those who do have jobs are maintained close to the lowest wage levels in the world: the minimum wage in San Salvador is $.30 an hour— less than $2.50 a day.

The free zone strategy in El Salvador is designed to take advantage of this unbelievably low wage rate—generally about one tenth of what U.S. workers in equivalent jobs earn. A U.S. "expert" on runaway shops and free zones stated that "El Salvador . . . can compete [for these investments] *because of its low wage*." The Salvadorean government has also attempted to keep labor unorganized, and, particularly in the runaway industries, has repressed workers' attempts to organize.

Other Central American governments are attempting to copy El Salvador's free trade zones. But this strategy cannot provide decent jobs to Salvadorean workers, as shown by the experience of the Mexican border industries (another runaway shop program). In effect, the Mexican border has been moving South, to Central America and the Caribbean, where governments give away more incentives and tax exemptions, where labor is cheaper and less organized, and where living conditions are worse. The Mexican experience shows that, at the first sign of higher wages or workers' rights, international capital, which has developed the technology for opening up and shutting down plants with great facility, moves on to more repressive and more exploited countries.

Moreover, this form of industrialization is no solution to the problems of unemployment in a country like El Salvador. It provides bare subsistence jobs to a tiny fraction of the work force, while the great majority of the unemployed gain nothing. Nor does it establish a production base oriented toward the needs of the population. In fact, if Salvadorean workers were employed producing goods for the domestic market, they would have to be paid enough to buy these goods. But at $.30 an hour, most workers can barely feed their families. In effect, El Salvador has been converted into a kind of service station in the international capitalist system.

The situation of El Salvador and the entire system of runaway shops and "free zones" has profound effects for U.S. workers: *for its purpose and effect is to discipline U.S. as well as Salvadorean workers*. First, when U.S. companies run away in search of cheaper labor overseas, they leave behind a mass of unemployed workers in the U.S. Second, even though workers in the U.S. are higher paid than Salvadorean workers, their wages and legal rights are currently under attack, and are further threatened by the existence of low-wage havens like El Salvador; because, when confronted by strikes or demands by U.S. workers, these corporations can always move overseas, or use the *threat* of running away to discipline U.S. workers and force them to accept real wage cuts, harsher working conditions, speedup or infringements on their rights.

The counterpart to the runaway shops, the other side of the shifting international division of labor, is the importation of low-wage Salvadorean workers into the U.S.—the new wave of immigration. To sketch the general outlines of the process:

Central America today is undergoing a rapid *proletarianization*, as the result of the intensified penetration (mainly by foreign capital) of the countryside. It is an extremely brutal process, as it entails the dispossession of the peasantry from their land, and their conversion into a working class. Some are forced to go to work for the new landowners on what was once their own land, which is now being concentrated into bigger and bigger plantations. But increasing numbers are being forced off the land altogether, and migrate to the Central American cities in search of work. However, since dependent capitalist/imperialist development in the cities generates work for only a tiny percentage of them, they either end up in the slums of those cities, marginal and jobless, or they are driven abroad—often without immigration documents—in search of a job, any job, no matter how poorly paid.

Although the great bulk of the undocumented workers in the U.S. are Mexicans, the flow of Central Americans has been increasing dramatically in recent years. They are concentrated particularly in California, although they are also throughout the country in cities like Washington, D.C. In Washington alone, in the late 1970's there were a reported 10,000 "illegal" (undocumented) Salvadoreans, and Salvadoreans accounted for 25% of all "illegal aliens" apprehended there.

This wave of Central American migration to the U.S. in the late 1970's and beyond is a direct result of the failures of the CACM and the attempted industrial development in Central America in the 1960's. Moreover, these are some of the many Central Americans who have *not* been employed by the free zones and runaway shops in the region. Rather than being incorporated into the economy, these Central American workers have been displaced and literally forced out of their country. Once in the U.S., their fate is scarcely better: as "illegals," they must take the lowest-paid, most degrading jobs—or remain jobless, swelling the ranks of the unemployed in the U.S.

What appears as an attack against undocumented workers in the U.S. is in fact part of the broader assault against the entire U.S. working class—part of the strategy of depressing wage levels and weakening the entire class by playing on divisions within it. By maintaining undocumented workers as a limitless reserve army, to be absorbed into or expelled from the U.S. work force at will because of their politically "illegal" status, the bourgeoisie can use them to depress wage levels of the entire U.S. work force.

The runaway shops and "free zones" in El Salvador show clearly that Central America has been viewed by international capital primarily as a source of cheap labor. But this is by no means the only example. In Guatemala the institutionalization of austerity policies took a somewhat different form in the late 1960's and 1970's. In the late 1960's, after a brief debate within U.S. policy circles over whether or not to push for a mild tax reform in Guatemala, Washington completely abandoned any attempt at a reformist policy for Guatemala. Thereafter, the U.S. promoted a form of "development" in Guatemala which was designed to pacify and stabilize the country *without* making any basic reforms; without in any way redistributing income to the working class or the poor.

The two primary U.S. objectives remained what they had always been—containment of the revolutionary movement and maintenance of Guatemala as a preserve for foreign investment. Within Guatemala's changing role in the international capitalist division of labor, this meant promotion of a new set of "productive" activities, oriented toward world market production—agribusiness, nontraditional exports, tourism and extractive mining. In the mid-1970's, significant deposits of nickel and oil were discovered in Guatemala, greatly increasing the country's strategic importance to the U.S.

These new panaceas, which were supposed to resolve Guatemala's balance of payments problems, trigger economic growth and provide new sources of employment, have in fact brought quick profits to a tiny group of Guatemalan investors, and almost no gain to the rest of the population. Basic indicators of poverty, unemployment and inflation have worsened, rather than improved. In Guatemala and throughout Central America, institutionalized austerity has provided the material basis for the growth of revolutionary political organizations, with an increasing base in the working class and marginal populations in the cities and countryside.

V. Resistance and Counterinsurgency

The monumental struggle in Nicaragua which led to the victory of the Frente Sandinista in July 1979, and the ongoing struggles in El Salvador and Guatemala today, are the outcome of centuries of exploitation and oppression, and several decades of active organizing to resist these conditions. We shall briefly sketch the development of these movements in the 1960's and 1970's, as background for understanding their immediacy today.

In a sense the history of these movements goes back to the 1930's (in Nicaragua and El Salvador) and the 1940's and 1950's (in Guatemala). The massive uprisings in Nicaragua and El Salvador in the early 1930's were so brutally repressed that they were followed by 25 years of military dictatorship, with relatively few initiatives by the resistance. In Nicaragua, the bourgeois opposition to Somoza attempted to oust the dictatorship through dozens of plots, uprisings and invasions, as well as through elections; but none of these efforts were well enough organized or had a sufficient mass base to have any real chance of succeeding. In the late 1950's, anti-Somoza activity among students and discontent in the countryside gave rise to a guerrilla movement, which took organizational form in 1962, with the founding of the FSLN.

Over the years, and learning from numerous defeats and errors, the FSLN developed a strategy of prolonged people's war, and in the mid-1970's built enough of a base to pose a serious threat to the government. In the last few years before the 1979 victory, the FSLN was able to unite with and lead certain sectors of the bourgeois opposition to Somoza and, of equal significance, to establish a mass base among urban as well as rural working class and marginal sectors. These were necessary preconditions for the victory of July 1979.

In El Salvador, following the 1932 uprising and massacre and a short-lived uprising in 1944, the military dictatorship ruled almost unchallenged for over 30 years. In the late 1960's, the labor movement launched a series of strikes, while the electoral opposition built its base—only to be denied the fruits of victory in the elections of 1972. By the mid-1970's, several revolutionary organizations had been formed and a guerrilla movement emerged, linked to mass organizations based among the peasantry, urban and rural workers, the great mass of the unemployed and marginally employed, and university students and professors. The process of unification among these organizations was completed in 1980—by which time the level of popular mass mobilization and the military challenge by the resistance had created a crisis which the Salvadorean government could meet only with extensive U.S. economic, political and military assistance.

In Guatemala, the experience of the unsuccessful 1944-54 Revolution was crucial—as guerrilla leader César Montes later put it, "a great source of lessons for us and . . . a real and living example of what a revolution is." In the early 1960's an armed socialist guerrilla movement emerged, drawing initially upon anti-government mobilizations by students and workers. By this time the futility of purely political-electoral opposition was clear, because *all* of the Guatemalan regimes since the U.S. intervention in 1954 were maintained in power by the U.S.; this was the logic of institutionalized counterrevolution after 1954. By 1966-68, the guerrilla movement was strong enough to require a major U.S.-sponsored counterinsurgency offensive, which succeeded temporarily in containing the insurgency, through wide-scale repression against the guerrillas and against entire sections of the population.

Recovering from its defeat in the late 1960's, the Guatemalan guerrilla movement greatly expanded its mass base in the 1970's and united with organizations in the labor movement. The particularity of the Guatemalan struggle is that at no time since 1954 has the country enjoyed any real "democratic opening"; the possibility of a bourgeois democratic solution has not existed since the overthrow of the bourgeois democratic Revolution, and repression has been relentless. The organizers of the Guatemalan resistance never doubted that their struggle would be protracted. But it is clear today that a movement and a people which have organized in clandestinity and survived the level of repression practiced in Guatemala cannot be extinguished by *any* means devised by the U.S.

The somewhat astounding rapidity with which these three revolutionary movements in the "backyard" of the U.S. have come to the forefront of struggle worldwide in the late 1970's is a direct result of material economic conditions created by U.S.-promoted economic strategies. The dependent industrialization of the 1960's and the cheap labor strategies of the 1970's have resulted in increasing *proletarianization* of the Central American population. Particularly with the strategies of the 1970's, *based* on maximizing capital accumulation through undervaluation of labor-power (i.e., wages less than what is required to produce and reproduce labor-power), the overall social direction is not toward social progress but toward ever more intense exploitation for those who fill the few jobs available, and absolute pauperization for large segments of the population.

These material conditions have contributed significantly to the development of revolutionary organization in Central America. In the early 1960's—before the beginning of the international capitalist crisis, the era of austerity capitalism and the decline of U.S. power worldwide— the U.S. had its last opportunity to experiment with a seriously reformist option in Central America. But the refusal of the U.S. ruling class to make *any* real reforms at that time, and the subsequent shift to an openly anti-reformist imposition of austerity capitalism on the region, closed off that option permanently. By this time, too, the structural changes in the capitalist world-economy determined Central America's development as essentially a cheap labor haven.

The political consequences of the above are clear. First, although none of the guerrilla movements of the 1960's gained sufficient base among the population or sufficient military strength to seriously threaten the existing regimes, their very existence and growth was testimony to the fact that basic social conditions had not changed from the so-called "reforms" promoted by the U.S. and its allies in the local bourgeoisie. The growth of these movements was a harbinger of the future in Central America. It was for this reason that even during the period of "economic reforms," the U.S. focused equally on counter-insurgency efforts.

Second, what began in the 1960's as guerrilla movements based largely in radicalized sectors of the petty bourgeoisie changed profoundly in the 1970's, as the structural social effects of unmitigated austerity capitalism became more widespread, and as the revolutionary organizations analyzed the weaknesses of their class base in the 1960's. These factors were determinative in enabling them to reorganize with a much broader working class base in the 1970's, rooted in the sectors of the population which quite literally have nothing to lose and a world to gain from revolutionary change. These, then, and not a communist conspiracy of any kind, are the bases of the struggles we are witnessing in Central America today.

VI. The Present Period and Future Prospects

No less significant than the international capitalist crisis and the generalization of austerity policies has been the decline in U.S. hegemony internationally, particularly since the U.S. defeat in Vietnam. This decline has meant, first, the intensification of inter-imperialist rivalry between the U.S. and the other Western capitalist powers. One fraction of the U.S. ruling class, which is transnational in its interests and orientation, has attempted to hold together the "Western alliance," for example through the Trilateral Commission. Over time, however, the Trilateral alliance has been subjected to increasing strains, as the U.S. ruling class is less able to coordinate international capitalist interests or to maintain hegemony over its counterparts in Western Europe and Japan. The U.S. has been unable to stop the erosion of the NATO Alliance and the emerging realignment of Western Europe economically and politically with Eastern Europe and the Soviet Union.

Second, the direct challenge to U.S. power worldwide has come from escalating resistance in the Third World. The U.S. emerged from the Vietnam War drained, isolated and defeated. Yet the potential for "more Vietnams" existed in many parts of the world, including Central America.

International decline has meant that the U.S. ruling class no longer has the power to set the terms of its relations with other countries unilaterally. U.S. options are more limited, and the U.S. is less able to force its will unrestrainedly on other nations through instant military interventions as it did, for example, in Guatemala in 1954, in the Congo in 1961, in the Dominican Republic in 1965. In general, the U.S. must negotiate its positions; and in many parts of the world, the U.S. has had to make concessions. Nevertheless, since the U.S. ruling class has always regarded Latin America as its natural sphere of domination, the response to defeats elsewhere was an intensified effort to preserve U.S. hegemony in this hemisphere. The brutal overthrow of the Allende government in 1973 was only the most extreme example.

With the U.S. defeat in Vietnam, with the lack of domestic support for foreign intervention, and with increasing isolation internationally, the U.S. ruling class had to make certain adjustments in its foreign policy. Tactically, in order to regain lost prestige internally and internationally, and in order to reconstitute its ability *long-range* to intervene in the Third World, the U.S. had to project a short-range policy of nonintervention and detente with the Soviet Union.

Detente policies did create, for a short time, an international climate that was less dangerous in terms of relations with the Soviet Union and more favorable to the struggles of oppressed Third World peoples. We might say that in some sense the Nicaraguan people benefited indirectly from this opening; they won their victory at a time when the U.S. was constrained from intervening directly and militarily to stop the overthrow of Somoza.

However, even during the last years of detente, beginning in 1976, Carter/Brzezinski went on the offensive against the Soviet Union by criticizing "human rights violations" there. But they could not call for "human rights" in the Soviet Union without making a show of advocating human rights elsewhere, hence Carter's "human rights policy" in Latin America. In fact, this represented no real commitment to human rights; it was a tactical adjustment to new realities in the world, and a platform for attacking the Soviet Union. Moreover, the ephemeral nature of the "opening" in the international situation and the fact that pro-detente anti-intervention policies were always tactical rather than long-range U.S. policy, have become clear in the increasingly provocative U.S. policies toward the Soviet Union since mid-1979. U.S. provocations of the Soviet Union in 1979-80 (in Cuba, in Western Europe, shelving the SALT II Treaty, the anti-Soviet alliance with the People's Republic of China, etc.) set the stage for the Soviet intervention in Afghanistan and gave Carter a new excuse for anti-Soviet policies.

Thus, Carter's foreign policy in 1979-80 catapulted the world from an era of detente into an era of Cold War, an era of increasing instability, unpredictability and brinksmanship. The "Carter Doctrine" reflected the U.S. government's desire to undertake an anti-Soviet offensive, and to assert U.S. power, *precisely at a time when actual U.S. power worldwide was declining.*

Within this general situation, the Carter Administration was forced to respond to the revolution in Nicaragua in 1979, once the Frente Sandinista had taken power. As is detailed in another article in this volume, this occasioned a serious debate within the U.S. ruling class over whether or not to extend aid to the new Nicaraguan government for reconstruction of its devastated economy.

Within the U.S. ruling class, the Nicaragua aid debate pitted Trilateralists (representatives of transnational monopoly/banking capital) against right-wing militarists (representatives of competitive industrial capital, e.g., the military-industrial complex). This was a drama of the new Cold War, part of a larger debate: how the United States should exercise its declining power in the world today—whether to continue pretending to wield unilateral power, or to make certain pragmatic adjustments to the reality of eroded U.S. power— and *how* to pursue a Cold War interventionist stance in the hemisphere.

The transnational bankers won the day temporarily, under Carter, with the decision to extend a $75 million U.S. aid loan to the Sandinista government. They had argued all along that this was the only way to keep Nicaragua out of the socialist camp, and to ensure Nicaraguan repayment of the $1.6 billion foreign debt left by Somoza (owed primarily to U.S.-based private banks). The longer-range effect would be to force Nicaragua into the intolerable situation of requiring austerity from the Nicaraguan people while paying off the debts accumulated by Somoza. This is, in effect, a longer-range political strategy for destabilizing the Nicaraguan Revolution (as contrasted with more immediate proposals from right-wing militarists for intervention by directly aiding *Somocista* exile groups, withholding all U.S. aid, etc.).

In the last months of the Carter Administration, the advance of the revolutionary movement in El Salvador presented the U.S. government with its most serious challenge since Vietnam. Both the outgoing Carter Administration and the incoming Reagan team raised military intervention as an option that could not be discarded.

The Republican Party platform adopted in the summer of 1980 stated opposition to aid for Nicaragua and support for exile groups plotting to overthrow the Sandinista government. Subsequently, while some Reagan advisers gave assurances of "no sweeping changes in U.S. policy toward Latin America," others stated that the model for Central America would be U.S. policy toward Greece at the end of World War II — a revival of the Truman Doctrine. While keeping open the option of outright intervention or the use of military force for "strategic limited objectives," the Reagan Administration has focused on Truman Doctrine-style massive military and economic aid, including the sending of military advisers. (This could be combined with the use of surrogates for U.S. troops, including ex-National Guardsmen from Nicaragua, Cuban exiles and mercenaries.)

The future development of U.S. policy will depend, to some extent, on the outcome of the jockeying for power within the Reagan Administration. On the one hand, there is evidence that the Trilateral Commission, which was a dominant force in shaping Carter policy, is attempting to play an active role in the Reagan Administration (e.g., through Trilateralist Vice President George Bush). On the other hand, most of Reagan's vocal foreign policy advisers come from right-wing think tanks, or are super-hawk military men or former Nixon-Ford officials to the right of Kissinger (e.g., Secretary of State Haig).

Even given this contention of forces, there is no question that the Reagan posture will be interventionist in one sense or another. However, the willingness to intervene must be matched by an objective ability to do so; and in this regard, they must operate within certain realities:

a) As seen above, since the defeat in Vietnam, the U.S. no longer dominates the capitalist world as it once did, and is no longer able to impose its will by unilateral action. Moreover, despite intense U.S. pressure, most of the European "allies" are not going along with U.S. policy in Central America. The social democratic government in Bonn, for example, has supported the FSLN in Nicaragua and the Frente Democrático Revolucionario in El Salvador. Both the Social Democratic and the Christian Democratic international movements have pursued an active role in Central America (though not always on the same side). Moreover, a number of Latin American governments such as those of Mexico and Brazil have their own interests and policies to pursue in Central America. The prospect of having to act in isolation from many U.S. "allies" may seriously limit what the Reagan Administration can do.

b) Adventurist right-wing policies on the part of the U.S. could provoke a more activist role in support of the revolutionary movements by Cuba or even the Soviet Union, and risk a larger confrontation in Central America. Certainly, if the Reagan Administration were to act on its verbal threats of a naval blockade against Cuba (to "punish" Cuba for supposedly supplying arms to the Salvadorean guerrillas), the conflict would be internationalized. Or alternatively, an overtly aggressive U.S. move into Central America (and/ or against Cuba) could be met by a Soviet response in other parts of the world. The world has changed greatly since the 1930's. No longer in a position of absolute hegemony, the U.S. today cannot warn the Soviet Union not to move into Poland, while simultaneously intervening directly and militarily in Central America. *Central America today is no longer simply the backyard of the United States;* the struggles there and any U.S. response have global implications, which limit the absolute freedom of action of the U.S. government.

c) This is a time of crisis in the national economies of the leading capitalist countries, most notably the U.S. Certainly, the easiest "solution" for the U.S. ruling class is to transfer this crisis onto the U.S. working class; hence, the austerity policies, which are being greatly intensified under Reagan. Yet at the same time, Reagan is calling for a vastly expanded defense budget; and certainly, any interventionist activity in Central America would be costly, since the revolutionary struggles there are too far advanced to be contained without a major U.S. effort. Thus, no major intervention abroad could be undertaken without consideration of the domestic consequences.

d) Also within the U.S., there is growing sentiment opposed to intervention in Central America. In fact, only 26% of the American electorate voted for Reagan in the November 1980 election; and of the 26%, many were protesting Carter's failures rather than voting for repressive, anti-working class policies at home or intervention abroad. Moreover, since mid-1979, polls have consistently shown that two thirds of the American people oppose U.S. intervention abroad, particularly in Central America.

An additional factor is the increasing involvement of the Church (especially the Catholic Church) in anti-interventionist activities—not unrelated to the increasingly vicious persecution of priests and Church officials sympathetic to the left in Guatemala and El Salvador; such pressure could weigh heavily on Reagan, who got a strong Catholic vote. Finally, a number of international and U.S. labor unions have organized significant pro-human rights campaigns and boycotts against the Salvadorean and Guatemalan governments. While these are only beginnings, and while the major U.S. media can be expected to support whatever Reagan does, nevertheless these currents in U.S. public opinion represent an important broadening of the traditional anti-intervention, pro-peace movement, and increasing working class participation in that movement.

Given these limitations, a Marine landing in Central America is probably not the most likely scenario. Nevertheless, the other options left to the U.S. government are still numerous and equally dangerous (e.g., a Truman Doctrine approach). In some regards, the options open to the Reagan Administration are similar to those that faced Carter. Dissidents within the Carter foreign policy apparatus argued in November 1980 that:

> Should President Reagan choose to use military force in El Salvador, historians will be able to show that the setting for such actions had been prepared in the last year of the Carter Administration . . . ("Dissent Paper on El Salvador and Central America," DOS, November 6, 1980, p. 10).

The Carter Administration decided to live with the Nicaraguan Revolution, once it was a *fait accompli* (although the U.S. had supported Somoza until it literally could no longer do so), but was determined at all costs to avoid repetition of the Nicaraguan Revolution elsewhere in Central America. Carter officials left open the "possibility" of direct intervention in the region and, according to the "Dissent Paper," various agencies were making preparations for an intervention. While mouthing a protest against "human rights violations" in Guatemala and El Salvador, the Carter Administration never really abandoned its support of either government, nor took any effective measures to stop the government/right-wing assassination campaigns in either country. Increasingly in 1980, "security" took priority over human rights as the determining factor of U.S. policy.

Within the context of the new Cold War policy globally, then, Carter's Central America policy was contradictory and hypocritical. *However*, the contradiction did moderate U.S. actions. Under Carter/Brzezinski, "human rights" policy was initially designed as a club to be used against the Soviet Union; but international opinion turned this diplomatic weapon back upon its inventors, forcing Carter to criticize "human rights violators" like Somoza in the U.S. sphere of influence. In short, the rhetoric of human rights became somewhat of a fetter on the policies of hemispheric security. *This is a fetter which does not bind the Reagan Administration,* and it is for this reason that the Reagan camp has taken great pains from the very beginning to denounce Carter's human rights policy. While Carter's proclamation of human rights policy was hypocritical, Reagan's abandonment of it is virtually a license for right-wing terror.

Beyond the conjunctural politics of the two Administrations, the revolutionary movements in El Salvador and Guatemala present the entire U.S. ruling class with longer-range problems— problems which were *not* posed by the Nicaraguan Revolution. For one thing, the Somoza dictatorship was viewed as somewhat of an embarrassment to the Carter Administration, and therefore an argument could be made for getting rid of it; in contrast, the U.S. approach in El Salvador (in the absence of a Somoza who had enemies among the *local* ruling class) has been to make the junta *appear* respectable.

Second, the revolutionary struggles in El Salvador and Guatemala are much more clearly working class based and led than was the case in Nicaragua; their political orientation is more clearly socialist; the targets of their movements are not one ruling dynasty, but virtually the entire capitalist classes of Guatemala and El Salvador. Moreover, the very pressures from social conditions (massive unemployment and poverty) would almost force revolutionary governments in these countries to move more rapidly toward socialist structures.

Third, it was one thing for (at least one wing of) the U.S. ruling class to accept as a *fait accompli* an isolated revolution in Nicaragua—one which they could attempt to control and manipulate through foreign aid credits, bank loans and debts. But the prospect of a revolutionary *bloc* in Central America (and the Caribbean/Cuba), including Guatemala, the country most strategically and economically important to the U.S. and transnational capital (with sizable foreign investments in oil, nickel, industry, etc.), is very different. While "domino theories" are red herrings in situations where the internal conditions for revolution do not exist, those conditions *do* exist in El Salvador and Guatemala today, and no part of the U.S. ruling class is willing to "lose" Guatemala. This is the reality underlying the vehement statements from all sectors of the U.S. ruling class about "drawing the line" in El Salvador.

None of the above considerations necessarily mean that the U.S. ruling class is planning to leave Nicaragua alone, long-range; indeed, it may well be that the Nicaraguan Revolution is an ultimate target of Truman Doctrine-style intervention in El Salvador and Guatemala. In a very real sense, the relative unity of the U.S. ruling class around some kind of interventionist stance in Central America changes the conditions which made the Sandinista victory possible in the first place.

Taking an even longer-range view, we may pose the dilemmas faced both by the U.S. government and transnational capital, and by the revolutionary movements in Nicaragua, El Salvador and Guatemala. On the one hand, the forces of capital are constrained internationally and domestically from unleashing their most direct fury against the Central American people—assuming some degree of rationality even within the Reagan Administration. A Truman Doctrine-type solution, or even a Marine-style intervention, could wreak horrendous destruction in Central America in the course of attempting to physically eliminate the "internal enemy," i.e., the mass movement (as happened in Guatemala in 1954); but neither can really crush the movements there. It is too late. There simply is no way the U.S. can "win" in Central America at this point, short of literally destroying entire populations.

On the other hand, the Central American movements face equally serious contradictions. The Nicaraguan Revolution is out of the grasp of *U.S.* imperialism, but in no way free of the vise of *transnational* capital. Indeed, like Poland and other socialist countries, Nicaragua remains vulnerable through its debts, and this places real constraints upon any transition to socialism. Furthermore, if and when the revolutionary movements in El Salvador or Guatemala take state power, they will face some of these same constraints. For example, if a revolutionary government in either country took the most obvious basic measures to raise wages for the working class, it would immediately be challenging transnational capital, which has used the country as a cheap labor haven.

Both sides in this international class struggle, then, are limited by the growing transnationalization of the world. One could even say that the present structure of the capitalist world-economy favors national liberation struggles, in the sense that transnational capital is not *necessarily* tied to the immediate interests of the U.S. government, and that the U.S. government no longer has the absolute freedom that it once had. But the tremendous power of transnational capital intensifies greatly the contradictions of socialist construction for newly liberated countries, and this will affect the fate of the people's struggles in Central America.

A final consequence of the above is the growing interrelationship between the development of the workers' movement within the United States and the struggles in Central America. The restructuring of the capitalist world-economy and the decline of the U.S. in the world have ushered in an era of austerity capitalism for the U.S. working class, which shatters for the foreseeable future any myth that the U.S. working class somehow "benefits" from the continued super-exploitation of Central American workers. Moreover, in this post-Vietnam era, it is clear that the overwhelming majority of the American working class does not support aggressive U.S. policies even in the name of "containing Communism." The so-called "Cold War consensus" has been shattered. It is for this reason that the Reagan Administration faces, even now, *before* the escalation of direct U.S. involvement in El Salvador, a significant and growing anti-interventionist movement within the United States.

In response to this movement, the Reagan Administration is building an offensive against vocal opponents within the U.S. of militarism and intervention abroad. The rebirth of McCarthyite witch hunting against left liberal institutions and the workers' movement is a clear response by the Reagan camp and the Congressional right wing to the threat of a broad-based peace movement—an attempt to revive ideological anticommunism in order to pave the way for support of right-wing dictatorships and U.S. interventionism abroad. At the very least, we can expect an operation similar to the massive (largely illegal) domestic intelligence campaign planned by Nixon during the Vietnam War. At worst, any U.S. decision to intervene directly and militarily in Central America would require more widespread repression in the U.S., a revival of McCarthyism.

The specter of repression against the anti-intervention movement within the U.S. is all the more real *because* the prospects for stopping a savage U.S. intervention (whether direct or Truman Doctrine-style) will depend largely on the American people. Longer range too, the prospects for the construction of socialism in Central America will depend significantly on the development of a working class movement in the U.S. which is able to destroy the capitalist system at its heart, and to dethrone *all* fractions of the U.S. ruling class, "domestic" and trans-national. In the words of Ruy Mauro Marini, elsewhere in this volume,

> It is for this reason that, along with the liberating forces on the move in Nicaragua, El Salvador and Guatemala, and arising along the length and breadth of Latin America, it is up to the North American people—*la palabra la tiene el pueblo norteamericano*—and the forces that can best express their historical interests.

The conditions exist for a broad progressive coalition or movement to oppose U.S. intervention in Central America; but this is understood perhaps sooner and more clearly by the Reagan Administration than by many sectors of the U.S. left. For this reason, Central Americans have reason to be concerned that this movement in the heart of the empire not be killed in its infancy. For this reason too, all progressive North Americans have reason to learn well one of the lessons of the Cold War of the late 1940's and the 1950's: that ideological anticommunism remains a powerful weapon which the U.S. ruling class can use to destroy the anti-interventionist movement *internally*; and that if anti-imperialists fail to combat anticommunism within their ranks, they cut themselves off from working class organizations and essentially preclude the possibility of an effective opposition to intervention abroad. Further, they would pave the way for a broadside attack against all progressive movements, as a direct consequence of failing to oppose repression against working class organizations.

It was the absence of a strong anti-imperialist movement linked to the workers' movement at the height of the McCarthy era that gave U.S. imperialism a free hand to intervene in Guatemala in 1954. It was the growth of a broad, progressive, anti-interventionist movement that was crucial in eventually forcing the U.S. out of Vietnam. And it is the rebirth of such a movement, which today because of the economic crisis could have a much broader working class participation and orientation, that can put a brake on the designs of the Reagan Administration to smash the popular struggles in El Salvador, Guatemala and elsewhere in the Third World.

—May 1981

Note on Sources

With a few exceptions, we have not included detailed references. The principal sources used (which may be consulted by interested readers) include:

1. For a broad historical and analytical interpretation, I have relied heavily upon the following articles by Marlene Dixon: "An Outline of Working Class History, 1917-1979," in *Our Socialism* (Theoretical Journal of the Democratic Workers Party) 2, 2 (May 1, 1981). "Rethinking 50 Years of American History: From Roosevelt to Reagan," *Plain Speaking* (News Journal of the Democratic Workers

Party) 5, 7 and 5, 8 (May 15-31, 1981 and June 1-15, 1981). "Responsibilities of the U.S. Working Class to Latin American Revolutionary Movements in a New Cold War Period," *Contemporary Marxism* 1, "Strategies for the Class Struggle in Latin America" (Spring 1980). By Susanne Jonas and Marlene Dixon: "Proletarianization and Class Alliances in the Americas," *Contradictions of Socialist Construction* (San Francisco, Synthesis Publications, 1980).

2. On the history of U.S. involvement in Central America, the following works by Susanne Jonas: "Revolution (1944-54) and Counterrevolution (1954-74)" in Section III of *Guatemala*, eds. Susanne Jonas and David Tobis (Berkeley, NACLA, 1974). "Test Case for the Hemisphere: U.S. Strategy in Guatemala, 1950-1974" (Ph.D. dissertation: Department of Political Science, U.C. Berkeley, 1974). "Guatemala" chapter in *Latin America: The Struggle With Dependency and Beyond*," eds. Ronald Chilcote and Joel Edelstein (Cambridge, Schenkman, 1974). "Nicaragua" issue of *NACLA's Latin America and Empire Report* (February 1976). "Central America as a Source of Cheap Labor for International Capital" (mimeo: San Francisco, Institute for the Study of Labor and Economic Crisis, 1979). "Reagan y Guatemala," *Cuadernos de Marcha* (Mexico, November-December 1980).

PART I

From the Struggle and Beyond

Revolution and Intervention in Central America

C. Martínez F.

Revolutionary struggle and victory in Nicaragua occurred at a time when the United States could not intervene without blatantly contradicting its own political line and becoming more isolated internationally. Successive internal crises in the Carter Administration reduced its maneuvering space and strengthened the pro-independence bloc of countries which, within the forum of the Organization of American States (OAS), flatly rejected all forms of intervention. Meanwhile, the Sandinista victory in Nicaragua, along with internal factors in both El Salvador and Guatemala, accelerated the development of revolutionary movements in those countries and heralded an early victory in El Salvador. There was a historical conjuncture. Nevertheless, in El Salvador, the vanguard organizations needed to discuss unity, to arrive at the tactics and logistical implementations of unity. Necessary as this was, it consumed much of the time of the conjuncture, and the process went out of phase: the situation developed faster than the revolutionary movement advanced.

Nevertheless, the advances of the revolutionary movement were sufficient to cause a reaction among some forces within the United States; these forces began to bring strong pressure upon their government, resulting in new threats against Cuba and arguments for an economic and political blockade of Nicaragua and Panama. Such pressure also encouraged the governments of Venezuela and Colombia to make alliances with the most reactionary sectors in the region and head up opposition to Central American revolutionary movements under the aegis of Christian Democracy.

Such were the ominous signs under which Ronald Reagan took office. From the beginning, he suppressed all advocacy for human rights, so he could fall back on direct intervention without going against his own political line. Intervention is his formula for recovering political prestige that has been undermined by the growth of revolutionary movements. To the same ends, he proposes strengthening the empire economically and politically—an idle dream. Unmindful that the hegemony which has been lost in recent years cannot be recovered, Reagan wants the United States to play the role it had in the 1950's. Imperialism cannot accept this loss of hegemony; thus Reagan is rushing into an attempt to recover U.S. hegemony in Central America, supporting repressive anticommunist governments and preparing to use armed intervention wherever necessary. His strategy is crystal clear: continue intervention in El Salvador to force acceptance of a chosen successor to the Christian Democratic junta, and intervene in Guatemala if necessary. Once the revolutionary movements in these two countries are under control, and since he knows that the submissive Honduran government would comply, Reagan would then establish an economic blockade against Nicaragua as a prelude to military intervention. Instead of direct intervention, this would use the governments and armies of Guatemala, El Salvador and Honduras as intermediaries.

United States strategy in Guatemala has led to an agreement with the Christian Democratic Party to support the government of Gen. Romeo Lucas García until the [1982] presidential elections, at which time the Christian Democrats will emerge as the compromise solution, the formula to hold back the revolutionary process. Yet it is a foregone conclusion that, given the present conditions in Guatemala, all kinds of contradictions will immediately arise between a Christian Democratic government, on the one hand, and the army and the oligarchy on the other. Even though events may take a different course, a steady advance of the revolutionary movement is to be anticipated, because it is the only alternative through which the people can come to power and establish a democratic, popular government.

This means that neither pressures brought to bear against Nicaragua, Cuba and Mexico, nor proclamation of a political solution in El Salvador, nor indirect intervention in Guatemala to assure the rise to power by Christian Democrats, will hold back the revolutionary process. Even an old-style direct intervention in El Salvador by the United States and its Marines would mean a setback for the movement, but never a definitive defeat; and the process would be similar in Guatemala. That is to say, the new conjuncture will demand more time and effort, while the Reagan government faces ever greater contradictions, both internationally and within the United States.

There has already been strong domestic opposition to Washington's recent return to militarism and interventionism. Senator Kennedy has accused his government of destroying hard-won progress towards world peace and international respect for the United States. The closer Reagan moves toward direct intervention, the more the opposition will grow. People who think clearly, like Senator Kennedy, understand that the empire is in a critical situation, and that if it employs force and intervenes, the correlation of forces and present conditions will not allow it to deploy its forces for very long. This is why it is to be hoped that Central American revolutionary movements will be able to defeat the counteroffensive; and that if the possible intervention in El Salvador and Guatemala were halted without having achieved decisive immediate effects, it would be a defeat for the interventionists, who would be obliged to withdraw by international pressures which the intervention itself would surely unleash.

Reagan understands that he no longer has as free a hand as he did during the electoral campaign. He will be his own worst enemy. But meanwhile, stressing his more aggressive policy, Reagan has publicly stated that the United States will eliminate human rights clauses from its international agreements, whenever these make relations with repressive Central American governments problematic. Paradoxically, such statements, like Reagan's overall militarist stance in foreign affairs, work in favor of the peoples who are fighting their way out of poverty and dependence. The road that Reagan has chosen will crumble beneath him as he moves along it; intervention and occupation will deploy his troops in a worldwide space so vast that it will swallow them. Imperialist forces will bleed very heavily indeed, both politically and economically, and to the extent that this happens, the North American people themselves will be increasingly victimized by economic instability at home — as is already evident in the trend of increasing unemployment and relentless inflation.

No kind of intervention, then, direct or indirect, can hold back the struggle in Central America, or in other areas where conflict rages. But intervention does mean a crueler, bloodier solution of the problems involved in the people's self-determination: governments throughout the world will judge how to deal with those whose greed brings the world to the brink of catastrophe. Intervention in Guatemala and Nicaragua today, combined with the intervention already underway in El Salvador, would be a process that could not be contained in Central America. Imperialism would be lighting greater fires than its resources can extinguish: a world ablaze will turn the empire to ashes.

DOCUMENTS FROM EL SALVADOR

The Role of Unity in the Revolutionary War: An Interview with Juan Chacón

CIDAMO

This is the major portion of an interview conducted on September 6, 1980 with Juan Chacón, who was a member of the Executive Committee of the Democratic Revolutionary Front (FDR) and general secretary of the Popular Revolutionary Bloc (BPR) of El Salvador. On November 27, 1980, Chacón and five other leaders of the FDR were assassinated by forces linked to the Salvadorean government junta. This interview was conducted by CIDAMO (Centro de Información, Documentación, y Análisis sobre el Movimiento Obrero Latino-americano) in Mexico, and originally published in Cuadernos de CIDAMO *No. 3 (Mexico, 1980).*

During 1980, one of the most important characteristics of the revolutionary struggle in El Salvador has been the development of unity between the various revolutionary, mass and democratic organizations. How has this come about?

The development of unity among the Salvadorean people is the principal factor in their revolutionary struggle for liberation. It is characterized by solid unity, a rock-like unity which is now irreversible. Our revolutionary, democratic and mass organizations had to take a series of steps that have now made it possible to consolidate. Previously the organizations existed independently of each other. That is, they developed separate fronts of resistance, each having its own strategy, tactics and methods of struggle, and this resulted in a lack of coordination between the struggles we waged. However, with the development of the revolutionary process itself, the growth of our forces and the beginning of a new stage in the people's war, these organizations find that they must unify and coordinate their efforts against the enemy—North American imperialism, the Salvadorean oligarchy, and the reactionary military. In practice, the ranks began closing among the mass organizations last October. In November and December 1979, an alliance was being consolidated. Unity was not achieved overnight, but followed a process of rapprochement until there was finally a convergence in tactical and even strategic planning.

The unification of revolutionary forces resulted from necessity, and practically every mass organization in our country anticipated it and included it in its strategy. However, each organization had its own idea of what that unity would mean and the methods to be used in achieving it. It is very important, that every organization, without exception, saw the unification of mass forces and the formation of a single, broad, united front as necessary for taking power. These steps had not been possible earlier for lack of agreement on the forms, principles and criteria by which to make the alliance among the organizations.

It was after October 15, 1979, when the North American imperialists unleashed one of their heaviest offensives against our revolutionary movement, that the movement realized the urgent necessity of beginning a process of unification among the revolutionary and democratic forces in our country.

It was the people's fighting that showed the unviability of the imperialists' goal. At the same time, those organizations and political parties which up until then had supported the electoral process as a way of taking power, and which formed part of the government along with the military in the hopes of establishing democracy, then became convinced that only through the struggle of the people and the total elimination of the military dictatorship could we make the profound changes needed in our society. In the wake of these events, a serious crisis developed among the heads of government which culminated with the resignations of practically all the cabinet members and of the three civilians in the junta. This was very important because it marked the beginning of a convergence in strategy among the revolutionary and the democratic organizations. Up to that point there had been two distinct positions. One favored elections and was supported by various democratic parties, including the National Democratic Union (UDN)—a revolutionary organization which sought the winning of power by peaceful means; the other position was that of the revolutionary organizations which sought to win power through armed struggle and the various means of fighting that the people have. These were the two predominant lines, the two chief ways in which people sought to win power. But following the treacherous events of October 15, and their tremendous failure, all the democratic and mass organizations realized there was only one road to victory: that of armed struggle and the use of the people's methods of combat.

After the complete disintegration of the first junta, there began a process of consolidating the revolutionary alliance until it reached the level of a revolutionary coordinating body. Thus the Political-Military Coordinating Council was founded in December 1979, which initially included the Popular Liberation Forces— Farabundo Martí (FPL), the Communist Party of El Salvador (PCS), and the National Resistance (RN). This was a very important development, because it meant coordination between the organizations which were the vanguard of the people, which had been directing the revolutionary war from its beginning and had been organizing among the people. The coordination of these forces had a far-reaching influence at the level of the masses and the organized sectors. A process of coordination and tightening of alliances likewise developed among the mass organizations, and in January the Revolutionary Coordinating Council of the Masses (CRM) was formed. It meant more than coordination among the revolutionary mass organizations, which included the Popular Revolutionary Bloc (BPR), the Unified Popular Action Front (FAPU), UDN and the People's Leagues (LP-28). It also meant the formation of a nucleus that could generate the broadest unity between the revolutionary and the democratic forces in the country. It was a central base on which we could build the broadest possible unity among democratic and revolutionary forces. There were various reasons for this. First of all, the CRM represented for us the alliance of the revolutionary sectors. Within it exists the worker-peasant alliance. We in the revolutionary organizations had long maintained that the basis for any alliance and any unity would have to be in a worker-peasant alliance, that it would be the nucleus for generating any sort of viable alliance. And for that reason we were all struggling to build that worker-peasant alliance. So now it is in the CRM that we have seen our aspirations take real shape; it is there that the forces of the proletariat and of the peasant class have converged. The other revolutionary sectors of society have, in turn, joined that alliance—such as the students, teachers, slum-dwellers, market vendors, public employees, etc.

In the second place, the CRM expresses the local power of the people. It is we in the revolutionary mass organizations who have initiated the construction of local power in the *barrios*, in the towns, in the precincts. In all the organizations, we have been building People's Committees, Precinct Committees and even Municipal Committees (the base of local people's power); they would eventually replace the present regime's structures of control. It is very important to point out all these factors, for they show the value of this kind of unity.

In order to win power, it was not only necessary to unite the revolutionary forces but also to join together with the powerful torrent of progressive and democratic forces in our country, thus completely isolating the regime and beginning to build a united political movement. The platform and program of the democratic revolutionary government played an important role in this. It was launched by the Revolutionary Coordinating Council of the Masses and then won the support of all the democratic sectors of our country. In April the process of unification took a further step with the creation of the Democratic Revolutionary Front, which became the broadest expression of our people's unity and the social and political base of the future democratic revolutionary government.

And so we developed that first stage, which then enabled us to move more swiftly toward preparing the conditions that would eventually see us take power. And here is an important point: Unity grows not only out of the need to defend ourselves against a common enemy as it unleashes a campaign of extermination against us. It is also born from the real possibility before us of taking power.

That is how we began our coordination, which in practical terms has opened the doors to greater mass involvement in democratic and political organizations. The birth of unity has given us more than a sum of our forces, it has in fact caused a multiplication of those forces; through that unity, we can deepen the consciousness among the people and incorporate them at a higher level in the struggle for winning power. Likewise, international support for us grows wider and stronger. The achievements of this first stage are very great, indeed, but in order to win we couldn't stay at that level of coordination.

The consolidation of unity was not a preordained fact, not a mechanical resolution by leadership, but a process which has unfolded in the practice of our daily lives. It is pressure from the masses, participation by the people and the advance of the revolution which make our organizations draw nearer, close ranks and take a united stand along tactical and strategic line.

It is in this sense that we have taken some very important steps in the process of consolidating our unity: the Political-Military Coordinating Council announced its reorganization into a Unified Revolutionary Directorate (DRU), preceded by the integration into that body of the People's Revolutionary Army-Party of the Salvadorean Revolution (ERP-PRS).

That event marked a qualitative leap in the development of our unity, because it conferred upon the people's movement a single leadership—we would now have a single strategy and set of tactics for our military and political fronts and on the international level. The DRU has announced that it has ready a plan for winning the war and that the people are only waiting for the signal to commence the final battle for victory.

The other organizations of unity, CRM and FDR, have likewise been consolidating themselves, to completely isolate the enemy and increase their influence among the people.

CRM has made a qualitative leap inasmuch as it no longer simply coordinates, but now has the capacity to direct activity. As such we don't think its title as Coordinating Council accurately describes what it now does. The Revolutionary Coordinating Council of the Masses now gives direction to the entire mass movement, and so its title is inadequate. However, the title has wide recognition and on that merit we keep it.

The FDR is likewise solidifying itself. On the one hand, the strength of the masses given to it by the CRM is increasing and on the other hand, the FDR is broadening, with the incorporation of new sectors. The participation of the democratic sectors has given FDR its pluralistic aspect and its capacity to draw together every sector of the people. This makes their role very important.

The democratic forces are not playing a merely decorative role in the FDR, and they know that—still, the imperialists have tried to describe it that way. These sectors of the movement have played a very active role, they are playing an active role, and they will continue doing so throughout the construction of the new society. We can truthfully say that the FDR has gained broad international support as the main embodiment of the unity of popular forces—more, it is becoming the social and political force that will in time create the democratic revolutionary government.

As of now, we can count on a unity that is irreversible. All our organizations have made a serious commitment—they will not abandon this movement at any time. This commitment includes the intention, from here on, to develop common structures, because in spite of common leadership our internal structures remain distinct from each other. An example is that, within the CRM, the BPR has kept its own structure, as has the LP-28 and each of its sections. With the political-military organizations, it is the same situation—the people's armies each have their own structure. But the strategy we project is the formation of a single organic structure. The same is true on an international level; everybody has their own structure and while they are coordinated, the goal is to move more and more towards forming common structures. In the future, there will be examples of such unified structures on the military, political and international levels.* That is the kind of perspective, the process which in the short range opens the doors to putting the people in power.

---

* On October 11, the Unified Revolutionary Directorate (DRU) announced the founding of the Farabundo Martí National Liberation Front (FMLN), which is charged with and structured for making strategic decisions regarding the direction of the revolutionary war. The FMLN is made up of the Popular Liberation Forces—Farabundo Martí, the People's Revolutionary Army and the Armed Forces for National Liberation; it is directed, politically and militarily, by the DRU. On November 11, the Armed Forces of National Resistance were also incorporated in the FMLN. [—CIDAMO]

Along with the process you have described, has there been a parallel movement towards unity within the labor movement?

Yes. The Salvadorean working class is very much part of that process, and is in fact the moving force in our revolution. In El Salvador, the largest social force is the working class. This includes, besides the industrial working class, the rural sector—the day laborers who collectively make up the largest social class in the country. So it is they, the working class, who are determining the direction of the revolution, while in firm alliance with the peasant class.

However, the admirable struggles by the labor movement had been taking place in a disconnected fashion, and there were different currents among the unions which created an obstacle to the development of a single union position. But by now those problems have been solved and the working class can face its enemies like a solid fist. What the various union organizations within the FDR have had to do is consolidate in a structure that will enable them, first of all, to prepare for the general strike that will take place along with the final offensive for taking power (which, while incorporating all the people, will have the union movement as its epicenter). In the second place, the new structure will enable the unions to lay the foundation for a single organization comprised of all workers, which will allow the labor movement to participate—in a conscious and organized way—in constructing the new society.

The consolidation we speak of is in fact the Committee for Labor Unity, made up of the Revolutionary Federation of Unions (FSR), the National Union Federation of Salvadorean Workers (FENASTRAS), the Salvadorean Federation of Unions of Workers in Food, Clothing, Textile and Related Industries (FESTIAVTSCES), the United Labor Federation of El Salvador (FUSS), the Union of Workers in Associated Industries (STIUSA), and the Union of Workers of the Social Security Institute of El Salvador (STISSS).

How do you evaluate the general strike of last August 13-15? Where does this event fit into the overall struggle?

In the first place, let me make it clear that this was not a general strike; we envision the general strike as accompanying the final battles for power. Rather, these actions were *paros*, general work stoppages, like the one on March 17, which was the first to be carried out by the joint forces. The latest work stoppage of August 13-15 had as its goal, first, to demonstrate the regime's inability to solve the problems of our country, to expose it as a government totally isolated from the masses; and to reconfirm the people's support for the FDR as their legitimate representative. It was also aimed at breaking the blackout that imperialism has tried to impose on our struggle and transcending national boundaries to tell people about what is really happening and the power of the revolutionary forces.

But the principal objective of the work stoppage was to begin moving to a more advanced stage of popular struggle.

How do we achieve these objectives? It's very clear. The enemy tried to hide the achievements of the work stoppage, boasting that it had been a failure. Ever since the *paro* was first announced, the government had carried out a publicity campaign to keep people from joining it. They also positioned all their armed forces in the capital, which is the nerve center of the country. The army and riot squads occupied streets, factories, public services, neighborhoods, etc., to force people to work and give an appearance of tranquility.

In spite of all this, the work stoppage was a tremendous success for the Salvadorean people. Without having to utilize all their potential, the people put the enemy on the defensive, as was shown by this wasted military action of the junta.

During the work stoppage, we gained more experience, there was greater organization of people by neighborhood, and mass participation was not limited to political actions, but also included actions with the militias and the people's army. Military encounters at the national level had results favorable to the revolutionary forces; these battles have been wearing down the enemy troops. For example, the FPL alone caused 810 enemy losses during the three days of the *paro* while 31 revolutionary *compañeros* were killed. This does not include the actions of the other political-military organizations.

The regime attempted to conceal all these achievements from the eyes of the world, trying to present a facade of apparent "tranquility," which they did by going house to house and forcing many people to go to work. There were workplaces of 200 or more employees where only 10 to 25 showed up. They forced transportation workers to work, while members of the junta strutted triumphantly through the streets.

This didn't break people's morale but it did confuse some sectors of the population, who let themselves be influenced by this demogogic nonsense.

Finally, we can be sure that the work stoppage dealt a severe economic blow to the ruling class, it showed the absolute political isolation of the military-Christian Democratic junta, and most important of all, it struck military blows against the military dictatorship. With this action, the people have climbed another step in their struggle, entering a new stage of the revolutionary war for seizing power.

An Interview with
Salvador Cayetano Carpio ("Marcial")

by Adolfo Gilly

Salvador Cayetano Carpio (whose nom de guerre *was Marcial), was a principal leader of the Farabundo Martí National Liberation Front (FMLN) of El Salvador, labor leader, communist militant, and military commander. A leader in the workers' movement since the 1940s, Marcial had left the Communist Party of El Salvador and founded the Popular Liberation Force-Farabundo Martí, which today forms part of the FMLN.*

In the following interview, conducted by Adolfo Gilly, Marcial was speaking for the FMLN. It was originally published in two parts in uno mas uno, *of Mexico, on January 4 and 5, 1981, prior to the elaborately staged elections which saw the downfall of the Christian Democratic government in 1982.*

Since the publication of this interview in the original edition of this volume, the Salvadorean movement suffered the tragic loss of both Marcial and his second-in-command, Melida Anaya Montes ("Ana María"). The Editors wish to express our profound sorrow at the death of these two great revolutionary leaders. At the same time we express our highest regards for the popular organizations which Marcial and Ana María helped to build. For it is truly a powerful testament to their leadership that the Popular Forces of Liberation (FPL) and the FMLN displayed such unity, courage, and determination in the face of these tragic deaths.

Before the interview with Marcial, we share with you here the communiqué with which the FPL announced his death in April 1983:

The Political Commission of the Central Command of the Popular Forces of Liberation-Farabundo Martí informs the Salvadorean people and the people of the world with great grief and revolutionary sorrow of the death of "Marcial," the first in command of our Central Command and Commander in Chief of the Popular Armed Forces of Liberation (FAPL) and member of the General Command of the FMLN.

The recent assassination of our Comandante Ana María was planned and executed by "Marcelo," who at that moment was a member of the Central Command of the FPL. The assassination of the *compañera* Ana María produced in *compañero* Marcial great revolutionary sorrow which deepened and caused an emotional crisis when he found out that one of the members of the Central Command who had been very close to him had been the organizer and executor of the crime. This led him to commit suicide on April 12 at 9:30 p.m., in a house where he was staying with his wife Enma and friends who were there at that time. The FPL, in the face of this lamentable tragedy, condemns this shameful crime committed by "Marcelo" in collaboration with other *ex-compañeros.*

With the death of our two top leaders, the FPL, the FMLN, and the Salvadorean people suffered two irreparable losses: two great revolutionary leaders who have given so much and who have contributed to the advance of the Salvadorean revolutionary process and contributed with self-denial and sacrifice for the development and consolidation of our organization in order to advance and develop the democratic-revolutionary unity of the FMLN/FDR. The hundreds of combatants of the FAPL, of the FMLN, and of all the people will carry on, until the ultimate outcome with redoubled energy, the objectives set forth by the two *compañeros*—the military defeat of U.S. imperialism and of the fascistic military puppet dictatorship.

We encourage all organized supporters and the Salvadorean people in general to be vigilant and alert not to allow themselves to be confused by the enemy's attempts to breed mistrust of the leaders and the directing bodies of the FPL and the FMLN in order to weaken and undermine their authority in the eyes of our people. We make a call to close our ranks to combat and defeat these maneuvers of imperialism.

We redouble our combative spirit against the aggressive policies of U.S. imperialism which, in its feverish desire to contain the Revolutionary movement, implements plans of aggression, psychological warfare, and covert actions. We reaffirm that these policies will continually be met by our high combative spirit and revolutionary decisiveness until the final victory of our combatants.

We, the FPL, express our gratitude for the efforts and facilities provided to our directorate by the Ministry of Interior of the Nicaraguan National Government of Reconstruction and by the National Directorate of the Sandinista National Liberation Front in clarifying facts behind the assassination of the Comandante Ana María. The Central Command will continue the investigations and makes a call to all of the members and supporters to tighten our ranks around the leadership bodies, the Revolutionary Council, the Central Command, and the Political Commission, in order to carry out the agreements of the last meeting of the Central Command, to strengthen and consolidate the Revolutionary Unity of the FMLN/FDR, to push forward with total sacrifice the political and military tasks, and to seek a just and dignified political solution in the interests of the Salvadorean people.

Political Commission of the Central Command of the Popular Forces of Liberation (FPL)-Farabundo Martí—Member of the FMLN

Signed,

Comandante Salvador Guerra, member of the Political Commission of the General Command and substitute Commander in Chief; Comandante Leonel Gonzales, member of the Political Commission and in charge of the organization of the party; Comandante Miguel Castellanos, member of the Political Commission and head of the urban front—April 1983

Interview with Marcial, 1981

What do you think of the latest reorganization of the Christian Democratic military government?

Undoubtedly the crisis of the military government has grown more severe in recent weeks. Their major weakness is now the economic situation. In November, the junta issued decrees designed to close off the flight of capital and slow down the internal deterioration of businesses, forcing them to leave part of their capital resources in the country.

The transnational corporations are leaving. The industrialists are leaving their factories with lower-level managers and factories are operating at 40% of capacity. In August, the indicators of economic activity had fallen to minimal levels. It seems impossible that the economy won't collapse.

But didn't the agrarian reform, fraudulent though it was, provide a certain social base for the junta in some rural areas for a while?

Surely this is what they wanted, but the agrarian reform backfired on them politically and economically. Economically, they didn't have enough technicians to encourage production and they lost lots of time in the first months. Furthermore, many of the technicians they had counted on actually sabotaged their own reforms. The infighting within the junta also manifested itself everywhere. In their limitless repression, the forces of tyranny began to assassinate entire groups that were part of cooperatives which they themselves had organized after the agrarian reform. Today the government believes this social base cannot be counted on, to the point that it is planning to militarize the cooperatives and even use the army for certain agricultural tasks, which would be another catastrophe for them. I'm sure you know that the person who designed the military junta's agrarian reform was a U.S. specialist who also designed the reform programs for South Vietnam and the Philippines, and it doesn't look like he did much better this time.

The whole junta is really a scheme of the United States, and more precisely the CIA. Colonels Abdul Gutiérrez, García and Carranza were bought off by the CIA through corruption a long time ago. When Molina was President, he pushed Humberto Romero through the army as his successor, against the wishes of many officers— especially the young military officers who wanted to put García into the presidency because they thought he was a sincere and progressive man. But Molina put Romero in as President and made García the head of the National Telecommunication Administration (Antel). García then took over Antel as if it was his own property; that's where he built his alliance with Abdul and Carranza and the three of them ran the enterprise for their own benefit and enrichment. The young military officers could not see this process of corruption and clung to their illusions about García. Thus, when the coup of October 15, 1979 overthrew Romero, the CIA was able to make its move by handing the government over to this trio. The young military officers, seeing García in there, thought they held power in their hands. Since then, the trio has been putting its people in other key positions, and we can see the results.

Generally speaking, we see a favorable evolution of the democratic spirit, including among certain army officers, which is caused by a triple crisis of the economy, the government and the army. It is the coming together of frustrations from the failure of the agrarian reform experiment and all the promises of reforms, and the understanding that the army cannot continue with unlimited genocide because it does not serve the goals that they seek.

And the soldiers?

The effects are more profound among the soldiers. You have to take into consideration the general situation of the army, despite the fact that it has fire power and receives constant aid from the United States. In recent months, imperialism has been convinced that the Salvadorean army is not capable of strategically defeating the popular movement. They carried out extensive efforts, concentrating thousands of soldiers in certain areas like Chalatenango. Afterwards they decided to wipe Morazán off the map. They amassed 4,500 men for the first stage, during 20 days of October, supported by tanks, helicopter artillery, planes and mortars. In the end they occupied the area, but FMLN units broke through, in small groups, and later regrouped their forces.

In other words, they achieved certain tactical objectives but not the strategic objective of the operation. This failure was aggravated by the fact that, in the course of the operation, they carried out massive assassinations of the population but were able to kill only a few guerrillas. They occupied terrain, but did not destroy the insurgent forces. This caused great confusion and demoralization among officers and troops. They felt guilty about the excess of bloodshed and frustrated because their strategic objective was not attained.

How have these partial defeats affected the overall relation of military forces at present?

They have led to a realization among the high echelons of the army and their Yankee advisers that strategically the army has been steadily losing its capability of destroying its enemy—the popular forces. Not because it is weaker than before, but because the guerrillas are getting stronger, so the previous tactic is not effective in attaining the objectives that the army set for itself. Thus the need for readjustments. There is demoralization among the troops, desertions, confusion among officers, growing doubt about the capability of the high command. You know that this counts a lot; to lose confidence in the military ability of your commanders is one of the worst things that can happen to an army. And every day, men like García, Abdul and other officers are losing the authority and respect of their subordinates.

Add to this another weighty factor: each day they are more and more drenched in the blood of their countrymen. And not all the officers and soldiers are hardened criminals. It's not nice to have to kill a child or a woman. And if the justification that the high command gave for these crimes was the necessity of wiping out the guerrillas, then, when this is not achieved, the wake of crime and genocide turns against them and demoralization deepens the contradictions in the heart of the army.

It is in this light that we must view the statements of the most reactionary officers, who blame the failure of their operations on the lack of unity, discipline and authority at the top. This is their excuse to justify a new centralization of political and above all military control, backed up by the chorus of Christian Democrats.

On the other hand, their growing international isolation weighs upon them, in spite of the efforts of the Christian Democrats to sugarcoat the situation.

This is the situation that the Salvadorean government came to face when it reached this latest crisis, which we can now define as permanent.

Given the critical military and economic situation, won't the junta be forced to devalue the currency as Somoza did just months before the Sandinista victory?

Aid from the Inter-American Development Bank is helping the junta to hold off devaluation. Some of the funds they have received are going to bolster workers' salaries, to keep the social crisis from exploding. Other funds are gobbled up by the agrarian reform. It's said that they have set aside $800,000 to help the refugees that now number more than 100,000.

There was a visible change recently in the general political tone of the Christian Democrats. Remember the optimism they displayed after the August strike, as if they had come out winners? Less than three months later, in November, they could not hide the crisis any longer, and Duarte and Morales began to declare that the economic situation was grave. The Salvadorean Industrial Association says that the country's economy is going through the *darkest moments of its history*. They call on us to tighten our belts in the name of patriotism. They have decreed restrictions on imports of luxury items. For example, for three months the government has prohibited the importation of vehicles and has said that if things get better they will reconsider this decision next January. But even so, lack of confidence grows among those who were once supporters, the investors retreat even more, and the economic and military crises fuel each other and have direct repercussions in the political arena.

We have discussed the state of the economy and of the army. How do you see the situation of the government and the latest reshuffling of the junta, with Duarte being named President?

This reshuffling reveals the degree to which imperialism lacks room to maneuver with the present regime, composed of reactionary military officers and Christian Democratic politicians. Carter would have wanted to cover up the fascist essence of the current regime, even while strengthening it. But this recent change has left that fascist essence more out in the open, since the two most discredited and reactionary types were promoted to top leadership: Abdul in the military and Duarte in the political arena. Duarte is the most servile; among the Christian Democrats, he is the most identified with the crimes and genocide. Abdul is the person most identified with the right wing, both within and outside the government; it is he who shares the job of D'Aubuisson and his death squads made up of National Guardsmen.

Is there still a division of labor for repression, then, between the official government forces and the supposedly paramilitary death squads?

Yes, but lately they mix together openly; people are arrested by soldiers in uniform and appear later as corpses disfigured by torture. Not long ago, in Amatepec, 60 young people were arrested by the army and the next day the corpses of 50 of them were found with signs written by the Unión Guerrera Blanca (White Warriors Union).

One more indicator of the breakdown of the regime is the incredible degree of cynicism and sadism in the assassinations that they commit daily. They take an entire family from their home, and the next day the

bodies are found strung up in the outskirts of town with their faces tied
together, as if kissing each other. It is repulsive to have to talk about
these things, but the world must know about them. In San Miguel, they
captured a very young female student and her boyfriend. The next day
they were both found dead; his headless body on one side, hers on the
other side with his head stuck between her legs. In December, disfigured
bodies began to appear with signs that read, "Merry Christmas, people.
We are ridding you of terrorists."

Such is government policy, now directed by the most noted
reactionaries.

*Why do you think they put in Duarte, with his Christian Democratic
cover, and not a military dictator without any go-betweens, who would
be more suited to these policies?*

You know quite well that this is not the first place where imperialism
has tried such a combination. Impelled by the crisis, this time they
made a patchwork repair of the formula that they have been following
since the coup of October 1979, but making it appear they had not
rejected their original plan. Carter and his party, after losing the November election, wanted to preserve their image for the future. They
wanted to be able to say, four years hence, that while they were in
power the United States did not rush head over heels into El Salvador,
but instead supported the Christian Democratic formula. Let Reagan, if
he wants to, take responsibility for other measures. This is why they
adopted such a patchwork solution, which in the end is turning out to
be the worst and most unbearable solution for them. It remains to be
seen if it will last, and how long. . . .

*Tell me what the situation is with the FMLN forces at the present
time.*

In recent months the revolutionary forces have grown much
stronger. The coordination that we have achieved by forming the
FMLN doesn't signify a mere increase in forces, but a qualitative
leap. It enables us to plan operations on a greater scale, to combine
small operations with large ones, to concentrate our fire power when
we decide to, to choose our objectives better and with greater possibilities
of success. The wearing down of the enemy forces matches our increasing
fire power. Their tanks are not invulnerable. The use of the equipment
they can count on is reaching a saturation point, since it has to be
transferred from one front to another, and then worn-out parts aggravate
the damage done by our fire power. We are now using bazookas, high
power mines, grenade launchers and mortars all the time. Other arms
will soon be brought into combat.

This helps to explain the failure of the recent army offensives, as
in Morazán or in the San Vicente volcano region. With these failures,

the army has shown that it is losing its capability of utilizing one of the fundamental factors in military strategy: the relation between concentration and dispersion. They don't have enough forces to place them simultaneously in all the places where they need to concentrate them to destroy the popular forces. Furthermore, those latest offensives have shown that even when they concentrate their forces in a particular zone, they are not able to liquidate our forces in that zone, and they leave us free to act in other areas. The fatal dilemma that the high command faces is, to use a popular saying, that their blanket doesn't reach: if they amass in one point, they leave the rest of the country open; and if they disperse, their forces are not sufficient to strike strategic blows.

On the other hand, the FMLN in the last months has increased its level of organization and structure, its operational capacity and its firepower. It is also evident how widespread the guerrilla activity (both of the insurrectional and militia type) and mass activity have been in the last weeks.

Instead of paralyzing our people as the enemy hoped, the assassination of the *compañeros* from the FDR generated an indignation that has translated into the participation of many people in the armed struggle at many levels. It is also evident that the people are going on the offensive more strategically in every way: militarily, insurrectionally and politically. This is what tells us that conditions are being created and the moment grows closer when the United Revolutionary Directorate (DRU) of the FMLN and the FDR will decide upon the formation of a democratic revolutionary government inside El Salvador.

The FMLN argues, and many of us share the belief, that if no external power intervenes in El Salvador, the insurrectional forces already mobilized are enough to guarantee victory for the Salvadorean revolution in the next year. But imperialism also knows this and its interventionist threats are growing more real all the time.

Certainly. Thus the necessity for everyone to support the battle that we are waging, and complete the job of internationally isolating the Salvadorean dictatorship. Our people need for all the peoples of the world to help hold back the interventionist hand of the United States. Let it be the Salvadorean people who resolve their own problems, freely exercising their right to self-determination.

What concrete forms do you in the FMLN see the danger of intervention taking?

There are various degrees of intervention, for which imperialism has different means at its disposal. Actually, intervention began some time ago, not only with the U.S. government's participation in the junta's programs, but also with military and economic aid and by sending military advisers. But now it takes more concrete and aggressive forms; among them, we can identify three levels.

The first would be to push for what we might call "humanitarian intervention." Carter's Administration, and especially Bowdler (Assistant Secretary of State for Inter-American Affairs— *Ed.*), has been claiming lately that a military deadlock exists in El Salvador, meaning that neither of the two sides can defeat the other. According to them, this deadlock is what's prolonging the horrible violence that is victimizing the people. They must assist "humanistically," then, to stop the bloodshed by proposing intervention by the OAS Commission on Human Rights or the "good offices" of democratic governments, so that a formula is found to intervene between the warring groups and stop the hostilities. This would be "merciful" mediation, a dangerous and hypocritical mask of imperialism.

But imperialism also has other, more militant means at its disposal. The second level consists of urging the governments of Guatemala or Honduras to intervene in different ways and carry out operations of military cooperation or direct intervention itself. The Honduran army is already systematically crossing the borders of our country to combat revolutionary forces. About a month ago the *compañeros* of the border region captured inside Salvadorean territory the Honduran commander of the Honduran town of La Virtud. To avoid incidents and provocations, they only disarmed him, accompanied him across the border and returned his weapons. Honduran troops systematically carry out raids and rape women in Salvadorean towns.

Presently the armies of Honduras, Guatemala and El Salvador are preparing "Operation Sandwich" to try to exterminate the guerrillas in the north. There is ample evidence, and denunciations have been made, including those of democratic and grassroots organizations in Honduras, that Honduras' army is turning over Salvadorean refugees to the National Guard of El Salvador, which assassinates them. The Honduran army is being armed by the U.S. government. Within this strategy, the peace treaty between Honduras and El Salvador is nothing more than a bloody pact against the Salvadorean revolution, conceived by the U.S. Department of State to consolidate a counterrevolutionary triangle of El Salvador-Honduras-Guatemala, and to try in this way to destroy our movement and launch an offensive against the Nicaraguan people.

On this second level, of using puppet armed forces, the present government of Venezuela is playing a nefarious role. The U.S. counts on the Venezuelan army for possible aggression against El Salvador. This army gives the most training, arms and credit to the Christian Democratic junta, despite the enormous repudiation of such actions by the Venezuelan people. In terms of training and military aid given to the Salvadorean dictatorship, Venezuela and Israel stand in second place after the United States. France sends no advisers, but sells sophisticated arms to the junta.

The third stage of intervention, now appearing with more dangerous contours than ever, is direct intervention by the Yankees themselves, a move of desperation if all other attempts to contain our revolution fail. The FMLN once again emphasizes the necessity for international solidarity from all countries to stop direct military intervention of imperialism in our territory.

The Salvadorean Struggle:
An International Conflict

Fermán Cienfuegos

The following analysis of the current situation in El Salvador reflects the position of the Unified Revolutionary Directorate (DRU) of the Farabundo Martí National Liberation Front (FMLN). Fermán Cienfuegos is the commander-in-chief of the Armed Forces of National Resistance (FARN) and a member of the general command of the FMLN. The FARN forms part of the FMLN, which is currently fighting to overthrow the Salvadorean civil-military junta. This article was originally published in the Mexican journal Proceso *on March 9, 1981.*

The situation in El Salvador in recent months reflects a crisis of hegemony, an expression of the profound crisis of dependent capitalism in our country. The disruption of all sources of capital accumulation is at the root of the social and political conflicts dominating the situation in El Salvador, where a key class, the Salvadorean proletariat, and its allies are struggling to build a new, more just and democratic society.

The Salvadorean revolution has broken away from many models. Those who have wished to view our revolution in terms of the Sandinista model have not only proven the impossibility of such a transposition, but also risk falling into some kind of disillusionment and frustration. The Salvadorean situation is particularly complex and in order to get close to the reality of it one needs to relinquish certain stereotypes.

El Salvador is experiencing a crisis of oligarchic power, which occurs at the level of articulation among the components of the ruling bloc: Government-Oligarchy-Army-Christian Democratic Party-United States. What are the relationships between these sectors of the ruling bloc and what are their contradictions?

Since late last year, the bourgeois-oligarchic sector has openly supported the junta. This sector is represented at the corporate-guild level by the Alliance for Production (Alianza Productiva) and holds various key positions within the government.

Nevertheless, their support for the junta's program is complex and contradictory, and inevitably carries within it the seeds of future conflict. The Alliance for Production supports the political goals of the Christian Democrats and the Army, predicated on defeating the revolutionary democratic movement. But this is not the case with the "community" economic program championed by the Christian Democrats. On the basis of a military defeat of the FMLN-FDR, the oligarchy would back up Duarte's project but not that of the Christian Democrats.

What is the explanation for this? Let's not forget that, after all, the coup of October 15, 1979, signified a relative unhinging of the oligarchy's power, in that it was a new situation with less than ideal conditions. For the oligarchy it was a matter of recovering government positions, which they hadn't really lost but hadn't been able to handle either. The representatives of the oligarchy's corporate interests, finding themselves in a delicate, complex and dangerous political situation, have been unable to reconcile these with their long-range goals.

This situation has caused shifts within the core of the oligarchy. Those with a more long-range political and economic approach have been pushed to the sidelines, in many far-reaching decisions, while those with a "do-it-now" approach and the most bellicose tendencies have gained much ground. This sector of the oligarchy views the present situation as a process of recovering political power it nearly lost to the bourgeois-reformist sector of the oligarchy which imperialism had wanted to impose.

The junta is definitely unable to govern. That it has ever governed is questionable. The Christian Democratic military regime has no popular support whatsoever, nor any national or international credibility. The continuous crisis of the regime, marked by constant desertions of its administrators and by an incapacity to implement even a small part of its programs, is now dramatized by total economic chaos, a chaos which, from many points of view, is irreversible.

Only one thing still holds up this government, and it is the same thing that props up all puppet regimes: imperialism's dollars and the political alliance of the most retrogressive sectors. The attempts to make a leader out of Duarte only add a touch of melodrama to a situation that is clearly untenable.

The bourgeois-imperialist undertaking of January 1980, based on an alliance of the Army with the Christian Democratic Party, the oligarchy and the U.S. government, did not come close to solving the contradictions that exist within the core of the Armed Forces. Instead, it created new conflicts and intensified the existing ones. The crisis of authority is rather apparent and is shown by the constant attempts on the lives of democratic officers. The fact that members of the military have no recourse except gunfire for resolving their conflicts shows the crisis of authority to be so severe that there is no way to keep the Army moving together, down the same road.

Due to the intensification of contradictions within the Army, we have been able to observe more clearly the workings of this arm of the state.

We see that the present Minister of Defense, Colonel García, holds the key to maintaining unity within the Army, while the key to political unity is divided between junta member Abdul Gutiérrez and Colonel Majano. Clearly the conditions are not exactly favorable to resolving the crisis of authority. Colonel Majano was persecuted and, after several attempts on his life, was imprisoned. This was intended to solve the crisis. But is there, in fact, an easy way out of this crisis? Is the problem so simple that the imprisonment of an officer will suffice to curtail a widespread democratic-technocratic movement within the Army?

Perhaps that would be the case if it were not for another fundamental issue. The FMLN is not only a political threat; it is above all a military threat. The U.S. government and certain big shots in the Christian Democratic regime openly recognize this, as demonstrated by the desperate and hurried manner in which the U.S. government has reinforced the junta militarily.

The point is that the "Salvadorean" Army is no longer capable of directing the war, strategically or tactically. With the January 10, 1981 general offensive, the FMLN gained the strategic offensive and all the bourgeois Army's attempts to regain it have resulted in major military defeats. This has had very far-reaching consequences—it leaves imperialism with no option other than intervention in order to try to defend a situation which is militarily indefensible. So imperialism converts the "Salvadorean" Army into a puppet army whose reins are held outside of the country; an army-of-occupation with its command center in the United States.

This clearly implies a reshuffling within the Army. Making the armed forces into a U.S. puppet is a direct blow to those officers of the nationalist school of thought, who uphold the motto "Salvation of the Homeland" and respect for the National Constitution. Thus, it isn't easy for the imperialists to transform the "Salvadorean" Army into a puppet army without deepening contradictions that already exist.

Meanwhile, the alliance between the Army and the Alliance for Production has grown tighter. However, the latter group, with a view to recovering economic ground, supports fascism and genocide without any reform measures. Thus the vicious circle is sealed and the door is shut on an already impossible situation. There is no "way out" except the open extermination of the Salvadorean people. The "Zimbabwe solution" is countered by the "Jakarta solution."

The Christian Democratic Party (PDC) has been reduced to a miniscule presence. Within it, a few personalities represent what would be entire sectors in other political parties. The present crisis, in dealing a blow to the ideological superstructure and thereby to the structures of the traditional political parties, has left its mark on the PDC.

The "leadership" of Duarte is nothing but an expression of the most abject and treasonous sell-out—a systematic genocide designed to assure maintenance of the circuits of capital accumulation.

Attempts are made to counter Duarte's fascism with the "clean" image of one Fidel Chávez Mena, a man who strives for a political solution to the crisis that will salvage not only the capitalist aims, but above all the image of the PDC, which is now quite bloodstained and discredited by its perpetration of genocide in El Salvador.

Individuals and tiny groups within the PDC take various positions, all of them based on the most rabid anticommunism, and none of them with any potential for providing leadership; their expression is limited to in-fighting.

These are some of the key aspects of the present situation in El Salvador:

—The U.S. plays a decisive and definitive role in the inner workings of the "Salvadorean" Army.

—The United States plays a decisive role in determining the fire power of the "Salvadorean" Army against the FMLN forces.

—The United States decides the continuation of Duarte and the Christian Democratic government. However, the efforts of the World Christian Democratic Union and the Venezuelan regime to find a negotiated and cooptive way out continue, and are increasing as the FMLN-FDR forces become stronger and the junta weaker.

—The United States intends to strengthen the most unyielding faction of the Army in order to strike hard against the FMLN militarily and thereby have the upper hand in any negotiations. This is what underlies the diplomacy game.

—The international situation is not favorable to a Vietnamization of the conflict; there are concrete pressures on Christian Democracy to find a political (negotiated) way out. This follows, in part, from a change that has occurred in the correlation of forces at the international level; certain powers that had supported the bourgeois imperialist aims of the junta are now reconsidering their positions.

—It is possible that the contradictions within the Army will intensify as a result of Colonel Majano's detention. However, the likelihood that the democratic constitutionalist movement within the Army could be thoroughly curtailed cannot be dismissed.

—The month of March appears to be decisive militarily. It is the month in which imperialism has proposed launching a decisive counter-offensive against the Salvadorean people and their vanguard.

—Nevertheless, the Reagan Administration has not found fertile ground in the Trilateral Commission for its warmongering positions.

The United States has felt obliged to pressure and blackmail its allies in Germany and Japan. This pressure comes without prior consultation and if the U.S. does consult them, it applies the threat of a "Soviet advance" in Central America.

The governments of Germany, France and England have not responded to the U.S. warmongering. On the contrary, they have been extremely cautious, signifying that there is little fertile ground for direct imperialist intervention. Thus the Reagan Administration is left with the uncomfortable choice of a unilateral intervention.

Since late February, imperialism has tried to recover the political initiative by launching a widespread political-diplomatic offensive with various aims:

a) To obtain the support, loyalty and commitment of its European and Latin American allies for its various plans.

b) To launch a campaign against the USSR and the socialist camp.

c) To reduce political-diplomatic support for the FMLN-FDR internationally by neutralizing certain parties or governments, and/or by recruiting new allies from sectors which are vacillating.

This is a huge political and diplomatic propaganda campaign that seeks to discredit the struggle of the Salvadorean people and win sympathy for the lost cause of the junta. It is not just a matter of trying to neutralize support, but involves stopping every kind of aid to the FMLN-FDR (weapons, humanitarian services for the refugees, money, etc.) and thereby loading them down with social problems.

The campaign is therefore very broad and far-reaching, and it convinces us that it is not just a question of defeating the FMLN-FDR militarily but of a definitive, long-term resolution.

d) To launch a campaign of diversionary tactics to cover up and justify the increasing, direct military intervention of the U.S. It isn't by chance that imperialist diplomatic tours have coincided with "Operation Black Falcon 4" in Panama, and "Operation Readex 1-81" at Vieques island off Puerto Rico.

e) To gain time, politically and militarily, for a final defeat of the revolutionary-democratic movement in El Salvador.

f) To alter the balance of forces within Central America on the basis of a broad strategy which includes aggression against Cuba.

The aims of this political-diplomatic offensive heighten international tensions. They make the situation in El Salvador first and foremost a "problem of national security" for the United States; they provide imperialism with lots of room to manipulate by use of blackmail; they renew the Cold War. The socialist camp is pushed to respond in the mode chosen by the imperialists—which could lead to a worldwide confrontation.

However, the fact that the U.S. has not encountered support for intervention opens up the possibility of a worldwide parliament, which through the United Nations could reach a negotiated settlement of the problem.

Because of North American pressure and the correlation of forces on a worldwide level, we can expect modifications (though not basic change) in the positions held by certain governments and their local political parties. The firm support expressed by Willy Brandt, the contradictions within the Socialist International (Costa Rica, Italy), the struggles between the Socialist International and the Christian Democrats (Venezuela, Italy), and finally the contradictions in the World Christian Democratic Union (Belgium, Holland, Switzerland), make up a complex panorama in which it appears that the position favoring a negotiated settlement is gaining ground.

Within the World Christian Democratic Union, positions have varied somewhat. There are sectors that persist in defending Duarte and his traitorous program while others express a range of positions from the deepest repudiation (Holland) to those who seek compromise formulas which at least exclude Duarte.

In this area we must say that the victories achieved by the Popular Social Christian Movement in El Salvador, member of the FDR and represented on the Political-Diplomatic Commission of the FMLN-FDR, have been invaluable.

The last meeting of ministers in New Delhi ratified the position of nonintervention in El Salvador held by the Movement of Non-Aligned Nations. There is a broad movement of countries which could form a wall of opposition to direct intervention. The FMLN-FDR greatly values the support of the Non-Aligned Nations, it considers this body to be of special importance strategically, and will make every effort to become an active member of it.

The FMLN-FDR also values the courageous position taken by the Mexican government. The fact that President José López Portillo refused to receive General Vernon Walters has special political and diplomatic repercussions that cannot be ignored. Brazil has adopted a cautious attitude, in that within the Andean Pact certain Venezuelan sectors are pushing for a compromise solution. Ecuador's firm support of the FMLN-FDR has become somewhat more neutral as a result of internal problems generated by its conflicts with Peru.

On a worldwide level, the imperialist efforts at direct military intervention have been relatively neutralized. For this reason, the United States at this time has no other way to carry out its interventionist plans than through limited maneuvers within Central America: a) Military support by the Guatemalan government for the Army and government of El Salvador. b) Setbacks in Belize's independence. c) Military support from the army and government of Honduras, including incursions into Salvadorean territory, attacks by the highly trained and well-equipped Honduran Air Force on FMLN encampments and, in an extreme case, the permanent penetration of Honduran armed forces into El Salvador. The Honduran Minister of Defense himself, Colonel Flores Queretín, acknowledges that his army has about 4,000 troops stationed along the border. Needless to say, those troops aren't there on an outing . . . d) Stimulating the activity of *Somocista* National Guards in Guatemala and Honduras, encouraging harassment and even an invasion of Nicaragua. e) Encouraging a political, economic and diplomatic blockade of Nicaragua. f) Activating the most fascist and backward groups in Costa Rica to persecute the anti-imperialist and opposition forces of that country. g) Openly violating the Panama Canal treaties and the autonomy of that nation. Pressuring and blackmailing the Panamanian government in order to force a change in its anti-imperialist policies, or neutralize it. h) Bringing about fundamental changes in Central America and the Caribbean by destabilizing the progressive and democratic governments of the region.

As we can see, the "El Salvador problem" extends beyond the borders of that country. Because of imperialism's plans for intervention on the one had, and the rising up of forces fighting for a new, just and democratic society on the other, El Salvador has become a focus of worldwide attention. At every conjuncture, the various North American administrations have chosen to support the darkest and most backward forces. We have the examples of the Shah of Iran, Nicaragua's Somoza and Cuba's Batista. And in all of those cases, the force of history prevailed and the old regimes were toppled by revolutionary governments. Sooner or later the forces of change will take power in El Salvador. The position that the United States adopts will determine, in the end, whether our future relationship will be one of open hostility or as good neighbors.

There is something which keeps imperialism from opening its eyes to the march of history: it is the steadfast bond that it inevitably maintains with the repressive forces of the dependent capitalist countries. This makes imperialism Public Enemy Number One to democratic revolutionary forces; in spite of it, history will march on.

The First Phase
of the General Offensive

Rafael Menjívar

This is a transcript of major sections of a talk given on February 17, 1981, by Dr. Rafael Menjívar, spokesman for the Democratic Revolutionary Front (FDR), and a leading Salvadorean intellectual. It was originally published in Informaciones de El Salvador *(Boletín de Prensa Internacional) No. 4-5, April, 1981 (Lima, Peru).*

It is important to begin with an analysis of the offensive of January 10, 1981, when the general offensive was launched by the democratic revolutionary forces, and in that light evaluate developments from then on.

The announcement of the general offensive implied a qualitative change in the struggle, both militarily and politically. Here it is important to clarify a point which perhaps was misunderstood and for which we are perhaps partly responsible. There were moments in which there was talk of a final offensive instead of a general offensive. The conception was of a general offensive—a tactical as well as strategic offensive—within which a series of movements would be initiated, eventually culminating in the final offensive. Thus, what began on January 10 was the general offensive, and within it also began the first movement or the first political-military wave.

This first wave, or first stage of the general offensive, had precise tactical and military objectives as well as political ones. Most of the military objectives were achieved. One of them, for example, was to consolidate the rear guard, that is, the areas which the people's revolutionary army controls. In effect, after all the military operations that took place, we find in areas such as the north zone, the central zone of San Vicente, Guazapa, Sensuntepec, that the goal of consolidating and strengthening the areas where the revolutionary movement is located was achieved. We cannot say at this time that we have liberated zones. They are almost liberated. Rather, they are zones which the enemy can penetrate but in which they cannot remain. So, we do think that this goal was achieved.

Another important objective was to cause the army to spread itself throughout the country, in order to prevent it from carrying out heavily concentrated attacks as it had been doing in the past. And in effect, the people's revolutionary army, the guerrillas, the militias, all moved throughout the whole country, attacking different military zones, thus forcing the enemy to disperse its forces throughout the territory.

The other objective, which was perhaps the one we achieved the least, was to sharpen the division that was developing within the army. Perhaps the problem is not that we were unable to accomplish this to a greater extent, but rather that there weren't ways, possibly due to our own errors, in which this division could *manifest* itself. Nevertheless, we know this division exists, as in the case of Santa Ana, where a large group of soldiers led by army officers rebelled and were able to "liberate" a Sherman tank and weapons, and blow up what was left. However, this phenomenon did not repeat itself in other places as we had expected. But without a doubt, the effects of the offensive itself are causing a sharper division among both the officers and the ranks of the army.

Another important factor was the mobilization of several large contingents of the revolutionary army, which were able to surround cities. The tactical objective was not to remain in those cities, but rather to take them and then leave. In fact, afterwards there was mobilization of the revolutionary army without it suffering great losses.

We think that an important indication of the degree to which we succeeded in striking blows against the junta militarily was the level of military aid it received from the U.S. during that period. The United States gave the junta helicopters, planes, ammunition and credit for $4.3 million to repair all the planes and helicopters that had been damaged. Furthermore, the U.S. sent 800 more Marines, making a total of 1,000 Marines in El Salvador who are labeled "military advisers"— and that seems to us like a lot of military advisers. In reality, they are lower-ranking U.S. Army officers who at this time are already directing the repressive actions in the cities and who are engaged in and leading the war against the revolutionary forces in the countryside.

Where we think there have been some problems is in the area of mass organizing. That is to say, we called for a general strike that was not able to consolidate and take hold completely. We think there were various problems. The first is that we had no effective military operations in cities such as San Salvador, San Miguel and Santa Ana—the more important cities with more industry and a larger number of workers. This limited the population's ability to evade the repression. So there was a lack of definitive military actions.

The other aspect has to do with the restructuring of our military, taking into account the mass movement. It may be necessary to restructure the revolutionary front of the masses, in the sense of increasing the cadre, who have been harshly repressed in those cities we mentioned, so they can lead the mass movement. For my part, I would add another phenomenon which has had great repercussions, in addition to the incredible repression in the cities where we saw the problems described above. In other cities of the interior, there were partial insurrections. This spoke, in large part, to the effect of the death of Monsignor Romero. The fact that Monsignor Romero, the spokesperson for vast sectors of the population, was killed, and that the church hierarchy has since switched to such an ambiguous position, has left the people not totally demobilized but certainly confused.

At this time we are, of course, continuing with our war plans. There would have been new phases within the general offensive which would have led us to the final offensive. But of course things have changed greatly. Reagan's decision to support the junta as much as possible, which was manifested in the delivery of 10 Hercules helicopters loaded with ammunition, tanks, planes and more soldiers, changes the situation. This is a factor that must be defeated not only internally in El Salvador, but especially internationally, by seeking the support of the peoples of the world and of the democratic governments of the world.

What Is the Model of U.S. Intervention for El Salvador?

The statements coming from Haig have been very clear. A State Department official stated that they were willing to support the Salvadorean junta up to the final consequences and in effect, they are doing so. I have pointed out before the similarities between Reagan and Hitler, who announced at one point everything he was going to do. There were a lot of people who did not believe he was going to do it when, in effect, he was almost at the point of succeeding. In the case of Reagan and all his advisers, I think he is ready to attempt everything he says. Whether he'll be able to succeed is another matter. That will depend not only on our stand in El Salvador but also on the actions of the other peoples of the world.

What does it mean to say "support the junta to the final consequences"? We understand it to mean that if the junta falls, as it is about to do, the United States would be willing to intervene in El Salvador. They have said it very clearly. They are looking for, and they have made this public, a way to launch a diplomatic offensive against the Socialist International, or involving the Socialist International, in order to derail — according to them — its support for the struggle in El Salvador. In my opinion, the United States is searching for several options. In the first place, they are attempting a maneuver through the OAS, in order to apply the Inter-American Treaty for Reciprocal Assistance which eventually would have the participation of those countries allied with the U.S. against El Salvador, such as the governments of Guatemala and Honduras (which has been militarily strengthened by the U.S.) and the support of the Herrera Campins government in Venezuela (which has provided the main support for the U.S. and for Christian-Democratic politics in El Salvador). And in the event that they are not able to carry out this plan, they would be willing, without a doubt, to carry out a full-scale, direct intervention in El Salvador. This intervention, according to their own plans, would not be limited to El Salvador, but would include Nicaragua and also would serve to strengthen Guatemala.

Given this reality, we have prepared ourselves for a longer struggle. We don't doubt for a moment that the U.S. will regionalize the conflict — which we do not wish to happen. This leads us to make a comparison with other types of interventions carried out by the United States in Latin America and other parts of the world.

I think there are two models that the United States always has in mind, one of which it obviously does not like. The first model is that of the invasion of the Dominican Republic in 1965, which was for the U.S. the most satisfactory in that they could localize the problem and leave the country very rapidly, with little loss of human lives (North American, of course) and at low political cost as well. The other model is that of Vietnam, where the conflict became a regional one, where the loss of American lives was high, the political cost was high and even the economic cost was high. Analyzing the Central American, Caribbean and world context of the situation, we think that in the case of El Salvador, the U.S. is not very likely to invade as they did with the Dominican Republic. In the case of El Salvador, as in Vietnam, we think they are going to make it a regional problem, because El Salvador cannot be seen outside the context of Central America.

Nicaragua has already warned, and it is quite evident, that an invasion of El Salvador would be immediately detrimental to the Nicaraguan Revolution. It would be practically an invasion of the Nicaraguan Revolution, which is already feeling the U.S. attacks and economic offensive through the denial of wheat, loans, etc. Also, we don't think this can occur without a reaction from the revolutionary movements of Guatemala, Honduras and Costa Rica. On the diplomatic level, we think that if Nicaragua is attacked, other countries in the Caribbean and the world will have to participate.

And then there is Mexico, a very important factor in our estimation. Mexico has had an anti-imperialist policy, not purely as a vocation, but because of very concrete interests of its own which make it take the side of the national liberation movements. Mexico has on its southern borders 80% of its oil, and 63% of its (natural) gas, and it has an oil pipeline; but it also sees very clearly that what the U.S. wants to do is close in through a hard-line policy in the Caribbean and Central America. We think that the United States is launching a very strong offensive, with many economic and political pressures, on a worldwide scale. We know it has launched a campaign against Mexico. Mexico has maintained a position of respect for self-determination, the same as Roldos [President of Ecuador, killed in a plane crash later in 1981.—Ed.], who practically elaborated a whole theory on the self-determination of El Salvador. Maybe there is something to the idea that the struggle over the Peruvian border is not far away. There is definitely the possibility of pressure being applied on Roldos so that he will change his position within the Andean Pact.

The United States is unleashing all forms of pressure against us, with the accusation that there is foreign intervention in El Salvador. That is nothing new. Since last April, the State Department and the Pentagon tried to prove in the Foreign Relations Committee of the U.S. Congress that Russia and Cuba were intervening. The only thing they achieved was to prove that Cuba was calling for the unity of all revolutionary forces, which is quite ridiculous if one is seriously looking for intervention by those countries. Then there are the provocations against Nicaragua, with the accusation that Nicaragua is sending arms and guerrillas by way of the Fonseca Gulf. Anyone with any knowledge of the situation in El Salvador, especially knowing the route by which the guerrillas allegedly reached El Salvador, would immediately see that it is an absurd claim. The guerrillas would have had to pass right in front of the island of Menguera, which has a helicopter base set up by none other than the United States. There has also never been proof of any captured or dead guerrillas. We think they will continue with these ridiculous claims. Their aim is to fool the American people, more than other people in the world who already understand the situation. The U.S. claimed not too long ago that they will present proof of Soviet, Cuban and Nicaraguan intervention in El Salvador, proof which is yet to be seen. This reminds us of their arguments during the U.S. intervention against the Arbenz government in Guatemala, when they fabricated a whole series of articles charging that there were submarines in Guatemala's Lake Izabal. Anybody who knows Guatemala and Lake Izabal can see how ridiculous this is. But in any case, there is a strong offensive. Our position is one of flexibility regarding negotiations with the United States but we also stand firm in defending the revolutionary process—as someone said, to the last man of the FMLN and FDR.

The Christian Democrats of El Salvador Are Isolated

Today we hardly dare to use the term Christian Democracy for what is left of El Salvador's Christian Democratic Party. In effect, it is basically a group of reactionary leaders, closely tied to Duarte and Calvani, which in itself is quite a charge to make in Latin America. We would not dare call it a Christian Democracy because the rank-and-file, the middle-level cadres and even some of the important founders of Christian Democracy are at this point in time part of the opposition— integrated into the Democratic Revolutionary Front, as part of the Popular Social Christian Movement. But what is most important in our judgment is that, despite U.S. pressures, Christian Democrats are little by little withdrawing their support for the junta. This is because the junta is embarked on a political venture which is completely outside any political spectrum in Latin America with Christian Democratic perspectives.

I remember the first meeting of the Christian Democratic International, called by Konrad Adenauer with the help of the State Department and held in New York in about June 1980. There were some Latin American and European parties present and they expressed support for the junta. In August, they called the second meeting, in Lisbon, where there was no support for the junta but rather the formation of a commission to investigate the Christian Democrats in El Salvador. At this time, we think that even the Central American Christian Democrats do not fully support the junta. As was stated in a document presented to the People's Permanent Tribunal recently held in Mexico, Christian Democrats from Nicaragua and Honduras are not supporting the junta. Thus there are only three countries that still support them. In fact, not too long ago, the Christian Democrats from Sweden sent a letter condemning the Christian Democratic junta of El Salvador and Christian Democrats as participants in that government. In Italy, there is increasing protest by the Christian Democratic Youth against support for Duarte. We believe that only the reactionary sectors, such as those headed by Calvani, who has even gone to each military base in El Salvador to talk with the soldiers about counterinsurgency, are supporting Christian Democracy in El Salvador.

The Progress Made by the Diplomatic Offensive of the FDR-FMLN

The work that we began more or less in May 1980, when the Democratic Revolutionary Front (FDR) began its first diplomatic offensive, has begun to take shape in international organizations, as well as in the positions taken by different countries. We think that an important example of that progress was the U.N. Resolution at the last General Assembly, in late November, early December. At that Assembly, the Revolutionary Democratic Front presented to the Third Committee a resolution condemning the violation of human rights and the participation of foreign governments in aiding the Christian Democratic junta. This resolution coincided with the murder of the leadership of the Democratic Revolutionary Front. There were good results in the General Assembly: 70 votes in favor of the resolution, 13 against—which forced the U.S. to abstain—and 40 abstentions counting the U.S.

We would also like to mention the Resolution of the Non-Aligned Nations, a very important force, in which there is concrete mention of El Salvador. This resolution calls for nonintervention in El Salvador and supports its right to self-determination. They gave their support to the national liberation forces. Along these same lines, there was the resolution by the People's Permanent Tribunal. Although this is not a governmental entity, it is an established Non-GovernmentalOrganization of the United Nations. Its resolution condemned the military junta and

U.S. intervention; it is important because of its practical links with the Bertrand Russell Tribunal and its successor, the Lelio Bazzo Tribunal.

There were also resolutions from political movements, such as the Socialist International, represented in different governments. During the past year, the Socialist International issued resolutions that were more and more favorable, more and more clear in their support for the Democratic Revolutionary Front and against intervention. We were able to get resolutions in San José, Costa Rica; then in the Dominican Republic, from the Latin American Section; then in Oslo last July and again last November. In spite of pressure from the U.S., the Socialist International made a strong statement against U.S. intervention and it also recognized and gave all its political support to the Democratic Revolutionary Front as the representative organization of the Salvadorean struggle. So, in these organizations, most of the nations and peoples of the world are supporting us except Venezuela, Honduras, Guatemala and the countries of the Southern Cone—which, according to statements by members of the National Action Front (FAN, the paramilitary organizations of El Salvador), are supporting the junta. Support for us comes even from the peoples of those countries and the rest of the governments of the world, some with a firm decision of support and others at least critical of the United States and the military junta.

From Insurrection to War:
An Interview With Joaquín Villalobos

by Marta Harnecker

The following interview was conducted by Marta Harnecker with Joaquín Villalobos, Commander-in-Chief of the Revolutionary People's Army (ERP), one of the political-military organizations which form the FMLN. Called "the most exhaustive analysis and review of the war to this day," the interview focuses on the strategical developments of the revolutionary movement since 1980. It was originally published in Punto Final *(Mexico), Number 204, November-December 1982.*

The Offensive of January 1981: An Error?

The strategy that oriented the military offensive launched by the FMLN in January 1981 had the objective—as I understand it—of attacking, or at least harassing, the military forces of the enemy concentrated in their barracks. In fact, this offensive was nothing more than a repeat of the Nicaraguan experience of September 1978. The present Chief of the High Command of the Sandinista Popular Army stated that "the great error" committed at this time was to attack "those points where the enemy was most heavily fortified," using the tactic of encirclement as the principal weapon. He recognizes that this tactic pins down the enemy, but "in a terrain which they dominate," and that in that way "it is not possible to solve the situation in favor of the revolutionary forces."

Could you tell me why this strategy was chosen? Was your decision influenced by the expectations of mutinies within the military and popular uprisings which in fact never happened, at least not to such a degree and of such intensity as had been hoped?

I think that perhaps the most important consideration would be to avoid reducing the offensive of January 1981 to the military problem per se or to the question of the tactics employed. It must be linked to the condition of the Salvadorean revolutionary movement and to what had been the development of the mass movement, which obviously generated high expectations concerning the insurrectional possibilities. This is what explains why that tactic—encirclement—was utilized.

The objective in the beginning was not to annihilate the army. We wanted the masses to rise up and then on that basis to apply different tactics ranging from the prolonged siege—with the support of the masses—of the barracks and outposts of the military to the use of measures that would force the army to move out and be susceptible to our attack while moving. For example, in the case of San Salvador, our intention was not to occupy the military garrisons, but only to harass them, while at the same time other units worked to lead the masses to an uprising in the shantytowns. Once this was accomplished we were going to try to force the army to move to reconquer the shantytowns, and while they were moving we would hit them.

We cannot say that our tactical abilities were well enough developed at that time to allow us to attack the enemy while in motion, or even while in the garrisons and barracks. Our fundamental aim was the uprising of the masses, and from here the military question would have to be derived. And we obviously combined this with the possibility that some sectors of the army would rebel. The explanation of why we could not meet all of our objectives is found in the weakening of the mass movement in the previous months, due to the terror campaign in the cities. Also, contradictions that existed up until then inside the army and between the different political factions inside the Junta were beginning to be resolved.

The enemy had already achieved a high degree of homogeneity around the Christian Democrat-Army and Reform-Repression program, and they were at their peak in the consolidation of these programs and of their homogeneity. Only now can we realize that they had reached that point and achieved those conditions. But at that time, after going through one of the strongest periods of mass struggle ever witnessed in

Latin America, it was very difficult to recognize this reality.

It is valid to ask the question: Does all this mean that an insurrection was impossible in El Salvador? I don't think so. What happened is that we let go the most favorable moment to launch an insurrection; in other words, there were other periods of greater strength in the mass movement, of very deep contradictions in the enemy camp; these were critical points of time during which we could have attempted to tilt the balance of forces in our favor and to take power.

Which were those periods?

I would say March-April-May of 1980 . . . If one thinks about it, at that time there were even bourgeois sectors open to establishing alliances with us, and they had political weight. They were still supporting a reformist position and had some possibility of action. In the army, to be specific, were Mena Sandoval and those who honestly believed in the coup of October 15. They were at their best moment within the army; there existed better conditions for conspiracy inside the barracks. Within the army there were great hopes regarding the revolutionary mass movement, even respect for it and a desire to participate in it. They had tried to set up talks with the Coordinadora Revolucionaria de Masas (Revolutionary Coordinating Council of the Masses).

With time, all this was weakened and the Right regained the initiative within the army, displacing these people. In addition, at that time international conditions were quite favorable to us; it was less difficult to force the USA to agree to a negotiated solution with the revolutionary movement. Afterwards, this aim required greater efforts, although I think that the North Americans are slowly starting to understand that they must reach a negotiated solution. At that time this was more feasible.

On the other hand, we had the mass movement. We are speaking now of March-April, 1980. The assassination of Monsignor Romero exasperated the masses. Everyone was waiting for an uprising; the revolutionary movement had the capacity to paralyze the whole country without resorting to military means; discipline was enough, since 90% of the working class and white-collar employees' organizations followed the leadership of the revolutionary movement. There was an organized revolutionary leadership at the level of the middle classes, within the working class movement, at the level of the teachers' movement, and a powerful mass movement in the countryside. Proof of this were the national strikes of March and June that had an impressive force: the whole country was totally paralyzed.

But I understand that the last national strike, in August, did not have the following that was expected.

The problem in this case was not one of lack of support from the masses. Very simply, the enemy had already started to impose systematic and massive terror, and the revolutionary movement did not have a strong enough military presence to permit the insurrectional expression of the masses.

By then the revolutionary mass movement was being gradually undermined, especially in the cities. In the countryside, the enemy began military operations that were the starting point for later efforts to displace the population from the FMLN's zones of control. We were truly weakened. On the other hand, our inability to meet the challenges of the situation in March was significantly influenced by the fact that we were lagging behind in the task of unity around a common political strategy; within the revolutionary movement we had not gone beyond an embryonic level of unity, and had not reached a unity with a greater political content. This fact accounts for the lack of an insurrectional strategy and a more correct political-military strategy.

If in March, April, and May of 1980, the FMLN had had the military force or the number of combatants that were available on January 10, 1981, and if these had been utilized as in later stages, I think there would have been an insurrection, independently of tactical problems. And possibly the enemy would have collapsed. On January 10 this was no longer possible, given the degree of terror imposed by the repressive apparatus. The masses by then demanded from their vanguard a higher level and quality of their military presence, in order for them to advance to a struggle of more definitive characteristics.

Let me clarify a point: Do you always think that a mass uprising must be accompanied by a mutiny in the barracks, or do you think that the insurrection could be successful even without a military mutiny?

This is an element that would have enormously contributed to the mass uprisings. There is a very important example, the case of Santa Ana. During the January 10 offensive, Santa Ana was perhaps the area which acquired the most insurrectional characteristics in the whole country. And this was so because the masses, when they saw the defeat of the military, due in part to a mutiny, recognized that this was a struggle of decisive proportions. The disarticulation of the army was, without a doubt, the element that ignited the mass insurrection. That is, in Santa Ana as opposed to the rest of the country, there were hundreds of people that joined an uprising in the neighborhoods around the town; they built barricades. It was the most important case of mass participation in the whole country, leaving 400 civilians dead. This took place in an area where the armed apparatus of the FMLN was inferior to the rest of the country. In short, the uprising of the garrison, of part of the soldiers, is an element that had an enormous impact on the will and disposition of the masses. But our plans by no means depended solely on this factor. We considered it only as an additional element.

If there had been no mutiny within the military, do you think that the uprising of the masses by itself could have toppled the government?

I think so. The strength of the mass movement was of such magnitude that, combined with a minimum of armed power—that is to say, with a much smaller arms-to-people ratio and with a military capacity much smaller than the present one, we could have provoked the insurrection of the masses and gone on to encircle and harass the barracks and garrisons. . . .

So the encirclement of the garrisons was then designed to take place with the participation of the masses?

With the masses . . .

Not only with the military apparatus . . .

Let me explain. I gave you the example of San Salvador, where we considered harassing and attacking the Air Force. However, our actions were directed at occupying the neighborhoods of Mejicanos, Cuscatancingo, all areas that are north of San Salvador and surround it almost completely. That was the principal part of our plan.

But wasn't the enemy capable of moving in force against you?

Yes, we knew that the army was going to come out.

And how were you going to confront the army when it reached those neighborhoods?

By surrounding it when it attempted to penetrate these zones, ourselves already having occupied important positions. For example, in Mejicanos we planned to maintain control over the approach routes. In other words, I think that the most important considerations were not questions of military tactics. We would have been successful if we had started the uprising of the masses. However, to achieve this aim, we needed, at that point in time, given the weakened condition of the masses that I described before, a stronger and more developed military apparatus than the one that would have been necessary in May 1980.

In April and May 1980, we did not have the necessary logistics nor the required armed apparatus. And when I say that we did not have it, I don't refer to the fact that it did not exist. I am saying that we did not have the degree of unity in the revolutionary movement necessary to generate the conditions to rapidly create that armed apparatus. No single organization, by itself, was capable of going into that battle. Now, if we had unified the armed apparatuses of all the organizations, then it is most likely that we could have responded to the situation. And we would have needed a minimum level of logistics, much smaller, in any case, than what was actually utilized.

I have stated that in the period of March, April, and May 1980, with 1,000 armed combatants we could have led the masses into insurrection and broken the backbone of the army.

According to what you are telling me, the dispersal of forces, or the attempt to encircle many garrisons, was a correct plan within the general scheme.

Yes, although not in absolute terms, but linked with the idea of mass insurrection. It was the weakness of the mass movement that necessitated a different scenario, and forced us to build an army and to use more developed military plans. In other words, revolutionary victory did not necessarily have to result from the perfecting of military tactics; there were periods in which victory was possible on the basis of a less developed military strategy.

I would say that the role played by the masses in Nicaragua made it unnecessary to so thoroughly develop a popular army. Obviously, there was a need to establish a military apparatus, but not in the same proportions as in our case. In El Salvador, of course, we are carrying on a struggle after the revolutionary victory in Nicaragua, and that affects also the policies of imperialism; there are new elements that in turn generate different conditions. Because of all of what I've told you, I don't believe you can judge the events of January 10 from the point of view of the tactics utilized during combat. I think the results would have been much better if a greater emphasis had been placed on the roads and highways; that is a necessary criticism, but it is not the fundamental one. What occurred is that the politically advantageous moment for the insurrection had already passed.

There were moments in the capital, during the period of January-February-March of 1980, during which the army, despite all its might, was incapable of controlling the mass movement, even though the masses were unarmed.

It wasn't capable, or it had not yet decided to use terror?

I would say that the army was incapable of dealing a crushing blow to the mass movement. The breadth and quality of the mass movement were such that it could not be dismantled with a single blow. In terms of quality, the mass movement contained solid clandestine and semi-clandestine structures, and in terms of breadth, it ranged from government employees to the workers of strategic industries, including up to 90% of the productive sectors, plus a peasants' movement deeply rooted in 12 of the 14 Departments in the country, covering over 90% of our territory.

The enemy required well over a year to weaken that movement and destroy its insurrectional possibilities, at least in the cities. What the army could not destroy were the mass reserves of the revolutionary movement and its capacity to renovate forms of participation. The movement was able to survive these difficult conditions and to leap ahead to create a powerful revolutionary army that would become its main instrument of action.

A Popular Army Is Formed Against Adversity

There are some who have stated that there exist no conditions in El Salvador for the operation of a guerrilla war, much less for the gestation of a popular army. I mean a popular army in the sense of permanent forces not linked to a specific territory, given the geographic and topographic characteristics of the country, i.e., a small country, without large mountains—conditions that prevent the existence of rear-guard zones within the country. In addition, El Salvador has a densely populated terrain, crisscrossed by multiple roads and highways that join the different areas. These analysts affirm that the only kind of armed struggle that is viable in such a country is a militia-type of struggle, intimately linked to an insurrectional strategy. I think that the best answer to these opinions is your concrete practice in the last months. However, I am interested in knowing your opinion in regard to these arguments.

The set of problems involved in this question is a very real one. Indeed, it is one of the major problems that had to be solved by the Salvadorean revolutionary movement in order to develop and grow in the military area. There did not exist rear-guard zones that were more or less impregnable, that provided even minimum conditions in favor of the formation of guerrilla detachments in areas where they could be protected by the topography itself. Those conditions do not exist in El Salvador. Additionally there is the problem of the multiplicity of means of communication.

With respect to the topography, the idea one gets when you talk about El Salvador is that it is all flat country, but then one sees documentary films and the mountains are there.

It is a mountainous country. It's a country of volcanoes. But to put it graphically, let's take an example. A typical volcano, like the many we have in our country, will have its slopes under coffee cultivation, and there will be a number of roads that are required to move out the coffee after harvest. The problem in other mountainous zones inhabited by poor peasants, where the soils are infertile, as is the case of Morazán, Chalatenango, and the northern part of San Vicente, is that they are very densely populated and are also crisscrossed with roads, with a large number of hamlets, small villages, and towns, with all the land under cultivation. There is no vegetation that could cover and camouflage the guerrilla units of the revolutionary movement. There exists neither the vegetation nor the isolation required for a first, preparatory stage. When the revolutionary movement started to form its bases in the countryside, it had to utilize methods of clandestinity as strict as in the city. One had to remain within the peasants' farms and provide them with military training, working at 2 or 3 a.m., using the same security measures as in the cities. In general, we can say it is a semi-urban condition. That had its disadvantages at the beginning, but it also had some advantages, because we were born and grew up in constant communication with the peasant masses. We have never been isolated from the masses. Certainly, as a result of the enemy's terror, there is a decline in the open participation of the masses in the cities. But, even though this limited the insurrectional possibilities, it did not prevent the creation of an army that would have never been possible without the participation, under new forms, of the masses.

That is the answer to your question. The Salvadoran revolutionary movement found the solution to the topographical disadvantages, to the problems represented by the population density. The answer lies in the high degree of organization of the popular movement, in the massive incorporation of the population into the revolutionary tasks, in the creation of new forms of participation. All of these constituted a strong basis for the creation of the guerrilla army. To say that we could only think about a struggle based on militias, linked to an insurrectional strategy, is to fall into a deterministic attitude toward one of the factors that comes into play in the building of a revolutionary strategy. The Salvadorean revolutionary movement found the solution to these problems in the enormous support of the masses and in the highly developed organizations it had among the peasantry. That has allowed us to create a rear-guard like the one we have today.

Today, almost two years after the offensive of January 1981, which is the factor that really allowed us to consolidate our rear-guard, the army has begun to abandon the majority of its minor positions inside our zones of control. We are starting to take control over not only the highlands that commanded those zones, of the hamlets and villages and a few roads; we are now dominating larger towns, major means of transportation, and also military positions of strategic importance. That implies to us a greater degree of development, greater ability to maneuver, more stability for our war fronts. A whole series of new conditions exist so that our plans and our offensives in the following months will have a greater magnitude and a much greater strategic importance.

Tell me, could these zones now be called liberated zones?

This is a difficult question. The fact that all our organizations have been careful in the use of this concept has to do, to some extent, with not having a neighboring country which made it possible to be self-sufficient in these zones. That is to say, we certainly exert control over these zones—military control, generalized political influence over the population—but we are not totally self-sufficient. We have organized forms of people's power with minimum conditions of self-subsistence, but we cannot be fully self-sufficient.

Aren't there small plots of land under cultivation that could feed the population?

They do exist and are the basis for the maintenance of the zones. What happens is that the terrain is so narrow that any incursion by the army, even though it cannot displace us permanently, is still capable of breaking our lines of supply, of dispersing us or taking away the cattle that we bring to these zones. Or they may burn certain crops. This is more of a problem in some zones than in others. The enemy cannot annihilate us, it cannot occupy our positions, or capture our arms, but it is still capable of keeping us more or less unstable since it can cut us off from our supplies.

It is sort of an ongoing siege.

That is perhaps too defensive a way to put it. You must consider that the zones of control cause a fundamental problem for the army, not for us. It is the army which must adopt defense measures to try to keep our zones surrounded, not only to interdict our supplies, but also to prevent these zones from growing. In this context, what then is the virtue of what is happening right now with the October campaign? [In October 1982, the FMLN began a very prolonged, nearly constant offensive.—Ed.] It is precisely the fact that the situation is turning around, and that the FMLN is extending its zones of control by occupying towns. The army must widen the perimeter of its siege more and more, making it weaker and more vulnerable each day. Now, even if the increased population represents some difficulties, the fact of having an extra 40 thousand people inside the zones under our control also brings about new possibilities for growth.

How long can the army maintain itself under these conditions, since we will continue occupying towns? How many population centers can the army surround? Which zones, which roads and highways will it be able to control? The army could even recover one or a few of the population centers it has lost, but will it be capable of maintaining them in its grasp? For the time being we are not so much interested in controlling territory as we are in hitting the army as hard as possible. In other words, the army's scheme can last for a while, but the zones of control will continue to grow. Then the supply problem would be solved, and perhaps then we would begin to use the concept of liberated zones. But also that concept would be temporal, because if the enemy is placed under those conditions, if it starts to lose such large areas, then its strategic collapse would come about sooner rather than later.

You were telling me that what made it necessary to create the people's army was the situation that developed after the failure of the insurrectional attempt of January of 1981.

The conditions imposed upon us the task of having to build an army. When the insurrectional alternative was eliminated, it became necessary to weaken and further fracture the army, on a purely military level; this made us develop and fine-tune our own military structures.

Which are, according to your experience, the minimal conditions needed to begin the formation of an army?

What is fundamental is to have a rear-guard, and that was precisely what was achieved on January 10. This offensive put the army on the defensive, forcing it to concentrate on its strategic positions. That gave us a few months at ease and allowed us to create the seven strategic fronts, the seven concentrations of forces and the rear-guard that permitted us to prepare new combatants. Even the enemy's offensives became schools for the training of fighters—the best schools of combative training. All those months, the months in which we resisted inside our positions, made us learn. We not only had the terrain to prepare our fighters, but we were also forced to solve the problem of learning military tactics in the daily clash with the enemy. We did not have a school where first the students graduated and then were taken to a theater of operations. We had the rear-guard and the theater of operations all mixed up in the same place, since sometimes the enemy forced us out of an area and we then had to come back to recapture it. Our people had to learn to do engineering work to protect themselves from artillery fire, from air bombardment, because there were daily occurrences. What turned Morazán, Chalatenango, and Guazapa into good schools for military contingents was the fact that during several months we had to fight, almost daily, against the enemy's efforts to annihilate us.

Another thing which helped in the formation of our army was that, for the January 10 offensive, the revolutionary movement decided to arm itself and carry out logistical plans. These plans, designed with an insurrectionalist mentality, basically started from two considerations: first, to have the people willing to take up arms—and the revolutionary movement had more than enough arms, even after the previous setbacks in the cities; second, to have financial resources, which were also available from the actions of the previous period. But it was not only the availability of a war chest and people willing to arm themselves that allowed us to carry out our plans. Above all, we showed the capacity to execute supply operations in a very difficult terrain; this capacity implied having plans, cadre, and organizational structures capable of achieving our goals by taking advantage of all the possibilities. If by January 10 we had not solved this question of logistics, it would have been very difficult to build the rear-guard. During 1980, the army began to launch military operations against what today are the zones of control, and the resistance that we put up at that time was much weaker than the one that began after January 10, when we were already armed. This, added to the fact of having established a rear-guard, allowed us to put up an effective resistance and get down to the task of building our army.

The other important thing is that we achieved basic supply levels, through the small actions of recuperation undertaken during the period from January to July-August of 1981, and by executing logistics operations to maintain our ammunition supply. That is another element that played a strategic role during this period. We no longer had a problem of weaponry, but now we needed to maintain a flow of ammunition to be able to resist the army. The army tried to surround us, maintained the offensive, sought to clash against our forces to deplete our logistics potential. They knew that if we ran out of ammunition they would have better chances to finish us off. Our ability to maintain our logistics disconcerted our enemy. When it seemed that a front had been depleted, after a few weeks it was back in action, and sometimes at an operational level much greater than the enemy thought possible.

You say you had many fewer arms than fighters willing to take them during the offensive of January 1981. But tell me, isn't there a difference between the willingness to take up arms during an insurrection and the willingness to build up a popular army, to move away from one's own town, etc.?

That is obviously so. To transform an armed mass into an army we had to improve our discipline, we had to foster a more strategical frame of mind—politically and militarily—during combat, a more far-reaching point of view to understand what a revolutionary war is. The fact that the revolutionary movement was capable of defending these rear-guard zones allowed us to modify the behavior of the military personnel, educating them along new lines, and to begin to move them—because of our very specific operational needs—to different theaters of operations. Of course, there were deficiencies at the beginning, but these began to be solved with time.

The events of March 28 [date of the national elections farce in 1982—Ed.] had the great virtue of forcing the revolutionary movement to act against urban centers. The enemy, because of the elections, brought the battle to the cities, and that obviously had an impact in favor of a change in our frame of mind. The revolutionary movement was also forced to move because we needed to bring our fronts in contact with each other, to upgrade the levels of cooperation. That began to create a new discipline in each fighter, since their participation was no longer limited to the question of defending an area or a position. This was one of the toughest problems to overcome during the first stage. The defense of an area is something which is linked more to a militia struggle than to anything else. To go from there to transforming the fighters into soldiers of a revolutionary army took us many months. It was difficult to leave behind that period in which we were on the defensive before the army's actions, and to move forward to the stage in which we determined whether combat was to take place.

The Defense of Positions: A Necessary Tactic

Starting from the point of view that the revolutionary war in El Salvador began in January 1981—which does not mean that armed struggle began then, since it had existed for several years but only as dispersed armed actions, lacking a global plan of confrontation with the enemy—could you tell me which are the main periods through which the war has developed up until now, and what is your evaluation of each of them?

In the first place, I would rather say that the war as a military phenomenon of strategic importance indeed started in January 1981. But the revolutionary war as such has existed throughout the last 10 years. This distinction is important because prior to January, two important phenomena took place. On the one hand, there was the development of cadre who would be the future leaders of the revolutionary army, those who could conduct the insurrection and later guide a revolutionary army. On the other hand, there was the ability shown by this armed apparatus to also organize a powerful revolutionary mass movement which led to the military confrontation with the enemy.

It is important to mention here the period of self-defense of the masses, a method employed by all revolutionary movements. The nuclei of combatants, of militia fighters, joined the demonstrations, the mass meetings; they took over factories, government buildings, churches. That was one of the most important expressions of the mass movement in El Salvador: a military presence, an armed presence within the movement. At the burial ceremonies for Monsignor Romero, an important role was played by the militia and the fighters. Many of them now hold leadership positions in the revolutionary army, although there is also a younger generation that grew out of two years of war.

Another important element is that armed struggle allowed us to accumulate basic capacities and resources for the following period of revolutionary war. I would say that January 10 represents the peak of this gathering of military strength, besides its enormous political importance. Someone has said that it was the introduction of the Salvadorean revolutionary movement to the international arena. At the level of national politics, it served the purpose of familiarizing the masses with the military potential of the revolutionary movement; they became more confident, as they saw that a new level of development of our forces was possible, at the moment in which open mass struggle—the most important instrument of action and presence of the revolutionary movement—was waning in face of the terror campaign launched by the enemy.

After the January 10 offensive followed a period that would play a very important role. We talked about this period in a previous question, when we explained the development of the revolutionary movement, particularly at the military level. After January, we could not start an insurrectional counter-offensive on short notice. It was obvious that what we needed to do was to strengthen our military power. The six months following January were a period of resistance, of consolidation of the rear-guard, of development of our forces, of achieving greater military ability. This period had its first expression in the July and August campaign.

Tell me: During that period, what instructions were given from a military point of view?

There wasn't a military plan for an offensive. We had no other possibilities than to make good use of the enemy's offensives to cause a weakening of their forces. We were successful. For the month of July 1981, the army had to admit 3,000 casualties between dead and wounded; they had approximately 400 dead, including 40 officers, for that period. This is an indicator of the extremely high cost to the army of these 6 months, during which time they tried to dislodge us from our position and attempted to annihilate our forces. The single major blow we sustained during the whole history of the war was on January 17, 1981, when one of our columns was enveloped in the western part of the country and over 100 combatants, including their main leaders, were killed during a heroic struggle to the last bullet, in the Cutumay Camones district in Santa Ana.

During the offensive?

Yes, during the decline of the offensive, in Santa Ana. After that, the army found hidden arms, and broke up our urban structures, but our casualties were never greater than five to eight militia members or fighters, mostly supporters and civilians. The fundamental tactic applied then by the revolutionary movement, the defense of positions, did cause some confusion.

Was the tactic of defense of positions an error on our part? I would say that the answer must include a consideration of the characteristics of the terrain in which we had to fight. Why? Because it is a very narrow area, and it is not possible to move around too much. What is the role of the defense of positions in weakening the army? It forces the enemy to assault our trenches. The 3,000 casualties of the army are a product of our defense of positions. In the case of Morazán there was an offensive in March of 1981 to try to capture Radio Venceremos. What did the army gain from it? Dozens of deaths and hundreds of wounded. The army invested millions of bullets, thousands of howitzer rounds, hundreds of bombs, and did not get anywhere after 22 days of trying to assault the FMLN's positions. Finally we had to move, but by then it was a different situation. What would have happened if during that period we had mainly employed a tactic of maneuvers? Most likely this tactic would have opened conditions for our annihilation by the army. Why? Among other reasons, because we had to move around with a mass of civilians.

Why did you necessarily have to take the civilians with you?

Because we depended on the masses. In other words, without those masses our rear-guard would have lacked both human reserves and supplies. The type of terrain forced us to depend on the masses in order to survive. We had to protect them and take them into consideration when designing any kind of military maneuver. The enemy has always considered this civilian mass a military objective, and that directly affected our forces. What was the result of this? That we were forced to impose heavy penalties on the enemy for each meter it advanced, so that when we had to move out, the army would be so weak that it could not pursue, having already spent many days continuously in combat. During the March offensive in Morazán, the army spent 22 days in campaign, 22 days on the offensive, while the FMLN resisted and maintained its positions. Even from the political point of view, that was an improvement. Why? Because there were political consequences when the army had to spend 22 days in campaign without any concrete results. However, we did not have sufficient forces to counterattack and hit the army with strength. So resistance was the main expression of the development and the military strength of the FMLN; it resulted in the enemy being incapable of regaining control over our zone. That had enormous political and military consequences for the enemy. The necessary defense of positions became a great success and was the principal tactic for that period . . .

Before we begin talking about the July-August campaign . . . You spoke more about the positive aspects of this period, of the defense of positions. Are there any elements of self-criticism that should be brought up?

Yes. I think there are two elements which are important to mention. One of them is the question of that bond between the revolutionary movement and the masses which, even though it had a positive effect within the overall context, allowing us to survive, also had a negative effect. It caused the dispersal of the armed power of the revolutionary movement, which had an impact in delaying the formation of its strategic operational forces. One of your questions alluded to a militia phenomenon, to which this dispersal of forces is most linked. What was most necessary then was the formation of a guerrilla army.

We had to choose the best terrain from the point of view of creating this army, one which could be defended and would weaken the enemy. We could not put this consideration aside and take into account only the need to defend the masses. But we did not always see this very clearly. With practice, reality itself, life itself, proved that this was an error and forced us all to begin applying a concept of concentrating our military power, our arms, and our cadre.

Another element which is important to emphasize is that the concept of defense of positions—although a correct notion, since it was a need of the revolutionary movement—weakened one aspect which should have been a permanent tactic of the revolutionary movement: the struggle on the roads and highways. The conditions imposed a given scheme on us, and we did not implement a tactic of attacking the enemy while it was moving—a tactic that, at the very least, could have taught us how to fight in those locations. At that moment, the fight on roads and highways and other means of communication was understood only as a harassment tactic, to contain the enemy. It was not understood as the fundamental tactic to annihilate enemy units.

Despite these critical assessments of this period, we had a correct formulation, in the context of the objective conditions of El Salvador at that time, starting from the needs of the masses and the characteristics of the terrain in which we had to fight.

The revolutionary movement at that time needed to preserve and consolidate its rear-guard. The application of a tactic of maneuver at that time would have been erroneous. Our forces still did not have the capacity to carry out maneuvers, and the terrain was so narrow that we could not constantly move from one zone to another. To leave our zone would mean falling into another of the enemy's theaters of operation, at a time when the army had the ability to sustain campaigns lasting 30 or 40 days. Besides, we carried a responsibility not only towards our nascent army, but also to protect the civilian masses, many times linked by family bonds to our fighters. Besides, this mass provided our supplies and made up our human reserves, from which new fighters could be trained. These considerations explain why it was necessary to carry on with the defense of positions.

There are two parts of the national territory over which the FMLN had control but lost it: the Conchagua mountain and the Cabañas front. In the case of Conchagua, the reasons why we lost our position were the characteristics of the terrain, the lack of a political presence among the population, and the proximity of the city-port of La Unión. In the case of Cabañas, we lacked a social base that supported us. Both fronts were reduced to a few small, more or less mobile units. It was the defense of positions that allowed Morazán and Chalatenango to become what they are now, that allowed the survival of Guazapa only 30 kilometers away from the capital. Without this defense of positions, the most likely outcome would have been the occupation by the army of certain positions, forcing us to move into the most disadvantageous areas, the most difficult areas, and we would have had many problems in trying to maintain the seven strategic concentrations of forces of the FMLN. In the case of San Agustín, which is a flat area with some nearby hills, despite the fact that the terrain is not the best, is less than optimum, the enormous mass support that we can count on allowed the survival of that front as an exceptional phenomenon. If Guazapa, just a few kilometers away from San Salvador, is a demonstration of the peculiarities of the war in El Salvador, the phenomenon of San Agustín is another important example. In flat terrain, full of plots of lands cultivated to cotton, without the least possibility of camouflage, one hour and a few minutes away from a strategic highway, another front of war persists because of the mass support it can rely upon.

In summary, the defense of positions played a fundamental role in that period of the war.

Enemy Failure To Occupy Radio Venceremos

Within six months after the January offensive, in July and the first days of August, the revolutionary movement was able, on the basis of the military experience accumulated during the resistance period, to improve its quality and take the military initiative. The movement left behind the period during which the main factor in deciding courses of action was the activity of the army and its capacity to launch offensives. For the first time, one of the enemy's military positions was overwhelmed, its forces surrendered, prisoners were taken, and weapons were captured. An important ambush was successfully carried out. Afterwards, the revolutionary movement was able to efficiently resist the counterattack of the army in the town of Perquín, Department of Morazán. Perquín occupies a strategic high area in the Department, and its importance is military, not political. Whichever side dominates this position can extend its control over practically the whole northern section of the Department. This allows the FMLN to bring together the lines of communication of its main positions in that zone of control. The aim of the army was to keep them apart.

Could you explain to me what this campaign was all about? What were its objectives?

For the first time we wanted to annihilate combat forces of the enemy. Up to that moment we had managed to weaken them, to maintain a harassment campaign. In this campaign we wanted to capture arms and take prisoners . . . we were successful. We combined a main operation in the Department of Morazán, the takeover of the town of Perquín, with ambushes along the approach routes to annihilate the reinforcements.

You wanted to take over the whole town, not only the garrison?

Yes, the whole town, plus an encirclement of the garrison to force its surrender. We took over the town and were effective in an ambush against the first reinforcements sent by the army, which were coming from the town of La Guacamaya; this has been traditionally the strategic position of the revolutionary movement in this zone of control, but had been taken over by the army during their March-April campaign. During the July-August campaign the army was forced to remove that force, to take it out of our zone of control. Our forces ambushed the army, recovered armaments, and occupied the position again. After this came the combined actions of sabotage of power lines and harassment along the roads and highways throughout the rest of the country. We added important operations inside the capital, like the sabotage action carried out by a compañero, a sergeant of the national police, inside the central police headquarters. Armored vehicles and parts of the building were destroyed.

What is your evaluation of this campaign?

Well, I think it would perhaps be of more importance to do a general evaluation of this and other campaigns, because the errors made will appear as a constant and it may be better to approach them as a whole.

After that campaign it was possible to maintain, in one way or another, different initiatives of some importance. From August to December we took advantage of our new experience and formed new forces, until December, when the army, again challenged by the presence of Radio Venceremos in Morazán, launched one of the biggest operations seen up to that time. But there were important tactical changes, with the army trying to penetrate deep into our zone of control to the place where the Radio was located. Small units disembarked mainly in the northern section of the Department, where we had only minimal

capabilities. During the initial stage of the operation, they were successful in disorganizing the front's defenses and forced us to undertake
maneuvers which weren't too well coordinated.

They launched their operation after having done a good analysis of
our tactic of defense of positions. They provided their units with high
mobility, used two support weapons per squadron to give them the
ability to attack our positions and dislodge our trenches; they concentrated large forces along our perimeter, occupying the areas to which
we could retreat. They captured one of the Radio's transmitters in an
ambush. They stated that the whole Radio had been captured, that
even the team who operated the Radio had been taken in as prisoners.
That was not true and they made fools of themselves. Within 20 days
Radio Venceremos was transmitting.

The shutdown of the Radio Venceremos became a big success for
the army, but it was an ephemeral one. They managed to deploy
their forces again in La Guacamaya, recovering the positions lost in
July-August. The offensive forced the FMLN's concentration of forces
to be constantly on the move to escape the enveloping maneuvers of
the army. It was a very difficult moment, but we were able to maneuver,
civilian masses together with the military forces. The army, as they saw
nothing come of their supposed victory, took revenge against the
civilian population in one of the worst massacres, killing over 1,000
people in El Mozote and other districts, utilizing troops of the
U.S.-trained Batallón Atlacatl. Later, when the army became tired, our
troops retook the initiative. This happened at the end of December,
approximately ... We surrounded La Guacamaya and annihilated the
enemy's position; even a lieutenant who was among those in charge was
killed in this action. We recovered La Guacamaya, and Radio Venceremos
went back on the air. This was a great victory; in contrast to July-August,
we not only had the initiative in our hands, but we also totally defeated
the enemy's offensive. One of the largest operations carried out against
our zone had failed, opening up an important new period in which we
were to have the initiative even during the enemy's offensives.

How many soldiers were in that garrison?

About 60 soldiers in La Guacamaya, and some more in El Mozote
and Arambala. If my memory serves me well, we captured about 25
weapons and a lieutenant, and a fair proportion of their force died. The
rest escaped our encirclement. In July-August we took a first step
forward, but they still had the initiative. From December to March we
permanently held the initiative; even during their offensives the revolutionary movement continued to hit them.

You were not limited to the defensive.

We were no longer limited to the defensive. The enemy's strength
was reduced and the course of events was increasingly determined by
what the FMLN did, not by what the enemy attempted to do.

New Tactics for the March 1982 Elections

The next period was from December 1981 to March 1982, and it was characterized by campaigns to pressure urban centers, followed by constant blows to annihilate minor positions of the enemy in Morazán and Chalatenango. One result was an important increase in the capture of weaponry. The FMLN's actions during this period were determined by the political context resulting from the electoral campaign. It would have been a serious error if the revolutionary movement had not taken into consideration the enemy's electoral process, or if only a superficial analysis had guided our actions. The electoral process defined, to a certain degree, the behavior of the masses and of the other national political forces, not to mention the attitude of all the international forces that carry political weight in El Salvador.

These factors also determined the military options to be adopted. The military process from December to March was characterized by the political content of the different actions. There was a need to put pressure on the urban centers, to carry out spectacular actions such as the one that took place at the airport, with the purpose of demoralizing the army and heightening the combativeness of the masses. During this period actions took place against the capital, Santa Ana, Usulatán, San Vicente, San Miguel—practically all the major cities in the country. The attack against the air force base at Ilopango on January 27, 1982, was a commando action which destroyed 70% of the airplanes and helicopters of the Salvadorean Armed Forces. This action shocked the army and provoked an acceleration of economic and military aid from the U.S. to recover what was lost.

The FMLN's military offensive of March took place in the context of continuous pressure against urban centers. There is still open debate on this topic. I generally evaluate it as a military and political success. If we go into details, to determine if our partial gains were larger or smaller than they could have been, then that's a different discussion. It is possible to debate whether the revolutionary movement was successful in influencing this whole period with all the force that it could dispose of, or whether because of tactical, military reasons, or because of an insufficient political commitment, we fell short of what could have been done. Then there is also the question of our unity: how the plan was elaborated, who held up one thesis and who had other opinions. All of these elements are part of this debate. The different forces did not all share the same political evaluation of that particular situation.

Let's leave aside these problems for one moment and talk about the actions of March 28. To transform this date into the beginning of the enemy's debacle we needed an action of strategic significance and an audacious employment of the forces of the revolutionary movement. Not to go out with 10 or 15% of our strength, but to use 100% of our forces. Without seeking a final battle, we still had to fight a strategic battle that could at least weaken the results of the election.

What were the fundamental characteristics of the plan for March?

Essentially the plan was to try for a military victory at some place in the country that would unleash an insurrectional process there and, if successful, then allow for two other developments: One, that the revolutionary movement could redeem for itself the force represented by the urban masses and in this way proceed along insurrectional lines that would accelerate the war. Second, that the enemy would begin to crumble and fall apart, so that the situation would then lead to a final offensive. The second outcome we judged to be the least probable of the two. What was important was to heighten the urban mass movement by means of a victorious action, which had to be fundamentally military in design. That is to say, we could not expect the masses to rise up by themselves, as was the scheme on January 10, but rather to start from military actions that, because of their success and precision, would give a big push to the masses. If that did not work, then our plan was to try to maximize the obstacles to the electoral process, and this we did manage fairly well. The results were felt with time.

What were the criteria for choosing the point where the political-military effort was to be concentrated?

I think that the area we chose makes the plan explicit. In the eastern part of the country we could have chosen a number of areas, but we decided on Usulatán for the following reasons: First, the weakness of the army garrison, made up of 300 to 400 men who could be forced to surrender if we maintained a siege for several days. Second, the front located there was capable of exerting pressure on the city, of surrounding the city and controlling its access routes and means of communication. Third, of the eastern part, it is the city where the urban masses have a higher political level, the best history and tradition of struggle, and therefore their participation in insurrectional actions was more likely. Fourth, the FMLN could concentrate there a good proportion of its forces, and it was possible for other fronts to cooperate militarily by controlling the access routes. Finally, in that front we had forces with greater experience in urban combat because of their frequent incursions into the cities.

However, the fundamental military objective for the first stage was not to organize the insurrection in Usulatán, but to ensure the isolation of the eastern region, and of that city in particular, from the rest of the country. This was necessary in order to maintain a prolonged siege against the garrison, starting with our own forces but progressively strengthened with the participation of the masses. We began with the assumption that a strategic collapse in one of the most important garrisons would provoke a general weakening of the army.

In other words, the plan depended to a great extent on your ability to prevent the arrival of reinforcements?

That is correct. Without that, the plan was lost, and we were totally aware of this fact. So, what happened? The first goal was accomplished, with the participation of hundreds of people in the Usulatán actions. We occupied the city for over one week, and reached positions within a few meters from the garrison. The whole eastern part of the country was destabilized, preventing the elections from taking place in four Departments: Usulatán, San Miguel, Morazán, and La Unión.

However, we did not achieve our fundamental objective, which was to overwhelm the Usulatán garrison after several days of siege. After the elections, the army recaptured the city. If reinforcements had not arrived, in four or five more days of siege we would have triumphed over the garrison, producing an important change in the balance of forces in the eastern part of the country. We already occupied three fourths of the city. We were fighting within 100 meters of the main garrison, and had begun artillery bombardment against their main positions. Over 500 people had joined in the struggle.

Why did that part of the plan fail?

Because reinforcements managed to break through into the city and the balance of forces changed. In the first place, the strategic approach routes were opened and the enemy was then able to transport important forces to the eastern part of the country. In the second place, our forces inside Usulatán concentrated their efforts on defeating the enemy inside and not on the approaching reinforcements. The siege plan was more carefully developed than our combat plan for the immediate access routes, which was insufficient. Most of our forces, the best combatants and leaders, were assigned to the siege, and we also concentrated there most of our firepower. On the other hand, not only were fewer forces assigned to the approaches to the city, but also they were dispersed because of how they were deployed. This made it difficult to attack the enemy with enough force to stop them or even just to eliminate some of their forces.

These errors or weaknesses of the FMLN became known to the enemy. Hence, to defeat us in Usulatán they did not attempt to go into the city right away. The fundamental part of their maneuver was a strategic encirclement of the whole city. We should have carried out that operation, and yet we allowed the enemy to do it because our forces were, for the most part, concentrated inside the city.

Did the plan for March include actions inside the capital city?

Of course. We knew that the enemy would concentrate its forces there, to give the impression of a country capable of carrying out an election. That is why we wanted the elections to develop in the context of urban combats. We planned to enter San Salvador on the 27th at night, to try to stay inside fighting during the day of the election,

March 28. We did not know if we could do it or not. Obviously the army occupies and controls the city of San Salvador, and its special forces are assigned to the capital. The army maintains strong defense lines to prevent penetration by our forces. However, we managed to break the defensive ring and moved inside the city, fighting there for approximately eight hours. But we could not stay throughout the whole election process.

The actions of March 28 left an electoral process in crisis, although the government, controlling the mass media, was able at first to project a different image. In fact, the elections took place in several of the country's Departments, and this served their political purposes, especially for the first moments of their international propaganda.

With the triumph of ARENA, the rightist party, and the apparent success of the elections, the army reached subjective conclusions for which it was to pay dearly. The army, considering that the guerrilla army had been weakened by the electoral process, took time out to dedicate itself to internal conflicts and didn't even imagine the significant improvement that the FMLN was to show during the June campaign. For all these reasons we do not feel that the battles of March ended in a defeat of our forces. We simply did not reach the strategic goals we had set. This occurred not so much because our overall analysis had been faulty, but rather because we committed tactical errors in the implementation of our plans. On the other hand, after these actions on the 28th, and in part because of them—as they became an important source of experiences for the revolutionary movement—the enemy fell into a process of increasingly difficult internal contradictions, the most serious period of contradictions in the whole history of our process.

The June 1982 Campaign: Beginning of the Army's Defeat

The enemy considered us to be defeated after they reoccupied Usulatán. We responded in June, and in this period a decisive strategic shift took place. The defeat of the Salvadorean army began, and the revolutionary movement advanced irreversibly toward victory. We demonstrated before the world that we could win the war. With the end of the electoral process our actions against the enemy no longer had to be determined by the political implications of a specific situation, a previous reality which had forced us to subordinate our military activity to the political demands of the moment. Our fundamental problem now became how to militarily crush the army.

We had to reach adulthood in the military arena. The tactic to be employed to defeat the enemy became the fundamental question. We needed to develop greater military efficacy, to move from the defense of positions to the war of maneuvers, from dispersion to the concentration of forces.

We summarized our previous experiences. A more military criterion began to be utilized in the design of our plans. Absolute secrecy became a fundamental prerequisite. In the previous insurrectional plans, their discussion at different levels, their mass content, and the necessary propaganda previous to their implementation, all alerted the enemy. Now we must rely on the surprise factor. The detailed debate of our plans has been eliminated, in particular regarding their political basis. Each force must now excel in obtaining the best results of its own actions, for this will advance the whole revolutionary movement.

Another fundamental change to make our operations more effective was the need to concentrate our forces and to put a special emphasis on attacking the enemy while it is moving about.

The "Comandante Gonzalo" campaign—named for one of the most important cadre to die in Usulatán, the second-in-command of that operation, vice-chief of the Southern Front and founder of the forces of the Southern Front—consisted in surrounding an enemy position to force the army to move, to attack the reinforcements as they tried to reach the encircled position.

Could you explain how that plan was implemented?

We encircled Perquín, one of the most important positions from the point of view of the terrain, in the Department of Morazán. It was a minor position, with about 50 soldiers, a small garrison. We were not interested in the position itself, only in attacking the reinforcements that we assumed the army would send in. That position is the most important one in the north, and of great utility for the army's communication with Honduras.

As we expected, the army moved in by air two companies to San Fernando, which is immediately west of Perquín, about 10 kilometers away. It also ordered the Perquín garrison to retreat, hoping to recapture the position later. Some did manage to escape, others were captured and taken prisoner, and our forces occupied the town.

At that time our plan was different from previous ones—reflecting very clearly the qualitative development in our tactics—since we no longer cared if we maintained control over Perquín. We obviously maintained the control over the town, but to advance in our major aim, we put the emphasis on surrounding the enemy's reinforcements, 250 soldiers that were assigned at that time to San Fernando.

Circumstances forced a new army movement to take place: Three companies were brought from Torola, southwest of San Fernando. That was the opportunity we were looking for. The enemy fell into our trap. We knew that a classical ambush had few chances of success, because the army already knew about our behavior, knew about our ambushes and harassment tactics, etc. Obviously their plan was to gain control of the high ground, that is, the strategic positions, to advance along the access routes without problems.

We had also prepared ourselves for that, to execute maneuvers to envelop the enemy while moving. In the end, it was the same ambush principle. The key problem was to annihilate an important army unit while it was moving. That was our line of reasoning. How could it be accomplished? The answer would be given by the terrain and the behavior of the enemy.

When we say that we maneuver, we mean that the ambush is prepared on the go—a more dynamic concept, more properly belonging to a war of maneuvers. That is what has given us the best results, because the army doesn't move anymore, almost by tradition. Besides, the distances are so short that they can get to a given point on foot, flanking the road; in other words, they not only move along the road but also along other routes, going through the elevated areas, etc.

All these elements must be considered by our forces. So, what do we need to do? Well, as we march we must begin to envelop the enemy force that is also marching, until it finally falls into an ambush. So what happened to the three companies from Torola that were trying to save the 250 soldiers surrounded in San Fernando? The army moved in by foot, and not only through the main road. When they detected us they tried to move through our flank, through a small canyon, at a lower spot in the area. We detected their maneuver, enveloped them, and finally annihilated their units while they were in that position. When you are in that situation it is extremely dangerous to occupy a low spot.

They got into that hole because of the great difficulty they were experiencing in trying to reach their objective along different routes. They could not go through the main road which comes from Gotera. All those elements helped us, but also made more difficult the action to annihilate them. The final results of this action were 43 prisoners, 80 dead, the capture of over 170 automatic rifles, 12 support weapons including light artillery, and thousands of rounds of ammunition.

And in the final phase we also reaped a military and political victory, when we shot down the helicopter that was transporting the Undersecretary of Defense, as he tried to reach San Fernando to improve the morale of the surrounded forces. Several days later, units of the FMLN captured the Undersecretary as he tried to escape towards Honduras.

This important defeat led the enemy to attempt an enormous counteroffensive, concentrating 6,000 men in Morazán, but it obtained no results except a weakening of its forces and the defeat of the Belloso Battalion, trained in the U.S. To confront this counteroffensive we used a new form of action that is applied in all the fronts: generalized sabotage of all kinds of transportation, along the roads and highways, and shutting down all transportation. This constituted a sharp blow to the economy which, added to the setbacks that the army was suffering in Morazán, forced the withdrawal of their forces. The army had to absorb the blow without being able to do anything to us. They had to withdraw without fulfilling their purpose of freeing the Undersecretary of Defense who had been taken prisoner when we shot down his helicopter. The Hondurans couldn't do much either, and got nothing but a strong condemnation.

A Leap in Quality

The new military concept used towards the end of the campaign, in about July 1982, which was to sabotage all forms of transportation, commercial, national, fuel transports, etc., is a better developed form of the notion of attacking the enemy while in movement. The army had to move to clear the roads, so we generalized harassment ambushes, which in this campaign were still small, but which in the next campaign, the October 1982 campaign going on right now, do play a fundamental role. In the future, our sabotage to transportation will reach strategic significance. Closing down, blockading the means of communication, harassment ambushes against enemy units trying to clear the roads to allow the movement of goods and the delivery of inputs for the cultivation of cotton, coffee, and other crops, all will become a fundamental part of our plans. The army is starting to be hit while attempting to clear the roads. This new modality, which forces the army to move and allows us to attack right when its defenses are lowered, is becoming a new law for the revolutionary movement; it is a leap in the quality of our forces. The army is forced to give up more terrain . . . but now we are really starting to talk about the October campaign.

Do you announce ahead of time that such roads cannot be used?

We do advertise each action as a way to show the strength of the revolutionary movement. These are orders that everyone has to obey. In itself that has political implications: the fact that the army is not capable of controlling the territory and that the revolutionary movement carries a certain weight in control of the situation. By announcing our intentions we also try to prevent harm to the population that, for reasons of necessity, needs to move from one place to the other.

Did civilians respect this measure, or did some people try to drive through the roads?

No, the measure was respected. It was a test of the forces that we had accumulated during the previous periods. And it was an effective test.

The only ones that moved were the military?

The military did move, and, well, during the first days so did a few commercial vehicles. However, since our ability to act against the highways is real, not fictitious, a few strikes were enough to enforce complete paralysis. There was no need to sabotage many vehicles for that to be really noticed. We can say that the two main highways in the country, the Panamerican and the coast highways, going from El

Salvador to the east and north, were 75% shut down, and traffic towards the west was also diminished by some actions, although they had less effect. This is a zone where the revolutionary movement does not have sufficient strength to act against highways; but towards the east and north, towards Chalatenango, transport was virtually paralyzed. And in the next campaign this happened with even greater strength. Even the army considered these actions as a test of forces.

After the June campaign, what followed?

The "Comandante Gonzalo" campaign was continued by the August operations. In other words, it was practically an uninterrupted plan, that diminished in intensity, of course, but that lasted three months: June, July, and August. Then came a lag during September and the first 10 days in October, when we started our next campaign. Even in this pattern we see an improvement of the revolutionary movement: Now we can take the initiative and start offensives much more rapidly than in previous periods.

The August operations were of great importance because they blocked the army's ability to move about. That was the role played by the ambush on the road to Ciudad Barrios, the occupation of Yamabal, the occupation of the San Carlos Hacienda near the Cacahuatique volcano. Together, these actions added up to the loss of more than an entire army company—between dead, wounded, prisoners, and captured weapons.

I understand that the Ciudad Barrios ambush was a classical operation. How could you do it if the army already knows about the methods you use?

It happened on August 7. This time the army did not take the necessary precautions to travel; it went aboard trucks and on the main road that leads to that city, which had been taken over by the FMLN that morning. To guarantee the ambush, we deployed our forces eight kilometers from the objective, and we created the impression that we were carrying out a harassment operation against the city, to encourage the enemy's movement. In this way they fell into a classical ambush, where we utilized mines and automatic rifles against the trucks as they went by, causing practically the complete annihilation of that whole group of reinforcements. This provoked a crisis in the movements of the army, which had a great impact on later military plans. The army lost maneuverability, and this weakened its minor outposts and positions. The other important factor is that we occupied a city of over 20,000 inhabitants, Ciudad Barrios, something we had never done before.

Before going into the present stage of the war, could you provide a summary of the main achievements of the June campaign?

The actions during the June campaign ended with the capture of the Undersecretary of Defense, the disarticulation of two army companies, the capture of over 200 weapons in a single front, Morazán, the forced withdrawal into Honduras of 250 surrounded soldiers, the participation of 6,000 Salvadorean and 3,000 Honduran soldiers in an operation against a single front that yielded not one positive result to them. They could not dislodge us from our positions and instead left behind 500 casualties and tens of prisoners. And, most fundamentally, we were able to show that we can win the war, and win it in a military sense. That was our aim when we planned the June campaign.

All of this was possible because of the sharp improvement in our tactics. The revolutionary movement went beyond the defense of positions and reached a stage of war of maneuvers; the control of the means of communication emerged as the fundamental element of its military tactics. This destroyed all of the plans with which the army had operated, and happened at the moment in which the army was beginning to progressively weaken. At the same time, this change in tactics allowed the revolutionary movement to open up a permanent logistical reservoir, through the capture of the army's weaponry.

When analyzing the statistical data on the war, from January 1981 to date, we find that we have captured over 1,000 weapons, with the highest percentage taken between June and October 1982. In Morazán alone, in the June-July-August campaign, we captured over 300 weapons. From a military point of view, to defeat an army is to capture its arms and to take its soldiers as prisoners, because if you only cause casualties, then you have a weakened army but one which can still remain in the field even after numerous casualties.

On the other hand, the revolutionary movement suffered greater losses during the harassment actions, trying to occupy positions, than now with a tactic of maneuver.

You had casualties and wasted ammunition . . .

Yes, large quantities of ammunition. Obviously, harassment actions can have a great political and military value in a given moment, but they accomplish nothing logistically.

In this campaign the revolutionary movement finishes battle with more logistics than we had to begin with, and with far fewer casualties than those suffered in any previous combat. That is a fundamental change. The casualties that we still have, which are fewer than before, are not due to direct combat against the enemy, because during most combats we hold advantageous positions. These casualties are mostly due to the fact that, since we are constantly on the move, we have no time to build defense structures, so enemy artillery is more effective as is the air force, with its helicopters and airplanes. This is what now causes our casualties. When we can build fortified positions, we lower our casualty rate. But we do not always have the time to do so when trying to outmaneuver the enemy, when we are running against time.

These are the main results of this campaign. Another positive result is that we were able to change the terms of the military debate within the FMLN. We changed the method with which we prepare our plans; they have become more practical, with less political debate. The fruits of all of this are being harvested during the October campaign.

Towards the Collapse of the Army's Morale

What are the aims of the present campaign, which began in October 1982?

In the previous campaign we wanted to prove that we could win the war. Now we want to push the army to the point where its morale will collapse. To beat an army it is not necessary to annihilate all its men, nor to capture all its arms, only to cause the collapse of its morale.

How can we achieve our aim? On the basis of deepening the three lines of the previous campaign: First, actions of strategic annihilation wherever possible; second, destabilizing the country through sabotage, fundamentally against transportation, power lines, telephone lines, and fuel; third, harassment ambushes and annihilation of minor positions. By deepening these lines of action, making better use of all our forces, and taking advantage of our high combative morale and the large efforts of all our fronts to further their development, we are making progress in our aim to provoke a collapse of the enemy's morale.

We are starting to see results: the strategic annihilation actions are already taking place in two of our fronts, Chalatenango and Morazán. The destabilization actions started on October 10 in Chalatenango, on October 12 in Morazán, and on October 14 we launched the national sabotage plan. The constant harassment ambushes along the highways, and the annihilation actions against minor objectives have multiplied . . . .We are 38 days into the offensive, and we have not noticed a decline in the quantity or quality of our operations. The army has been dealt three severe blows already: the one in El Jícaro-Las Vueltas, in Chalatenango, and the ones in Perquín and Corinto and Morazán, with the loss of three army companies.

In a single month, we have taken 210 prisoners; killed over 200 soldiers; wounded 343; captured 422 automatic rifles and 25 support weapons, including two 120mm heavy mortars and over 100,000 rounds of ammunition of different calibers. We have shot down one helicopter, destroyed a small tank and over 12 military trucks; important actions have taken place in Guazapa, where we have also captured arms and ammunition, only a few kilometers away from the capital. The ambushes along strategic highways are numerous, and actions of annihilation against minor outposts are constant. It has become a fact of life for the revolutionary movement to capture arms and prisoners. The eastern part of the country is practically paralyzed economically since the start of the campaign, without transport or electrical power. Fuel is scarce since we have destroyed over a dozen fuel trucks. Water is rationed. The railroad is paralyzed due to our sabotage of the bridges and engines. All these facts will have an effect on the cotton and coffee harvests.

In the central zone there are four Departments affected to a greater degree by our sabotage of power lines: San Vicente, Cabañas, Cuscatlán, and Chalatenango. The Troncal del Norte highway is also closed down because of our constant sabotage.

In the capital city sabotage actions are also continuous, and have affected the city's transportation system. Electric power is 50% below normal, and sometimes we manage to cause total blackouts. All the strategic electrical power systems have been sabotaged. Thousands of telephone lines are also out of service.

In the western part of the country we have managed to partially close down the transportation system, by destroying railroad cars, buses, and trucks loaded with coffee. Electrical power is also starting to be affected in the west. Commercial transportation from Guatemala has been paralyzed by our sabotage actions. By prolonging and sustaining this situation, and by continuing with our military operations, we will put the army in a difficult position.

We are far from depleting our military activity. The rational use of our military power, combined with the enemy's general weakness, has allowed our troops to rest and replenish their strength, assuring the continuity of our efforts. This is one of the most important accomplishments of the "Heroes and Martyrs of October of 1970 and 1980" campaign. [In fact, by mid-1983 when this volume went to press, the FMLN's offensive had continued nearly non-stop since October 1982—Ed.]

This is a very important practical step forward, which places the enemy in a difficult position concerning their mobility and dispersion of forces. They are definitely aware that they cannot control the national territory, that they must give up more and more terrain, that their forces must be concentrated in defending their strategic areas. There is no other possibility. Moreover, during the course of the campaign we carry out actions that reinforce the enemy's awareness that they must concentrate on defending strategic positions. One such example was our attack against the oil refinery located in what was presumed to be their safest territory, the western area, their deep rear-guard, where the revolutionary movement, because of the terror campaign, had been forced to scale down its activity. We attacked the refinery with several Chinese RPG-2 rockets, producing "considerable damage," as was recognized by the government itself, forcing a reduction in their output and in the distribution of fuel to the rest of the country.

That attack, our actions along the highways, and our sabotage in the capital city, have forced the army to dilute its concentration of forces. The elite units are used to control roads and highways, while the army continues to lose its remaining positions in our rear-guard zones. By now we have taken over six population centers in Morazán and three in Chalatenango, aside from the 19 towns that the army has abandoned already but that we haven't occupied. We are now in control of vast new areas, which is also a great improvement.

Another element, aside from the conquest of new terrain, is the decline in the army's morale. It is reflected in two facts: First, there are more prisoners taken than killed or wounded soldiers. Their troops now have a marked tendency to surrender. They prefer not to fight in order to save their lives. Another proof of their demoralization is that they refuse to move. This is not the result of a military option in favor of defensive tactics; it reflects lack of morale, fear that the troops may be disarticulated or annihilated. Another element of the same phenomenon is that increasingly they are talking about operations that simply do not exist, or operations that militarily do not make any sense—such as operations against the civilian population, a policy against people who may have the inclination to join our forces. Today this policy has a limited importance, insofar as our units are each day advancing and the army is giving up terrain of strategic importance to us.

Only after the FMLN's offensive had gone on for 30 days, and as a result of their loss of terrain, the army finally concentrated their forces and launched a counteroffensive against our positions in Chalatenango, with the cooperation of forces of the Honduran army. The cost of this counteroffensive will be very high, not only from the point of view that it will weaken the army in Chalatenango, but also because our offensive activity has not diminished and will not diminish. We will continue to hit them, and the army will have to leave Chalatenango without any success at all. Apparently the main purpose of their offensive is to recapture some of the towns they've lost to raise the morale of their troops. We are more interested in hitting the enemy than in holding terrain, but, in any case, the army will continue to lose ground throughout our campaign because they don't have sufficient strength to stay put. To maintain certain positions is to continue to offer us military targets.

Could you please tell me concretely what the October plan in Morazán was?

To date, the October plan has not been completed. Our plan, in concrete, was to confront the army with these alternatives: either they would give up terrain because they decided not to mobilize and we would continue occupying positions and extending our zone of control, or they would mobilize, in which case our plan was to achieve the annihilation of major units.

What did the army choose? At first, they opted to give up terrain, abandoning territory that for us offered greater areas of maneuverability to solve the supply problem. Now, in the process of occupying six towns and in the ambush on the Corinto-Sociedad highway, on November 8 in Morazán, we have annihilated and captured the weapons of two companies and have disarticulated and put out of combat another two. We have practically put an entire battalion out of commission in a month. Prior to this, they could maintain a broad encirclement around our zones of control to impede the arrival of supplies in order to weaken our social support base. Now that option is being eliminated, as our theater of operations and zones of control have extended.

The October campaign in Morazán began with the encirclement of more than 100 soldiers in an important location and the occupation of three towns practically at the same time. The towns of Torola and San Fernando were taken in the first hours of combat, and the army's positions at Perquín were surrounded, ending with the occupation of the town and the surrender of the majority of the forces there, including the captain in charge of the company.

This presented the army with a situation which theoretically obliged them to make a strategic move. However, the army did not, so we searched for other targets: the occupation of the town of Carolina, in the northern part of San Miguel. This added to the quantity of terrain at our disposal, and now practically the northern part of the Department which borders Honduras was in our hands. On November 18, on Corinto-Sociedad highway, our forces annihilated another enemy company which was heading towards Corinto as reinforcements. Nearly 100 arms and some military vehicles were captured, and 62 prisoners, including two officers, were taken. Later, our forces occupied Corinto.

It is very significant that now the army argues that the lost positions are not important, after having made large-scale operations to keep them in the previous two years of the war—operations in which thousands of men and millions of dollars were invested, many soldiers were wounded or killed, fortifications were built, and millions of bullets, artillery shells, bombs, etc., were spent.

The problem of holding the terrain in the case of El Salvador is a serious problem for either side. El Salvador is too small a country to afford one the luxury of losing terrain. If the army is losing terrain, it is because it is losing the war.

To say that the zone bordering Honduras has no strategic importance is absurd. There is an entire corridor in the northern parts of Morazán and Chalatenango which is controlled by the FMLN, making communication with the Honduran army difficult. The closest position to the border held by the Salvadorean army in Morazán at this time is 30 to 35 km from it. This represents a weakened position for the enemy, including for the Honduran army's interventionist plans.

The Strategic Importance of Radio Venceremos

I'd like you to explain again, although it was touched upon somewhat previously, how it is possible that the enemy has not been able to destroy Radio Venceremos? What role does it play in the war, and what are the principal lines it follows in disseminating information?

Radio Venceremos was begun essentially with the January 1981 offensive and afterwards became the main target of the army. The operations launched in March and April attempted to capture the

Radio. I believe that here one can see with great clarity how the defense of positions became a political-military victory, because the defense of positions resulted not only from forging the bond with the masses, from problems represented by the narrowness of the terrain, but also from the necessity of defending a political and strategic instrument such as the Radio.

The Radio forced us to keep a fixed position, to try to wear out the enemy, to try to prevent the enemy from reaching the Radio, or to at least make it so that if the enemy did succeed in reaching the Radio, they would be so exhausted that they would either have to retreat from the zone or we would force them out later. It seemed militarily crazy that an irregular movement, a guerrilla army, could defend a position, but what it was doing was protecting that political tool and, besides, it was creating a political situation by demonstrating that the army had to take 20 days to occupy a small chunk of terrain . . . .

Now, as the revolutionary movement began to take initiatives, the Radio was no longer the enemy's principal target. Instead, it tried to jam it. Another tactic was tried because the enemy was convinced that the only way to shut down the Radio was to win the war. And why? Because now the initiative taken by the revolutionary movement confronts the enemy with other problems, which are our offensive actions. At this moment the Radio is protected not only by the forces that are there to defend it but also because the military offensive actions taken by the revolutionary movement are its best defensive ring.

Also, there are possibilities of starting other stations and other fronts, and we are even at the point of transmitting on FM directly to the capital city. This was one of the achievements of the previous June campaign, and it is almost a luxury that the people can listen to us every night on a simple radio. This is fundamentally the way in which Radio Venceremos was able, in the first stage, to develop and become more and more a political and propagandistic instrument of the revolutionary movement at a strategic level.

At this moment we are waging battle against jamming by transmitting the program on two frequencies simultaneously: short-wave three times a day and once daily on FM for San Salvador. Now, in relation to the role that it has played in the war, it is important to point out that one of the most important instruments used by the army after January has been the informational blockade both at the national and international levels . . . . The role of Radio Venceremos has been precisely that of breaking the informational blockade, allowing other information. It has also become an instrument expressing the complexity of the Salvadoran process; it instructs the masses, it participates in the diplomatic battle, it participates in the debate with the army, it proves that we are winning the war.

It is a dynamic instrument and an official voice through which the FMLN puts forward its positions before the international community.

The wire services take its word as the official word of the Salvadorean revolutionary movement, and thus its significance increases since it plays a role in the diplomatic war, in the battle against intervention.

If Radio Venceremos was born to foment a possible insurrection on January 10; if it was the instrument which permitted us to inform the people that we were wearing out the army on our battle fronts, while carrying out resistance during January-June 1981; if it was the instrument that allowed us to prove that we were taking the initiative in the July-August campaign in Perquín, Morazán; if it was the instrument that allowed us to prove that as long as it was alive, we were advancing and that we were invincible when the offensive was launched against it in December; if it was an instrument for agitating the masses and orienting them in the context of the electoral campaign of March 28; if it was the instrument that allowed us to communicate our disposition towards a political solution, towards mediation, towards dialogue, towards the search for peace; if it has accompanied the strategic course of the war, now it is the instrument that proves that we are breaking the army.

The Radio reaches the army. The army is one of our most avid listeners. Captured soldiers have told us this, and we know it through our own intelligence work in the army. Why? Because there's a policy of disinformation within the army. Officials believe more in what Radio Venceremos says than in what García says and in what the high command instructs them. Why? Because the Radio does not invent even a single prisoner. Its informational policy has been to stick to the truth; in other words, to not say anything unless it's taken from reality. This has given us a great deal of prestige with the masses and even with our own adversaries.

For a case in point, within the army, when the June campaign was undertaken in which Castillo was captured, there were a large number of officers who did not believe there were prisoners, who did not know because no one informed them. And, what happened? The Radio came along and gave names, places, and concrete proof. This led them to use their own channels of information to investigate as to the whereabouts of the companies of the Third Infantry Brigade that were sent as reinforcements. And they began to verify that what we have been saying is exactly the truth.

This was a policy that was maintained from the moment that the Radio was born. The masses acquire confidence in us. We defeat the army's informational policy and we avoid also falling into the mistake of falsifying data to project a shallow spectacularity. . . .

Policy on Prisoners

You tell me that one of the positive elements of the last two campaigns is that there have been many prisoners taken. Is this due to a policy change on the part of the FMLN? Because I have the impression that in the beginning, the Salvadorean revolutionary movement wanted to annihilate the enemy; that the fundamental objective was not to take prisoners.

The Salvadorean revolutionary movement suffered from the influence of certain factors that explain how such manifestations did crop up within some of the FMLN forces. But this should not be considered as a case isolated from the actual conditions, without trying to see what the starting point was. One must remember the effervescent past of the masses of the Salvadorean revolutionary movement as well as how, within what was insurrectional enthusiasm, the necessity logically seems to be to hit the henchman, to execute the traitor. This obviously had an impact on the initial structuring of the revolutionary army and provoked differences within the FMLN with respect to the necessity of taking prisoners which, from our point of view, would provide benefits in every sense—not only in the military sphere but also in the human sphere, in the political sphere, in the social sphere. From the military point of view, taking prisoners deepens the demoralization of the army.

Did you have to struggle against spontaneous tendencies within the population in order to achieve this objective?

Effectively, yes. For example, we confronted situations of this type in the period after the October 1980 offensive in Morazán. When our forces regrouped, the first thing they began to do was to execute paramilitary personnel. The leadership ordered that these executions must cease, that the paramilitaries should not be touched, that it was necessary to speak to them, to raise points that would allow them to realize that they were wrong and to use a political approach to defeat them. And, what was the logic of our policy towards them? It was the problem that 90% of the paramilitaries belong to peasant families. Although some of them can be considered a little like a lumpen phenomenon within the peasantry, people with distorted minds, etc., for the most part the masses that in this case made up ORDEN, the paramilitary organization of the army, were peasants who because of ignorance, pressure, or really believing that they were right, got involved in it.

The same happened with the army. The masses were pushing for execution, but had we allowed ourselves to be influenced by fanaticism, by a series of subjective sentiments of the masses, that would have been incorrect. We could not in any way get into a policy of elimination, of exterminating these people simply because they were armed against us, or because they betrayed the people. We had to adopt other forms of struggle with them that included political struggle, even giving them political instruction when we had the possibility of taking them prisoner. In order to defeat the strategic enemy of those same masses, which is the army as a structure dominated by the fascist high command, it is also necessary to have a policy directed towards saving part of that army.

In a war that has lasted two years, in which there is a very wide-ranging confrontation, deformations in our own people can be provoked. And, what do we obtain from the policy of taking prisoners? It allows that our combatants learn to respect the loser, that they have a humane response, that in war and in victory they do not act with the arrogance of a victor incapable of understanding the problems that at times have led the soldiers to take up arms against us, which could have happened because of ignorance, because of error, etc.

Now, concretely, what results have you had in practice with respect to this policy with the prisoners?

In practice the principal result is that 10 to 20% of the prisoners captured have been incorporated into our own forces. The political treatment and the humane treatment that they were given was such that they made the decision to join our ranks to continue fighting. This proves that it was erroneous to think that a solution was to kill them or to adopt strong measures against them, discounting the sensitivity that these men could have for a revolutionary project.

On the other hand, prisoners have been freed unconditionally. The only one we haven't let go is the Vice Minister of Defense. The rest have either been handed over to the International Red Cross or they have been freed immediately after the fighting. This fact causes these soldiers to change their image of the revolutionary movement; they carry with them an image that the enemy does not allow to be seen. They are able to see that this is the highest expression of humanism, even in combat. The fighters care for the soldier that they find wounded, they give him food, treat him as a comrade and little by little, all the preconceived ideas that he had are broken and he realizes that he is as much of the people as they themselves are. This also carries political benefits, since those that leave take this message to the rest of the army. And the word is spread that surrendering is not an act of humilia-tion—that it is a way to save one's life, certainly, but also that it is a way to stop fighting for something that has no meaning for them. It makes no sense to die defending the interest of a few officers. That is something they are understanding more and more.

This is an aspect of our battle against the most reactionary sectors of the army and we are winning it. Even Gen. García himself, in an interview, said once that he could not accept the return of prisoners officially because this implied that they would continue surrendering. But several weeks passed and the same General was officially accepting that the International Red Cross would receive the first prisoners. And, after several weeks more another delivery of prisoners was accepted, and new deliveries of prisoners are being prepared. The high command has been forced to assume this attitude because the prisoners become a pressure within the armed forces with respect to their return. This policy also sends a message to the sectors that have some sensitivity that it is possible to reach an understanding with respect to the war problem and to search for other forms of solution to the conflict.

Reasons for the Discontinuity in the Offensive

One last question. After what you have told us, there is no doubt that there have been great strides forward in the revolutionary war in El Salvador and that each time there is a shorter interval between campaigns. Nevertheless there are those who think that there is a certain slowness on your part to pass on to new offensives. What can you say in this respect?

The absence of continuity is not determined by a conservative will but rather it is determined by the same characteristics that the war assumes. The vacuum that appears between the distinct stages is due to a real expansion of our forces. And this was of greater importance once we arrived at the stage of forming our army. Here, the physical exhaustion, the exhaustion of supplies, the exhaustion of logistical reserves is something very real. The enemy himself passed from campaigns of 20 days to campaigns of 8 days and later to campaigns of 4 or 5 days.

Why? Because each time the exhaustion factors affect him more, because his behavior is that of an army and therefore the exhaustion factor weighs more heavily upon him. There have been moments in which physically we had to stop. There are those that have argued for the need to maintain a quantitative continuity, in other words, to be on the move, acting, continuously. We feel that it is preferable at a given moment to stop, to make an overall reassessment, and to look for a new strategic target against which we can use 100% of our forces with the goal of achieving a significant change, a turnaround in the situation. You get better results by executing a group of actions in one period than you get from the quantitative sum of operations that are not united within a maneuver.

The 10th of January had that virtue. We could have used all our armed potential accumulated for January 10 in another way, more spaced out, more continuous, with successive operations. That would have been a grave error. We would not have stopped the enemy. Now, to have stopped it, to have strained it at the same time, what did it mean? It meant the quartering of the army, the cessation of offensives and the possibility for us to gain time to secure ourselves in given territories. Now, did that bring a period of relative stability? Yes, it did, but it was for our benefit. The same will be true at other stages.

We have achieved a strategic accumulation of victories which will be expressed in a final culminating moment. But because of the characteristics of our situation, because of the decrease in the insurrection potential—especially of the urban masses—the offensive cannot be maintained in an ever ascending spiral, as occurred in Nicaragua in the last 6-8 months of the war. In Nicaragua I would say that at times the masses themselves got ahead of military actions. In other words, the Sandinista Front made the determination to take a neighborhood between today and tomorrow and as the hours passed in that time slot the masses took that neighborhood, and the military units would arrive to secure it. But that was a different situation from what ours has been. We have to start with our own forces, with the supplies that our forces carry, with the exploration of the terrain, with the assurance that our arms have ammunition, with the knowledge that the plan is complete. All of these factors come together in order to carry out operations. The forms of participation of the masses are different from those of an insurrection and, therefore, our army has at times almost regular characteristics.

Now, since this tactic of attacking the enemy while in movement allows you to resolve logistical problems, doesn't that permit an acceleration in the rhythm of the campaigns?

After the campaigns of June, some of us were asking, why stop? It must be remembered that with the encirclement of our zones by the army in which there were, counting Salvadoreans and Hondurans, more than 8,000 men, our food was depleted. How were we going to continue military operations? Obviously, several weeks had to pass in order for us to continue. But, what was the army's situation after those operations were carried out? The analysis should not be based only on the situation in which the revolutionary movement found itself, but also on the weakening of the army. The problem is who recuperates more rapidly, them or us.

And, precisely what can be derived from this situation is that now the time necessary for recuperation of the FMLN forces is shorter than for the army. Thus we say that the October campaign could mean, if optimum results are obtained, the end of the offensive capability of the Salvadorean army. The army can continue to act, to harass our positions, but without achieving any military result. And what does this signify? That we are clearly going to begin to resolve the supply problems and we are going to resolve them in two ways: by a generalization of mass support for the revolutionary army and because the increased terrain gives greater possibilities. The annihilation of army units provides arms, ammunition, and logistics, and the arms allow us to incorporate new fighters from the masses. In other words, other factors appear. And what does this imply? It implies an ascending spiral in which the continuity of operations will be constant and no vacuums will be produced.

Now, what will be the form in which the masses participate in this final phase of the war? It is difficult to make a prediction about this.

First, it must be repeated that the masses never have been absent from the revolutionary process, that without the masses we would never have been able to create the powerful popular army which we have at present. Now, it still remains to be seen whether the masses are going to mobilize at this point in an insurrectional form, or in the form of a general strike, or by way of a massive incorporation into the revolutionary army. What we know is that the popular war advances with giant steps, that the struggle itself consolidates more and more unity among our forces, and this allows us to hit the enemy each time more forcefully.

The Salvadorean revolutionaries are aware of the dimension of our struggle for the future of Latin America, and also we see clearly our responsibility for peace and liberty on the Continent. The levels of war and victory that we have reached, in spite of the fact that we fight against a dictatorship that receives vast support from U.S. imperialism, have been possible only thanks to the heroism of our people and to the ability and self-sacrifice of the combatants and leaders of the FMLN forces who have responded to each moment of the war with the spirit and wisdom necessary to give life the ideals for which generations of heroes and martyrs who preceded us in the struggle for the liberty of our country offered their lives.

Given all of this, if imperialism stubbornly insists on impeding our people from building their own destiny, we are sure that it will suffer a deeper defeat than in Vietnam, since nothing can stop us from winning our freedom. Our people and their vanguard are determined to win and WE WILL WIN.

DOCUMENTS FROM NICARAGUA

Sandinismo, Hegemony and Revolution

Sergio Ramírez

This speech was given at the Central American Congress of Sociology in July 1980 by Sergio Ramírez Mercado, member of the Junta of the Government of National Reconstruction of Nicaragua. A short section describing measures taken by the government in relation to capital accumulation under Somoza has been omitted. It was published in Spanish in Barricada *(Nicaragua, July 8, 1980) and subsequently in* Cuadernos Políticos *No. 25 (Mexico, July-September 1980).*

When the motley columns of guerrilla fighters entered Managua on July 19, 1979, when thousands of victorious combatants raised their liberating rifles high, there had been two decades of mortal combat on our continent; of doubts and dissension, of theoretical recrimination, of watching and waiting through a long revolutionary night. And then the light of history shone upon a new praxis, for a wise, heroic vanguard had joined together all the elements required to construct the circumstances of victory according to a new model. They led a people's war to break the hard, dead shell of a ruling system that had endured half a century of pressures, and then they smashed it completely, leaving only a trace of all the repressive, criminal, and ultimately genocidal violence.

The people of Nicaragua triumphed in arms, in insurrection; the Sandinista Front triumphed through mobilization and organization of the masses; it triumphed through its leadership of diverse social forces, thus proving the efficacy of complex alliances; it moved to victory with a successful military strategy and a successful political strategy. Sandinismo was established in Nicaragua as a historical project with irreversible consequences. A people's project, anti-imperialist in nature, it smashed to pieces the pathologically rigid system of internal rule which North American armed intervention had imposed; it cut forever the bonds of an old and vicious dependency, the archetype of subjugation and plunder in Latin America.

The victorious Sandinista project is a historical project, which means that its nature, its hegemony and its consequences cannot be subject to risk or to negotiation. For the Sandinista project was not born of accidental circumstances, of some chance turn of history; it is the result of a whole social dialectic deeply rooted in old realities of oppression and exploitation, of brutal foreign occupations, of national sovereignty sold out in time payments, of a nation forever in critical danger of ceasing really to exist, of obtrusions engineered by the imperial power that designed, armed and stabilized the predatory Somoza dynasty. To explain Sandinismo, then, is to explain a nation built upon a foundation of people's forces, for it is the people who have historically defended the nation, who have assured its survival and its final victory.

The most critical conjuncture in our history came in 1927 when General Sandino decided to take action against the foreign occupation forces: this was as much a class option as it was an option based on nationality. As a result of the class alignments that had developed under foreign intervention, Sandinismo raised its banners both against imperialism and against the traitorous oligarchy. It was the common people— miners, craftsmen, day laborers—who took up the historic project of our nation at a time when the liberal sector of the oligarchy (or the conservatives, which is the same thing) complacently watched the nation gradually dissolve. Weak and alienated, servile and obsequious, the oligarchy played their sorry role as intermediaries of imperialist power, for whom they organized the widely heralded elections that were so well guarded by U.S. Marines and for whom they administered the imperial banks, railroads and customs.* It was Sandinismo that undertook responsibility for the nation at that time, and would do so again, because both as idea and as reality, the nation is defended in war and survives thanks to war. The people's hegemony was identified once and for all with liberation, and sovereignty was guaranteed to be people's sovereignty.

Military dictatorship, the new model of domination installed after the Sandinista battles of 1927-1933, wallowed in unlimited submission to imperial power, as had the former oligarchic traitors. Thus there was no change but rather an exacerbation of the fundamental, latent contradiction in our history: the contradiction between people and dictator, between Sandinismo and Somocismo, between nation and imperialism. The poor, who had been the soldiers of Sandino's Army for the Defense of Nicaraguan National Sovereignty, were to fight again, with ups and downs, until this contradiction was finally resolved by the complete

---

* U.S. control of customs was, of course, an extremely flagrant violation of national sovereignty —*Ed.*

destruction of the whole political and military apparatus that foreign intervention had engendered.

And so, the victorious Sandinista project is a national project, a people's project, whose hegemony was achieved when it displaced the old regime and took power through armed struggle. This is the only way a new social project could be put into effect, the only way to realize the will for change that rises primarily from the interests of the vast majority, from the masses who come to take their hegemonic place in history. This process cannot be explained in any way except from the perspective of the people.

There have been other ruling social forces that, at different stages of their growth, came into contradiction with the dictatorship and, towards the end, these contradictions sharpened. These forces lost the historical opportunity to become consolidated as alternative models and thus bring their own projects to power. When the Sandinista-led insurrection reached a decisive phase, the irreversible force of the masses swept these other sectors into the struggle to defeat the dictator-ship; but the liberation war was not theirs, and it was the war that defined the nature, the quality and the advisability of the alliances needed for victory.

This concept is important for defining the role played by alliances in the development of the revolutionary project, which, in one year, has produced fundamental changes in our national reality, and which is endowed with the political will and the strategic capacity to make this transformation more profound, and to consolidate social change.

* * *

In recent months we have been battling tooth and nail on the political front to defend our victory in choosing definitively for a people's army and a people's revolutionary state able to undertake political change on revolutionary terms. This choice obviously implied rejecting the option so dear to anti-Somoza ruling sectors, and to the U.S. diplomatic apparatus since the period of mediation, in October 1978. They would have refurbished the National Guard, washed its bloody hands and entrusted it to enforce the security of a new form of domination; they would have tolerated an institutional coexistence with "decent" and "upstanding" elements of Somoza's Liberal Party. Thus they would have defrauded the people, made it impossible to bring the people's political project to fruition, and left the historical contradiction between the nation and imperialism unresolved.

The unifying character of the Sandinista project is sustained by many political alliances and participation in it is open to the most varied sectors, but those alliances are indeed subject to a real hegemony. This is not only because the revolutionary vanguard has assumed political leadership of the process, but fundamentally because hegemony over the whole historical project was established by a choice of forces and a definitive settlement of forces. That choice is irreversible in political terms; and most importantly in historical terms, and in terms of the consolidation and development of an economic program under the people's hegemony. Given the political will that directs the Sandinista project and the nature of the social forces upon which it rests, its future development will be determined by the sum total of forthcoming conjunctures, by the ebb and flow of tensions in our immediate geo-political surroundings, and ultimately, it goes without saying, by the correlation of forces in the world.

We cannot hope to walk this road without suffering. Although the absolute triumph of the people in arms displaced all other options, options which failed to be concretized as alternatives to the dictatorship, that does not mean the struggle is over. Nor does it mean that Sandinista power, people's power, does not still face a permanent challenge.

Outside of a few skirmishes and as yet unsuccessful attempts at organizing armed counterrevolution, the struggle is now taking place principally in the ideological arena. The main thrust is an attempt to destabilize the revolutionary process politically. A call is made for returning to accepted standards, based on trying to take out of context all the dynamic and necessarily abnormal factors implicit in the revolutionary process, which has dislocated the country's whole social tradition in less than a year. These factors are treated as abstract anomalies, in order to justify demands that the revolutionary leadership hasten a return to classical, institutional normalcy.

There is cunning, daily praise of the familiar virtues of the democratic panacea: elections that are free, and, one would hope, well-guarded, like the good old days; orderly, alternating terms in office and due handing over of the gold-stitched presidential sash; a strict division of powers *à la* Montesquieu, with stipends for legislators, if possible. All this alternates with a seemingly healthy and innocent attack on the forms of people's power brought into being by the revolution. On the surface, the attack questions only the legality of those forms and not their very existence; yet such fine points are but a mask to conceal the underlying attempt to turn back the revolutionary project, to reverse its gains.

For underneath, there is a whole struggle to contain and halt the revolutionary process; to freeze its actions, warp its course, enmesh its tactical apparatuses in strategic frustration; to dissolve its mass support now organized through the neighborhood committees, trade unions and rural workers' organizations. Meanwhile, there is praise of immaculate democracy, of the infallible kingdom of private property, unique in its efficiency, for free enterprise doesn't permit challenges to management, whereas the state makes everything go to hell. Dreams of a paradise lost.

The forces now in conflict with the revolutionary process still follow the scent of their class interests; they understand that the Sandinista people's project is a national project, a project for definitive consolidation of a national anti-imperialist state. Therefore, their ideological offensive aims to gut the state of its Sandinista content so that a return to normalcy would bring a change in hegemony.

This is a game of many stratagems, among them the feints of democratic legitimacy, of liberal conscience offended by the close relationship between the Sandinista Front and the state—indeed, they say, remember how Somoza mixed the interests of his family and those of the state! They demand that the Sandinista People's Army be antiseptically cleansed of its Sandinismo and of its political nature—indeed, the finest military tradition is that of being constitutionally apolitical as in the Southern Cone! They try to make the word *pueblo*, people, into a very abstract and cross-class term, in order to separate the people from the vanguard—which, of course, was brave and intrepid during the war and led the way to victory, but that need not mean that the vanguard represents the people or embodies their hopes! Because the revolution was made by the people and, in the vocabulary of those who were displaced, the "people" of course means *everybody*.

Then, too, although the Sandinista Front has never made rhetorical use of the term socialism, the dislodged class hurries to coin its "socialism with liberty," in order to castrate the whole historic force that such a concept carries. Then they roll up to the front their second-, third- and fourth-hand battering rams of the anticommunist crusade to protect the sacred values of patriotism and religion from the dangers of communism which tears babies from their mothers' arms, burns holy images, shuts churches, carries off the small farmer's four cows and establishes what *La Prensa* has called a new, infallible and inquisitional faith.

Now, since there is a present danger that all these calamities may befall us, a danger that the liberties so dear to all Nicaraguans will be lost if we are unable to construct an original model, the wise ideologues of the counterrevolution paternalistically advise us to be original, to achieve socialism without sacrificing the freedom of man. But they are speaking of freedom only as an ontological category. They would not look into history to find a model for social action. They would never look into a history which, like our own, is only now beginning to emerge from the long night of pain and poverty, of abandonment and outrage. They do not deal with the transformation of a republic with few schools and less hospitals, a Nicaraguan republic of the poor and ragged, of those who starve without land or shelter, of jobless and marginal people who root for food in garbage dumps. In the republic of the wise men, there is only a false humanism that says social reality should be dominated by freedom in the abstract—meaning, the freedom of the few. Those few, frankly, now experience limits on their previous freedom, which was not an abstract matter at all but rather the very concrete freedom to mercilessly exploit the many who never had any freedom of choice.

The national, Nicaraguan character of this revolution is not in question, as the counterrevolution contends, when it points to the danger of copying models. Our revolution is national because it is Sandinista, and historically Sandinismo implies the people's hegemony. If the course of its own development leads our revolution to repeat structural changes carried out by other revolutionary processes, this happens, quite simply, because we are resolving a dialectical contradiction generated by the fact of being a poor country now engaged in overcoming and destroying unjust structures, in moving towards true independence. In this we structurally resemble so many marginal countries that have found their road to liberation in armed struggle, all the countries that are now seeking and will surely find their road to liberation in armed struggle, if reason watches over their weapons and if truth is on their side.

Our revolution will have to create its own model, in the dynamics of the conjuncture and taking into account our own social conditions. But we will never comply with counterrevolutionary demands that the revolution change its popular nature in order to be unique and unlike any other; that it alter the spectrum of alliances so as to weaken the revolutionary hegemony of the popular classes; that it cease to deepen its achievements; that it freeze the process of structural change at a point where the balance is favorable to reactionary interests.

That is why our enemies become so angry when we insist that this revolution is of an irreversible nature, that there can be no return to the past or to any of the alternatives already condemned to failure. The revolution is irreversible in nature because the masses have taken their place in history; the poor and common people have awakened, and they are learning how to make history. And they will not run the risk of reversal, the risk that has proved so costly in other circumstances and in other latitudes of Latin America. For reversibility and irreversibility are necessarily opposites. And in order not to risk reversal, the Nicaraguan people have the arms with which they won victory for the Sandinista project, arms which they will use to defend reason and justice, which are also on our side.

Patria Libre o Morir!

(A Free Homeland or Death!)

Managua, Free Nicaragua

July 5, 1980

The Masses Move Forward, the Bourgeoisie Encounters Limitations

CIDAMO

The article presented here was originally published by CIDAMO, the Centro de Información, Documentación y Análisis sobre el Movimiento Obrero Latinoamericano in late 1980.

The efforts of the bourgeoisie to hold back the revolutionary process grew sharper in every area of class struggle during the period between Alfonso Robelo's* resignation from the Junta of the Government in April 1980, and the collective withdrawal of bourgeois members of the Council of State in November. This is basically because, while the bourgeoisie has had the economic and political space in which to further its own interests, the growing organization of the working class and its participation in the Sandinista revolutionary program have developed into a process which will be very difficult to reverse.

In fact, the popular nature of the democratic process that began on July 19, 1979 was established from the start by the conditions under which Somoza's dictatorship was defeated. The masses, who participated so fully in the insurrection, did so independent of bourgeois institutions. This reality, first embodied in the Movement of the United People (MPU), grew in scope with the unification of the Sandinista National Liberation Front (FSLN) and the formation of the Sandinista People's Army, which has played a key role in broadening mass organizations and in containing the counterrevolution since the defeat of the dictatorship. Under these conditions, anti-Somoza sectors of the bourgeoisie had no choice but to participate in the Government of Reconstruction and National Unity, accepting a secondary role and enjoying limited support.

Counterrevolutionary Maneuvers
Of the Bourgeoisie

As the autonomy of the working classes grew, the bourgeoisie suffered a representational crisis, because none of the traditional political parties proved capable of representing its interests. Costly as this had been under Somoza, under the new circumstances it could mean a greater defeat for the bourgeoisie. Thus it is not surprising that

---

* Alfonso Robelo, leading industrialist and part of the bourgeois opposition to Somoza, was a member of the Government Junta from July 1979 to April 1980, when he resigned and denounced the Junta and formally went into opposition to the government. — *Ed.*

bourgeois demands upon the Sandinista government were first formulated by a trade organization, the Private Enterprise Council (COSEP). Their main demands were: depoliticizing the army, disbanding the militia and the Sandinista Defense Committees (CDS); repeal of the publications law and the emergency law; enactment of a law of property guarantees *(Ley de amparo);* establishment of a Council of State; municipal and presidential elections without delay. Economically they sought reduced state intervention; an end to land confiscations; an end to "unfair competition" in the distribution of basic consumer goods by the CDS and the government's basic foods outlet, ENABAS; an increase in financing, etc.

The newspaper *La Prensa* was another instrument of bourgeois representation during this period. In April 1980, the owners decided to change editors, taking a sharp turn to the right. From that time on, bourgeois positions on the most diverse subjects were published in *La Prensa* and widely disseminated both at home and abroad.

Robelo's resignation was part of his effort to place himself and his party, the Democratic Nicaraguan Movement (MDN), at the head of the bourgeoisie. This is clear from his announcement to a business group that he disagreed with the government's "alarming deviations"; it is also clear from his program, despite his call for a "free and Nicaraguan socialism." Robelo's resignation, occurring just a few days before the opening session of the Council of State, was the first sign that one sector of the bourgeoisie was willing to make a break with national unity and go over to the opposition, with no regard for the way in which they were sabotaging an institution upon which the bourgeoisie itself had insisted—the Council of State.

But Robelo's attempt to dominate the bourgeois forces failed when, after some hesitation, the COSEP and other parties decided not to follow the MDN initiative to boycott the Council of State. They considered that they did not yet have sufficient domestic support. In the months that followed, class struggle was characterized by intensified bourgeois activity aimed at gaining strength within the country, which included insistence upon immediate elections as well as an increase in the number of incursions from Honduras by counterrevolutionary bands of ex-soldiers from Somoza's National Guard.

Tension between the business sector and the government slackened after the Sandinista national leadership reaffirmed the pact of national unity, while adopting such measures as repeal of the emergency law, enactment of the law of property guarantees, cessation of land confiscations, and naming two new members to the Junta. This forced Robelo to draw back temporarily and to declare his support for the defense of the revolution, given the actions of the counterrevolutionary bands. The MDN also became part of the Council of State. Nevertheless, these were not signs of a bourgeois retreat. Businessmen stepped up the pace of disinvestment in factories; the Conservative Democratic Party challenged Rafael Córdova on his participation in the Junta. These actions by the bourgeoisie went together with terrorism and demands for immediate elections to form a panorama of growing confrontation.

The counterrevolutionary bands had three clear objectives: provoking the Sandinista government and the mass organizations; creating bases of operations within the country; and crippling the revolution by murdering the nine members of the FSLN national leadership. The participation of businessmen and large landowners in the organizing and financing of the counterrevolutionary bands has been clearly established on several occasions. Particularly significant has been their support of plans to assassinate the national leadership of the FSLN—plans directed by former Defense Minister ex-Colonel Bernardo Larios—and the smuggling of thousands of arms into the country, discovered when COSEP vice-president Jorge Salazar was killed by the army in an escape attempt. At the same time, *La Prensa* with its campaign against the National Literacy Crusade has, in effect, provided a propaganda cover for the counterrevolutionary murderers of literacy workers. During this period the bourgeois parties also engaged in provocations—they sought to create confrontations between the government and sectors of the population whose sympathies they could then capture to widen their own support, which had dwindled to certain petty bourgeois sectors. Here again, *La Prensa* played its role, with a nationalist, anticommunist ideological campaign.

One major bourgeois provocation took place at the end of October in the Atlantic Coast town of Bluefields. Reactionary forces instigated a series of protests against the presence of Cuban health and literacy workers. Sandinista national leadership was able to resolve the conflict through dialogue with the people on the Coast (whose circumstances, earlier on, had prevented them from becoming significantly engaged in the struggle against the dictatorship).

The positions that business had taken and the marked swing to the right in the United States, especially in Central American policy, encouraged Robelo to launch a new electoral campaign, despite the government's very firm announcement that elections would be held in 1985. The MDN, on the pretext that a rally at Nandaime had been prohibited, staged an attack on a Sandinista office in Managua and burned the FSLN flag. *La Prensa* unleashed a vicious campaign against the government and finally, on November 12, COSEP, the MDN, the Conservative Democratic and Social Christian parties, along with the Christian Democratic leadership of the Nicaraguan Workers Central (CTN) withdrew from the Council of State. However, the government crisis they tried to provoke did not take place because the social base of the bourgeoisie was simply too limited and the combative response of the working masses far too strong.

The Strength of the People's Response

During the period since the fall of Somoza, the majority of the Nicaraguan people have come to a much clearer understanding of the nature of bourgeois organizations and the role they play. One sign of this is the rapid development of the people's own organizations: the Sandinista Workers Central (CST), the Rural Workers Association (ATC), the Luisa Amanda Espinosa Women's Association, the Sandinista Defense Committees (CDS), etc. But the political consciousness of the masses has also been expressed in struggles to unseat those members of local government juntas who did not represent the people's interests; in rank-and-file challenges to the CTN leadership; in worker demands to nationalize businesses engaged in capital flight; and in overwhelming support for the decision to hold elections in 1985. There has also been outstanding mass participation in the militia. One important example is that of the Comandante Ezequiel Brigade, comprised mostly of urban and rural workers from Monimbó and Estelí, who took less than a month to wipe out a counterrevolutionary band which had been operating throughout the northern part of the country.

Thus the masses have shown a high level of political maturity and fighting spirit in their attitude towards the bourgeoisie, and have refused to become engaged in provocations. This attitude was apparent on November 19. Nearly a quarter of a million people gathered that day in the Plaza of the Revolution, joining the FSLN and the government to demonstrate anti-imperialist national unity by their energetic condemnation of provocations from the business sector and by reaffirming their commitment to the tasks of production and defense of the revolution.

Intellectuals and the Sovereignty of the People

Rosario Murillo

In September, 1981, a meeting of Latin American and Caribbean intellectuals was held in Havana, Cuba, to discuss the serious threat which today challenges "the sovereignty of the peoples of Our America." "At that meeting," states renowned Cuban author Roberto Fernández Retamar, "in light of the serious risk of extinction facing all humanity these days, a risk beyond any philosophical, religious or political ideas, we issued an open letter to the people and intellectuals of the United States which inspired a warm and fraternal response."

Out of that call, a second meeting on the sovereignty of the people of the Americas was held, this time in Mexico City in September, 1982. Representatives from the Institute for the Study of Labor and Economic Crisis, along with some 40 other North Americans, joined with many intellectuals from throughout the American continent in a very necessary "Dialogue of the Americas."

Unfortunately, in what was an angering—and revealing—statement about the primitive state of the progressive intelligentsia in the United States, some prominent U.S. personalities refused to participate because an invitation had not been extended to a certain counterrevolutionary poet-in-exile who has become a cause célèbre in some social democratic circles. In their failure to join this critical dialogue, these intellectuals contributed nothing to the struggle for liberty and justice for which they so self-righteously profess to speak. They served only to perpetuate the isolation, ignorance and backwardness of the progressive U.S. intelligentsia at a time when dialogue and unity of the world's peoples are ever more necessary.

To further stimulate the dialogue called for by our Latin American compañeros, we are publishing here a powerful and challenging statement made at the September 1982 Mexico City meeting by Rosario Murillo of the Nicaraguan delegation. Rosario Murillo is a widely respected poet and Secretary General of the Sandinista Cultural Workers Association.

We have come to Mexico, this land that is our sister in solidarity, to participate in the "Dialogue of the Americas" representing the Nicaraguan Revolution. Before all else, we wish, in the name of our people, our artists and intellectuals, our Revolution, to greet our sister people of Mexico and their President, the intellectual Don José López Portillo, that great friend of Nicaragua who has done so much to push forward an exemplary policy of solidarity with the peoples of Latin America. We take advantage of this forum to express, once more, the recognition of our people for the fraternal, unconditional, and consistent support we have received from the government and people of Mexico who have done so much to aid in the consolidation of our beautiful Sandinista Revolution.

We have come to this meeting representing our Nicaraguan writers and artists, but, in a deeper sense, we are here in representation of our people—our heroic and long-suffering people who after years of courage and struggle won our definitive freedom in 1979, achieving our dearest dream, the victory of the greatest poem ever written: that of a people having won its liberation.

And so we have come to speak with you about hope and life. Because our people live in the constant offering up of hope, providing life with a future, responding to the challenge of rebuilding a country we inherited in ruins so that we may keep it beautiful and defiant for our future generations, keep it in dignity—the dignity we carry in our veins from the time of Diriangén, Andrés Castro, Sandino, Rigoberto, Carlos Fonseca [historic revolutionary heroes—*Ed.*], the dignity with which thousands of our heroes and martyrs made fertile the road we now travel, the dignity and commitment we still admire today in those who continue to fall beneath our enemies' bloodying rage.

But we said we have come to speak with you about hope and life. And this is possible only because we have a revolution in Nicaragua, because our people are a revolutionary people and because we—Nicaraguan intellectuals and artists—represent here the energy and the fervor of a revolution in progress, a revolution which, in spite of multiple tensions, threats, and concrete aggressions, continues its route, sure in the optimism it sees reflected in our people's eyes; solid in the hands of our workers fertilizing fields; alive in the weapons with which we respond to the enemy's fire, checking his rampage of death and destruction.

And so, because we speak in our people's name, we can speak with hope in our eyes—in spite of the war we hear, in spite of the shadows that darken our present and dim the future of Our America.

In February of this year, we celebrated in Managua the first ordinary meeting of the Permanent Committee of Intellectuals for the Sovereignty of the Peoples of Our America. At the time this meeting took place, the Reagan administration's provocations against our

Revolution, the declarations being made by the principal spokespeople of the United States government, and the movement of troops in the area all pointed to a very serious situation in Central America. El Salvador and Nicaragua were the continued target of these aggressions. The Managua meeting, for that reason, took place in a prewar atmosphere, and the discussions and resolutions emerged out of a threatened, ambushed, and embattled reality, but also from a reality of a people's combativeness, work, and organization. The organization of a people in self-defense, and engaged in—among other things—the cultural and artistic tasks natural to the struggle to preserve our gains, to preserve our sovereignty, to preserve this battle aimed at maintaining peace.

And so, before coming to this event, the Nicaraguan delegation discussed the theme it had been assigned for this paper. Faced with the possibility of developing ideas which might contribute to deepening the various theoretical alternatives related to the concept of sovereignty— and living as our Nicaraguan intellectuals and artists do the reality of such an intense daily struggle, a struggle launched precisely in order to preserve that sovereignty won by our people on July 19th, 1979—we decided to use this tribunal in order to explain, once more, the concrete contents of our struggle. We decided to expose the factors which every day bring the danger of aggression against our sovereignty, freedom, and independence closer, and ever more dramatic, the factors which daily threaten the peace won by the blood of Nicaragua's most precious sons and daughters. We decided to use this forum in order to denounce the concrete acts which today threaten our sovereignty—Nicaragua's sovereignty and the sovereignty of all the peoples of America—and to condemn the concrete acts which today cause us to once again live the prelude to war. And we decided to make our intervention in these terms because we are sure that everyone here is interested in dealing with concrete problems and concrete ideas aimed at making more effective the commitment of intellectuals, in particular, the progressive sectors of America and of the world in general. It is a commitment we must assume in order to avoid this war. Because today's struggle for sovereignty in America is the struggle to preserve peace, it is the struggle to avoid war, and to maintain the principles of independence and self-determination for the peoples. It is the struggle against imperialism.

Humanity today lives one of its most critical moments. This is something which has been spoken of, discussed, and denounced throughout the world with ever greater urgency in recent times. The international economic crisis reflects the weakening of unjust forms of production and trade which have been imposed on great areas of the world. Today the poor countries, without sufficient means for their development, sink further and further into debt in an effort to deal with the crisis, and they continue to pay the price of the irrational and inhuman relations of exchange between nations. These unequal relations operate by underselling our products, the fruit of our sweat and labor, until all that remains of us is the sickness and death of our undernourished peasants and workers, who are exposed to every kind of risk in order to buy at ever-increasing prices the medicines, machinery, parts, and supplies which we need to work and to live. Our countries continue to be the object of the irrational looting of our natural resources or of the looting—for it is nothing but looting—hidden in the multimillion dollar profits of the international financial institutions on which we are forced to depend. We are denied the possibility of technical development for the processing of our primary resources, and we are criminally blackmailed with the productive and nutritional needs of our peoples. Millions of human beings throughout the world die of hunger or are undernourished. While all of this continues, the political and military tensions are more threatening every day. We are witnessing the prelude to the third war which not only we, but all of humanity, are obliged to try to avoid.

And this irrational, unjust, illogical, and inhuman economic policy is the structural support of those who continue to risk humanity's most sacred and vital interests. It is the structural support of those who reject the initiatives designed to avoid the use of force in international affairs; who refuse to sign nonaggression treaties; who refuse to ratify the SALT II agreements; who turn their backs on a dialogue regarding the freezing of strategic weaponry and the prohibition and destruction of nuclear arms; who promote the war in the Malvina (Falkland) Islands; who invade and murder in Libya; who interfere in the free countries of Africa and retard their liberation processes; who direct and advise the genocide in El Salvador; who maintain the criminal blockade against Cuba and retain Guantanamo Base; who refuse to comply with the Panama Canal treaty; who support, arm, and train the ex-Somoza guards and organize the counterrevolutionary bands in Nicaragua; who destabilize, spy, intrigue, instigate, and plot in order to keep the peoples of the world from moving forward; who would deny us our right to the future and who would indeed deny humanity its future.

When we left our country, the XVII Regional Conference of the United Nations Food and Agriculture Organization (FAO), in which ministerial-level delegations from the American countries are taking part, was in session. They were discussing the problems of nutrition and development in Our America and in the world. At the opening session of this important international event—whose realization in Nicaragua is evidence of the recognition given by the countries of the world to the agricultural transformations wrought by the Nicaraguan people's Sandinista Revolution—the Coordinator of the Government Junta and member of the National Directorate of the FSLN (Sandinista National Liberation Front), Commander of the Revolution Daniel Ortega Saavedra, said in speaking of our country's current situation within the above-mentioned international context:

At this juncture, Nicaragua is twice-over a victim, on the one hand, gripped by international economic injustice, and, on the other, attacked, both economically and militarily, by those who try to impose their hegemonic policy.

Nicaragua, which in December, 1972, sustained material losses for $1 billion, as a result of the earthquake, according to ECLA reports;

Nicaragua, which during the last years of struggle against the tyranny [of the Somoza dictatorship], sustained losses for over $2 billion according to World Bank estimates;

Nicaragua, which as a result of the recent floods in May, 1982, sustained losses for $357 million, according to ECLA reports;

Nicaragua, a poor country, which in a decade has suffered losses for $3.4 billion in damage to its economic and social infrastructure and productive activity, as well as other material damage, and has had thousands of people killed, wounded, or affected by natural disasters, is today the victim of the hegemonic policy which fosters political isolation and economic aggression; a policy which:

• hinders the approval of loans in international bodies;
• encourages armed aggressions with their resulting casualties;
• organizes the blasting of bridges, transport vehicles, and machinery;
• fosters domestic destabilization;
• orders the violation of our territorial waters and air space;
• promotes confrontation and war between fraternal peoples;
• through its criminal actions, forces hundreds of farmers to leave their cultivated areas, thus affecting our people's efforts.

But that punitive will crashes against the extraordinary effort of our people in revolution to survive and to advance in the midst of adversity.

We feel it important to quote this part of Commander Ortega's speech because it clarifies even more the panorama of struggle to which we have been referring. Throughout the world—in America, in Central America, in Nicaragua today—the struggle for sovereignty is the struggle for peace, the battle to avoid war. "The most beautiful victory we can win," as one of our leaders said, "is that of the war we are able to avoid."

The efforts of the Nicaraguan government nationally and internationally to keep peace in the region of Central America are well known by all. These efforts have ranged from the peace initiatives brought before the United Nations by the Coordinator of the National Reconstruction Government in October of last year, through the exposition made by Nicaragua before the U.N. Security Council in March of this year, to the diplomatic offensive carried out by leaders and functionaries of our government who have traveled extensively on special missions, visiting friendly countries and governments to transmit our Revolution's desire for peace. From the proposals for dialogue presented by our country to the U.S. government; the projected meetings of heads of state of the area; the meetings between defense ministers; the talks held in the border zones through the patient and mature attitude of our leaders, of our people, of our Army, of our militia; from the simple refusal to respond to enemy provocations wherever they may occur, to the blood of our heroes and martyrs shed by the counterrevolution's armed aggressions in cities, towns, and border areas across our country. This will for peace, laced with dignity and courage, finds concrete expression in the smile of young Brenda Isabel Rocha, a brave 16-year-old militiawoman. She responded to the attack of a counterrevolutionary band in the northern part of the department of Zelaya, fighting until the last of her comrades died alongside her and she herself was badly wounded. She lost her right arm, but refused to allow them to defeat her spirit as a youth, a militiawoman, a Sandinista, a revolutionary. "I've lost an arm," she said, "but I'm willing to give the other, and my life if necessary, to defend this people's Revolution!"

This is the concrete aspect of our struggle for sovereignty: this people's heroism, this determination to win or die, and the courage displayed by the heroic militia of San Francisco del Norte, where another band of counterrevolutionaries struck a few weeks back beneath the banners of "God, Country, and Patriotism," murdering four humble peasants and kidnaping ten more whose whereabouts are unknown even today. There too, these agents of death and destruction were confronted by the undefeatable spirit of Sandino, by the heritage of Leonel Rugama, a young militiaman who preferred to have his arms cut off than to allow them to wrench his weapon from him and see it used by the enemies of his people, enemies who would like to see a return to the bitter past which our Revolution has uprooted once and for all.

These are the voices that rise up against war. This is our people's conscience, and it is also the struggle of our intellectuals and artists who, while carrying out their creative work, live as our people live, in the heart of our people. Artists like Andrés Valle, painter and stage actor who, on his job as a cameraman for our Sandinist People's Army television, fell in battle against the [counterrevolutionary] bands only a few months ago. Artists like those who in March and April of

1982 joined dozens of cultural brigades and traveled across the country with their poetry, their music, their dance, their theater, their painting, aiding in the people's organization for defense. Artists like those who throughout these three years have so often had to put aside their literary, musical, or artistic vocation in order to take on necessary bureaucratic tasks, to comply with ministerial or state functions; in short, to make the Revolution. Artists in the People's Militia who have lived for months at a time in the mountains, in the reserve battalions, participating in activities as important as the moving of the Miskito people to their new homes provided by the Revolution. Intellectuals, like many among the leadership of our Revolution, including novelists, poets, and anthropologists, who have had to assume duties of state before those of their own vocations. Poets like the common men and women among our people who write on their nation's walls—now that our people know how to write—"THEY MAY DIE OF NOSTALGIA, BUT THEY SHALL NOT PASS!"

We said that we came to speak about hope and life. And that's what we're doing. Because in spite of the situation of grave threats and criminal acts that we have denounced today; in spite of, or along with, this situation, you must have gleaned from our examples of heroism, of courage, of struggle, and of the will to work, the love for life on the part of our people, our intellectuals, and artists. You must see that in Nicaragua hope and life are real things, elements of struggle, spearheads in the battle against the possibility of war.

In the midst of concrete threats and aggressions, the Nicaraguan people continue making their Revolution. The Literacy Crusade which brought light to 89% of Nicaraguans, the Popular Education Centers which coordinate the follow-up aspects of that campaign, and the health programs, and particularly the People's Health Campaigns, with the participation of thousands of voluntary brigadists, have made possible a real reduction in the index of endemic diseases and epidemics. The land reform, which has played such a determinant role in the economic, political, and social transformations demanded by a revolution, has increased the peasants' share of our country's arable territory from the 3% they owned in 1979 to 20% today. The incentives of every kind (economic, in infrastructure and services) to the production of foodstuffs in order to guarantee the people's sustenance; the policy of subsidies which greatly benefit the worker through price control in correspondence with real income; housing projects, cultural projects, sports projects, all of which—in the midst of our real and serious difficulties—are proof of our will to go on living, to go on waging the battle to preserve these gains, to continue our effort, our sacrifice, our heroism if necessary, because we have a right to life, to a free present, and to the luminous future we want to build.

What do we expect, what do the Nicaraguan people and the Nicaraguan Revolution expect, from this meeting? After the first Meeting of Intellectuals for the Sovereignty of the Peoples of Our America in Havana at the end of 1981, thousands of North American writers and intellectuals at a meeting in New York signed a document in solidarity with Latin American intellectuals in their struggle for sovereignty, thus responding positively to the call for a meeting like the one we attend today.

Almost a year has passed since then and, as we have seen, the situation in Our America has not varied. Today, in fact, it is even more serious. Now, more than ever before, the countries of Latin America require the concrete, effective solidarity which, as during the imperialist aggression in Vietnam, points up the contradictions between the warlike, adventurist, and imperialist policies of the U.S. administration and the attitude of its people.

The North American people and intellectuals, who showed so amply their abhorrence of their government's policies during the decade of the 60s by demonstrating against the crimes committed in their name in different parts of the world, must once again respond to the call of the peoples. Symptomatic of the discontent and repudiation which is beginning to make itself felt are the mobilizations for peace taking place in many cities throughout the United States, as well as the constitution and consolidation in the U.S. of networks in solidarity with peoples in struggle in other parts of the world.

The North American intellectuals, artists, writers, scientists, and journalists have an important role to play in the struggle, particularly at this moment which is so crucial for humanity. They must be the forgers of public opinion among their own people. It is up to them to help tear down the wall of misinformation, of ignorance, and of helplessness with which the enemy attempts to surround them, in an explicit effort to neutralize the possibilities of opposition. It is up to them to expose the continuous lies woven around Latin America in an effort to divert the people's struggles and profound sense of justice. It is up to them to break through the silence, raise their voices, speak with the force of truth and with the force of the muscle and the blood of our peoples in combat, and speak out with the extraordinary vigor of a consciousness awakened to the need for development in a changing world. It is up to the intellectuals of the United States, perhaps more than anything else, to build a solid wall against the prospect of war: a war which would affect everyone, even the North Americans themselves. A war which would have tragic consequences for everyone, even for the North American people. A war which might even mean the extinction of all peoples, even those who inhabit the United States.

It is up to the intellectuals of the United States today to gather up the freedom banner from the heroes of its own independence; to inject with new vigor the mystique of its own battles against colonialism; to impregnate their words and actions with the spirit of justice and liberty which characterized their forefathers and foremothers out of their own heroic tradition; to propose the end to the aggressions, the end of interventions, the end of threats, of blackmail, of blockade; to work for an end to the imperialist policies of the United States of America; to work for peace!

While you in the United States will most probably be holding seminars, conferences, campaigns, and lectures; while you are writing articles in magazines and newspapers or holding exhibits in solidarity with the peoples of the Americas; while you are carrying out what we decide upon here today, our brothers and sisters in El Salvador will continue their frontal battle to win their independence. The sons and daughters of that nation will continue to die determined in the conquest of their freedom, sovereignty, and independence. Among them, or simply as part of them, the Salvadoran intellectuals, many of whom, like the leader Eduardo Sancho, or like the unforgettable Roque Dalton, have temporarily exchanged their poetry for a gun and a place in the revolutionary leadership, will continue to fight and continue their road to victory or death. In many Latin American countries, intellectuals will continue to be persecuted, tortured, and "missing," like our exemplary Alaide Foppa, like Paco Urondo, Rodolfo Wash, Haroldo Conti. . . . In Chile, in Paraguay, in Uruguay, in Haiti . . . in Nicaragua, we will continue to respond. Perhaps you by heading a conference on sovereignty and peace; perhaps one of our intellectuals in a militia battalion, in a health brigade, at an international conference . . . or writing, painting, acting, contributing to the cultural development of the Revolution. Perhaps one of us, too, as in the past, by giving his or her life for the defense of their country, for sovereignty, for peace.

All this is possible in Nicaragua in the coming months, as it has been possible and real throughout these recent years. All of the foregoing is possible in America. The war, as we have said, is also a real possibility. It is up to you—it is up to us—but more to you who are able to confront the enemy on his own territory, to struggle against injustice and crime, prevailing in the world. We must stop continuing wars, or else accept the final war.

While you return to your homes, to your jobs, to your books and projects in the United States, we will return to the very real possibility of war. We do not want war. We fought to achieve peace and we will do everything in our power to preserve it. But, if in spite of all our efforts, if in spite of all the efforts that our Revolution realizes in all areas, we cannot prevent war, we will assume it with the same courage, the same determination, the same sacrifice with which in the past we confronted intervention, the Somoza dictatorship, and the continuous imperialist aggressions. We will respond with the heroism of Andrés Castro. We will respond as in 1856. With the heroism of Zeledón. As in 1912. With the incomparable will and bravery of Augusto C. Sandino. With the will and the faith in victory of Carlos Fonseca. With the indomitable spirit of Rugama, of Ricardo Morales, of the Sandinist National Liberation Front.

For us, the struggle for sovereignty is the struggle to preserve peace. Our role as intellectuals in this struggle cannot be other than that of any human being whose heart beats in his people's hands. Our commitment is to struggle for sovereignty and, in Nicaragua today, that means preparing ourselves for defense.

And this is why we are here today, speaking of hope and of life, telling you that in our homeland, where we come from and where we will soon be returning, there is a people working, sacrificing itself, fighting. There is a people standing firm, with tenderness in its eyes and nurturing its dream. A people, in short, preparing itself "with love in the bullet and its heart in the mouth" to continue making its Revolution. To light its way to its future! To continue to hold up the poems of Rugama and Gordillo which come from the hand and the genius of the people. Like the poem we mentioned before: "THEY MAY DIE OF NOSTALGIA, BUT THEY SHALL NOT PASS!"

DOCUMENTS FROM GUATEMALA by the Guerrilla Army of the Poor (EGP)

The Guatemalan Revolution

The EGP is a leading revolutionary organization which has been active in Guatemala since the early 1970's. These articles originally appeared in Compañero, *the international magazine of the EGP. Several were written prior to the 1982 coup analyzed in the final section of this book.*

Introduction

The Guatemalan revolution is entering its third decade. Ever since the government of Jacobo Arbenz was overthrown in 1954,* the majority of the Guatemalan people have been seeking a way to move the country towards solving the same problems which were present then, and have only worsened over time.

The counterrevolution, put in motion by the U.S. government and those national sectors committed to retaining every single one of their privileges, dispersed and disorganized the popular and democratic forces. However, it did not resolve any of the problems which had first given rise to demands for economic, social and political changes. These demands have been raised again and again in the last quarter century, by any means that seemed appropriate at the time, and have received each time the same repressive response as in 1954.

---

* Jacobo Arbenz was President of Guatemala from 1951 to 1954. The Arbenz government, the second government of the 1944-54 "Guatemalan Revolution," was a period of democracy, nationalism and anti-imperialism, and instituted many needed reforms for the Guatemalan working class. In June 1954, the U.S. government sponsored the overthrow of the Arbenz government by counterrevolutionary forces.—Ed.

For one part of the popular movement it was soon clear that only an armed struggle would allow the people to remove from power the tiny group of representatives of national and foreign interests, who are the only beneficiaries of a system that produces widespread misery for the rest of the population. This conviction produced the revolutionary guerrilla movement of the 1960's. However, an important segment of the popular and democratic movement still harbored the illusion of solving the country's problems within the institutional framework set up by the counterrevolution.

A high price was paid for this illusion. The revolutionary movement, politically isolated, was defeated militarily by an army trained by the U.S. in the counterinsurgency techniques learned in Vietnam. With the temporary defeat of the armed movement, this army was left in charge. It worked to systematically and brutally eliminate all protests, all demands and, finally, all possibility of participation within institutional channels.

At the same time, an economic development model based on exports has led to an ever-greater concentration of wealth in the hands of an ever-smaller group, while increasing the misery of most of the population. Today, those who hold political power use the state apparatus to increase their power and wealth still more, reducing to civil and economic impotence not only the worker and peasant majority, but now also the middle classes and those business sectors uninvolved in the plundering. To govern under these conditions, the government has had to move from pressure to repression, from electoral fraud to physical elimination of opponents, from sporadic crime to systematic crime, from selective repression to massacre and genocide.

The temporary defeat of the armed movement at the end of the 1960's did not demonstrate the impossibility of armed struggle, but rather the need to link more closely armed struggle and the entire spectrum of popular and democratic struggles around economic, social and political demands. Or, better, the need to incorporate all the people in a process of popular revolutionary war, with armed struggle as the center of the process. By different routes, with ideas that put the accent on mobilizing this or that sector of the population, with different degrees of success, the scattered remains of the revolutionary movement of that first decade re-initiated their activities on new premises. These were years of patient and anonymous work, of slow and laborious advances, of difficult convergence among the different organizations and political positions.

But the conditions created by the accumulation of basic, unresolved social problems, the spread of dictatorial power to all areas of life, generalized repression and the concomitant destruction of all other forms of political participation, made it clear that the armed overthrow of the repressive regime is a prerequisite for any kind of change. The basis was laid for the historic convergence of the armed revolutionary movement and the popular and democratic movement. The popular and democratic sectors were now convinced that their objectives could not be reached within the ever-narrower margins set by the government. The coming together of the armed struggle with other forms of mass struggle implies that more and more, the struggles of the popular organizations assume paramilitary forms and underground organizational methods, while the armed struggle assumes more of a mass character.

The convergence of the armed revolutionary movement with the popular movement marked the beginning of accelerated growth of the armed organizations. At the same time, it gave rise to a more congruent development of the different political positions and projects. As a result, a tendency towards unity was generated, which since then has taken more concrete form and has become consolidated among the Guerrilla Army of the Poor (EGP), Rebel Armed Forces (FAR), Organization of People in Arms (ORPA) and Guatemalan Labor Party (PGT). As all other forms of participation and all other viable alternatives have disappeared, the revolutionary organizations have become the focal point, drawing together all the popular and democratic forces, all aspirations for change and all expressions of protest.

The strategy of popular revolutionary war put into practice by the revolutionary organizations projects the development of the guerrilla war through a gradual accumulation of forces, and its extension throughout the entire country starting from the places where the revolutionary forces already have a firm base.

Today, the extension of the guerrilla war and the qualitative growth of guerrilla units are occurring faster than ever before. The revolutionary organizations' actions now cover more than half the country, including the most densely populated zones and those of greatest economic importance. This has only been possible because of the will of the entire population to fight, which is reflected in the massive incorporation of the people into the ranks of the revolutionary organizations, in some areas by the hundreds and even thousands. Entire towns are organizing themselves to establish contact with the revolutionaries. In the urban areas, among workers, students and other sectors, something similar is happening. The problem today for the revolutionary organizations is to develop all this potential and provide effective leadership.

The development of the Guerrilla Army of the Poor and the other revolutionary organizations has allowed the armed revolutionary movement to move from the initial phase of creating a base, to a superior phase. The first phase was characterized by armed propaganda actions, which consisted of the military takeover of towns and large farms to transmit the revolutionary message to the population, avoiding direct combat with the army. During this phase, guerrilla units of the

EGP occupied hundreds of localities, speaking at times to thousands of people and demonstrating with deeds the way to confront, arms in hand, the violence of the oppressor regime. The message and the example of the revolutionary combatants, born among the local people and speaking their native languages, resulted in the massive incorporation of the populace.

The government's repressive forces, unable to strike at guerrilla forces fed and protected by the population, directed their blows against unarmed civilians. But repression has only strengthened the determination of the Guatemalan people to fight and underlined the need for armed struggle as the only way to change things. People have learned to organize armed self-defense to resist the repression and protect their leaders and organizations. Armed propaganda actions continue, but now guerrilla activity has grown and reached a higher level.

The present phase of revolutionary activity is characterized by increasingly important and frequent battles against the army of the government. In the already consolidated Guerrilla Fronts, the revolutionaries have gained the offensive. From July to November of 1980, the EGP alone carried out 15 ambushes of army troops and 17 attacks on barracks, outposts and other fixed positions—and this doesn't include the many actions of our sister organizations. These actions caused several hundred government losses, and numerous quantities of arms and munitions passed into the hands of the revolutionaries. In August, our new Comandante Ernesto Guevara Guerrilla Front in Huehuetenango province emerged publicly; since then its members have taken over seven municipal capitals in addition to tens of towns and villages. Throughout the country, dozens of actions to distribute revolutionary literature took place.

The government army has been forced to increase its detachments in the most important towns, but in so doing has been forced to abandon many posts it can no longer protect. In an attempt to contain the insurgency, the army has stepped up forced recruitment, although it has had to stop recruiting soldiers in the areas dominated by the influence of the revolutionary organizations. Since these zones take up practically the entire central and northwest, Indian-populated highlands, the government has opted to increase its troops through recruitment among the ladino (mixed Spanish-Indian) population of the impoverished eastern region. There, the regime is also trying to exploit the discriminatory attitudes of certain sectors of the non-Indian population, product of centuries of cultural oppression and discrimination against the Indians. But as the revolutionary war spreads to this region, the army will run up against limits to this policy.

The government's defensive policies also include pressing the military reserves into active service and increasing the number of police, downgrading their civil functions and assigning them military duties in the largest towns. This is also true of the treasury and customs police. The creation of numerous private police forces and gangs of thugs at the service of large landowners and government politicians has also been encouraged.

The confrontation between the government of Gen. Romeo Lucas García and the Guatemalan people thus begins to take on a more military character. The government has completely abandoned even the slightest effort to ameliorate the misery or repression, even those efforts which might prolong its own existence. Rather, Lucas is counting on his close ties to the Reagan Administration which has promised to provide him with all the aid he needs. The public support voiced by the U.S. government has already resulted in a newly aggressive attitude on the part of the security forces which, sure that the granting of massive military and economic aid and an ending of criticism by U.S. officials of human rights violations are imminent, have increased the terror campaign against ever-widening sectors of the population, including respected journalists and world-renowned intellectuals.

On an economic level, the Lucas government has also made clear that there will be no concessions. To pay for the mounting costs of war against its people, the government has increased those taxes affecting the popular sectors, while at the same time providing million-dollar tax cuts for the most reactionary sectors of private enterprise. With the full authorization of government ministers, the prices of necessities like beans, cooking oil and sugar have risen to never-before-seen levels which turn them into luxuries for the majority of Guatemalans.

In an attempt to channel popular discontent, the official political parties have announced an early start to the March 1982 presidential electoral farce. But even they no longer believe in such spectacles, after two sucessive electoral frauds and the assassination of the leaders of the legal opposition. Even the most reactionary groups have begun to call for postponing the elections in order to deal with the national crisis.

Today it is clear to all Guatemalans that any opposition, any project for change, is viable only if it is centered around the revolutionary organizations EGP, FAR, ORPA and PGT. Conscious of the responsibility this implies, the four revolutionary organizations have in the past year taken decisive steps towards achieving revolutionary unity. The unification process has already resulted in the execution of coordinated plans of increasing importance. It has also given rise to a consensus on important strategic and tactical points and joint initiatives. The unification process is irreversible. It corresponds to the rise in the militancy and will to fight of the people and to the convergence of all the forces and aspirations of Guatemalans around the same objectives and around one sole task: the overthrow of the criminal Lucas government and the establishment of a revolutionary, popular and democratic government.

The Struggle of the Guatemalan People and International Solidarity

Today the eyes of the world are focused on Central America. The rising revolutionary, popular and democratic struggles have transformed this region of pacified, docile "banana republics" into one of the world's most intense areas of conflict.

The Nicaraguan Revolution gave the final death-blow to the decades-long, shameless Somoza dictatorship, and in so doing, marked the beginning of a new conjuncture, a new set of conditions in the area. It dismantled the strategic military structure promoted by the United States and the local reactionary governments, and broke up the submissive transnational economic bloc represented by the Central American Common Market (Mercomun). Within the context of the popular revolutionary war already underway in other Central American countries, the victory of Nicaragua's popular insurrection confirmed the validity of armed struggle as the method for achieving the liberation of our countries. It creatively enriched the plans of the political and social forces participating in the revolutionary struggle, and accelerated the process of developing mass consciousness throughout the area, imbuing thousands with confidence of certain victory. And in a very significant and important way, the Nicaraguan Revolution opened the region to new factors of political interest and of international solidarity.

It is within this framework that Honduras has entered a period of popular and democratic struggles, generated by deepening internal contradictions much like those characteristic of the other Central American countries, and also by the militant example set by its neighbors. Costa Rica is threatened by an economic crisis that has dealt blows to the workers and middle-income sectors, and now threatens the internal stability of the country as a whole. The struggles of the workers have extended nationally and, in a slightly different vein, the heart-felt solidarity of the Costa Rican people unwaveringly supports the struggles of sister nations, and is nourished by them.

The resolutions passed in the United Nations and Organization of American States that Belize should be granted its independence in the course of 1981 are one more example of support for the progressive forces in the region, and express a total rejection of the Guatemalan government's belligerent positions.

In El Salvador, battles are being fought at this moment that will be decisive in determining the future freedom of that heroic people, and of the other peoples in the area. In spite of a succession of repressive-reformist measures that become ever more desperate, the Salvadorean masses, under the leadership of their revolutionary organizations, are demonstrating once more the strength of a people in arms who have decided to take their destiny into their own hands. And in Guatemala, our people have massively, militantly, and in an organized fashion become incorporated into the different tasks required by the revolutionary popular war, under the unified leadership of their revolutionary organizations: the Guerrilla Army of the Poor (EGP), the Rebel Armed Forces (FAR), the Organization of People in Arms (ORPA) and the Guatemalan Labor Party (PGT).

The panorama has never been as favorable for the triumph of the revolution in the area as it is today, and in the face of this, the reactionary local and international forces, with the new President of the United States, Ronald Reagan, at the head, have already begun to mobilize. Armed attacks and provocations of all kinds aimed at the Sandinista government have increased all along the borders of Nicaragua. Within the country, ex-Somocistas and counterrevolutionaries from the private sector conspire against the people.

The U.S. government, and the banks under its control, pressure and condition economic aid to Costa Rica in exchange for assurances from that government that it will align itself with the blood-stained government of El Salvador and lend itself to imperialist maneuvers in the zone. The new U.S. government also threatens noncompliance with the Panama Canal treaties—result of a historic victory won by the Panamanian people— and threatens to increase its use of the yankee military bases entrenched in that country for actions directed against the peoples of Central America.

The United States government is also doing its best to isolate Honduras from the wave of changes shaking the Central American region in order to convert it into a springboard for aggressions against the other countries in the area, by pouring massive amounts of funds in its direction. This same intention lies behind the recent "Peace Treaty" signed by Honduras and El Salvador under intense North American pressure; the same can be said of the agreements reached by the armed forces of Guatemala, El Salvador and Honduras to coordinate their actions against the heroic people of El Salvador.

As the more subtle forms of intervention prove to be inefficient, the number of U.S. military advisers to El Salvador increases, and the allocation of massive financial and military aid to the government of Guatemala can be seen coming up in the not-so-distant future. The United States continues to pressure other governments on the American continent to collaborate in rescuing the Salvadorean junta; and the danger of a military intervention, whether overt or disguised as something else, becomes more real every day. Voices of protest and warning from democratic and progressive forces the world over can already be heard in the face of this threat.

Sides have been taken; and crucial moments in the confrontation are near.

The Guatemalan Revolution

In the present conjuncture of agitation and social change in Central America, the struggle of the Guatemalan people is decisive in determining an outcome favorable to the people of the region. Guatemala is the country with the largest population, and its economy is the dominant one in the area because of its relatively higher level of development, which also implies a corresponding political and social influence. The discovery of considerable oil and mineral reserves in the northern part of our country gives it a specific geopolitical importance within the regional panorama.

At this moment, the reactionary Central American forces and imperialism are attempting to mount the bastion for counterrevolution on Guatemalan territory. The reactionary forces which carried out the 1954 counterrevolution with U.S. support, overthrowing the democratic government of Jacobo Arbenz, and the current Guatemalan government and its army, are giving refuge to the Somocistas in exile, and supporting the Salvadorean oligarchy and the government of El Salvador.

The one reason these forces have not intervened on a larger scale and more aggressively against the Nicaraguan Revolution and the Salvadorean people is that the struggle that we, the Guatemalan people, are waging against them inside the country prevents them from having the breathing space to do so.

Because our struggle stems from the need to find solutions to our most immediate problems, and because the government totally ignores our situation, and in fact makes it worse, it is a struggle that grows with every day. The need for land to plant our food on, for fair wages and job security, for housing, education, health care and a decent life, are deeply felt by the immense majority of our people, who suffer rapidly worsening conditions in all these areas. The best lands in the country are concentrated in the hands of a tiny few, while thousands of peasants try to survive with no land at all, or on minuscule plots of eroded and exhausted soil. The large *fincas* (cattle, coffee, cotton and sugar cane plantations) produce for export, leaving only the worst land, and less and less of it every day, to satisfy the nutritional needs of the population, besides being the cause of endemic seasonal unemployment.

Industry is dependent on and controlled for the most part by the transnational corporations. It offers few jobs, and is primarily dedicated to production for export, because of the extremely low buying power of the impoverished Guatemalan masses. Thousands of children die unnecessarily of curable diseases, and thousands of teachers are unemployed, in a country where more than half of the population is illiterate. Living conditions worsen every day for the majority, despite the much-touted "development projects" that in reality only end up being an excuse for ransacking the national treasury and pushing the country further into debt.

While our people remain in this miserable situation, one of the worst on the American continent, a small minority tied to foreign interests benefits from the poverty and exploitation. They are the people who own huge extensions of unused land, while a shortage of basic grains exists throughout the country; they are the people who rob the Indians of the few lands still left to them; they are the people who get wealthy off the badly paid labor of superexploited workers. They are the same people who have handed over more than half of our territory to the foreign companies that exploit our oil and nickel resources under onerous conditions for our country.

Out of this minority, a group has evolved in the last few years that is in the process of establishing itself as the most powerful of all. This new group arose as a result of the Guatemalan army's counterinsurgent offensive, under the guidance of U.S. advisers, against the revolutionary movement during the decade of the 60's. The army was able to defeat our first guerrillas, and as a result, military officers went from being the ones who carried out the dirty work in order to preserve the interests of the ruling classes, to being partners and participants in those same interests.

This new group, which controls economic, political and military power, uses state resources and the public sector of the economy to increase its wealth, and to reproduce itself. It is composed of a small clique of military officers, functionaries and businessmen who control the power of the state and use it to rob and hoard land, make shady business deals with the people's money and with international aid, and plunder the national reserves. They have become millionaires overnight, through a process of monopolizing and concentrating wealth in a way comparable only to the economic power accumulated by the Somoza family in Nicaragua. Their greed leads them to hoard credit at the expense of small and medium farmers and industrialists, and to impose their immediate economic interests over and above, and even against the interests of other sectors of private enterprise.

For many years this bureaucratic bourgeoisie attempted to dress their exercise of power in institutional clothing, but two successive, blatant electoral frauds, and their total, violent intolerance of any and all opposition, have destroyed all semblance of legitimacy. There have been years of institutionalized corruption and submission to foreign interests, of setting up state-owned monopolies for the exclusive benefit of the ruling clique, of costly construction projects completely unrelated to meeting the most pressing needs of the popular sectors, and many times left unfinished or nonfunctional due to the incompetence of the persons heading up these projects and the out-and-out robbery of the assigned funds. This corruption has reached its peak in the present government of Lucas García.

But it has been the use of systematic, brutal and indiscriminate repression unleashed by the Lucas clique against the people that has sealed the people's total rejection of this government, its army and other repressive forces, and those sectors that support them. At this point, repression is the only recourse left to this group in order to stay in power against the will of the immense majority of the population; the use of repression is the only means enabling it to continue reaping benefits from exploitation and repression, while ignoring the demands for basic necessities made by the people.

It is in this context that they have massacred Indian peasants whose only crime consisted in defending their lands, their towns and their lives. In Panzós, Chajul, Cotzal, Río Negro and in many other places, the massacres have left hundreds of victims. And those who protest against the institutionalized repression have also been killed. The most well-known case is the massacre of the Indians, and students and workers who supported them, who were burned alive in the Spanish Embassy in January of last year. In the countryside, towns and villages are occupied and ransacked by the army, as soldiers rape the women and murder the peasants, men, women, old people and children alike.

Labor, peasant and student activists and leaders, and those Christians who identify with their people, are systematically persecuted, kidnapped, tortured and assassinated along with their families. The government has resorted to forms of terror which go as far as the kidnapping and massive disappearance of more than 40 labor leaders as they attended a meeting held at their legal union headquarters in June and August of 1980, and the indiscriminate machine-gunning of students at the University of San Carlos in July of last year.

The repressive forces of the Lucas government have brazenly assassinated the leaders of the democratic opposition, like Manuel Colom Argueta and Alberto Fuentes Mohr, in addition to hundreds of their middle-level cadre. They have murdered the Guatemalan intelligentsia, or forced them into exile; the same fate has befallen scientists and people in the technical professions. They have even lashed out against the rank-and-file and middle-level cadre of the weak and rightist Christian Democratic Party, despite its unprincipled, undefined, pro-imperialist positions.

Lucas and his clique have brought down the entire institutional scaffolding of the country through their inability to govern, their corruption, their submission to foreign interests and arbitrary use of power, but mainly through their crimes and total lack of respect for the human rights of the people in the country. They have been the first to violate their own laws, as well as international norms and laws. They have responded to even the discussion of possible solutions to the acute economic and social problems plaguing the country with intimidation and the machine gun. They have attempted to subjugate the entire population through force and terror.

This situation has led the great majority of the Guatemalan people to the conclusion that as a first step towards satisfying their needs and aspirations, they must overthrow the government of Lucas García and the clique that acts as his support. The desire for a better life, for professional and personal development, for an end to exploitation and discrimination, for social progress and peace, cannot be satisfied under the current regime. Therefore, a broad alliance of all the sectors of society who consider their interests and their future affected by the Lucas government has become both possible and necessary, an alliance of all the sectors of society whose common task is the overthrow of this government in order to make way for a different one that will be capable of solving the urgent problems of the nation.

This goal can be reached only with the establishment of a revolutionary government, a popular, democratic government, a government that will be the common creation and instrument of all of these forces together.

The new government that we have in mind will have to implement profound changes in the type of development our country undergoes. Dedicated today to seeking profit for the enrichment of the few, its goals will have to be reoriented to meeting the basic and immediate needs of the majority. The new government will have to guarantee organized, mass participation in decision-making on economic and political issues, with poor workers from the countryside and the city, Indians and ladinos, all participating. It will have to respect and take into account the many points of view of all sectors and forces that compose it.

But the overthrow of the criminal Lucas government and the establishment of a revolutionary, popular and democratic government will be achieved, under the concrete conditions in our country, only through a struggle with arms in hand. Only through widespread guerrilla struggle and the creation of the popular army will we be able to break the backbone of the army, the sole genuine support of the present regime. Only backed by the use of arms will our people be able to construct a broad political front including all the democratic, popular and revolutionary sectors. Only by basing itself upon the armed power of the people will the new government be able to consolidate, and bring the great social transformations desired by our people to fruition.

This is why the revolutionary vanguard organizations will have to play a principal and decisive role throughout this process. Only the revolutionary organizations have proved themselves capable of outlining and establishing a coherent and realistic alternative that does not and will not compromise with the dictatorship. At a time when the democratic political parties, the unions and the university—that is to say, all the legal forms of organization—have been dealt serious blows, obliging them to put into practice new and more radical forms of struggle, only the revolutionary organizations of our country's poor have been able to develop their forces, dealing progressively harder blows to the regime. This is why the committed, truly popular and democratic sectors have approached the revolutionary organizations and tend to converge more every day around them as the pivotal point of the struggle.

International Support

Although the struggle to overthrow the criminal Lucas government and to establish the revolutionary, popular and democratic government will fundamentally be the work of the Guatemalan people, its implications reach beyond the national frontiers. Many of the aspirations and interests of our people coincide with the interests and aspirations of sister nations and with those of democratic and progressive governments and forces in other countries on this continent and throughout the world.

Our people share with others the desire for a world where peace, disarmament, justice and respect for the rights of individuals and peoples prevail. The present Lucas regime is an example of savagery known the world over, and offends the human conscience. It tramples on all norms of human coexistence and defies international law and convention as it burns down embassies, kidnaps and tortures defenseless citizens. This behavior presents a constant threat to stability in the region and an affront to the countries with which it maintains relations. It presents a situation wherein all peoples and democratic governments throughout the world must of necessity revise the economic, diplomatic and political relations which they maintain with a government based upon assassination and crime, and they must instead seek out the people of Guatemala through their representative organizations.

On an international level, the Lucas government consistently aligns itself with the most repressive and racist governments, those which are dependent, submissive, criminal and willing to sell out their country's resources. Lucas is a loyal ally of the racist South Africans. His government maintains close and friendly relations with the government of Israel, which in turn provides arms, training and military advisers to raise the technical level of the repression against our people. On this continent, the present regime is the closest friend of the gorilla dictatorships of the Southern Cone; in sabotaging efforts to form a democratic bloc, it has given dictatorships throughout the continent one more expression of support for their genocidal and interventionist actions.

The interests of our people coincide with those of people in the other countries that are faced with similar problems of dependency and distortion of their economies. Along with the other fundamentally agro-export economies, Guatemala is at the mercy of an international market whose behavior is beyond its control, and whose terms of exchange have been historically unfavorable to Guatemala in its trade with the highly developed capitalist countries. The transnational corporations operating in our country seek plentiful and cheap natural and human resources, plunder the country at their whim, never taking into account the needs of the nation now, or the needs of future generations. In this context, the Lucas clique is an accomplice and minor partner of these interests, indiscriminately handing over the resources of the country to benefit its own greed. And on an international level, in the face of problems common to the peoples of Latin America, Africa and Asia, the present government behaves like a scab that creates divisions and obstacles to the formation of a common front. Only the revolutionary, popular and democratic government will be able to take the necessary steps to establish relations of equality and mutual respect with other countries that will serve the real national interests.

Among the problems having to do with the natural resources, we must point out the situation of countries like ours that possess oil and other strategic resources. In the last few years, the Third World countries that produce these resources have taken positions to defend them in the face of the unlimited voracity of countries with higher rates of consumption, especially the United States. In answer to this redefinition of the terms of dependence, the U.S. government has responded with the concept of "areas of strategic interest," proclaiming the right to intervene in situations which the U.S. government perceives as a threat to the supply of "its" oil. This self-centered and imperialist doctrine constitutes a risk for all of our countries that we have to denounce and fight against as a group.

In broader terms, we must reject the attempt on the part of the pro-militarist sectors in the United States to assume the right to intervene in any part of the world where they believe their geopolitical interests to be at stake, these interests being defined exclusively in terms of a supposed confrontation with the Soviet Union. This doctrine has begun to serve as a pretext for a U.S. intervention in Central America. It has been received enthusiastically by the Lucas clique, which sees in a U.S. military intervention its only salvation from the revolutionary combativeness of the Guatemalan people. This doctrine threatens not only the Central Americans; it violates the right of every country in the world to its independence and self-determination. It must be defeated today in Central America because what happens in our presently struggling countries will affect, to a great degree, the future of other peoples of the world, especially on our American Continent.

The Tasks of Solidarity

The overthrow of the Lucas government and the establishment of the revolutionary, popular and democratic government—which will also be nationalist, anti-imperialist and expressing its solidarity with the demands of the poor, dependent countries—require tasks to be performed at the international level.

At this moment, the struggle to dismantle imperialist plans for intervention and interference in the area is a first priority, of utmost importance. This intervention may be direct or indirect, overt or covert. In whatever form it takes, it brings with it serious risks of becoming an international issue and of threatening world peace. Constant denunciation and blocking of interventionist plans will give our people the space needed to confront and overthrow our internal enemies.

The Lucas government, totally isolated and besieged by the revolutionary forces within our national borders, seeks to supply itself through other governments with the means necessary to increase the repression and to give itself a minimal facade of legitimacy before the international community of nations. But on this plane, its isolation is also steadily increasing. One example was seen in the recent vote-taking with respect to Belize, where not even the other reactionary governments of Central America supported Lucas. International tribunals and organizations condemn his crimes against the population, and the tourist boycott of Guatemala continues to grow. But now the new U.S. government plans to reverse the situation in favor of the repressive clique in power by supplying it with massive doses of economic and military aid.

The struggle to continuously increase the international isolation of the Lucas regime, to prevent it from being granted or receiving economic, military or diplomatic aid, to strip it of any legitimacy in international forums and leave it standing completely alone, will accelerate the day of its downfall.

Aware of its weakness and isolation, the Lucas government has contracted the services of the same public relations firms that tried to sell their image of Somoza to public opinion. These firms, together with the big North American news agencies, want to convince the world that in Guatemala there is a battle between two extremes, that the revolution is imported from outside our borders and not the necessary result of explosive internal conditions; they characterize the Lucas government as "centrist" and incapable of controlling the violence. This campaign of false information seeks to prepare world public opinion for a possible intervention, and to justify supplying aid to an unpopular government that has lost prestige. The battle against dissemination of false information and for making known the truth and the fighting spirit of our people will bring the moment of victory closer.

And as the complement to denunciation and isolation of the regime, there is the construction and development of active and militant support, in all possible and necessary forms, for the Guatemalan people and their organizations.

With the massive and generalized incorporation every day of our people into the revolutionary process; with the multiplication of guerrilla combat throughout our national territory; with the unified forces of the revolutionary vanguard organizations EGP, FAR, ORPA and PGT; with the growing contradictions between the government and other sectors of the ruling classes and their national and international isolation, our struggle approaches victory. We know that our people can count on the solidarity of sister peoples, and of all the democratic and progressive forces of America and throughout the world. And we will respond to this support with our daily and consistent actions. All people, friendly and sister forces, can rest assured that our people will not disappoint them, will not forget them and will take our struggle to its already approaching triumph.

The Indian Guerrilla Fighters

For more than half a century, Guatemala has held a strong attraction for different types of foreign visitors: students, artists, tourists and businessmen. Archeologists, ethnologists and linguists have encountered ancient Mayan cities in our country, micro-societies with pre-Columbian traits, living laboratories of Mayan tongues. Artists have delighted in the singular beauty of the textiles and other crafts found in the colorful highland marketplaces. The tourist, uninformed, has sought rest and distraction in the indigenous local color, unaware of what lies beneath the elaborate scenario mounted by the tourist business. Many young people have settled permanently in villages and towns, believing they would find a paradise of simplicity and quiet among the Indians. The more pragmatic businessmen detected favorable conditions for investment; in tourism, among other things. These visitors have returned to their countries with newly learned skills, inspiration and projects. The tourist left with anecdotes and gifts, unaware that he had been the victim of an outrageous trick: the travel agencies gave him an adulterated product, a distorted image of the Indian component of Guatemalan society. However, in the last few years, visitors with a more discerning eye have gone back to their countries with many unanswered questions and serious concern about the indigenous population of Guatemala, over their living conditions, their role and their future. Recently, the hotels in Antigua, Panajachel and Huehuetenango have been abandoned by tourists; the archeologists and other foreign researchers have been leaving; businessmen have ceased investing their capital in the country; and the young dreamers of peace have become aware of the state of war convulsing the countryside.

On January 31, 1980, newspapers the world over headlined the horrendous massacre of 36 people in the Spanish Embassy in Guatemala, transformed into a blazing bonfire by the repressive forces of General

Lucas García's government. Of these 36 people, 27 had engaged in a peaceful takeover of the embassy as a last resort, to denounce before the civilized world the genocidal repression practiced by the army in the northwestern part of the country. Among these were 23 Indians: Quiché, Ixil, Achi and Cakchiquel peasants from the areas under attack by the soldiers. In May of 1978, in the town of Panzos near the nickel deposits exploited by the International Nickel Company—INCO, a multinational corporation with headquarters in Canada—more than 100 Kekchi Indians were also massacred by the army in the public plaza as they protested the robbery of their lands.

Every day more peasant families in that area are being forced off their lands. These recent instances are but two examples, the most widely known, of the already unstoppable struggles of the Guatemalan Indians and of the criminal response on the part of the government to any show of discontent. But little has been said about the work stoppages and strikes carried out by the agricultural workers and sugar cane cutters, the coffee and cotton pickers—Indians, for the most part—who, side by side with workers not of Indian origin, claim their rights, organize, and mobilize for struggle. Also, little is known outside the country about the takeovers of towns and farms by guerrilla forces of Indians in arms, who communicate the ideas of the Guatemalan revolution in their own Quiché, Ixil, Mam, Kanjobal and other Indian languages; and almost nothing is known about the constant battles waged in all parts of the country by Indian guerrilla forces against government troops.

What has happened? What is now going on? How can one explain the contrast between the falsely normal image of a day at the market in the plaza at Chichicastenango or any other town in the highland, and the thousands of primarily migrant sugar cane workers who come together at a crossroads near the southern coast to demand, machete in hand, their right to a just wage? What is it that has transformed the quiet worker in the cornfields from the provinces of Quiché and San Marcos into a determined guerrilla warrior? What has driven the tranquil Ixil, Mam or Kanjobal Indian women weavers to replace the loom with a weapon turned against their oppressor?

The Minorities That Are the Majority

Of the seven million people in Guatemala, four million are Indians, descendants of the peoples who inhabited Guatemalan territory at the time of the Conquest, who, in turn, were descended from the great line of the Maya-Quiché. In 1524, these peoples, represented in greatest numbers by four groups—the Quichés, the Mames, the Cakchiquels and the Kekchis— constituted nationalities that were related through their ancestors, but whose languages and customs had become differentiated to a greater or lesser degree over time; and who vied among themselves for land and power. They were undergoing a process of change, and generalized conflict. Socially and politically, the Mayan-Quiché people were well-structured, well-versed in agriculture, architecture and astronomy—exemplified by the Mayan calendar they lived by. They had varied and complex forms of cultural expression, developed around a maize culture.

Their military defeat at the hands of the Spaniards was followed by the plundering of their lands, the subjugation of the population to laws and institutions which reduced them to slavery, and the imposition of a different religion and culture from their own. Spanish domination was total: military, economic, political and ideological. The Mayan-Quiché peoples were completely subjugated. At the beginning, when they were forced into slavery, there was a drastic reduction in numbers of the native population. Soon they were subjected to new forms of exploitation. The Indians were divided up among the *conquistadores* along with the lands, and the right to ownership included not only the product of the land and the mines, but also the work of men, women and children. They were forced to pay tribute in many ways.

During the 300 years of the colonial period, the Spaniards imposed measures of control and segregation which served to further increase the fragmentation of the indigenous population, already divided into different ethnic groups with their own languages and customs. They grouped the Indians into small communities, the so-called "Indian towns" and forced the inhabitants of each community to wear distinctive dress. Thus they broke down the ethnic groups into small concentrations. The Indians were conveniently relegated to these small groupings, and were obliged to work on the lands of the *conquistadores* according to the demand for labor. So it was, with the forced labor of the Indians, that the cities were built, and the roads, and bridges and aqueducts.

On the basis of this system of oppression and exploitation and the need to justify it, an ideology was developed that characterized the Indians as inferior beings, full of defects and incapable of governing themselves, who could not enjoy the same rights as the *conquistadores*. With time, discrimination against the Indians became part of the ideology of the ladinos (mixed Spanish and Indian ancestry). The Indian culture came to be regarded as a subordinate, negated, contemptible culture, even by the poor and oppressed ladinos.

The ethno-cultural contradiction in Guatemalan society originated in the relationship between the Spaniards and Indians, where one dominated the other, and was reinforced by the ideological mechanism of discrimination used by the *conquistadores* in their oppression of the Indians. Today, the racial content of the contradiction has been necessarily reduced as a result of the high degree of intermarriage. Nevertheless, an ethno-cultural contradiction continues to exist, a product of those old ideological mechanisms, although the terms within which there is domination have been modified. On the other hand, the ethnic border between Indians and ladinos no longer corresponds to the class structure of present-day society. But despite this fact, the current system of exploitation makes use of the cultural oppression and discrimination developed in pre-capitalist periods to its own advantage.

The culture of the Indian peoples of today is the product of 400 years of a way of life centered around the communal peasant economy based on the cultivation of corn; it is also the product of interaction with the world of the Spanish, and then the world of the ladino, incorporating, in a very particular way, elements of Western culture and especially of the Christian religion. There are differences in richness and vigor among the cultures of the different ethnic groups. The sense of identity has also changed over time. Once determined by the ethnic group—the conquered nationality: Quiché, Mam, Cakchiquel or Tzutuhil—it was later centered in the smaller group, the "Indian town" of the colonial epoch: Chichicastenango, Nahualá, Patzún. Still later, under capitalism, the borders between communities break down and give rise to a feeling of solidarity, identification and affirmation of the consciousness of being "Indian" in general, without losing each group's specific identity.

The Situation Today

The end of Spanish colonial rule with the independence of Guatemala in 1821 changed nothing for the Indians, who continued to be oppressed, exploited and discriminated against. With the growth of capitalist agricultural enterprises as a result of the "liberal revolution" of 1871, the process of monopolizing large extensions of the best land—the *latifundios*—and their concentration in the hands of a few landowners accelerated. For a long time, the Indian peasants from the highlands, where there were still large reserves of land, were required by law to go down to the coast to pick coffee. As land began to become scarce as a result of plundering, exhaustion of the soil and the growth of the population, the increasingly small plots of land were not enough to provide sustenance for whole families. Poverty and need took the place of laws; these were what forced the Indians to seek seasonal employment on the coffee plantations. Many communities resisted and, to avoid having to work on the plantations, began to work new lands in more isolated wooded areas or any usable land, even steep hillsides. As available lands were used up and the needs of the impoverished Indian population grew, entire families including women and children ended up going to work on the plantations.

Since that time, the poor peasants, *minifundistas* (owners of sub-subsistence plots), have had no other choice than to migrate periodically to the coast, if they are to survive. This reality constitutes one aspect of the inextricable relationship between the *latifundio* and the *minifundio*. The other aspect is the landowners' reliance on this migrant labor force, and the convenience of its poverty. This system, which requires hiring additional workers during the harvest, increased the seasonal mobility of the Indians. This, together with the growth of commerce, gave rise to more and more contact among the different communities and ethnic groups, increasing the ties between them as Indians. Within this process of capitalist transformation, the Indian peasants have become wageworkers part of the year, or semi-proletarians. The rural semi-proletariat, on the increase each year, is estimated to include at least 650,000 Indian families. It constitutes the fundamental labor force for agro-export activity, the mainstay of the Guatemalan economy.

Upon becoming agricultural workers, the Indians come in contact with a new kind of life. They come to experience exploitation, different from the poverty suffered in the highlands. For the first time, they are working for someone else, the landowner, the boss, and are paid a salary that is always insufficient. At the same time, within sight are the well-built homes of the landowners (who have other residences in the city, since they don't live on the farms); there, for all to see, are the luxurious cars, the airplanes, the machines. The Indians discover that the money they receive in exchange for their work is not enough to buy what they need in order to survive, on the farm itself where the food ration is not enough and later on in their towns. Still less does this pay suffice for accumulated debts incurred in buying medicines, fertilizers and seeds. They see how their salaried work goes hand in hand with unfair treatment, tricks and abuses in the allotment of work tasks, and in the weighing-in of a day's picking during harvest time. They are subjected to constant surveillance and to the violence of the bosses' and government's repressive forces. They see that the poor ladinos, equally dispossessed of their lands, also work as day-laborers on the same farms. Their whole vision of the world, of themselves and of others, is affected as a series of elements previously unknown, or interpreted differently, become part of daily life. Even the notion of time and its use has to change, because the long hours spent working for pay leave little time for religious rituals and craft work. Moreover, their craft work is also increasingly framed within capitalist relations, becoming at-home labor dependent upon local, national and even transnational commerce.

In the Indian towns themselves, a process of proletarianization also takes place. Thousands of Indians from the provinces surrounding the capital, needing monetary income because they have no land to live from, commute to the city on a daily or sometimes sporadic basis, in search of domestic or other service jobs; some work for a fixed salary, others on a contract basis. The majority do not completely abandon peasant life, and regularly return to their communities, where other members of the family continue to cultivate plots of land which they either own or rent.

The process through which the Indians become wage workers is a violent one, full of insecurity and suffering. It is doubly painful for the Indians because this process is accompanied by discrimination. In fact, many become aware for the first time of individual and collective discrimination as they live through this process. Exploitation, while it brings together the Indian ethnic groups as Indians, also brings them closer to the ladino workers, as workers.

The transition imposed by the capitalist system upon the indigenous groups, from a peasant economy and way of life to the sale of their labor in exchange for wages in agricultural or industrial enterprises, coupled with the ever-increasing incorporation of ladino ways of life and customs into their culture, leaves no future for the Indians. Their misery will continue to grow, accompanied by the loss of their culture as a result of the loss of their lands and destruction of their communal life style. And, on top of all this, the perpetuation of discrimination. The revolutionary popular war, and the ethnic affirmation of the Indians in the process of this war, today offer the only alternative and future solution to the ethno-cultural complexity of our country.

The Indians in the Revolutionary Popular War

One characteristic is peculiar to Guatemala, and distinguishes it from the rest of the Central American countries. In our society, there will be no revolution without the incorporation of the Indian population in the war, and without their integration with full rights into the new society, a society which the Indians must help to build. The more than 20 Guatemalan Indian groups constitute, as a whole, the majority of the population. But in addition, the Indians are also the fundamental factor in agricultural production for export (coffee, sugar cane and cotton), and in the production of foodstuffs. They make up the bulk of the rural semi-proletariat. Their role as producers of the wealth gives the Indians both strength and rights: strength to wage the war, and an undeniable right to participate in the construction and leadership of the new society.

In Guatemala, the Indian and ladino workers are standing together at war against the present regime. The descendants of the Maya-Quiché, oppressed, exploited, repressed and discriminated against for more than four centuries, and after hundreds of rebellions and local uprisings that lacked clear prospects and were mercilessly put down, are rising up today in a struggle for clearly defined revolutionary objectives. This is the most fundamental fact in the present history of Guatemala. It is the first time that the Indians are aligning themselves fully with a political, revolutionary program that contains their most deeply felt demands. The Indians are not only supporting the popular revolutionary war, they have also assumed in it the principal role that corresponds to them. They are the fighters and guerrilla cadre of the revolutionary organizations. It is their incorporation that has allowed for the development of the ideas, the methods and forms of organization of the revolutionary struggle. It is their combative spirit that has resulted in the massive growth of the popular and revolutionary organizations. The Indians are fighting in their towns, on the ranches and farms and in the mountains, carrying out the work of the war together with their ladino compañeros. The military actions that are causing many and constant losses to the army and other repressive forces, the ambushes, takeovers of towns and ranches, and attacks on enemy posts, are the work of guerrilla units made up fundamentally of Indians, and supported by the indigenous population in the zones where the guerrilla forces operate. This presence of the Indian people in the popular revolutionary war—in all its forms of struggle—is a political and military fact that the present government can no longer deny or contain. It is critical to understand this particularity of the Guatemalan revolutionary process, in order to fully understand the magnitude and depth of the revolutionary transformation which the country is undergoing.

The present system reproduces and takes advantage of the discrimination against the Indians that the exploiters of past times practiced and imposed upon the entirety of the population as the dominant ideology. It maintains the idea that the Indian is inferior, in order to set ladino and Indian workers against each other, and to perpetuate amongst the Indians a submissive and resigned attitude. For this reason, the elimination of cultural oppression is a central objective of the revolution and is only possible in the framework of the revolutionary process. If the Guatemalan revolution does not solve the dual problem of exploitation and cultural oppression suffered by the ethnic groups, it will not be a real revolution.

In fact, the first steps towards a solution have already been taken in the revolutionary struggle which unites Indian and ladino workers around the same objectives, confronting the same enemy. And it is in the course of the revolutionary struggle that the ethnic Indian groups recover and develop their own identity, that of revolutionary Indians, joined through war with the rest of the poor—Indians and ladinos—who are the builders of our new society.

Communiqué from the EGP to Those Christians Who Struggle Alongside the People

THE GUERRILLA ARMY OF THE POOR— EGP—IN THE FACE OF THE LATEST REPRESSIVE ACTS AGAINST TRUE, COMMITTED CHRISTIANS, EXPRESSES ITS

SOLIDARITY AND CALLS ON THEM TO PARTICIPATE
IN THE PATH OF HOPE OF THE POPULAR REVOLU-
TIONARY WAR.

During the last month, the Lucas government and the army have intensified their campaign of assassination and intimidation against Christians, both priests and nuns and lay preachers. The only reason these good people, from Guatemala and other countries, have been massacred and continue to be threatened is that they have come into close contact with the poor of Guatemala and have understood through their own experience that the society of exploitation, repression and discrimination in which we live is incompatible with the principles and practice of true Christianity.

Although the government has created a climate of terror, falsely accusing the church of abandoning its role in order to get involved in politics, the truth is that every day there are more Christians, both on a base level and throughout the hierarchy, who, faced with the grave misery and merciless repression suffered by the majority of Guatemalans, have stopped supporting and giving a facade of legitimacy to the voracious interests of the rich and the government. They have come to the conclusion that to put an end to this situation, profound and integral changes in our society are needed. And that therefore, those who maintain the injustice, crime and contempt towards the majority must be denounced and defeated.

Christians play a large role in increasing the consciousness and organization of our people, and have turned their faith into a generous force for the liberation of Guatemala. Thus they have won, through their own efforts and their own vocation, a prominent place in the popular struggle and in the Guatemalan and Central American revolution. We have all known many heroic examples in El Salvador, Nicaragua, Honduras and Guatemala.

Those Christians who have raised their own level of consciousness as they have taught others, those who have known how to commit themselves to the liberating struggles of the poor because reality showed them on which side justice lies, and on which side lie the physical and moral forces capable of building a new society, should understand that for now we face an enemy whose bestiality has already been felt by six native and foreign priests, hundreds of lay preachers, above all among the Indian peoples, and thousands of Christians: men, women and children of the Guatemalan people.

This enemy will have to be confronted and destroyed. He will have to be stopped at all cost from continuing to attack those forces which form part of the people fighting for their liberation. The entire people will have to fight so that there are no more mass kidnappings of union leaders in broad daylight, so that no more young, useful lives are torn apart and no more young bodies thrown onto the streets of the city, so that the enemy cannot go on massacring peasants, raping women, killing young people in the markets and plazas, burning huts and fields, and bombing villages and towns, as is the case now with the Ixil and other Indian peoples.

All our people, most of whom are Christian, will have to unmask and confront this enemy so he no longer profanes our religious beliefs and in order to stop these beliefs from being used to give legitimacy to the Lucas government, as was the case with the beatification of Brother Pedro.*

The EGP calls on all true and committed Christians to denounce all these things nationally and internationally; to support all the people in their confrontation with the genocidal Lucas government and to take all necessary measures to avoid becoming easy prey of the repressive forces and official death squads of the government and of the rich. For although it is true that martyrdom for Christians has a high moral value, our people, for years exploited and mercilessly massacred and discrim-inated against, want you standing in struggle for justice; our people ask you to be unbreakable, with your moral forces intact and renewed, carrying out the daily work of the revolution until you see fulfilled your hopes and yearnings for a revolutionary victory and the building of a New Guatemala.

The revolutionary struggles of the poor of Guatemala and Central America have entered a decisive phase, where internal and external conditions favor victory as never before. True, committed Christians should understand that, when peaceful means to reach justice have been exhausted, revolutionary violence is legitimate and just. The Guatemalan people exhausted these means years ago, and for this reason the EGP has understood that the revolutionary violence of the poor in the necessary and inevitable path of the popular revolutionary war, is the only way to achieve victory.

All the lay preachers, priests, nuns and religious, Catholic or Protestant, have an open door in the Guerrilla Army of the Poor if they want to share with us the unshakable struggle we are waging in the countryside and in the city. There is a place for each and every one on this path of hope for all the poor of Guatemala. In our country one cannot be a Christian and not be a revolutionary. One cannot love his fellow human beings and not play a serious and concrete role in the popular war, whether this be in the guerrilla organizations or in the different militant mass organizations. In any of the work taken up

---

* "The beatification of Brother Pedro" refers to a television propaganda ploy by the Guatemalan government, an attempt to use a saint to legitimize the government's "call for peace." —Ed.

by true and committed Christians, they can count on our fullest revolutionary solidarity.

HASTA LA VICTORIA SIEMPRE
EJERCITO GUERRILLERO DE LOS
POBRES

Guatemala, July 1980

Letter From the EGP
to the North American People

The following letter originally appeared in Compañero, *the international magazine of the Ejército Guerrillero de los Pobres (Guerrilla Army of the Poor, EGP) in late 1982. The translation was provided by* Compañero; *minor editing has been done for this publication.*

We, the Guatemalan revolutionaries and patriots of the Guerrilla Army of the Poor, wish to share with you the situation of our people, their struggles and sufferings as well as their hopes and aspirations. We would also like to tell you about those who have exploited our natural resources and profited from the efforts and the misery of Guatemalan workers. Above all, we need to let you know about the suffering that successive U.S. governments have wrought on our people by supporting the small wealthy elite in Guatemala that has imposed an oppressive and antidemocratic regime in our country. It is this very same support that the Reagan administration is planning to increase today.

With this letter we hope to contribute to tearing down the wall of misinformation and silence that conceals the reality of Guatemala from the world. This wall has been imposed by those who are interested in hiding the horror our people are enduring, as well as the hope that springs from struggling by every conceivable means. Finally, we hope to win your solidarity with our cause of liberty, democracy, justice, and peace for our country.

Guatemala is a small country which covers some 41,420 square miles and has a population of 7.5 million. It is located in Central America, and borders with Mexico to the north and west, El Salvador and Honduras to the east, and newly independent Belize to the northeast. Nearly two thirds of our population lives off the land, on small subsistence plots where corn and beans are grown and on large.plantations—*fincas*—dedicated to the cultivation of export crops, mainly coffee, cotton, sugar cane, and bananas, as well as cattle. It is to these plantations that thousands of peasants—*campesinos*—migrate every year to work as temporary labor because their plots of land are insufficient to feed their families year round. It is on these *fincas* that 71% of the country's exports are produced.

In contrast, the industrial sector is poorly developed, employing barely 4% of the economically active population. Guatemalan industry produces mainly consumer goods (food, textiles, beverages, shoes), and is largely controlled by multinationals, both through direct investment and through technological dependence. This is why the vast majority of Guatemalans are peasants. Furthermore, roughly half of the population is Mayan Indian; they form one of the 22 ethnic groups that inhabit the northern and western highlands and the mountain ranges of our country. The Indians, the majority of the population, have long been subjected to a barrier of discrimination and cultural oppression erected by the wealthy elite, both national and foreign.

A high percentage of our exports, 33%, go to the U.S., and most of our imports come from your country as well, 34.6%. Out of 456 transnational firms that operate in Central America, 125 do so in Guatemala, 31% of the total; of these, 101 are U.S. firms, which make up 81% of the total.

Out of total foreign investment in Guatemala, U.S. firms own 88% in agribusiness, with 21 firms; 73% of the banking and financial institutions, with 5 firms; 90% in the retail business and services with 8 firms; 71% in mining and forestry, with 4 firms, and 81% of transport and tourism, with 8 firms.*

Because of the way our society is organized, there is great inequality between the living and working conditions of millions of poor people and the opulence and squandering of a few thousand wealthy people, both national and foreign. Their standard of living and lifestyle are similar to that of the ruling sectors in highly developed countries, and they enjoy privileges which are in brutal contrast to the generalized misery of the working population.

The grossly unequal access to our country's resources and wealth is best exemplified by the distribution of land: 2% of all landowners own 70% of the arable land, monopolizing the most fertile land. The average wage in the countryside is $1.50 for an arduous day of work, a sum which is totally inadequate to meet minimum daily needs for a family. This situation is aggravated by a chronic lack of jobs: 35% of the population is unemployed, and there is an even higher percentage of underemployment. The social consequences are staggering: according to 1982 figures, two out of three Guatemalans are illiterate; three out of four Guatemalans live in inadequate housing, and there is a shortage of

* Figures from Castillo Rivas D., *Acumulación de Capital y Empresas Transnacionales en Centro América*. México, Siglo XXI, 1980.

1 million housing units. Eight out of every ten children under 5 years of age are undernourished; commonly curable diseases are the cause of 80% of all deaths. Such is the situation in a country famous for its natural wealth and hardworking people.

The ruling sectors have historically maintained this outrageous situation, in which the people are deprived of even the most basic rights, through the use of violence. When workers and peasant masses have organized and attempted to change this state of affairs through trade unions and grassroots pressure, the wealthy and the government with their Army and gangs of assassins have responded by prohibiting or dissolving all legal popular organizations, eliminating free expression, perpetrating scandalous electoral frauds, kidnapping and assassinating leaders, and massacring entire populations.

It is this reality of misery and terror which has led thousands of Guatemalans into a struggle to change an inhuman situation. Our struggle has deep social and national roots, and in no way stems from the so-called East-West confrontation, as the Reagan administration would try to have you believe.

Given the situation in our country, what role have successive U.S. governments played? Have they in any way contributed to improving the living conditions of our people, to guaranteeing or at least respecting our sovereignty, to helping our people obtain the basic rights to which they are entitled? Or, on the contrary, have they supported the land-owners and wealthy businessmen so that this sector can continue to be a privileged minority, all under the pretext of guaranteeing the national interests of the USA?

The history of relations between your country and ours is full of political maneuvering, diplomatic pressure, economic blackmail, corruption, impositions, and contempt for our own national interests, which are repeatedly subordinated to foreign interests. Threats of and actual intervention are ominously present. A few examples should suffice to illustrate our point. The monopoly of the United Fruit Company over the most important economic activity in the country, which lasted well into the late fifties, earned Guatemala the tragic name of "Banana Republic." Even more tragic was the armed intervention which in 1954 overthrew Jacobo Arbenz's democratic government (1951-54). Arbenz set out to foster independent capitalist development and democratic liberties in our country. As has been revealed by U.S. leaders of the period—Eisenhower, Allen Dulles, etc.—that intervention was planned, promoted, organized, financed, and led by the U.S. government through the CIA.

During the sixties, the counterinsurgency program that was carried out in Guatemala under U.S. auspices, financing, and advisorship, was modeled on programs being carried out in Vietnam: so-called "Civic Action," and the use of terrorist practices against the population.

During this time, 373 Guatemalan officers were trained in U.S. counter-insurgency training camps, there were many U.S. advisors in the country at the time, and there was a military base with close to 1,000 Green Berets.

Since 1954, successive U.S. administrations—to varying degrees and using diverse methods—have set about the task of creating an army trained and ideologically instructed to commit the most horrendous crimes against its own people. The Guatemalan Army has been trained to massacre children, women, and old people, and to destroy their homes and crops, using weapons and techniques provided directly by the U.S. or through its allies, such as Israel.

And what has been the Reagan administration's attitude since it took power? The Reagan administration's plans to bolster the Guatemalan Army in its war against its own people are becoming increasingly evident. Reagan has already officially expressed his intent to renew military aid, suspended during the Carter administration because of the obvious crimes committed by the Army and various security forces. Fearing rejection by the American people and Congress, the administration is planning to renew direct aid gradually. But in the meantime, the Guatemalan Army is being given essential military items through third parties, and military aid has been disguised as spare parts and civilian equipment. What has this meant in practice?

In 1981 the Reagan administration granted the Guatemalan Army $3 million worth of trucks and jeeps for military transport. These trucks are used to transport genocidal troops that raid villages in the Guatemalan highlands, massacring entire populations. Cessna passenger planes and civilian helicopters equipped for offensive operations have been sighted bombing and strafing civilian populations. The Guatemalan Air Force has at least 14 UH-1H (Huey) helicopters, well known for their role in Vietnam, also made in the USA. The U.S. government also supplies the genocidal Guatemalan Army with spare parts and ammunition. $250,000 in military training funds have been proposed for fiscal year 1983 as a formal step towards obtaining Congressional approval for renewing direct military aid. The Reagan administration has taken steps to obtain the informal approval needed to sell $3.7 million in spare parts for helicopters. At the same time, $50 million have been proposed for alleged development programs in the Western highlands where the population is being massacred indiscriminately. These funds will clearly be used for military purposes, to build garrisons and erect strategic villages, also reminiscent of Vietnam. These emplacements are being used by the Army to relocate people who have been expelled from their communities by the official scorched earth policy, a policy that has already displaced over one million people, and totally disrupted their economic, family, social, and cultural lives.

Attempting to hide its crimes, the Army blames the guerrillas for the massacres that its own troops are committing. But according to an Oxfam America report, out of 115 U.S. citizens living in Guatemala who were interviewed, 69% believed that the Army and right-wing paramilitary groups are responsible for the massacres.

The Army not only massacres the Guatemalan people. It has also killed three North American priests in recent years. The last priest to be slain was James Alfred Miller on February 12, 1982, and the people of the U.S. have yet to see a report on the investigation into his assassination.

Whatever direct aid is granted by the U.S. government at this point will only complement aid granted through third parties. Galil rifles, Uzzi submachineguns, Arava transport planes, and other standard military equipment are all made in Israel and sold to the Guatemalan government through Marcus Katz, a well known dealer in Israeli arms. In this way the Guatemalan government has been kept generously supplied during the last few years, while the U.S. government has not had to dirty its hands directly and has been able to maintain the appearance of respect for the human rights of the Guatemalan people. Nevertheless, we know that this systematic flow of military supplies to our country can take place only with the express approval of the U.S. government.

The steps the Reagan administration has taken so far in regard to Guatemala foreshadow a more intense intervention, similar to the one directed against the Salvadoran people. Reagan wants to make the war in our country his own, siding with the powerful and with those responsible for genocide. While he sends millions of dollars in aid to murderous regimes in El Salvador and Guatemala, Reagan suspends all aid to the heroic Nicaraguan people, and is imposing an economic blockade on them. Reagan is also spending millions of dollars to destabilize the Sandinista revolution, and is providing the Somocista bands with political and military support.

Faced with an unjust situation of exploitation, oppression, repression, and dependence which blocks any possibility of achieving basic demands through legal forms of struggle, the Guatemalan people have developed their own organizations. These are the Guerrilla Army of the Poor, EGP; the Rebel Armed Forces, FAR; the Organization of the People in Arms, ORPA; and the Guatemalan Workers Party (Leadership Nucleus), PGT, which have now come together in the Guatemalan National Revolutionary Unity, URNG. They are waging a popular revolutionary war, and have called on the people to struggle to take power and set up a revolutionary, patriotic, popular, and democratic government based on five programmatic points that can be summarized as follows:

I. The Revolution will eliminate once and for all the repression against our people and will guarantee to our citizens the supreme rights of life and peace.

II. The Revolution will lay the foundation for resolving the basic needs of the great majority of our people by eliminating the political domination of the repressive rich, both national and foreign, who rule Guatemala.

III. The Revolution will guarantee equality between Indians and Ladinos, and will end cultural oppression and discrimination.

IV. The Revolution will guarantee the creation of a New Society, in which all patriotic, popular, and democratic sectors will be represented in the government.

V. Based on the principle of self-determination, the Revolution will guarantee a policy of non-alignment and international cooperation which poor countries need in order to develop in the modern world.

We, the revolutionaries and patriots of the Guerrilla Army of the Poor, realize that you, the North American people, are subjected to the disastrous effects of the Reagan administration's warmongering policies and its support for the weapons manufacturers. We must all unite to confront those who oppose the people's sovereignty, social justice, and world peace, in defense of their own selfish interests.

Finally, we call on the North American people, democratic and progressive forces, the young, Christians, ethnic and national minorities, to take all the necessary steps to block any increase in military and economic aid and every other form of intervention by the Reagan administration on behalf of the military government in Guatemala.

We ask you to tear down the wall of silence and misinformation, to denounce the crimes commited by the government and the Army, and to make known the advances in the struggle being waged by Guatemalan revolutionaries and patriots.

We also call on the North American people to redouble your efforts in support of the thousands of refugees produced by this cruel war, and to broaden and deepen your solidarity with the struggling Central American peoples. In this way you too will come closer to realizing your own aspirations and demands.

This will be the best contribution you can make to our struggle.

Hasta la Victoria Siempre
GUERRILLA ARMY OF THE POOR (EGP)

Seven Keys to Understanding the Central American Crisis

Edelberto Torres-Rivas

1. Introduction

At the beginning of the 1970's, neither the popular forces, nor the vanguard, nor least of all the social scientists of the region, would have been able to predict the dimensions of the crisis that would so deeply shake Central American society some years later. An understanding of events—if such is possible—does not imply the ability to control their course, much less to prevent them from occurring. Predictions concerning the future, as Hannah Arendt has on other occasions pointed out,[1] are nothing more than projections of ongoing processes; that is, what would happen were there no human intervention nor unexpected developments.

And it is precisely the unexpected, the unforeseen, that constitutes the uniqueness of a revolutionary process. During the first years of the 1970's, defeat was a common experience in all countries and surely in all leftist organizations: defeat, if we consider the pure meaning of the word, alludes not only to defeat at the hands of superior forces, but also to a perhaps transitory loss of direction. The Guatemalan guerrilla movement was almost totally disorganized between 1966 and 1970, and in March 1970 General Carlos Arana Osorio, the man responsible for counterinsurgent operations that took more than 10,000 lives, was elected President. The Sandinista National Liberation Front (FSLN), founded in 1959, was defeated in Pancasán in 1963, while its urban fraction was almost entirely wiped out in Managua in 1969. In 1971, the Conservative Party signed a new electoral alliance with Somoza for the umpteenth time, and following the earthquake in 1972, the Somoza dynasty enjoyed one of the greatest moments of power in its long history.[2]

In El Salvador, a broad coalition of Christian Democrats, Social Democrats and Communists won overwhelmingly in the presidential elections of 1972; however, Col. Molina succumbed to fraud and violence by the military in an act of force widely supported by bourgeois coffee planters. Only Honduras presented a relatively different picture, with a new type of peasant movement that supported and used violent acts and, in fact, expropriated land that legally was not deemed private property. In this country, it was the landowners who were in a precarious situation.

The Salvadorean experience plays an important role in Central America, which was already steeped in political violence and characterized by the slow consolidation of military dictatorships. In effect, the defeat of the electoral alliance led by Napoleón Duarte, the present head of the Salvadorean government, was decisive evidence for the self-generating capacity of a system that, moreover, did not show signs of weakening. This provided the opportunity for a group of moderate forces with a Kennedy-type reformist program that had widespread popular support to begin a process of "democratization of the political system"; this was a successful example of what other coalitions had tried to implement as a project of "democratic reconstitution, with development." After the defeats of the popular movements, impossible to report in detail here, diverse political forces appeared on the scene, fighting in support of a similar proposal, an option that was intended to be nurtured by the mistakes or defeats of the revolutionary left and the excesses of conservative power.

The government of José Figueres (1970-74) in Costa Rica represented the materialization of this "third" force option. However, the social forces that supported this model of "democratic reconstitution, with development" were weak in Guatemala and Nicaragua, and suffered new setbacks even in El Salvador, where the country was undergoing a gradual process of political "hardening," characterized by the existence of a militarized state apparatus. In the middle of the 1970's, this "third" force hopelessly disintegrated, some of its members joining the armed struggle. It was a period marked by the political destruction of a process which is problematic anyway—that of attempting to create a democratic alternative. This option always implied partial integration of the popular sectors, and it was exactly this feature that repeatedly showed itself to be difficult or impossible to achieve.

In other words, up to about 1975, the crisis that was coming to a head in Central American society had, at least for the dominated classes, the mark of adversity. Any act could be unforeseen, but could occur; the events that did take place were in fact a series of "unforeseen acts" which prove that, as Proudhon warned, the vigor of the unforeseen exceeds the caution of statesmen. It was not until recently that doubt was cast upon this *ex post facto* reasoning: contrary to what the Romans believed, God was not always on the side of the great batallions.

The nature of the crisis that rocked the entire region, particularly in Guatemala, El Salvador and Nicaragua,[3] cannot be understood if one adheres to classical models of political crisis or to abstract formulations of models. Of course, only idiots believe that crises are the product of "foreign" plots—treacherous Soviet conspiracies that make the dominoes fall, one by one, while the United States strives to keep them standing in place. Here is an important theoretical challenge, not so much because destiny plays an important part in the political arena, but because it is difficult to find a plausible explanation for these historical facts.

2. The Scenario of the Crisis

It is the peculiarities of Central American society which define the general framework of the process we seek to analyze here. These peculiarities are the result of the historical formation of bourgeois society in Central America, of the state, and in particular, of its classes. While this observation is necessary as a starting point, it does not explain the Central American crisis as a result of unsolvable economic problems that are then translated into the surface appearance of a political structure. The notion of capitalism in crisis, which is probably applicable to other aspects of this analysis, is not at all germane or useful at this point. To attribute the economic condition to the state/political apparatus would be a gross simplification of a process whereby capitalist development takes place under particular historical conditions.

This assumes confusions based on a dubious duality: the crisis as a process of "maturation" resulting from the formation/accumulation of problems, along with the "revenge of those who long for bread," the revolt of the poor who have been so abundantly produced by this system.

At this point it would be appropriate to outline some facts and propose some hypotheses in order to define the scenario of this critical conflict. First of all, after World War II, but particularly during the 1960's and 1970's, Central America went through the most important period of growth and economic differentiation in its history. There were crises and stagnation, but when viewed over time, growth was important and, above all, it was greater in comparison to earlier periods. If these important socioeconomic changes had not taken place—for example, the strengthening of capitalism—many things that offer an explanation would not have occurred. The purely economic crisis that is frequently talked about in Central America today really has a three-fold explanation. It is the result of development (not stagnation) during the last few years, foreign influence, and recent political conflicts.

In the post-World War II period, the economic system seemed to unfold as a result of external dependence, so that the old model of agricultural exportation gave way to one that promoted internal development stimulated by a plan for a regional common market. Important efforts at import substitution (by industrialization) and agricultural diversification were developed and supported by state aid. These projects are mutually independent because of state policies concerning the allocation of resources and the final destination of the product. A feature of this double mechanism of capital accumulation is that it is not realized by different social classes (in conflict) but rather by local, economic family-groups and foreign capital, both dependent on external demand, and at present subject to international finance capital.

Central American society continued as an agrarian society. There was important growth and diversification with the emergence of new products for export (cotton, beef, sugar). This growth was based on renewed concentration of landholdings, extensive cultivation of the land, and taking over the best land. The agricultural sector concentrated on high levels of production for export and on extremely low levels of production of food for internal consumption. It was an economy that produced capital (but no food), practically exhausting agricultural resources while the population doubled. In this way, the primary sector contributed in a contradictory way to the functioning of the system as a whole: it did not generate employment and income, and threw some 40% of the population onto the threshold of absolute poverty.

The agriculture of the internal market— historically, a deficit— plunged deeper into crisis in a radically new context: the partial destruction of traditional subsistence economies by very dissimilar things, such as the utilization of fertilizers or the penetration of finance capital. In addition, the growing role played by money in agricultural trade at all levels, has made the *buying power* of the rural sector even more vulnerable. The fact that Central American economies were not inflationary during the post-World War II period, but only afterwards (1974-75), cannot be underestimated. Inflation was a new and unknown phenomenon in societies that were monetarily very stable. It can be explained in part as the result of the development of capitalist social relations throughout all social spheres.

This set of factors has had a profoundly favorable effect on the accumulation of capital, in part through the production of absolute surplus value and in part through increases in productivity that are not matched in wages. In other words, economic growth has only increased social differences. The mechanisms of accumulation in the sector of import substitution created a new center for the concentration of wealth. A resource as scarce as capital was definitively put into the hands of a few, and given excessive protection by the state. This partially explains the weaknesses that are apparent today in the plan for regional economic integration. Of course, this extreme industrial protectionism did not damage export agriculture, but rather directly harmed the *craftsmen* (both rural and urban), the producers of basic foodstuffs, and the sectors whose capacity to organize and to defend their wages was very weak.

The state always appears at the center of all of this. All roads lead to the state, wherever the bourgeoisie is involved: the concentration of banking capital and access to public credit, interest rates, customs and duties regulations, fiscal exemption policies, taxes and the repression of unions. All this constitutes a permanent subsidy of capital at the expense of labor, under conditions that go beyond what is considered "normal" in other Latin American societies. This type of political capitalism gives the state a particularly crucial aspect today and reduces the social importance of the bourgeoisie as a *class*. Functionally, the bourgeoisie are highly concentrated, that is, they hold a monopoly over all productive forces as a result of the advantages they obtain through absolute control of political power.

In this context, the so-called conflict between growth and distribution is a deception; not so much because it implies a feature inherent in capitalist growth, but because the distribution of wealth is at any moment a political problem that depends on the capacity of the working class to organize independently and fight for wages and other corporatist demands. These have been relentlessly repressed over the last 25 years.

The state serves necessarily as a center for favors and repression, without abandoning its bizarre neoliberal ideology. This is not classical liberalism, since it implies the active intervention of the state on behalf of national and foreign capital. This explains why the formation of ruling classes is protected on all sides: protected from other sectors, from agricultural/industrial contradictions, from demands for higher wages. The process of Central American economic integration takes place without the social expansion of the internal market (without increasing the income of the vast majority); external financing is sought in order to avoid tax reforms.

Given this type of growth, social differences increased in quantity and quality. As a result, social polarization became not only greater but also more visible and deliberate. But it is not that the viability of the "model" has been exhausted; rather, its "additive" character seems to point now to limits on the expansion of the internal market, and it cannot stop the growing instability of the regional market. International causes of the crisis should not be underestimated, as imperialism is responsible for some of the basic contradictions. Political conflicts put the final touch on an economic scenario that was definitively favorable to the development of the crisis we are considering.

3. The Intra-Bourgeois Struggle

The exploited can benefit from crises that are provoked by the bourgeoisie itself, as occurred in 1848 in France and in many other historical situations around the world. "The name given to the revolution at the beginning," says Marx, "will never be written on its banners on the day of victory . . . revolutions should get their tickets of admission to the official scene from the ruling classes themselves."[4]

The Central American revolutionary movement was born out of an intra-bourgeois crisis, as that crisis was generated in different situations and with a rhythm imposed by the contradictions it had to resolve. In any case, in the 1970's, the revolutionary movement did not grow out of direct confrontation with a monolithic reactionary power. It grew over a period of time in response to a crisis of hegemony in which conflicts within the ruling classes were superimposed on the contradictions arising from the ascent of the masses.

The intra-bourgeois struggle in Central American countries does not have a common origin, nor does it take the same form from country to country. Nevertheless, underlying the differences is a common pattern in the way the bourgeoisie perpetuates itself or resolves the contradictions of oligarchic domination and of the bourgeois society in formation. "Oligarchy" refers not so much to the form of the state and the development of its material apparatus, as to a political-ideological rule of the agrarian classes, based on the "natural" exclusion of the dominated and on an identification between the dominant interests (the coffee planters, *par excellence*) and more general interests—those attributed to the nation. It is a nonexistent nation, built on a cultural identity that *excludes*. In this way, the problems of the oligarchy were resolved—incompletely—and are now superimposed on the crisis of the formation of the modern bourgeois regime.

The bourgeoisie is not and has never been a homogeneous class, not even during the period of expansion after the 1950's; its internal differentiation results from the unequal, combined and uneven form of capitalistic development.[5] This differentiation is intensified in agrarian societies where capitalist relations of production become generalized through external effects.

The intra-bourgeois crisis is the result of changes within the ruling class and between this class and the state. These changes start with new relations of dependence and the conflicts that begin to arise with the subordinate classes. More specifically, the crisis is the result of the political situation that accompanies this internal differentiation, where the internal base for primitive accumulation is altered (i.e., agrarian accumulation), and comes under the domination of foreign capital and new sectors of commercial and manufacturing activities. In other words, the perspectives for economic expansion after World War II provoked the first signs of a critical situation for the bourgeoisie, whose base is agrarian and backward, and who saw in international capital an ally more than a business partner—an evil that could not be avoided.

Capitalist development of agriculture, provoked by external demand, cornered the *latifundio* and produced a "capitalized" agrarian bourgeoisie which is open to new options on the market. The economic integration of Central America, as said before, was a program of forced substitution of imports of consumer goods, and brought about more differentiation. But it was the political conditions set to broaden the bases for accumulation and reproduction, conditions linked to external factors, that precipitated adjustments in economic interests. These political conditions manifested themselves as tensions and conflicts reflected in the state—the place where they are usually resolved—and not in the market, where they originate. Intra-bourgeois competition thus becomes an institutional crisis.

In Guatemala, politics and the national-revolutionary mobilization of the masses—until 1954—stimulated a transitory bourgeois unity, the product of fear. Immediately afterwards, there were bitter conflicts at the top. As in other countries, these were generally expressed in the form of military conspiracies, coups within the military and divisions within the army. It was through a military *putsch* that the bourgeois factions fought it out and resolved their differences.

In El Salvador, differences did not surface as much because of the traumas of the 1932 peasant insurrection. They did appear in 1948, then with the government of Osorio, and finally in 1976 under the military dictatorship of General Molina and his agrarian policy. But it was in Nicaragua that struggling bourgeois factions maintained a constant split which could obviously be characterized as intra-bourgeois competition (Somoza, the Bank of America, the Bank of Nicaragua) and, moreover, corresponded to conflicting political parties.

More than a mirror that reflects what happens around it, the state is the scene of conflict, where the bourgeoisie disguises the fact that it is an *actor* of history in order to appear as an anonymous institutional power, which only political games can unmask. Because of this, the intra-bourgeois differences caused institutional shake-ups. How well we know that the state is not the state-of-the-bourgeoisie, neither is it the state of everyone. The bourgeoisie proceeds in this way because it is through the state that it can reach class unity, by putting the state at its service, and because in backward societies the relative margin of autonomy is substantially lower. The state, then, is formed where the *dominant* social forces are formed. This also occurs among the *dominated*, but in an opposite form: in the party.

It is obvious that the intra-bourgeois crisis did not facilitate the creation of organisms of democratic participation, although their evident absence in the political life of Central American society cannot be attributed to this factor alone. But dictatorship is also a political form for solving the contradictions of capitalist development within the bourgeoisie itself, through the restructuring that occurs inside it, and thus through the difficulty of maintaining the old system of alliances.[6]

The intra-bourgeois crisis in the region has two additional characteristics. The first is the lack of its own political organization and the absence of bourgeois leadership of multi-class movements of any significance. We are referring to the organic articulation of its own political interests by a class that defines itself through the exercise of power. If it is true that the existing political crisis is also the crisis of all forms of party organization in general, then this is even more true for leftist sectors. There were never right-wing parties in crisis, because they did not exist. The bourgeoisie did not need this channel for mediation/participation because its representation in the state is direct and total, and because only a liberal democratic state needs parties. But there are exceptions; in Guatemala, the extreme right managed to consolidate the National Liberation Movement (MLN), the "party of organized violence," according to its leader Sandoval Alarcón. And in Nicaragua, the commercial "aristocracy," later transformed into a commercial and financial elite, succeeded in maintaining a small but respected Conservative Party. The most characteristic of these groups is the National Liberation Party of Costa Rica, a true expression of social democracy in a society where the working class does not make up the majority of the population. The remaining parties are multi-class, with middle-class cadres, transitory, organized only with a view to elections, with ambiguous programs and not self-identified politically as bourgeois.

The second characteristic of the intra-bourgeois crisis is the absence of any dominant ideological analysis of a bourgeois character and capable of building hegemony. In fact, the Central American bourgeoisie did not form its big political party, nor did it have its undisputed national leader; instead, it espoused the poorest of ideological defenses — that of anticommunism — as a justification for governing and a pretext for repression. The poverty of this position is that it is not really an ideology; it negatively defends the status quo, without proposing an alternative doctrine or even offering an ideological and intellectual form of bourgeois affirmation.

Finally, the importance of the intra-bourgeois crisis changed noticeably in the decade of the 1970's, when the army appeared as the pivot of an authoritarian structure that seemed momentarily to end internal differences. In any case, the crisis as an expression of internal conflict was not over; but more importantly, the crisis did cease to qualify and condition relations with the oppressed classes. In effect, the present unity within the counterrevolutionary bourgeoisie is answered by the exploited classes in open conflict. The Central American political crisis is not an expression of secondary, unsolved contradictions within the dominant class, but rather an open class struggle that questions the very foundations of bourgeois domination.

4. The Character of the Popular Movements

Undoubtedly Latin America is living through a new period of rising popular struggles. Since 1975, the mobilization of workers and peasants has resulted not only in a more precise definition of their interests, but in a new type of radicalism, which is creating an independent popular movement. Certainly this deep-seated resurgence of social conflict is not new to Central America, but from the beginning the people's movement there had several particular characteristics which explain the role that it plays today in the crisis.

For a long time, the oppressed sectors rarely tested their capacity for direct confrontation with bourgeois power. The great political movements of the postwar era in Central America (the general strikes and the political-military movements which either put an end to or checkmated the traditional dictatorships of Ubico in Guatemala, Hernández, Martínez in El Salvador and Carias in Honduras) had a multi-class composition, but an unequivocally bourgeois or "protobourgeois" leadership. After 1950, the popular demonstrations always had a spontaneous character, and although these social movements are not *amorphous*, they appear to be so because social backwardness prevents the political action of the class from becoming homogeneous. Trotsky once said that backwardness confuses everything. The "mass" as a social factor does have its own interests, capable of being specified. However, when we are dealing with either heterogeneous social groups or social groups constrained by traditional practices, there is a tendency toward the "corporatization" of protest, and it is well-known that in this short-term strategy, the demands are particular economic ones that require immediate satisfaction. That is both the weakness and the strength of economist positions.

In the immediate postwar period, the workers' movement tended rapidly to become part of the popular movements. Both struggles almost always grew out of a *generic* discontent in which one could just make out the initial goal and the precise profile of the enemy. All of this is related to the absence of an organic tradition; and the extreme weakness of trade union organization explains the spontaneity of the popular movement, which started by going beyond "what was foreseen" and ended up not exactly in failure but in retreat. In spite of this generic character of discontent, there were worker, peasant and student demonstrations, as well as attempts at organizing which served to link important social movements. More than once, a proletarian action was undertaken only to be violently repressed. In the early years of the postwar period, it was difficult to appreciate the behavior of the class, in its organizations and programs, strictly at the trade union level. The influence of the artisans and the general coexistence of noncapitalist with capitalist relations cut through society and left their mark on society and on the popular movement.

Nevertheless, already at that time and certainly later on, we can see the following characteristics of the Central American popular movement:

a) Whenever the worker and peasant movement organizes itself, it does so autonomously, independently of state control (for example, from the Ministry of Labor) or the bosses' support. Having had only fleeting experiences with class collaborationist leadership, and not being established enough to make compromises or deals, the working class took action characterized by opposition to the political order. Consequently, it had a semi-legal character which incited both the intolerance of the bourgeoisie and more or less unavoidable police repression.

With its many possibilities of cooptation—the Church, agencies of imperialism, corruption—why was the Central American bourgeoisie unable to exert even partial control over the organizations of workers and peasants? Whether out of weakness or virtue, it is true that bourgeois politics always found it hard—or did not even try—to construct its ideological and organizational dominance over the working class. Is this a bourgeoisie that had lost its *chance* to consolidate its power by means of a populist alliance, or a bourgeoisie that intended all along to consolidate itself by authoritarian control over every passing demand? The independent character of working class organizations together with the inability of the bourgeoisie to control them produced, among other things, the following two results: on the one hand, violent repression and the outlawing of social confrontation; on the other, the demand for political democracy, which would subsequently become an extremely important working class demand. Both must be remembered when we examine the current crisis.

b) Probably because of the characteristics mentioned above, the union movement is "illegal" (but only to the extent that the regime cannot make it legal and assimilate it). Therefore, popular demands emerge from the opposition and tend to grow outside of the legal system. No reformist policy can prosper if it does not resolve and absorb the most elementary social conflicts in a normal and predictable manner. Even before the current crisis, whatever has been popular has been suspect and has led to repression. Because of this, there is a secondary characteristic of the workers' movement, the fact that it was always local in character, generally confined to the capital and only later struggling to expand.

c) The impossibility of a social pact similar to those with which South American societies repeatedly experimented has, in the Central American experience, a characteristic which could be classified as *anti-populism*, undoubtedly produced by that uneasy relationship between the "oligarchical" character of political domination and the recently formed world of capitalist relations. The truth is that social protest, either geographically localized or limited by its organizational forms, gradually tended to overflow the boundaries imposed by its corporatist origin, and rapidly took on a political dimension. During the seventies, but even before as well, it was often the case that the most modest trade union demand tended to be formulated in an uncompromising way and became a threat to the established order. The speedy deterioration of trade union struggle, in the absence of institutions of bourgeois cooptation (mass parties, business unionism, populist ideologies, etc.), forced the struggle to rise rapidly to a strictly political and national level. The corporatist perspective was quickly abandoned, more because of bourgeois intolerance and repression than class consciousness. The truth is that the popular sectors were being formed in the context of a national-popular experience of a new type. Of a new type because of its revolutionary practice.

We have not given examples but many could be cited, such as the immediate politicization of student demands, industrial labor conflicts, street demonstrations. When these were repressed, there were times when union and particular corporatist demands escalated into national and universal protests that had their effects on state power: the resignation of a chief of police, the Secretary of State or the President of the Republic himself. In short, the organizational and ideological backwardness (which is ending in this decade) seemed to have been compensated for by a militancy not limited to wage and cost-of-living demands. This is a contradictory quality of backward situations which produces frontal confrontations with the system. Failure only stimulated resistance, and out of this pattern of development, the working class emerged strengthened and not weakened. It was out of defeat, not domestication, that the current revolutionary movement in Central America emerged—that collective, popular will which today has stalemated the Central American bourgeoisie.

Since 1975, the revolutionary process has contained new characteristics which began to develop out of the circumstances described above. There are ruptures that signify the triumph of subjective factors, and there are continuities in a long-standing tradition which do nothing but reinforce those factors. The culmination of all of this is a popular presence of a new type which is expressed in a new form of organized demands, new historical protagonists and new ideological-political elements.

It is significant, first of all, that both university and secondary students have slowly stopped being the key protagonists of political protest. They played a fundamental role in the struggle for democracy, but their function as surrogate actors for other classes has lost its relative importance, if we look at them in terms of their status as student. Out of the school system and the universities have come numerous militants and cadres who are of prime importance precisely because they have lost their status as students.

Secondly, it is important to point out the failure of leftist political parties to organize and lead the people's popular struggles. This applies particularly to the older ones, the communist parties. For years the only representatives of the working class and the peasantry, full of experience in underground work, the brutally beaten victims of unremitting state repression, the communist parties were never able to turn their ideological seriousness into a vanguard practice. Perhaps their fundamental error resides in the fact that to various degrees they granted the bourgeoisie a leadership role in the bourgeois-democratic revolution, a historical error which led to more than one important defeat. Paradoxically, the tragedy of those parties has been that they knew the landed oligarchy prior to knowing the bourgeoisie, and exaggerated the revolutionary role of the latter. Their theory of stages in the social development of the revolution made them forget the links between the two dominant classes. This led them to a search for different power blocs and alliances in each period, which were imputed by theory but negated by reality. In their search for alliances precluded by history, they did not foresee a new revolutionary crisis which would pose the possibility of new class alignments. When that crisis came, they were left unarmed, politically and militarily.

It is not possible here to make an inventory of the different national experiences of the various communist parties. The Guatemalan Labor Party (PGT) after 1960 accepted armed struggle as the fundamental form of class struggle. It joined in that struggle with all the ad hoc *foquismo* of that period, and came out of the experience practically liquidated. The Communist Party of El Salvador, always closely linked to the urban masses, joined the Revolutionary Coordinating Council of the Masses (CRM) and later was linked organically to the Farabundo Martí National Liberation Front (FMLN) and the Unified Revolutionary Directorate (DRU). The two socialist parties of Nicaragua, weak both organizationally and politically, linked their anti-Somoza stand to the bourgeois leadership of the Democratic Union for Liberation (UDEL) led by P.J. Chamorro, in 1974. One of these parties continues today and conducts labor opposition, which is not only reactionary but profoundly backward.

Despite these errors, one must grant the communist parties of Central America an invaluable endogenous quality. Out of these parties (in particular the Guatemalan and Salvadorean) have come almost all of the most important organizations and revolutionary cadres. The present political-military organizations in these countries (known to everyone) are like successive spin-offs from a common core. Even the Sandinista Front counted on the "transfer" of valuable cadres from the two socialist parties.

The displacement of the "party" by the "movement" has not yet been sufficiently analyzed. However, it is not a degradation of the Leninist organizational structure, but rather the functional adaptation of a political structure to the needs of a military struggle. At times this displacement becomes a provisional response to the eruption of the masses and makes all existing structures obsolete in the face of action that was practically unforeseen. The communist parties were left behind by this situation, which just shows the profoundly popular character of the crisis.

Let us examine rapidly the character of the *new* organizations and the new protagonists. We are referring to organizations that either emerge or reconstitute themselves self-critically in accordance with two types of experience: the nonfunctioning of the party and the defeat of the guerrilla *foco*. During the sixties, this duality (party and *foco*) was a tragic functional division of tasks: the mass movement led by some and the armed insurrectional struggle led by others. The divorce was quick and bloody. Today, the so-called political-military organizations (to emphasize their dual unity) have taken on those experiences and are working out an original and productive combination of various forms of struggle through concrete praxis.

In this sense, all the experiences are original. In Guatemala, the Rebel Armed Forces (FAR), with strong influence in the trade union movement; the Organization of People in Arms (ORPA), based exclusively in rural areas, especially in regions with peasant-Indian populations; and the Guerrilla Army of the Poor (EGP), probably the most experienced organization, are carrying out successful multifaceted activities on the theory that mass struggle should lead to armed mass struggle of a national character, although following somewhat the model of army-building in order to defeat another army.

In El Salvador, the experience is relatively different but marked by the same concern for developing all possible forms of confrontation imaginatively and boldly. In some cases, the guerrilla group engages in mass work and "produces" its front, combining trade union and popular forces; in others, the group penetrates the already existing workers' movement and contributes to its strength; finally, the guerrillas engage in political work in the countryside and firmly establish their presence. Such is the experience of the Popular Revolutionary Bloc/Popular Liberation Forces-Farabundo Martí (BPR/FPL), of the Armed Forces of National Resistance/Unified Popular Action Front (FARN/FAPU), of the People's Revolutionary Army/People's Leagues LP-28 (ERP/LP-28), and of the Communist Party/National Democratic Union (PC/UDN).

The experience of the Sandinista Front is equally diverse and probably better known. The long series of defeats—the product of a narrow military conception and other internal factors— split them into the three already-known groups, each of which went on to engage in political tasks following a particular conception of the struggle against the dictatorship. The necessity of doing political, urban mass work was added to the conception of a prolonged people's war, and later came the insurrectional strategy which combined all these forms of confrontation. In Nicaragua, they put together—for the first time in Latin America and in an original form—guerrilla warfare in the countryside, insurrectional forms of urban struggle, the general strike, work among peasants, work in neighborhoods and factories. This effort included winning over an important fraction of the smaller bourgeoisie and intellectuals, until the Sandinista National Liberation Front (FSLN) was surrounded by a ring of mass political organizations which gave an extraordinary strength to its military actions.

The popular organizations that emerged after 1975 made a radical break with traditional forms of organization and control. The Sandinista

Front closely resembles the image of a popular army. But it is an army that knew how to *surround* itself in the final offensive with mass organizations, practically the entire people, from whom it received total support. This is why we say that in the struggle against Somoza, the state confronted the society. The organizations currently being formed in Guatemala and El Salvador do not properly constitute a party, but they are also not an army. They are multi-class movements which adopt the *front* as a transitional form, with a political-military structure at the summit and a wide dispersion of mass organizations at the base, all held together by links that are not always organic or ideological. What is the national-popular principle of these genuine though unexplained coalitions of masses that recruit from all sectors of society?

Breaking with traditional forms of participation implied a double internal movement (the reflection of socioeconomic changes taking place in the interior of Central American society) expressed in the new organizational forms discussed above and in the active presence of new participants. Undoubtedly, it is the peasants and the marginal sectors who are the new subjects of political praxis, and their mere presence destabilizes the system. Even without raising the most traditional peasant demand, parceling out the land, the existence of an independent peasant organization constitutes an immense act of civil disobedience. Even when it is peaceful, the process of peasant participation is experienced as a profound crisis of authority. Only by knowing the social and political backwardness of Central America can one grasp the importance of this: it is the end of fatalism, of a chiliastic ideology that only revolutionary violence can break.

The popular struggles reached a new level after 1975 because violence became a way by which people were immediately incorporated, because violence came to constitute an equally immediate response to violence. Thus the conflict took on dimensions unknown up to that time. The organization of the masses in the countryside took on a dimension of "defeat in advance" for the bourgeoisie, because for many years independent organization had seemed impossible. Repression and control could not be overcome by traditional means. Let us only mention that in El Salvador the bourgeoisie had organized the Precinct Patrols, the National Guard, the army, the police and ORDEN. The latter was formed as a political police force, from the middle strata of the peasants. Its purpose was to control the peasant sector from the inside and repress it from the outside. The Military Commission in Guatemala and the *Jueces de Mesta* [appointed village officials—*Ed.*] in Nicaragua also are or were extremely efficient organizations for making the peasants themselves carry out military intelligence, espionage and open repression among themselves.

The armed struggle of the peasants and groups of the socially marginalized brings to the conflict a violence that is also new. The capacity of the marginalized for destruction—properly channeled

—was tested in the Sandinista militias, which recruited from the urban unemployed. The Salvadorean popular forces have a similar experience in a society where the declassed sectors have for a long time made up a respectable majority, and it is not merely urban. Their sudden entrance into the history of social conflict is not new, but it has always been marginal. However, when they do surface, they are always against the status quo. The marginalized make up a powerful, elemental force, which they themselves unleash. To organize them for a violent response turns out to be almost natural to their own social existence. The experience of Nicaragua, however, teaches us that it is extremely difficult to channel their energies into constructive work, deliberated political action, and the development of a socialist consciousness.

Our analysis would not be complete without acknowledging the important contribution of religious groups. They deserve a separate analysis and a more fitting interpretation of the way in which Christian groups come to "discover" the reality of misery and the exploitation of the masses, and thus give the ministry a popular character: to love reality is the precondition for beginning to know it;[7] to know it is the precondition for changing it. The rank-and-file Christian movements, formed by priests and laymen of the most diverse denominations, became themselves protagonists in the people's struggle and literally fused with the masses. The practice of these religious and lay movements translates itself into a decodification of the traditional doctrine of the hierarchical church and into a political and ideological proposition: liberation theology. Criticism of the system strengthens Christian faith in the practice of loving thy neighbor. But now the neighbor is the next-in-line, the exploited. Thus the act of faith becomes deeply subversive within the framework of traditional culture, subversive in the sense of undoing what was expected to be done. Moreover, it is a directly political act.

With the unity of the political and military organizations comes a congruence of the dominated classes. This includes those who, although not exploited, are nevertheless marginalized, and the *coexistence* of different forms of radical consciousness within the popular movement: classical Marxist thought, Jacobin rebelliousness, the will of the petty bourgeois radical democrat, the sensibility of left Christians and the deep pre-capitalist hatred of the marginal elements, especially the indigenous ethnic groups (in Guatemala). This sum of social forces acquires an even clearer definition in the struggle itself. There, it is necessary to overcome many real difficulties so that unity "coagulates" in a powerful organic front, so that it is no longer the sum of the organizations but rather a truly national vanguard. The national classes are now the classes exploited by the system; they are finally making their presence felt and thus giving political meaning to the popular, national character of the history which they are writing and of the alternative they propose.

5. The Counterrevolutionary State in Crisis

For a long time, the game of appearances mystified analysis and strategies. Alterations in the relations of class forces in Central American society were not foreseen in the sixties when everything pointed to the making of the *exceptional state*, that is, a power which deals with a crisis situation. Like any other form of social relations, this type of state is a "hybrid" because it surfaces in order to remedy a *particular* form of crisis. We have tried, perhaps unsuccessfully, to analyze this crisis in the previous sections of this article and we will now sum it up: problems of hegemony within the power bloc and in that bloc's relations to the masses.

The exceptional state surfaces in a form that is not necessarily extreme, in order to stabilize the political regime in crisis; this does not always presuppose the possibility of resolving the crisis. The realignment of classes expresses itself in the state as a military dictatorship. The army is the only force that can stand at the center of the stage when the fractions of the bourgeoisie cannot reach agreement and, above all, when the uncontrolled popular sectors appear on the scene. The exceptional state in Central America is a counterrevolutionary, military dictatorship.

This dictatorship took form in Guatemala with the coup of March 30, 1963, which prevented the election of Dr. Juan José Arévalo and placed the armed forces at the center of power, as a state institution. In El Salvador, although military men have always been in the forefront of the government, it was only with the coup of January 25, 1961, that the army was definitively institutionalized as the executor of state power.[8] In Nicaragua, the "plebeian" dynastic structure of the Somozas already assured the control of power, with direct support from the pretorian guard. In all three cases, military dictatorship produced similar effects:

a) Regimes based on the systematic exercise of repression and, after 1975, on open, generalized terror.

b) Regimes that therefore express a great vacuum of hegemony, originating within the dominant bloc and permeating the entire society. These are weak states but militarily armed to the teeth.

c) Regimes that cease to base themselves in institutions where consensus and the ritual of class representation are traditional. Thus the total devaluation of the parliamentary function, the disrespect for the judicial process and the uniformity of a rightist press (a notable way of ending freedom of the press) leave the electoral process in a poor position to provide legitimacy.

Here we face a power that violates its own rules, that does not respect its own system of legality as a means of defending itself from the oppressed classes, a power that will not fulfill the promises it has made when its own interest is at stake. For example: in Guatemala, when General Ríos Montt, the real winner, was set aside by General Laugerud in 1974; or El Salvador in 1978, when General Romero was the recognized winner over General Claramount in a fraudulent election. These are only two isolated examples; the crisis of confidence strikes directly at the petty bourgeois preoccupation with democratic formalities.

For one or another reason, the state first lost its capacity to control and later its capacity to disorganize social struggles. The crisis of the state affects the entire society. It becomes a real issue when the masses, led by Marxist-oriented, political-military organizations, slowly but inexorably win space, recognition and influence. This produces a fatal situation for the bourgeois order: the *objective* conditions created over the years by the socioeconomic structure, which are an accumulation of problems permanently deferred, can now be expressed *subjectively* through the boldness and strength of popular organization. This situation, in particular the victory of subjective conditions, explains the character of class struggle, the rupture that produces the *isolation* of the military dictatorship. But it does not explain the ultimate nature of the crisis.

This has to be sought in the way in which this rupture is produced within the state and within the dominant class. Class contradictions are not produced outside the state; rather, they cut across it, in all of its dimensions. State terrorism as a policy is simply the response to these contradictions; what we call the "flight in advance" of the bourgeoisie is yet another inevitable reaction.[9] By virtue of this "flight," the Central American bourgeoisie now has its roots as a dominant class abroad rather than in the political arena where it attempts to be the ruling class.

What this contradiction implies is that the bourgeoisie, by virtue of its monopolistic nature, the (relative) concentration of wealth at its disposal, and its partnership with foreign capital, is politically weak because of its inability to form alliances. The conduct of the Nicaraguan bourgeoisie was different because it was isolated by an anti-Somoza front. The bourgeoisies of the rest of Central America appear to be equally alone and defend themselves as such, while counting on imperialism's support. The opposite occurs in the exploited classes. There, the popular offensive is precisely a broad front which defines itself as the nation-in-movement. This was undoubtedly the case in Nicaragua. With the general strike of June 24-25, 1980, the revolutionary movement in El Salvador was closely approaching the Nicaraguan example. Guatemala should follow the same course. Only by winning a large majority will victory be assured.

To sum up, the state institutions for bourgeois domination are in crisis (elections, parliament, cooptation, peasant passivity, etc.). The dominated sectors are putting to a test the bourgeoisie's ability to rule. For many years, the bourgeois response has been terror and violence.

This elicits similar responses. If power is the ability of one class to satisfy its immediate and historical interests, then the local bourgeoisie has renounced its future and that of the nation, with a deliberate forcefulness that at times seems suicidal. We know this is not possible, but the course of events does not assure the reproduction of the bourgeoisie as a class; nor can the existing political forms assure the reproduction of the bourgeoisie as a class in relation to the system of relations of production. The political reproduction of society is no longer a sure thing. The state, therefore, becomes an openly counterrevolutionary power as shown by its daily activity in Guatemala-El Salvador. This crisis of the state, thus constituted, becomes a crisis of the system itself.[10]

6. What Are the Popular Forces Fighting For?

What is the revolution all about? It is not something static, predictable from theory, but a *will* that creates its own programmatic responses in the course of practice. Obviously, one does not start from zero, but the theory is a function of the type of society that one intends to *destroy* and not so much of the type that one wants to *create*. In other words, the revolutionary process does not start with an already established rationality, with a coherent ideology that asserts in a positive way the creation of a counter-model for society. In the Central American revolution, an ideological backwardness confronts the social movement.

The Nicaraguan Revolution, which is moving at a velocity that would displease the taxonomists, has not fallen into the error of defining itself *prematurely*. One reason for this, among others, is that the crisis of the bourgeois system of domination, the bourgeois crisis proper, has not yet been resolved, although we cannot doubt the popular character and strategic strength of Sandinista power.

Because of the objective conditions set by history and North American imperialism (and also the international capitalist system), the Central American revolution today is neither bourgeois nor socialist. Today the programs of the political-military organizations, and in general of the whole people's movement, differ from those of the 1960's. They are both more mature and more realistic. They should be understood as the strategy of a revolutionary-democratic revolution, the objective expression of a transition between an unfinished bourgeois revolution and an incipient socialist revolution. The nature of the revolution should not be confused with the forms of struggle used to carry it out. One would think that only socialism could be proclaimed from the barrel of a gun. But armed struggle, the "savage" explosion of the masses, is part of a process that today is aimed at creating a popular, democratic and revolutionary power.

Within the context of conditions in Central America, does this process have an anti-bourgeois character? Obviously, yes. Winning national independence, the liquidation of the *latifundia*, establishing democracy and the development of the forces of production, etc., are all unrealized goals of bourgeois domination in the stage of imperialism. The failure of the bourgeoisie to accomplish tasks inherent to its class conditions means only that these tasks will have to be accomplished in spite of and *against* the bourgeoisie. What makes this possible is the coalition of forces in which the proletariat and peasantry play a primary role.

The programs of the popular movements unequivocally aim for this first revolutionary-democratic stage. The seizure of power is the condition for its fulfillment. From there, with the conquest of state power and with the winning of a new majority, one can embark upon the road to socialism. And as Marx said, the process of social revolution "cannot derive its strength and character from the present, but from the future. It cannot begin its task until it rids itself of all superstitious veneration of the past."

It is not useful to search either for the originality of the crisis or its resolution. The lesson is more modest. The people's movement and its vanguards exist as such because they have been able to unearth the authentic character of the process of revolution (revolutionary-democratic), win over the masses, and find the way to develop the revolution (the armed struggle and the combination of different forms of mass struggle) looking toward the future but rooted in the best local tradition (the anti-imperialist image of Sandino, the incorporation of the indigenous peoples, etc.). And they have understood, perhaps without reading Gramsci, that one must act with the great pessimism of intelligence and the optimism of the will.

7. The International Dimension

The revolutionary crisis in Central America has a *decisive* international dimension. It is not possible to analyze it here because the focus of this effort was to examine *internal* factors. However, we cannot avoid mentioning the important role that international factors played in the Sandinista victory and how they are working *against* the Salvadorean revolution. Two stances of North American imperialism can be clearly seen. With Carter, the central problem was to put together a viable, controlled and limited democracy as a response to the inter-bourgeois crisis and the rise of the masses. This was a serious error, because the FSLN made the strategy of consolidating a "third" force (neither Sandinismo nor Somocismo!) impossible. With Reagan the geopolitical vision gained primacy, and the objective has become the establishment of order at any price. It is because of this that the myth of Soviet intervention in Central America has been re-created. But above all, it is because this is an area where the North American policy of containment could easily and fully succeed. That is the policy which would restore wounded pride within the United States and reestablish the confidence of allies abroad. It is not in Afghanistan or Iran or Angola that the United States can make up for its defeats. It is in El Salvador, Guatemala or Nicaragua.

Intervention is no longer a threat. It has already happened directly in El Salvador and is about to happen in Nicaragua.

NOTES

1. Hannah Arendt, *Sobre la violencia* (Mexico, Cuadernos de Joaquín Mortiz, 1970), p. 12. She adds that "A futurologist's dream can come true only in a world where nothing ever happened."

2. Paul Ocquist, Nicaragua, *La lucha Sandinista por la Democracia* (Quito, ILDIS, F. Elbert Foundation, Series Materiales de Trabajo, 1978), Num. 21, p. 29. This source is cited, as others could have been, for a fact on which there is complete agreement.

3. In this analysis, we shall refer particularly to these three countries.

4. F. Claudín, "La superación del Estado Burgues." *Teoría Socialista del Estado* (Editorial Mañana S.A.), p. 132.

5. The differences generated within the bourgeoisie originate in the different functions performed by capital—commercial, industrial, finance, etc.—and the contradictory development of its sectors, the various ways of relating to foreign capital, the competition for credits, and the formation of the finance sector.

6. After the war, there was a rupture in the traditional alliance with the peasants, natural allies of the bourgeoisie. This was an agrarian bourgeoisie, that eventually lost the support of its tacit ally, over whom it had always had hegemonic control. Remember the peasant revolt in El Salvador in 1932, the revenge against agrarian reform in Guatemala after 1955, and the massive peasant (land) invasions in Honduras during the 1960's.

7. *Coyuntura actual y vida cristiana* 4, 31 (August 1980), p. 361.

8. The military proclamations that accompanied both coups seemed to have been written by the same hand. The army, in its earlier internal deliberations, that is to say, "democratically," acquires consciousness of its mission to keep order. And as the only institution not dependent on the vote, that is to say, on the whims of the people, it seizes the state apparatus.

9. Data for 1978 indicate that deposits by Central American capitalists in Swiss banks are reaching 9 billion francs, which would be the third largest amount kept in Swiss banks. Obviously, this is not productive investment, which is located today in Mexico, the USA and other financial centers.

10. The economic intervention of the United States in El Salvador is more important than the military intervention and obeys the same reasoning, the same cause. We have purposely not examined the international dimension of the crisis, only because of the truly provisional character of this investigation.

The Nicaraguan Revolution and the Central American Revolutionary Process

Ruy Mauro Marini

The triumph of the Nicaraguan Revolution in 1979 represents to a certain extent the result, and at the same time the beginning, of a new stage in the cycle of social struggles that was opened up in Latin America by the Cuban Revolution. The long interval between the two revolutions can be explained by the counteroffensive launched by the United States following the Cuban Revolution and after a radical revision of U.S. foreign policy, which came to be dictated by the doctrine of counter-insurgency. Basing itself in the native ruling classes, and utilizing the Armed Forces as the main instrument for the implementation of that doctrine, the U.S. confronted the wave of insurrectional movements of that time in Latin America and other parts of the world with a stance that was highly military. The objective was, as is the norm in any war, not only to defeat but above all to annihilate the enemy.

In 1959, from the point of view of its imperialist interests, the U.S. not only was able but also was forced to proceed in that manner. The world capitalist economy was in its full expansive stage and in that context the U.S. economy, as well as U.S. ideological and political influence, had no rival. No one except the anti-imperialist, popular movements was challenging U.S. hegemony at that time, which was why those movements were perceived as the enemy to destroy. At the same time, the senseless hostility of the U.S. toward the Soviet Union made it difficult for the U.S. government to focus its attention on those movements, and thus it was forced to seek a certain level of agreement with the socialist bloc. In other words, the policy of counterinsurgency rested upon the policy of detente, so both had to function hand in hand during the decade that followed. The fact that detente would open up possibilities for the Soviet Union and other socialist countries to exert influence in the areas where insurrectional movements were unfolding did not enter into U.S. calculations. For this error they paid a price later on.

By 1979, the situation had changed radically. The capitalist world went from prosperity to a phase marked by serious upsets, of which the crisis in the international monetary system was only one indication. It was also marked by sharp recessions, particularly those of 1974-1975 and including the current one. U.S. supremacy was being challenged in many ways by the European capitalist powers, particularly Germany, and by Japan. In the peripheral capitalist countries, after a brief setback, the insurrectionist movements gained new strength and achieved resounding victories in Asia and Africa, that favored the Soviet Union in the worldwide balance of forces. The conditions which 20 years before favored the U.S. offensive—crystallized in counterinsurgency— have changed considerably and thus demand new responses. Although coming from different perspectives, both Carter and Reagan are bent on finding those new responses.

It is not our intention, however, to focus our attention on the implications for U.S. policy of this new stage in the revolutionary process, which was opened up in Latin America by the Nicaraguan Revolution. Rather, we are interested in analyzing why the methods of counterinsurgency will not suffice to stop the revolutionary process, or, more simply, the rise of mass movements in Latin America, taking into account the internal causes which motivate them. We then would like to point out some of the implications of this for Latin America and the United States.

The Nature of the Process

In analyzing what is happening today in Central America and in Latin America as a whole, we see first that the social movements taking place there are not the result of backwardness but rather the result of progress. More precisely, they are the result of the type of economic progress experienced by that region. The penetration of foreign capital, which was the counterpart of counterinsurgency, and intense economic development beginning in the 60's have had a very strong impact on the class structure of Latin America. These factors have also caused shifts in the alliances and agreements on which the state is based.

Parallel to the rise and consolidation of an agrarian, industrial and financial bourgeoisie, closely linked to foreign capital by way of direct investments or loans, we have also seen the living conditions of the urban and rural working masses grow worse and their composition change. Thus, the peasantry has not only had to suffer growing exploitation, but has also undergone brutal transformations in its way of life, particularly because of the rapid process of proletarianization, which has created a new agricultural proletariat and augmented the urban proletariat. At the same time, the urban proletariat has changed in character as a result of the industrialization of the 60's, due to pressure on its artisan sectors and the formation of a modern industrial working class which is more concentrated and in better objective conditions to organize itself. Meanwhile, the petty bourgeoisie also suffered a process of liquidation, giving way to new middle classes of an increasingly salaried character and based primarily on the growth of the service sector.

Thus came the end of the old political structure in which a markedly rural oligarchy held the reins of state power. Now the state rests on a more complex class alliance composed of the remains of the old oligarchy and the new bourgeois fractions, which extends to the higher levels of the petty bourgeoisie. At the center of this new configuration of power are the Armed Forces, themselves undergoing an internal process of transformation. This process is serving to 1) make their anticommunist ideology more extreme, 2) provide them with new forms of organization and discipline, and 3) link them directly to property-owning groups by their occupying management positions in the business sector and their acquiring land and stocks, and by the personal relations being developed. Upon this base, then, is erected a highly exclusive system of domination which is organized around an authoritarian state, almost always of a dictatorial type, and which consecrates the primacy of the military institutions.

It is in this context that the political forces leading the revolutionary movements in Latin America today have come to exist. In many cases they are new forces, constituted in the late 60's and early 70's. Others are forces which, having been practically destroyed by the counterinsurgent offensive, reorganized themselves within the framework of new conditions imposed by that offensive. The Sandinista National Liberation Front (FSLN) is a combination of both. It encompasses the experience of past efforts which did not succeed, and it organized itself in its current form at the beginning of the last decade. In any case, these political organizations are not inexperienced in clandestine methods of work, nor are they characterized by open organic structures like those which had to face the counterinsurgency offensive and be destroyed by it. Today, _these organizations are born in the very heart of counterinsurgency itself; they have learned to organize and work under the strictest clandestine conditions, with cadres trained in the art of operating under the most brutal repression._

This fact alone differentiates the conditions under which the present revolutionary struggle takes place. But it is not the only difference; the old vanguards of the masses were defeated not only because of their organic and operative conditions, but also _because of their ideology._ In effect, with the rise of the new bourgeois fractions which came into conflict with the old oligarchy in the 50's and 60's, the popular movements felt called upon to participate in that conflict. They have been strongly influenced by the methods of action defended by the rising bourgeoisie, particularly the electoral processes, broad mass mobilizations, etc. In that context, Guatemala is the model. But since the establishment of the counterinsurgency regimes, the popular movements have been excluded from the political arena. They have had to develop in the extralegal arena. Furthermore, they have had to function politically under conditions in which politics are defined by the bourgeoisie and imperialism as war, in essence leaving politics to the police and military apparatus.

The new vanguard organizations have had to understand this reality. But having done that, they are now functioning with complete awareness of it. That is why they have broken away from illusions of stable alliances with fractions of the bourgeoisie, alliances with the possibility of building new societies through the installation and development of bourgeois democratic regimes. The Chilean counterrevolution of 1973 has done nothing but confirm them in their decision to make this break. That's also why the new vanguards have emphasized the military component which every political struggle contains. The existence of armed vanguards today derives both from the fact that they represent popular movements which are not subordinate to bourgeois leadership and the fact that these movements must survive and triumph under conditions of counterinsurgency, the ultimate expression of which is the military character of the state.

Thus are derived the main characteristics of the Central American revolutionary movements of today. First, there is the internal distillation, in terms of the cadre, organizational forms and methods of action. Second, the striving to unite the popular movement as the central condition for developing a struggle independent of the bourgeoisie and the different bourgeois fractions. Third, a policy of class alliances which allows for agreements and compromises with sectors of the bourgeoisie but does not give any bourgeois fraction an integral part in the revolutionary social force—and this, by the way, influences the policies of alliances on the international level. Fourth, a political-military strategy based on the creation of revolutionary military power, not by means of divisions within a regime's armed forces, but rather by incorporating the masses of people into a people's army, led independently by the revolutionary organizations.

The success of that strategy in Nicaragua has sped its implementation in El Salvador and Guatemala as well, although the vanguard forces in these countries have in no way simply imitated the Nicaraguan process. The specific character of their struggle and organizational forms, of the process by which they implement their strategy of class alliances, of their strategic and tactical military plans, indicates that what the Salvadorean and Guatemalan forces have taken from Nicaragua is less a model than an inspiration to carry forward their own politics, founded on their particular national conditions.

Some Implications

The process currently taking place in Central America has many implications. Notable among these is the formation, for the first time on this continent, of a bloc of revolutionary states: Cuba, Nicaragua and most recently Grenada. At this stage it is still only a tendency toward a movement, but it opens up great possibilities for the revolutionary movements of the area because of the political and material support they could receive from such a bloc, the significance of which is heightened by the fact that one of its members is located on the continent itself.

But the importance of the Nicaraguan process is not limited to this development. Its impact is felt very directly, especially in the Central American region. For one thing, as we have previously pointed out, the Nicaraguan Revolution has become a source of hope and inspiration for the Guatemalan and Salvadorean movements, regardless of the fact that these movements maintain their particular characteristics. The unity achieved by the Salvadorean movement and the current process of unification underway among the Guatemalan revolutionary forces have been considerably influenced and accelerated by the experience of the FSLN. Moreover, the effects of the Sandinista Revolution in Central America go beyond the revolutionary movement and affect the balance of forces in the whole area, causing abrupt shifts in Costa Rica and Honduras and serving to strengthen Panamanian nationalism. Pressure from the U.S. on those countries serves only to further polarize the political forces and radicalize the situation. All this has made Central America a *critical area*, a weak link in the imperialist chain which threatens to become even more important in that sense than Southeast Asia in the past decade or the Middle East today.

This is true also because the Sandinista Revolution transcends Central America and radiates towards the rest of the region, particularly Mexico and the nearest of the Andean Pact nations. The progressive shift to the right in Venezuela, Colombia and Ecuador radicalizes the situation, as does the rightward trend in Costa Rica and the conversion of Honduras into the bastion of U.S. imperialism. This is all the more true because the rightward shift runs counter to the trend that sparks the popular movement—a movement which, as indicated previously, is stronger now than before the intensification of the counterinsurgency campaign and also has had a positive influence on the development of the left in those countries.

Nicaragua and Central America's revolutionary process in general also intervene indirectly in the power play between the stronger nations of the area and the U.S., a play which revolves around the renegotiation of the status and new interests of those nations. This is especially clear with respect to Mexico, whose Central American policy is guided by criteria very different from and, in fact, in open contradiction to those of the U.S. But the same phenomenon can also be seen with respect to Brazil, and in a different sense with Venezuela, Argentina and even Chile.

Brazil has achieved a remarkable economic development since the end of World War II. This development, especially since the mid-60's, has been characterized by relations established with Western Europe and Japan which have served to reduce the economic pressure of the U.S. and, consequently, its political importance in Brazil. The fact remains, nevertheless, that the U.S. continues to be the superpower of the capitalist world, the sphere in which the Brazilian military government consciously inserts itself and attempts to assert its subimperialist schemes. Consequently, there must be a revision of the existing relations between the two countries that includes a whole gamut of still unresolved issues. Central America *per se* is not among those issues for Brazil, which has always regarded that region as being under the direct influence of the U.S. and outside of what it considers its own sphere of influence (South America and southern Africa in particular). Nevertheless, in the eyes of Brazilian subimperialism, Central America is an important chip with which to negotiate. This is why Brazil includes its eventual support for U.S. policy in Central America in the general package of pending issues to be negotiated with the U.S. The magnitude of that package makes the process of negotiation very difficult and actually makes Brazil very reluctant to fall into line with the policies that the U.S. wants to impose in the capitalist camp with respect to Central America.

With regard to Venezuela, following the difficulties it had with the United States because of its support for the Nicaraguan Revolution (which was encouraged by the Social Democrats at that time), it has now been brought back into line. Steps in the same direction have already been taken in the case of Argentina, by tightening relations with that regime following the replacement of Videla with Viola. [General Roberto Viola, ex-Commander in Chief of the Army, replaced General Jorge Rafael Videla as President of Argentina on April 4, 1981.—*Ed.*] The current process of rapprochement with the Chilean military government, and that country's rabid anticommunism, will most likely produce similar results.

Nonetheless, in every one of these cases, the U.S. government is nowadays forced into a position of more formal "politicking," in the sense that it has to discuss and negotiate its positions. The days are long gone when it could impose its will without appealing to the Latin American bourgeoisies. The OAS itself, formerly the forum which blessed undisputed U.S. hegemony over the continent, has now become an organization difficult to control and likely to produce important defeats for U.S. policy, such as its open opposition to Somoza and any intervention in Somoza's favor on the eve of the Sandinista victory. For this we can thank Mexico, with its clearly apparent position, and Brazil with a less visible one.

Because it has been forced to deal politically with Latin America, the United States under Carter favored the democratic institutionalization of the military regimes there. Although such processes do not lead to full democratization, they do open possibilities for participation by the bourgeois opposition, and to a greater or lesser degree, depending on the country, for participation by certain sectors of the popular mass movements. This indicates a relative flexibility on the part of these regimes. If this were to take place without compromising bourgeois and imperialist domination, which is the reason for seeking to build the armed forces as the fourth power in the state, then the United States would not have to deal with monolithic, powerful and arrogant military governments and would have enough maneuvering space to carry out its objectives.

Conclusions

The revolutionary Central American movement has turned that area, which was formerly an unshakable cornerstone of U.S. imperialist domination, into a critical zone. The movement has been helped by the relative weakening of U.S. economic power in the context of the current world crisis, and by the contradictions that have arisen between the United States and the rest of the imperialist powers of Europe and Japan. Another factor is Latin America's economic and political diversification, which has given rise to more powerful states with interests of their own that are not antagonistic to those of the U.S., but still conflictive. These factors have aided the development of the insurgent forces in Central America. But the determinant factor has been their reorganization, following the application of counterinsurgency policies, and their ability to operate in the midst of counterinsurgency. In fact, they have turned the exploitative and repressive nature of the regimes into a legitimation of their struggle, in the eyes of their people and the world.

The Central American revolutionary movement has thus opened up new perspectives for popular and progressive forces throughout the continent. Under Carter, the United States' perception of this situation led it to attempt a reaccommodation of its dominance by pushing for the institutionalization of the dictatorial regimes and for a new image. This process has been complicated by the sharpness of the class contradictions in Latin America, and their international effects. Under Reagan, the North American response has been to fortify counterinsurgency activities in Latin America, without abandoning the line of favoring institutionalization, as is demonstrated by continued U.S. support for the civilian-military regime of El Salvador. But if each of these lines of action (institutionalization and counterinsurgency) separately appears inadequate to the task of containing the rise of social struggles in Latin America today, then their combination, far from strengthening the imperialist strategy, creates contradictions that do not promise much success.

At this crossroads, the United States will have to use all its imagination to find responses that can deal with what Latin America is undergoing today. So long as it insists on looking for answers whose purpose is to reverse the present situation and relive the past, that is, so long as the U.S. attempts to reestablish its domination over the region as it was in the past, then the responses it gives are unlikely to prove successful. The United States will have to take to heart the idea that *the power and autonomy of the Latin American people's movement, especially of its working class, and the political capability of the new vanguards that have arisen in the past decade, will force a radical redefinition in U.S. relations with the region and, in contrast to what has been the rule through the last century, the quest for a relationship not based on subordination and exploitation.*

The U.S. ruling class and its state, as it is structured today, are obviously not capable of moving towards such a radical change. This is a task that falls to the popular movement of that country, and constitutes one of its greatest responsibilities in the transformation of U.S. policy which the Latin American revolution is demanding. The popular forces of the United States are prepared for this, through such memorable struggles and victories as those which were at the root of changes in U.S. policy toward Vietnam. Today this line of action is again needed, with even greater emphasis and greater possibilities of victory— particularly if one recalls that Latin America is not a foreign reality to the United States but part of its own internal composition, by virtue of those millions of immigrant workers who are directly exploited by U.S. capital, not to mention the Puerto Rican people. It is with those groups, and in alliance with other abused minorities, that the U.S. working class, progressive forces and the country's leftist organizations will have to focus their actions in order to guarantee a future that is different from the one promised by a Carter or a Reagan. As in the case of Vietnam, their formulas mean not only the diverting of resources and the sacrifice of youth in a foreign war to preserve the U.S. ruling class, but also *an internal conflict, the tearing apart of the United States itself.* The state of the U.S. ruling class will take advantage of this conflict to repress the people of that country, subject them to a political oppression unprecedented in U.S. history, and chain them to an exploitation made worse by the cost of maintaining such oppressive policies.

It is for this reason that, along with the liberating forces on the move in Nicaragua, El Salvador and Guatemala, and arising along the length and breadth of Latin America, it is up to the North American people—*la palabra la tiene el pueblo norteamericano*—and the forces that can best express their historical interests.

Notes for a Manifesto

Pablo González Casanova

The United States government is advocating a philosophy of world destruction—what else can politics based on "might makes right" mean today? The belief in its imperial manifest destiny leads the U.S. government to assume the right to intervene and the right to invent reality. Implicitly or explicitly, the present government is declaring its right to send arms, military advisers and Green Berets to fight against the people of El Salvador.

Those who govern the United States engage in falsifications and fabrications of reality when they say that the USSR, Cuba and Nicaragua are arming terrorist groups against the [Salvadorean] government junta, which is a U.S. ally and protégé. They falsify reality when they say that all who have rebelled against tyranny are terrorists. They falsify reality by inventing a conspiracy on the part of the socialist world. They falsify reality by refusing to recognize the very existence of the Salvadorean people, and again, when they say that the government of El Salvador really represents the people of El Salvador. And they falsify reality by using all of the above arguments to support the conclusion that they have the right to counterattack in order to guarantee their national security.

All these falsifications and fabrications by the U.S. government imply a logic of violence, and reveal enormous stupidity. They foretell growing physical violence, and are absolutely useless for solving any of the problems facing the United States. In fact, they pose a grave threat to the very survival of the United States.

As falsehoods, these distortions and lies have shocked the world with their brutality, which is both outrageous and idiotic. As political arguments, they are open to various interpretations. Does a decision to go to war lie behind these arguments? If that is the case, the lies signal a holocaust for the North American people. Or are they merely meant to blackmail the socialist countries and world democratic forces and thus extort the right to wage a colonial war against an unarmed people with impunity? If that is the case, they are threatening another Vietnam.

Our days are not the days of Queen Victoria. We live in historic times, given to people's liberation and self-determination. Which is to say, today the world's peoples and many of their governments know how to fight when their rights are violated.

The struggle for national sovereignty and for the common good has become a practical matter. Neither Nicaragua, nor Cuba, nor Mexico can stand idly by as the government of the United States intervenes against the people of El Salvador. The logic of survival moves them to fight against an already foreseeable triple U.S. intervention and against its possible effects. U.S. intervention with the junta as intermediary is like a Vietnam prologue. United States intervention by means of an international conflagration with Honduran participation against Nicaragua would be a repetition of the war between North and South Vietnam. Direct intervention by the U S. army would imply the vietnamization of Central America and the Caribbean. Would it stop there?

If the governments of Mexico, Cuba and Nicaragua were to believe it prudent to give the United States free rein to intervene, not only would they be unable to control their own peoples, who would see such conduct as treason and suicidal cowardice, but they would also be creating conditions in which sooner rather than later U.S. imperialism would strike at their own governments and natural resources. For that reason, these countries, and many others, cannot allow the United States to assume the right to intervene in Central America and the Caribbean. Therefore, it is neither metaphor nor wishful thinking to say that El Salvador could be the beginning of another Vietnam, and even more dangerous for the United States.

U.S. action against El Salvador marks the beginning of a process of war in Central America and the Caribbean. It is clear, from reading statements of high-ranking U.S. government officials, that El Salvador is only the beginning. The actions taken and threats made against the people of El Salvador carry an ominous message for the world and for the North American people. It is clear that there has been a decision to solve social problems by force, and forcibly so. In this there is the logic of a strong state grown weak, seeking to impose authoritarian decisions: first, upon those who are weaker, or those deemed weaker; next, upon the cowards, or those deemed cowardly; and then upon the prudent, or those believed to be prudent. The actions against El Salvador now imply the decision to continue using the same politics of force, once the United States becomes stronger.

It is not only the peoples of Central America and the Caribbean who feel the threat of the new policy of the U.S. government. Canada and Europe also see themselves threatened, as do Angola and Ethiopia, the Arab world and Iran, Indochina, the USSR, and many peoples throughout the world, including the people of the United States. Not only do the peoples of the world feel threatened, so do the governing classes; not only the proletariat, but also the property owners. Those whom the U.S. government can humble today, it will plunder tomorrow. Therefore, worldwide responses follow the logic of survival. This logic is widespread, but is as yet insufficient and ineffective in many places.

Peoples and governments that seek peace as a form of survival must begin by taking practical measures to prevent the defeat of El Salvador. That is, they must fight for Salvadorean sovereignty against the escalation started by the new and deplorable Reagan Administration, which threatens the whole world as it goes step by step down the road to a new Vietnam.

The world *is much stronger* than the United States government which is threatening it, and the world must force the recognition of another philosophy, beginning now, beginning with El Salvador. The capacity for reason and the strength of the peoples of the world *must* insure respect for the reason and the strength of each and every people's sovereignty. The rights of nonintervention and of self-determination are facets of one basic right, which is the people's right to sovereignty. Whoever respects the sovereignty of the Salvadorean people will also respect that of the North American people, and will help to keep them both from war. Those who insure respect for the people's sovereignty will insure world peace.

All democratic and revolutionary organizations throughout the world, all democratic and socialist countries, must fight to raise the consciousness and the will of all peoples in defense of the Salvadorean people, and put an end to all aid to the Salvadorean military junta which is waging a war against its own people.

In El Salvador, the only possible political solution will emerge once the principle of nonintervention is really put into practice. No intervention against the People!

There must be a United Nations resolution against all aid to the military junta, stopping it so that the people can exercise their sovereignty and decide how they shall be governed. The United Nations must demand the right of international solidarity with the Salvadorean people, as a right in accordance with the U.N. Charter and the U.N. responsibility for world peace.

Respect for the sovereignty of El Salvador is the road to peace.

PART 2

U.S. Strategies for Counterrevolution

Economic Expansion, Political Crisis and U.S. Policy in Central America

James F. Petras and Morris H. Morley

Introduction: Overview

Central America is in the center of conflict between social revolutionary and counterrevolutionary forces. An unprecedented level of right-wing governmental and paramilitary repression is matched by the most inclusive, far-reaching left-wing mobilization in recent history. This historic confrontation which is unfolding before us at the present moment is the product of 25 years of rapid and uneven capitalist growth and transformation, which have unmercifully exploited and uprooted millions of peasants and workers and destroyed locally anchored communal productive systems. Trade expansion, industrial growth, the commercialization of agriculture, and the extension of urban space are testaments to both a period of sustained economic expansion and a process which has left in its wake a vast army of underpaid and unrepresented wage laborers. The predominant "outside and above" capitalist development model has also led to the creation of a mass of semi-employed and unemployed workers in urban and rural Central America. According to a recent study under the auspices of the United Nations' Economic Commission for Latin America, "a significant segment of the [Central American] population—possibly over 50%—lives in what could be described as extreme poverty by any reasonable criteria."[1] Open unemployment in the region as a whole currently stands at between 8% and 15%, while underemployment is estimated as approaching 50% of the economically active population.[2]

Capitalist growth in the region has occurred within a socioeconomic and political framework which includes: 1) the continuity of the traditional ruling class increasingly diversifying its holdings, but retaining its family-based source of political and economic power;[3] 2) rulership through military or civilian-police state regimes with familial and economic ties to the ruling class and to military and police agencies of the U.S. imperial state; and 3) multinational corporations, primarily from the United States, but increasingly from Western Europe and Japan, with links to traditional ruling class groups, as well as to the economic and political agencies of the U.S. imperial state.[4] This Triumvirate of traditional family-based capitalism, multinational corporations and military rulers has provided the framework for capitalist growth for almost a half-century in the Central American countries of Nicaragua, El Salvador, Honduras and Guatemala.

The growth of capitalism in Central America and the transformation of the social structure have had differential effects on the region's class structure. On the one hand, growth has been accompanied by the concentration of capital, as evidenced by the activities of the Somoza family in Nicaragua. The "clan" fortune increased from around $60 million in the mid-1950's to an estimated $400 - $500 million in the mid-1970's— encompassing estates and agricultural businesses, processing industries, industrial enterprises, communications and banking, and foreign investments.[5] On the other hand, repression of wage and salary demands has contributed mightily to the process of steady economic expansion. In turn, these twin processes of wealth concentration and sustained levels of repression have induced the growth of radical popular movements which link their demands for immediate improvement with a transformation of the social structure.

The social movements in Central America have grown in the past decade from small, urban-based groups of skilled workers and intellectuals to broad-based mass organizations. These include an extremely wide range of wage and salaried workers, extending to practically all major industries and services, landless rural wage workers, smallholding peasants and, significantly enough, a growing number of indigenous communities.

The dynamic growth of capital, with its voracious appetite for new sources of land, labor and resources has drawn into its vortex practically every segment of society. The expanded accumulation process which has fueled economic expansion has at the same time provoked the most comprehensive opposition. By subordinating a great variety of social classes to the common yoke of repression and exploitation, by monopolizing all mechanisms of legality and representation, the process of capitalist development has *homogenized the conditions of heterogeneous social classes* (salaried, wage, unemployed, smallholders, etc.) and has *created the basis for a broad unified social revolutionary movement.*

U.S. political and economic policy must be analyzed within this process of growth, repression and popular mobilization. Decades of financial assistance and military aid were geared essentially to *promoting* and *supporting* the capitalist development programs and the repressive regimes which preceded the current period of unrest. Through public and private loans and investments, through direct governmental programs, and through their influence in shaping the policies of the so-called international banks (World Bank, Inter-American Development Bank, etc.), Washington policymakers sought to promote the economic infrastructures, financial institutions and industries of Central America. At the same time, U.S. military assistance, arms sales and training programs were directly linked to the maintenance of dictatorial regimes supportive of U.S. policy goals in the area. In other words, the efforts of imperial state agencies and personnel were directed toward "building," protecting and nurturing state regimes that undertook to free markets, control labor and incarcerate trade union leadership.

Beginning in the early to mid-1950's, U.S. policy became increasingly linked with those sectors of the Central American ruling class involved in industrial and financial institutions and less tied to the direct ownership of land. The shift in economic activity did not, however, lead to any change in policy toward the political and social status quo. The convergence of U.S. policy and investor interests with those of the Central American ruling classes thus led to a historic compromise in which successive U.S. administrations sacrificed democratic rights in exchange for capitalist economic opportunity and U.S. strategic interests. For the rulers of these countries were not only willing to promote "open" economies in the interests of foreign capital accumulation; they were also agreeable to direct involvement in U.S.-promoted operations against nationalist and/or anti-capitalist states in the region (the overthrow of the Arbenz government in Guatemala in 1954, the invasions of Cuba in 1961 and the Dominican Republic in 1965, the counterrevolutionary activity currently being directed against the present Nicaraguan government).

The fundamental challenge to this long-standing U.S. policy came with the military defeat of the Somoza dictatorship in Nicaragua in July 1979. The overthrow of an erstwhile American ally by a mass-based, poly-class movement under the leadership of the Sandinista guerrillas and the initiation of a democratic-revolutionary process in Nicaragua sent shock waves throughout Central America, which had immediate reverberations in Washington. The Carter Administration, fearful of a new wave of revolution in the region, embarked upon a series of political maneuvers designed essentially to sustain U.S. economic and strategic interests, and to prevent the success of new revolutionary struggles.

Capitalist Growth and Political Crisis

The political crisis in Central America is the product of capitalist expansion and the consequently increasing class polarization which has put the issue of a class-anchored social revolution on the historic agenda. The crisis is not the result of "stagnation and underdevelopment," the incapacity of capitalism to transform society, but is rather the social consequence and political framework within which the transformation is taking place.[5a]

The last two decades provide abundant evidence of the capitalist transformation of the economies and class structure of the region. Autocratic rule created optimal conditions for capitalist expansion, as reflected in the growth rate in the Gross Domestic Product during the period 1960 to 1978.

The growth of diversified economies, as multinational and local capital increasingly invested in industrial enterprises, is rather strikingly illustrated by the changing pattern of U.S. investments in Central America, especially between 1970 and 1979. Whereas in 1970, manufacturing accounted for approximately 12% of total U.S. investments, by 1979 this figure had grown to more than 33%—clearly indicating the extent to which manufacturing had become one of the preferred areas of investment for metropolitan capital.

Between 1960 and 1978, all countries in the region experienced steady rates of industrial growth, despite variations between economies and over time.

The increase in Central America's agricultural production and the parallel rise of its role in world trade has essentially been a function of mechanization of the rural sectors. This process of mechanization is indicated by the tremendous increase in the use of tractors and the expansion of irrigated land. Nicaragua, for example, as the following tables show, experienced an almost fourfold increase in both the amount of land under irrigation and the number of tractors in operation in the agricultural sector.

Gross National Product Average Annual Growth Rate, 1960-1978 (percentage)

Honduras	4.20
El Salvador	5.55
Guatemala	5.80
Nicaragua	6.50*
**Mexico	6.10
Panama	5.60
Costa Rica	6.25

Source: World Bank, *World Development Report* (August 1980), pp. 112-13 (*=1960-1977).

** NOTE: For the purposes of this study, Mexico has been included.

U.S. Direct Investment In Central America (excluding Mexico and Panama) ($ millions)

	1970	1979
All Industry	624	895
Mining and Smelting	10	24
Petroleum	160	72
Manufacturing	74	304
Transport		75
Trade	380	102
Finance and Insurance		56
Other Industries		262

Source: U.S. Department of Commerce, *Survey of Current Business*, Vol. 52, No. 11 (November 1972), pp. 30-31; Vol. 60, No. 8 (August 1980), p. 27.

Growth of Production: Industry
(percentage)

	1960-1970	1970-1978
Honduras	5.2	5.9
El Salvador	8.5	7.0
Guatemala	7.8	7.6
Nicaragua	11.0	7.3*
Mexico	9.1	6.2
Panama	10.1	.7
Costa Rica	9.4	9.1*

Source: World Bank, *World Development Report* (August 1980), pp. 112-13 (* = 1977).

Growth of Production: Agriculture
(percentage)

	1960-1970	1970-1978
Honduras	5.7	0.8
El Salvador	3.0	2.7
Guatemala	4.3	5.3
Nicaragua	6.7	5.4*
Mexico	3.8	2.1
Panama	5.7	2.4
Costa Rica	5.7	2.5

Source: World Bank, *World Development Report* (August 1980), pp. 112-13 (* = 1977).

Irrigated Land, 1961-1976
(thousands of hectares)

	1961-1965	1976
Costa Rica	26	26
El Salvador	18	33
Guatemala	38	62
Honduras	60	80
Nicaragua	18	70
Panama	15	23

Tractor Use, 1961-1976

	1961-1965	1976
Costa Rica	4,311	5,700
El Salvador	1,800	3,000
Guatemala	2,250	3,750
Honduras	331	1,050
Nicaragua	450	1,316
Panama	789	3,800

Source: James W. Wilkie, ed., *Statistical Abstract of Latin America, Volume 20* (University of California at Los Angeles: Latin American Center, 1980), p. 39.

The agricultural sector has also continued to expand since 1960, though at a slightly slower rate than industry; and, as one would expect, the growth has not been in food production.

A major consequence of this mechanization process has been an accelerated rate of displacement of landless laborers from the countryside into the large population centers, where they have swelled the ranks of the unemployed and underemployed urban poor. The agricultural work force as a percentage of the total work force has declined significantly in every Central American country since 1960.

While Central American agriculture has mechanized and increased its role as an exporter of rural commodities, the pattern of land ownership, highly concentrated in a few hands, has not changed at all. In Guatemala, 2% of the landholders own 70% of the land (1980); in Honduras, 0.3% of the landholders own 27.4% of the land (1975); in El Salvador, 1% of the landholders own 57% of the land (1978); and in Nicaragua under Somoza, 1.4% of the landholders owned 41.2% of the land.[6]

One of the more notable features of the region's economic development since 1960 has been the central role of the so-called service sector. While agriculture's contribution to the Gross Domestic Product has declined to less than 30% in every country with the exception of Honduras, and while industry's contribution has grown steadily, "services" still account for the greatest share of Gross Domestic Product in each Central American economy (approximately 50%). The capacity of this sector to maintain its position within these economies over time reflects a pattern of economic growth characterized by large-scale, nonproductive investments. The entrepreneurial activities of high military figures, bankers and family elites, in the form of heavy investments in high-rise offices, luxury housing, commercial buildings and other urban real estate, have directly shaped and promoted this type of development.

Central America's economic expansion has been, in large measure, export-based. The following table shows that during the 1960's, the region experienced a dynamic upsurge in trade, with an average annual growth rate in excess of 8%. During the 1970's, exports continued to grow, although at a slower rate in all countries with the exception of Mexico.

Sectoral Distribution in Gross Domestic Product
(percentage)

	Agriculture		Industry		Services	
	1960	1978	1960	1978	1960	1978
Honduras	37	32	19	26	44	42
El Salvador	32	29	19	21	49	50
Nicaragua	24	25.2	21	26*	55	51*
Mexico	16	11	29	37	55	52
Panama	23	16.1	21	—	56	—
Costa Rica	26	18.6	20	27*	54	51*
Guatemala	30**	25.9	—	—	—	—

Source: World Bank, *World Development Report* (August 1980), pp. 114-15; Inter-American Development Bank, *Economic and Social Progress in Latin America, 1979 Report*, pp. 15, 21 (*1977, **1960-1964 annual average contribution).

Sectoral Distribution of Labor Force: Agriculture (percentage)		
	1960	1978
Honduras	70	64
Guatemala	67	57
El Salvador	62	52
Nicaragua	62	44
Mexico	55	39
Panama	51	31
Costa Rica	51	29

Source: World Bank, *World Development Report* (August 1980), pp. 146-47.

Growth of Merchandise Trade Average Annual Growth Rate Of Export (percentage)		
	1960-1970	1970-1978
Honduras	11.1	2.9
Nicaragua	9.7	5.6
El Salvador	5.6	0.6
Guatemala	9.0	3.4
Mexico	3.3	5.2
Panama	10.4	2.2
Costa Rica	9.4	5.9

Source: World Bank, *World Development Report* (August 1980), pp. 124-25.

While primary products still make up a significant proportion of exports, the shifting pattern of foreign investments, into economic sectors apart from the traditional agro-mining centers of production, indicates that the countries of the region can no longer simply be referred to as "banana republics." In 1950, a single primary commodity accounted for 80% to 90% of total exports; by the late 1970's, no country was dependent on any one product for more than 50% of its export trade.[7] The growth of industrial investments has stimulated the expansion of nontraditional exports throughout the region. Even though the local economic elites continue to invest heavily in commercial agriculture, and primary commodities are still the predominant exports, they are less central than in the past.

The Central American development "model" has been substantially dependent on large-scale inflows of finance and investment capital, principally from U.S. sources and the international banking community. Overall U.S. private investment in Guatemala, Honduras, Costa Rica, El Salvador and Nicaragua, for example, grew steadily between 1963 and 1970, rising from $539 million to $624 million.[8] During the 1970's, however, the total American investment "stake" increased in size by approximately 40%.

At the same time, finance capital from metropolitan and private banking institutions began to assume a commanding role in a number of countries in the region. Between 1970 and 1978, gross inflows of medium and long-term loans jumped approximately threefold in Guatemala and Nicaragua, tenfold in El Salvador, almost elevenfold in Mexico, over thirteenfold in Costa Rica and around fifteenfold in Panama.

Merchandise Exports: Primary Commodities
(percentage share of total)

	1960	1977
Honduras	98	90
El Salvador	94	80
Guatemala	97	83
Nicaragua	98	83
Mexico	88	71
Costa Rica	95	76

Source: World Bank, *World Development Report* (August 1980), pp. 126-27.

U.S. Private Investment in Central America
(1980)

Guatemala	$260 million
Honduras	$250 million
Costa Rica	$210 million
Nicaragua	$160 million
El Salvador	$145 million

Source: *New York Times* (July 9, 1980), p. 10.

Public and Publicly Guaranteed Medium and Long-Term Loans Gross Inflows
($ millions)

	1970	1978
Honduras	29	163
Guatemala	37	107
El Salvador	8	80
Nicaragua	44	142
Mexico	782	8,606
Panama	67	986
Costa Rica	30	396

Source: World Bank, *World Development Report* (August 1980), pp. 136-37.

Ratio of External Public Debt To Value of Exports Of Goods and Services
(percentage)

	1970	1978
Honduras	3.0	8.6
El Salvador	3.5	3.1
Guatemala	7.4	1.8
Nicaragua	10.6	17.3
Mexico	24.1	59.5
Panama	7.6	62.0
Costa Rica	10.0	23.4

Source: World Bank, *World Development Report* (August 1980), pp. 138-39.

External Public Debt Outstanding and Disbursed

	$ millions		% of GNP	
	1970	1978	1970	1978
Honduras	90	591	12.9	34.9
El Salvador	88	333	8.6	11.0
Guatemala	106	374	5.7	6.0
Nicaragua	155	964	20.6	45.8
Mexico	3,238	25,775	9.8	28.7
Panama	194	1,910	19.0	84.1
Costa Rica	134	963	13.8	29.3

Source: World Bank, *World Development Report* (August 1980), pp. 138-39.

This accelerated dependence on external sources of financing was accompanied by a massive growth in the region's external debt. In Panama, the external public debt as a percentage of the Gross National Product grew from 19.0% in 1970 to 84.1% in 1978. Over the same time span, it rose from 20.6% to 45.8% in Nicaragua, from 12.9% to 34.9% in Honduras, and from 13.8% to 29.3% in Costa Rica. Comparable trends were also evident with regard to the debt-exports ratio. Between 1960 and 1978, Panama's external debt rose from 7.6% to 62.0% of the value of its exports, Mexico's grew from 24.1% to 59.5%, Costa Rica's increased from 10.0% to 23.4%, and Nicaragua's moved from 10.6% to 17.3%.

As a result of these developments, a number of regimes increasingly came to view access to overseas financial capital as crucial to their continued ability to refinance existing foreign debt structures.

Over time, and in the absence of state structures seeking to promote redistributive socioeconomic programs in the context of nationally anchored development strategies, these parallel processes—the commercialization of agriculture, the growth of industry, urbanization, and the permeation of Central American economies by foreign capital—have had a profound impact in creating the social movements and class conflicts that more and more dominate the political horizon in the region.

Class Transformation and Class Struggle

The nature of Central American economic development has rendered major changes in the class structures of the region. Accompanying these shifts has been a massive concentration of population in the cities: in most countries between one-third and one-half of the population is now located in major urban centers.

In rural Central America, the commercialization of agriculture has increased the number and importance of rural wage workers; at the

Urban Population as a Percentage Of Total Population

	1960	1980
Honduras	23	36
Guatemala	33	39
El Salvador	38	41
Nicaragua	41	53
Mexico	51	67
Panama	41	54
Costa Rica	37	43

Source: World Bank, _World Development Report_ (August 1980), pp. 148-49.

same time it has uprooted peasant populations, depressed the conditions of production of the petty commodity producers, and maintained large segments of the population at the margins of economic life. The Mexican experience well illustrates the exclusionary nature of these development schemas. Between 1953 and 1975, according to a World Bank study, changes in the country's highly unequal income distribution were "small or non-existent." The number of "poor" families in the agricultural sector declined by a mere 2% (54% to 52%) over this 22-year period. In 1975, the World Bank still categorized as "poor" some 1.5 million landowning families and 850,000 landless families—or 76% of all families residing in rural Mexico.[9] El Salvador, on the other hand, presents a striking example of rapid and massive proletarianization of the agricultural population: from 11% of the total number of peasants in 1961 to 29% in 1971, to 40% in 1975, to an estimated 65% in 1980.[10] Similarly, in Guatemala the growth of a landless or near-landless peasantry (owning insufficient land to maintain a subsistence living) had reached enormous proportions by the early 1970's.[11]

The transformation of the class structure in the countryside has led to wider and deeper involvement of rural populations in agrarian social movements and in struggles for unionization. In Guatemala, following a period (1966-1972) of violent rural repression by the state, guerrilla movements re-emerged in the countryside, where a great deal of their efforts were focused on the development of labor and peasant unions. At the same time, ongoing land conflicts and government terrorism (e.g., the massacre of at least 100 Kekchi Indians by the army in Panzós, Alta Verapaz in May 1978) have contributed to a growing militancy on the part of the peasants and have increased their openness to the political and economic appeals of the guerrillas. In the northern province of Quiché, a center of operations of the Ejército Guerrillero de los Pobres (Guerrilla Army of the Poor), many villages have been under military occupation since the mid-1970's.[12]

In El Salvador, since the announcement of the so-called agrarian reform in March 1980, the army, security forces and right-wing death squads (operating in concert) have stepped up the level of repression and counterinsurgency operations in the countryside—especially in the most impoverished rural areas (Chalatenango, Aguilares, etc.) where peasant political organization is strongest.[13]

Even in "stable" Costa Rica, rural wage workers have begun to organize in pursuit of social and economic demands. In February 1979, for instance, some 4,200 banana plantation laborers, around 80% of whom were represented by the Unión de Trabajadores de Golfito, went on strike against their imperial-capitalist employer, United Brands, over management's continued refusal to negotiate a new collective labor contract. The workers' demands encompassed salary increases, improved holiday and social benefits, and a reduction in the workday from eight to six hours. Their strategic location in the economy—bananas are the second most important export crop—at a time of a decline in Costa Rica's foreign trade position forced the Carazo government to intervene directly in the dispute. An official mediator granted immediate wage increases ranging up to 30%, with the understanding that the social demands would be incorporated into the eventual new labor contract.[14]

In urban Central America, the growing concentration and centralization of industry has led to an increasing concentration of labor which, in turn, has facilitated organization and struggle. The proportion of industrial workers has been steadily growing over the past two decades—though their proportion in the labor force in 1978 varied from 14% in Honduras to 26% in Mexico. More significantly, the proportion of "service" workers, largely underemployed or unemployed workers, has jumped tremendously since 1960. In Nicaragua, for example, the following table shows that, while the percentage of industrial workers actually declined between 1960 and 1978 from 16% to 15%, the "service sector" almost doubled in size, going from 22% to 41%.

Sectoral Distribution of Labor Force
(percentage)

	Industry		Service	
	1960	1978	1960	1978
Honduras	11	14	19	23
Guatemala	14	20	19	24
El Salvador	17	22	21	26
Nicaragua	16	15	22	41
Mexico	20	26	25	35
Panama	14	18	35	47
Costa Rica	19	23	31	48

Source: World Bank, *World Development Report* (August 1980), pp. 146-47.

The integration of a significant proportion of rural migrants into the factory system has provided them with a class-anchored frame of reference through which to act politically. The mass of migrants, however, excluded from stable wage employment, are systematically concentrated in urban slums, as a result of the organic ties between the state and the real estate investors: state subsidies, expenditures and loans facilitate the expansion of big real estate interests and the eradication of lower class communities. The state links to expanding real estate capital have, in recent years, provoked mass opposition among squatter settlements throughout the region.

The region-wide growth model, based on economic incentives for those "above and outside," has not only produced changes in the class structure but also led to precipitous declines in the standard of living for wage and salaried groups—especially salaried employees within the public service sector. Real wage levels fell by 25% in Nicaragua between 1967 and 1975 and by 30% in Honduras between 1972 and 1978.[15] In El Salvador, workers experienced a substantial decline in real wages during the decade of the 1970's, while the value of the minimum wage in Mexico declined during 1977, 1978 and 1979 as inflation continued to outstrip wage gains.[16] In Costa Rica, inflation and the erosion of living standards among industrial workers and public employees translated into increased strike activity by these groups beginning in late 1979.[17] In fact, spiraling prices for goods and commodities were a feature of most area economies during the 1970's. While the average price index for the region rose by only 13% between 1950 and 1970, it increased by 74% during the 1970 to 1977 period.[18]

The general and chronic deterioration in economic conditions served to unite adversely affected fractions of salaried and wage groups. The combined impact of externally induced inflation, declining standards of living, and autocratic-predatory states has led to united actions across class and occupational lines against the existing regimes. In Nicaragua, a broad-based anti-dictatorial movement incorporating multiple class participants succeeded in overthrowing the Somoza dictatorship in July 1979.[19] In El Salvador, workers, peasants, urban slum dwellers, university students, independent professionals and churchpeople, under the aegis of more than 20 popular organizations, political parties and labor federations, have coalesced (and allied themselves with rurally based guerrilla movements) to pursue the struggle to oust the military-dominated junta currently in control of the Salvadorean state.[20] In the late 1970's, the resurgence of rural struggle in Guatemala was accompanied by a growing urban labor militancy, principally among public sector employees, as the military regime sought to contain demands for union recognition, growing inter-union activity in the form of solidarity strikes, and opposition to rising inflation and lowered standards of economic life.[21]

The expansion of capital in the region has not been a linear upward progression, but rather has followed a cyclical pattern. The fluctuations have led to the incorporation of labor into the work force at low wages during the upswing, and the expulsion of labor in the downswing, undermining the limited gains and the possibility of cumulative incremental gains. The introduction of the workers to factory or plantation organization preceding the layoff provides them with a class perspective through which to challenge the social order. The "disorder" generated by capitalist instability on workers' lives forces them to seek to "reorder" the class system.[22]

The diversification of capital beyond the agro-mining-export centers of production has led to the proliferation of points of class contestation within the economies of Central America. The overwhelming majority of worker strikes in El Salvador during 1977 and 1978, for example, were concentrated in the construction and manufacturing sectors of the economy.[23] In sum, the growth of state-local-multinational capital has created new class formations and new class conflicts.

Generalized class conflict and multiple class demands challenging the old paternalistic and personalistic forms of domination go beyond the collective bargaining framework, laying claims for a new social and political order. Emerging from the sometimes turbulent movements in opposition to existing state regimes is a fourfold challenge: 1) to the forms of rulership, 2) to the social order; 3) to the external linkages; and 4) to the economic development model.

The attempts by the autocratic regimes to contain the growth of proletarian class consciousness through the promotion of state-controlled bureaucratic organizations (sometimes described as "corporatism") undermine the reformist organization which attempts to mediate the struggles between the state and "society." The lack of reformist representation within the state is combined with economic and political struggle. Even the immediate issues of contention—salaries, wages, working conditions—are set by the state. The resolution of the immediate issues requires resolving the issue of the forms of rulership. The quasi-political monopoly exercised by the Triumvirate mentioned above and the development strategies pursued (free market, cutbacks in public spending, state penetration of private organizations, etc.) marginalize small local capital, pauperize public employees, and undermine the prerogatives of church and civic association leaders—forcing them to go beyond criticism of specific policies and to question the economic model in its totality.

The mobilization of multiple strata and classes in society, and the opposition to the social order, external linkages and economic model, move toward a low level of civil war. One major consequence is the drying up of investment funds, as factories are closed and large amounts of capital are shipped out of the country ($90 million from Nicaragua during July-December 1977, $300 million from El Salvador during 1978, $100 million from Honduras during 1980).[24] The crisis of the regime is manifested by internal divisions between those who seek to make "concessions" and those who want to "go to war." In society, alternative sources of authority are created—a pre-revolutionary situation emerges. In the crisis, the multinationals and their states seek to substitute new partners—replacing the military dictators and plantation owners with representatives of local industrialists and small and medium-size firms. In turn, the local members of the Triumvirate may lay claims to "nationalism" by attacking foreign intrusions, while simultaneously accelerating the outward flight of capital ($315 million left Nicaragua during January-June 1979, $1.5 billion fled El Salvador during 1979-1980).[25] The common fear of social revolution, however, prevents any decisive breaks within the Triumvirate and, in the end, it unites to attempt to prevent the new mass-based movements from taking power.

U.S. Aid Policy Toward Central America

The crisis in Central America is a very complex, multi-layered phenomenon that touches every aspect of society and polity. It cannot be reduced to either a "political" crisis, a problem of underdevelopment, or to a set of discrete social problems. This is a "constitutional" crisis, in the sense that what is at stake is the very foundation of the social order. The challenge posed is one that involves reversing historical relationships, transforming the social order and sustaining the development of the productive forces. This is no easy task, given the central position of the U.S. within the region. The U.S. government is attempting to cope with this revolutionary challenge through a combination of repression and reform, with the former clearly in ascent.

The U.S. government's support for Central American dictatorships has been manifested through a vast program of bilateral and multilateral economic aid and various forms of military assistance. Between 1953 and 1979, Washington provided the ruling classes of El Salvador with $218.4 million in economic aid and $16.8 million in military loans and credits. This sum was more than matched by the World Bank, Inter-American Development Bank and other U.S.-influenced multilateral banks to the tune of $479.2 million. The Guatemalan oligarchy received $526.0 million in U.S. economic aid and $41.9 million in military assistance, in addition to some $593.0 million from the "international" financial institutions. The Somoza clan in Nicaragua was the recipient of $345.8 million in U.S. economic aid and $32.6 million in military assistance, while the "international" agencies channeled $469.5 million into its coffers. In Honduras, the ruling political and economic elites benefited significantly from these same sources: $305.1 million in U.S. economic aid, $28.4 million in U.S. military assistance, and $688.0 million from the "international" banks.

The long-term, large-scale involvement of the U.S. in Central America, both economically and militarily, has been to a considerable degree responsible for sustaining in power repressive, autocratic regimes which refuse to deal with underlying social and economic problems persisting into the present period. Economic assistance largely benefited the entrenched oligarchies who, in turn, utilized much of these funds not for developing the productive forces but rather for speculative investments, luxury purchases, or for transferral to foreign bank accounts. The military assistance and training programs acted to enhance the repressive capabilities of these state regimes wedded to development strategies based on "open" economies and coerced labor forces.

Even the much vaunted Carter "human rights" policy did not change the preexisting economic relations between the U.S. and Central America that were, in large measure, responsible for creating the social and political unrest. U.S. economic assistance to the military juntas in Honduras, Guatemala and El Salvador during 1980 totaled more than $125 million, notwithstanding the enormous rise in the number of government opponents assassinated and tortured by the armies, security forces and paramilitary "death squads" of these countries over this 12-month period.[26] According to the El Salvador Human Rights Commission, more than 13,000 deaths were recorded in 1980, the overwhelming majority at the hands of the security forces and the paramilitary groups.

U.S. Economic and Military Assistance to Central America, 1953-1979*
($ millions)

	1953-1961	1962-1969	1970-1979	Total 1953-1979
Mexico				
economic	342.1	518.4	1,672.1	2,352.6
military	3.6	4.0	7.2	14.8
Nicaragua				
economic	46.2	116.2	183.4	345.8
military	1.9	10.4	20.3	32.6
Panama				
economic	67.9	173.4	341.9	583.2
military	0.1	3.0	11.8	14.9
Costa Rica				
economic	71.5	115.7	118.0	305.2
military	0.1	1.7	5.1	6.9
El Salvador				
economic	14.3	115.1	89.0	218.4
military	0.1	6.5	10.2	16.8
Guatemala				
economic	134.7	170.8	220.5	526.0
military	1.5	18.3	22.1	41.9
Honduras				
economic	37.9	75.9	191.3	305.1
military	1.1	8.0	19.3	28.4

*Includes U.S. Export-Import Bank and other U.S. government loans.
Source: see source for chart on next page.

Economic Assistance From International Financial Institutions,
1953-1979
($ millions)

	1953-1961	1962-1969	1970-1979	Total 1953-1979
Mexico	153.6	971.8	4,746.7	5,872.1
Nicaragua	33.8	86.3	349.4	469.5
Panama	15.4	37.8	535.5	588.7
Costa Rica	18.8	75.9	587.7	682.4
El Salvador	24.7	57.4	397.1	479.2
Guatemala	21.6	76.1	495.2	593.0
Honduras	32.5	85.7	569.8	688.0

Source: U.S. Agency for International Development, Statistics and Research Division, Office of Program and Information Analysis Services, *U.S. Overseas Loans and Grants and Assistance From International Organizations, July 1, 1945 - September 30, 1976*, pp. 43, 47-48, 53-55, 183-85; U.S. Agency for International Development, Office of Planning and Budgeting, Bureau for Program and Policy Coordination, *U.S. Overseas Loans and Grants and Assistance From International Organizations, July 1, 1945 - September 30, 1979*, pp. 45, 49-50, 53, 55-57, 218-22.

In Guatemala, the growth of mass popular trade union movements, the radicalization of the highland Indian communities and the growing effectiveness of the guerrillas did cause the Carter White House to apply some pressures, largely in the form of a temporary cutback in military credits. This was an effort to force the regime to modify its repressive policies: to be more selective in their application and to combine state control with limited social reforms. The refusal of the military-landlord ruling class to modify its rulership led to some friction between Washington and Guatemala City but did not stop the flow of economic assistance.[26a]

Continuing its government-to-government economic assistance, the Carter Administration at no point exercised its economic "muscle" in the multilateral banking institutions to limit the gross human rights violations in the region. During 1979 and 1980, it supported International Monetary Fund loans of $65 million and $77 million to Somoza in Nicaragua and the Salvadorean junta respectively.[27] Furthermore, in December 1980, Washington did successfully flex its economic "muscle" in the Inter-American Development Bank *in support of* a $45.4 million agrarian reform loan to El Salvador, to be drawn from the Bank's special operations fund, in which the U.S. holds 62% of the capital.[28]

While U.S. *economic* policy remained consistent under Carter, there were, as previously noted, some cutbacks in military aid, notably

Major Israeli Arms Sales To El Salvador 1974-1978		Israel Aircraft Industries Sales In Central America, 1973-1979	
Quantity and Item	**Delivery**	**Country**	**Equipment**
25 IAI-201 Arava STOL transport aircraft	1974-1979	El Salvador	18 Ouragan, 6 Fouga, 5 Arava
200 9mm UZI submarine guns	1974-1977	Guatemala	8 Arava
200 80mm rocket launchers	1974-1977	Honduras	12 Super-Mystere, 3 Arava, 1 Westwind
18 refurbished Dassault Ouragan fighter bombers	1975	Mexico Nicaragua Panama	25 Arava 14 Arava 1 Westwind
6 IAI Fouga Magister trainer aircraft	1975		

Source: Institute for Policy Studies, *Background Information on the Security Forces in El Salvador and U.S. Military Assistance* (March 1980), p. 12.

Source: "Problems From the Barrels of Israeli Guns," *Latin American Weekly Report* WR-80-19 (May 16, 1980), p. 9.

in respect to El Salvador, Nicaragua and Guatemala. Yet these were essentially conjunctural responses over discrete issues at particular moments in time, and did not denote a defined, consistent opposition to repressive military regimes in that area. The government of General Romeo Lucas García in Guatemala, for example, continued to make cash purchases of American weaponry between 1977 and 1980 worth $4.7 million, under the Foreign Military Sales program.[29] Selectivity was the byword—in some countries and respects, military assistance was cut back for limited durations of time and in others it was not. Beyond that, the real impact of U.S. arms sales policy was substantially minimized by the emergence of Israel—a strategic Washington ally and "regional policeman" in the Middle East—as a major exporter of military supplies to the Central American dictatorships during the 1970's. Israel supplied 81% of El Salvador's foreign arms purchases between 1972 and 1977, and 98% of Somoza's arms imports during the final year of his rule.[30] The above table presents a detailed breakdown of major Israeli military sales to El Salvador between 1974 and 1978.

The largest single Israeli arms exporter to Central America has been the state-owned Israel Aircraft Industries (IAI), which has found a ready market for its products—especially the ARAVA, a tactical transport aircraft particularly suited to counterinsurgency warfare.

In late 1979, in the context of a heightened social class struggle in El Salvador and the growing consolidation of the Nicaraguan Revolution under Sandinista leadership, the Carter Administration decided to terminate its policy of selective arms constraints in favor of a policy of directly arming the terrorist juntas in Central America. Between the military coup of October 1979 and the resignation of the first civilian-military government in January 1980, Washington shipped $205,541 worth of riot control equipment and reprogrammed (with Congressional assent) some $300,000 in International Military Education and Training funds to El Salvador.[31] In April 1980, the U.S. government repro-grammed $5.7 million in military aid for El Salvador and submitted a request for an additional $5.5 million for the junta in Fiscal Year 1981.[32]

At the same time, Carter also obtained Congressional support for the reprogramming of $3.53 million in Foreign Military Sales credits to the Honduran regime and for an increase of International Military Education and Training funds from the budgeted Fiscal Year 1980 of $225,000 to $347,000. The Honduran military was further permitted to lease at least 10 U.S. Bell Huey helicopters, while welcoming dozens of U.S. military advisers who entered the country during 1980.[33] In Fiscal Year 1981, the White House and the Pentagon expected the Guatemalan junta to expand its purchases of military hardware through the Foreign Military Sales cash program.[34]

The long-term continuity in U.S. economic assistance—despite changes in political administration—mirrors the long-term capitalist interests in Central America and the basic support for local ruling groups by all U.S. Presidents, whether Republican or Democratic, liberal or conservative. The limited change in military aid policy under Carter reflected a variety of factors: the relative importance of the human rights lobby within the Executive branch; the shifting nature of the bureaucratic debate over tactics and strategy; and the political changes taking place within the Central American countries.

The human rights lobby was strongest in the early part of the Carter Administration. In the years between 1976 and 1978 it was able to push legislation which successfully limited U.S. military support for specific regimes (Guatemala, El Salvador). By 1979, however, the more conservative forces within the State Department and the National Security Council had effectively isolated the human rights proponents within the foreign policy bureaucracy. This, in turn, was followed by a reopening of the military aid "pipelines" as the U.S. government moved to actively support repressive pro-capitalist military regimes in Central America (as well as in other parts of Latin America and the Third World).

The major change in Washington's policy was the recognition, in the aftermath of Somoza's overthrow in July 1979, that a major effort had to be made to forge a coalition of civilian business groups and the army to provide a *political*, as well as a military, solution in other

Central American countries experiencing a resurgence of anti-dictatorial and class struggle. The central concern of U.S. policy was first and foremost to undermine the revolutionary popular movements and preserve the existing armed forces. Irrespective of whether these armed forces engaged in declared wars on their own populations, Washington's pressure for reforms has always been subordinated to that intent.

In the first instance, the effort was made by the White House to forge an alliance between the right-wing armed forces and reformist social democratic groups in El Salvador following the October 1979 coup which ousted General Carlos Humberto Romero from office. The effort was doomed to failure. The social democratic representatives in the junta could not generate any significant support for reform programs, while the armed forces were killing scores of workers and peasants— literally on a daily basis. As the reformers abandoned the coalition government, U.S. policy shifted speedily to the political right.

With the collapse of the civilian-military junta in January 1980, new, more malleable Christian Democratic politicians were brought into the regime to maintain the illusion of civilian authority within the ruling coalition. The sudden increase in U.S. military aid now reflected an attempt to combine repressive policies against the popular movement with limited economic reforms. The locus of economic change was in Washington's attempt to benignly sacrifice the short-term interests of segments of the local landowning class—through land reform—in order to reformulate a political bloc that subordinated peasant property owners to multinationals. The refusal of landowners to submit to U.S. tactical maneuvers and their desire to exclude the new U.S. political clients from a share in effective governmental responsibility set the stage for the new triangle. By mid-1980, at least 10 Cabinet members or high-ranking civilian officials had resigned from the government, as the U.S. government became forcibly allied with the terror of the military, security forces and paramilitary organizations such as the 50,000 to 100,000 member ORDEN. At the same time, Washington attempted to convince the ultra-right to share power with its increasingly compromised, impotent and isolated middle-sector client groups.

U.S. policymakers still proclaimed the viability of the regime, while the Salvadorean ruling class withdrew $1.5 billion in the midst of the 1979-1980 political crisis. U.S. Agency for International Development officials continued to insist that the junta's agrarian programs were designed to help the poor, while economic resources were channeled to a government controlled by large landholders and financial groups who siphoned off the bulk of the funds for their own use. During 1980, according to Socorro Jurídico (Legal Aid Office of the Archbishop of El Salvador), some 8,062 peasants, workers, students, trade unionists, professionals and churchpeople were assassinated in *non-military* confrontations with the security forces, paramilitary groups and Salvadorean troops commanded by U.S.-trained officers.[35] Hundreds more opponents of the regime "disappeared" after being arrested.[36]

Meanwhile, in the absence of the prosecution of a single military official, the Carter Administration perversely continued to label the regime a "moderate," "reformist" and centrist government and to engage in a determined effort to focus the blame for the violence on nongovernmental paramilitary organizations. Select cutbacks in U.S. military aid were in no way designed to undermine the internal discipline and cohesion of the armed forces. While on occasion condemning the "extremists on the right," the "human rights" Administration continued to support the military which practiced the violence and provided the recruits for the right-wing terrorist groups.

Washington's formula for reviving military aid to the Salvadorean armed forces in late 1979 was the same as in the past: the defense of economic privilege, support for the "integrity of the military" and opposition to social revolution. What was different was the attempt to forge a coalition between the military and the civilian middle class liberals to undercut the polarization emerging from past and present economic policies.* Through the facade of a controlled civilian regime, token reforms and an intact military, U.S. policymakers hoped to defuse public criticism at home and abroad, without endangering corporate economic and strategic interests. By December 1980, this policy had led neither to reform of the underlying conditions generating mass discontent, nor to a lessening of the level of repression by the regime. What it left was basically an escalating civil war and the threat of new U.S. interventions in the region.

Washington's attempt to defend traditional economic interests and sustain the Central American armed forces by creating a new set of civilian-military coalitions, through controlled and restricted elections, was the other side of the coin of its policy of continuing economic support to a military intent on physically destroying the revolutionary popular organizations and their supporters. Both the so-called "moderate civilians" and the extremist military were wedded to the same destructive ends. A brief survey of recent U.S. policy in the post-Somoza period is useful in demonstrating this approach and the extent to which it has, or has not, been incorporated into the foreign policy outlook of the Reagan Administration.

From Carter to Reagan: U.S. Policy in
The Post-Somoza Period

By the fall of 1979, all of Carter's campaign promises of 1976 had vanished: contrary to the earlier human rights commitments, global

---

* A similar strategy was followed in Honduras, as the Carter Administration sought to defuse a burgeoning mass movement by enlisting traditional conservative and liberal civilian politicians to participate in elections—while the military excluded leftists, social democrats and even Christian Democrats.

arms sales and the overall military budget were on a pronounced upward spiral. Among the primary recipients of new "security assistance" aid programs were an array of military and autocratic regimes in Central America, the rest of Latin America and other parts of the Third World which had previously been criticized for widespread violations of human rights. The appearance of a new aggressive U.S. posture toward the Third World, which went hand-in-hand with the armaments build-up, also served to distract attention from internal U.S. problems (inflation, unemployment, declining standards of living and the energy crisis) which were themselves transformed by Carter into instruments for external confrontation. Hostility toward OPEC, etc., became a tool for sustaining internal cohesion within the U.S. and avoiding potentially divisive cleavages between consumers and corporations.

The first major step toward reactivating the Marines was the effort by the U.S. government in June 1979 to secure passage of a resolution in the Organization of American States calling for the creation of a hemispheric military force to intervene in Nicaragua to prevent a Sandinista victory.[37] The failure of the resolution to gain support within the regional body, and the fact that Washington was not in a position to intervene unilaterally in Nicaragua, should not obscure the profound shift that had taken place in U.S. policy and its consequences for the immediate future.

In the fall of 1979, the Carter Administration accelerated efforts to create a 100,000-person Rapid Deployment Force capable of intervening within hours in any area of the world. The "new interventionists" also proposed the creation of a hemispheric military "peacekeeping" force—which would have required a complete conciliation with the worst dictatorships in Latin America. The efforts to reconstitute a post-Vietnam domestic constituency that would support the "new interventionist" policy reached a hysterical pitch with the effort by Carter and his National Security Adviser Brzezinski to fabricate a Soviet military threat in Cuba—an effort so transparently fraudulent that even the Washington political establishment was soon forced to reject it. Nonetheless, the incident was part of a singular bellicose pattern—a drift toward "direct action." In fact, out of the non-threat of Soviet troops in Cuba, Carter was able to set up a Caribbean Joint Task Force in Florida to police the area and prepare for possible interventionary actions.

In summary, military resources and public opinion were again being mobilized to defend imperial interests under the ideology of "defending ourselves against aggression," i.e., national security. U.S. policy had come full circle since 1976: the policies, rhetoric and instrumentalities of the 1960's and early 1970's are being refurbished for the 1980's.

The transition from Carter to Reagan has been accompanied by a remarkable degree of continuity in the area of foreign policy. While the "new interventionist" framework undergoes further elaboration and extension, however, some shifts in strategy are already clearly discernible as regards Central America and other parts of the Third World.

As part of its overriding goal to revitalize U.S. capitalism both at home and abroad, the incoming Administration intended to further downplay human rights considerations in the execution of foreign policy, and to seek closer ties with autocratic military regimes in the Third World—regimes that supported U.S. political-strategic interests and accorded foreign capital a central role within their development schemas. One of the major recommendations contained in a report prepared by Reagan's State Department Transition Team on Latin America was the following: "Internal policy-making procedures should be structured to ensure that the Human Rights area is not in a position to paralyze or unduly delay decisions on issues where human rights concerns conflict with other U.S. interests."[38] Subsequently, the head of the Transition Team, Ambassador Robert Neumann, put it more bluntly in an address to a group of Foreign Service Officers, declaring that such "abstractions" as human rights had no central place in a foreign policy that wished to pursue "American national interests."[39]

The other side of this coin was the new rhetoric that defined support of pro-capitalist, pro-U.S. "moderately repressive [sic!] autocratic governments" as compatible with the "national interest."[40] In language that recalled the Johnson Administration's "Mann Doctrine"* (which formalized U.S. support of military dictatorships in Latin America and described them as "pre-democratic" phenomena), a senior Reagan foreign policy adviser on Latin America was quoted, in part:

"We must maintain our interest in promoting democracy without getting disillusioned because there's a military coup in Honduras and the generals didn't respond the way we wanted. . . ." A Reagan administration, he said, would structure Latin American policy on the idea that democracy and not military dictatorship is the best protection against Communism, but it would recognize that democracy in some cases can be instituted too rapidly.[41]

At the operational level, the new policy is currently focused largely on the Central American region, with particular attention to El Salvador.

In late November 1980, Reagan's Latin American policy advisers personally "assured" leading representatives of El Salvador's business community "that the new administration will increase military aid, including control equipment, to security forces fighting leftist guerrillas."[42] On January 17, 1981, the outgoing government, utilizing special executive powers that circumvented the need for Congressional

---

* Named after Thomas Mann, Under Secretary of State for Economic Affairs, 1965-66.—*Ed.*

assent, authorized an emergency $5 million package of lethal military assistance for the Salvadorean junta.[43]

In early March, the Reagan White House announced its intention to provide a further $25 million in new military aid and increase the number of American military advisers in El Salvador from 25 to 45.[44] By the end of the same month, total Fiscal Year 1981 U.S. military appropriations for the junta had risen to $35.4 million.[45] In Congressional testimony at the end of March, acting Assistant Secretary of State for Inter-American Affairs John Bushnell stated that the Administration would authorize the dispatch of 56 Pentagon advisers to El Salvador, including a number of Special Forces personnel experienced in counterinsurgency warfare.[46]*

For Fiscal Year 1982, the Administration has requested $26 million in direct military aid to El Salvador and an additional $40 million from the misnamed "Economic Support Fund" which, in practice, operates as a weapons assistance "support fund."[47] These current and projected increases in military aid to the regime in San Salvador in part reflect Reagan's decision to forego the Carter strategy of attempting to disassociate the junta from responsibility for the terror — preferring, instead, to support the militarization of civil society, if that is what is required to defeat a revolutionary popular movement which has put the issue of state power on the immediate agenda.

Like his predecessor, Reagan is continuing the program of large-scale economic assistance to what is now pictured as "a moderate government . . . looking forward [sic!] to legitimate elections. . . ."[48] Bilateral aid from the U.S. Agency for International Development for the current Fiscal Year stands at $63.5 million, but will be doubled if Congress can be persuaded to support a further $63.5 million in "emergency" economic assistance.[49] Of even greater (potential) significance is the reported Administration plan, utilizing various imperial state agencies and the multilateral financial institutions (World Bank, Inter-American Development Bank, International Monetary Fund), that would channel an estimated $429.5 million in economic assistance to El Salvador before the end of the present Fiscal Year. In pursuit of this goal, Washington has apparently let it be known that it is prepared to apply considerable pressure on allied governments in Western Europe, Japan and Canada to contribute a substantial proportion of the total amount under the aegis of the "international banks."[50]

The military juntas in Honduras and Guatemala have been visibly encouraged by the advent of a staunchly anticommunist "business" Administration in Washington and the shifts in Central American policy

---

* Apparently, some 20 to 30 Israeli military advisers are also currently involved in training Salvadorean government forces in anti-guerrilla warfare tactics. See "Latin Letter," *Latin American Weekly Report* WR-81-13 (March 27, 1981), p. 8.

that have followed in its wake. Honduras will receive $5.4 million in military assistance during Fiscal Year 1981 and a proposed $10.7 million (the third-highest appropriation for the entire region, exceeded only by the requests for El Salvador and Colombia) during Fiscal Year 1982.[51] While Guatemala is not expected to receive any direct U.S. military aid before the end of Fiscal Year 1982, the new U.S. "policy line" has coincided with an acceleration of the terror campaign against urban and rural opponents of the regime. In January 1981, for example, almost 400 people were killed by the military. In the first week of February, at least another 85 peasants were assassinated in a "scorched earth" attack on two villages in an area northwest of Guatemala City, by army units reinforced by helicopter gunships.[52] Later that same month, *Amnesty International* released a detailed report on the repression which documented in great detail the regime's role as the *only* author and practitioner of the "official" and "unofficial" terror:

> . . . people who oppose or are imagined to oppose the government are systematically seized without warrant, tortured, and murdered, and . . . these tortures and murders are part of a deliberate and long-standing program of the Guatemalan government. This report contains information, published for the first time, which shows how the selection of targets for detention and murder, and *the deployment of official forces for extra-legal operations,* can be pinpointed to secret offices in an annex of Guatemala's National Palace, under the direct control of the president of the Republic.[53]

Toward the revolutionary government in Nicaragua and its devastated economy, on the other hand, the Reagan Administration has adopted a policy of diplomatic hostility and cutbacks in previously authorized economic assistance. In a verbal message relayed to Managua in February, and supposedly originating from a staff member of the National Security Council, the American Embassy was informed that "the question is not whether U.S.-Nicaraguan relations were good or bad, but whether there will be any relations at all."[54] Subsequently, the White House announced that it was withholding disbursement of the final $15 million of a $75 million economic aid package authorized and released by the Congress in late 1980.[55] At the same time, an official of the Agency for International Development acknowledged that a $9.6 million shipment of vitally needed food supplies (wheat) could not be completed until approval had been given at "the political level."[56]

Secretary of State Alexander Haig justified the aid suspension on the grounds that Nicaragua was providing arms to the guerrillas in El Salvador. Although, according to the State Department, the arms flow has since been halted, the economic funds remain frozen.[57] Furthermore, the Reagan Administration has drastically cut the level of proposed

U.S. economic assistance to Nicaragua during Fiscal Year 1982 (via the Agency for International Development): from $33.2 million proposed by the Carter White House to a mere $13.4 million.[58] Nicaraguan officials have recently expressed growing concern that this policy of economic denial might soon be expanded by Executive branch policy-makers to include efforts to prevent possible large-scale international banking credits from reaching Managua.[59]

Conclusion

In retrospect, the limits on U.S. intervention in the mid and late 1970's in Central America reflected several conjunctural factors. In the case of Nicaragua, to take the most striking example, the extent of mass internal support for the Sandinista regime increased the cost of direct involvement, threatening to bog down the U.S. in an endless policing operation. Diplomatic efforts in the Organization of American States failed to secure regional support for military intervention, while the opposition of Western European and Latin American social democratic and liberal governments (and parties) to U.S. policy threatened to destroy the efforts to reconstruct alliances within the Western world. Given these conjunctural constraints, U.S. policymakers were unable to work in a single channel (direct intervention) or with a simple set of alliance partners: the circumstances dictated flexible, political tactics in pursuit of rigidly set economic imperatives that continue to characterize and shape Executive branch decision-making.

U.S. policy tactics will vary substantially with contexts in which Washington will not always be able to control and dictate its optimal solution. U.S. policymakers will continue to support *viable* dictators: those firmly in control over the population and state apparatus and promoting American economic interests. In periods of *emerging insta-bility*, Washington may support conservative (civilian) factions of the opposition or "reform" military groups *if available*. In highly polarized situations, the U.S. will support reformist-liberal coalitions against revolutionaries *if necessary*. Finally, in strategic areas, the U.S. will directly intervene to prevent social revolution, when lacking any of the previous alternatives. As the cases of Nicaragua and El Salvador illustrate, the forms of U.S. interventionism do not always take the most direct (military occupation) or reactionary (in any absolute sense) direction, but rather reflect the *relatively most reactionary position*, depending on the context.

In Nicaragua, the U.S. attempted to substitute conservative opposition figures for Somoza, preserving the National Guard and preventing a Sandinista victory. This move occurred, however, on the eve of Somoza's overthrow, when virtually all of the major urban centers were under the control of the revolutionary forces. Hence, U.S. policy shifted after July 1979 toward an effort to support and bolster anti-Sandinista and reformist elements within the governing coalition and the society at large—a strategy that is still in operation. The $75 million economic aid package passed by the U.S. Congress and finally released, after months of delay, in September 1980 exemplified the Carter Administration strategy. Nearly two thirds of the funds were stipulated for use by the private sector—reflecting an obvious effort to improve the position of the conservative propertied groups in Nicaraguan society. With the advent of the Reagan presidency, the continuing application of external economic pressures on the Nicaraguan government has been complemented by the provision of increased U.S. military assistance to area dictatorships hostile to the Nicaraguan Revolution.

In El Salvador, the U.S. attempted a preemptive coup: in the face of a profound polarization in which practically all of civil society was ranged against the Romero regime, Washington promoted a center-right coalition in late 1979, coopting liberal Catholics, social democrats and reformist military officials, while maintaining intact the existing state apparatus. The timing of the change in El Salvador was a response to the lesson learned in Nicaragua, where it was impossible to create alternatives in an open insurrectionary situation. Nevertheless, after three months the Salvadorean reformers realized their ineffectiveness and withdrew from the government, forcing the U.S. to call upon the most reactionary wing of the Christian Democratic Party to maintain the fiction of a coalition government. The shift from inflexible dictatorial rule to conservative but "flexible" military control (including openings to conservative civilian politicians) clearly reflected the growing recognition in Washington of the importance of timing its political tactics in gauging its activities vis-à-vis the emerging political and social struggles in the Third World. The current Reagan strategy of promoting the militarization of civil society in order to defeat the popular movement is further evidence of this new tactical sophistication on the part of the imperial state.

A proper conception of U.S. policy toward Central America must follow the multiple tracks which it pursues, as well as its capacity to shift tracks depending on the contextual situation, and depending specifically on the scope and depth of the class struggle. In periods of *individual* protest, Washington will continue to collaborate with the regime, with occasional public criticisms of its "excesses." In situations of *incremental growth* of the opposition, where collective conflicts are local and uncoordinated, it will continue to work with the regime, criticize the lack of tactical flexibility, maintain ties with the civilian conservative opposition and support repression of the revolutionary left. In periods of *mass mobilization*, U.S. policy will be to strengthen the conservative, electoral opposition forces and promote alliances with sectors of the military—and even try to entice opportunistic and unprincipled sectors among the social democrats to isolate the revolutionary left. A coup against the incumbent power holder may be encouraged, and foreign aid and support of reformist policy declarations may accompany the switchover, as long as the revolutionary left is kept out of power and effectively repressed. If these political maneuvers fail and there exists the imminent likelihood of a politico-military victory by a movement led by social revolutionaries—especially in a country designated as "strategic"—the use of a Rapid Deployment Force, or some variation thereof, by the United States cannot be discounted.

Given the rising mass movements, especially in Central America and the Caribbean, and given the increasingly interventionist orientation in the U.S. government, the 1980's promise to be a period of growing confrontation. U.S. interests in preserving or only marginally changing the repressive state apparatuses, and wholehearted U.S. support of the "free market" economic policies in the region, are inevitably in conflict with the broad-based pressure for dismantling the same repressive state structures, nationalizing multinational properties, and redistributing income and other forms of wealth. As the populations of the region change from being passive human rights victims to active protagonists of revolution, the U.S. government shifts from being a "critic of repression" to a promoter of intervention.

NOTES

1. Gert Rosenthal, "Economic Trends in Central America." *CEPAL REVIEW, Second Half of 1978,* p. 47.

2. Ibid.

3. For a discussion of family-based corporate capitalism in Latin America, see Maurice Zeitlin and R. E. Ratcliff, "Research Methods for the Analysis of the Internal Structure of Dominant Classes: The Case of Landlords and Capitalists in Chile." *Latin American Research Review* X, 3 (Winter 1965), pp. 5-61.

4. For a detailed analysis of the U.S. imperial state, see James F. Petras and Morris H. Morley, "The U.S. Imperial State." *REVIEW* (Fernand Braudel Center for the Study of Economies, Historical Systems, and Civilizations) IV, 2 (Fall 1980), pp. 171-222.

5. See "Nicaragua: How the Local Boys Made Good." *Latin American Economic Report* VI, 4 (January 27, 1978), p. 27.

5a. See, for example, Edelberto Torres-Rivas, "The Central American Model of Growth: Crisis for Whom?" *Latin American Perspectives* VII, 2&3 (Spring and Summer 1980), pp. 24-44.

6. See Clifford Kraus, "Guatemala's Indian Wars." *The Nation* (March 14, 1981), p. 306; "Honduras: Land Seizures." *Latin America* IX, 21 (May 30, 1975), p. 165; data from Amnesty International as reprinted in Institute for Policy Studies, *Background Information on the Security Forces in El Salvador and U.S. Military Assistance* (March 1980), p. 2; Inter-American Development Bank, *Nicaragua: Proposed Loan for an Agricultural Recovery Credit Program.* Internal Document, No. PR-1083 (November 25, 1980), p. 5.

7. Gert Rosenthal, op. cit., p. 49.

8. U.S. Department of Commerce, *Survey of Current Business* 45, 8 (September 1965), p. 24, and 52, 11 (November 1972), p. 30.

9. World Bank, Latin America and the Caribbean Regional Office, *Income Distribution and Poverty in Mexico.* Staff Working Paper No. 395 (Washington, D.C., June 1980), pp. 20-22.

10. "El Salvador: One Hundred Years of Crisis on the Land." *Latin American Regional Reports: Mexico & Central America* RM-80-03 (March 21, 1981), p. 5; "El Salvador: Reform Imposed From Above." *Latin American Weekly Report* WR-81-10 (March 6, 1981), p. 10.

11. See Edelberto Torres-Rivas, "Guatemala—Crisis and Political Violence." *NACLA Report on the Americas* XIV, 1 (January-February 1980), p. 20.

12. See "Guatemala: Peasant Massacre." *Latin American Political Report* XII, 22 (June 9, 1978), p. 175; "Guatemala Massacre Points to Growing Peasant Resistance." *Latin American Regional Reports: Mexico & Central America* RM-80-02 (February 15, 1980), pp. 1, 3; "Guatemala: Guerrillas Put the Military in a Sweat." *Latin American Regional Reports: Mexico & Central America* RM-81-01 (January 9, 1981), pp. 5-6.

13. See "El Salvador: Counter-Insurgency Moves Into Overdrive." *Latin American Regional Reports: Mexico & Central America* RM-80-06 (July 11, 1980), p. 5.

14. "Costa Rican Banana Workers Win Big Pay Increases." *Latin American Economic Report* VII, 9 (March 2, 1979), p. 72.

15. "Deepening Crisis Alarms Nicaraguan Private Sector." *Latin American Economic Report* VII, 17 (May 4, 1979), p. 133; "Spotlight on Honduras." *Latin American Regional Reports: Mexico & Central America* RM-80-05 (June 6, 1980), p. 8.

16. World Bank, *El Salvador: An Inquiry Into Urban Poverty.* Internal Document, Report No. 2945-ES (November 5, 1980), p. iii; Harold Jang, "Civil War in El Salvador." *New Left Review* 122 (July-August 1980), p. 15; "Mexico: Fall in Real Wages Threatens Labour Unrest." *Latin American Regional Reports: Mexico & Central America* RM-80-01 (January 11, 1980) p. 5.

17. "Costa Rica: Grapples With Inflation and Labor Problems." *Latin American Economic Report* VII, 33 (August 24, 1979), p. 26.

18. Gert Rosenthal, op. cit., pp. 51-52.

19. See James Petras, "Whither the Nicaraguan Revolution?" *Monthly Review* 31,5 (October 1979), pp. 1-22; Harold Jang, "Behind the Nicaraguan Revolution." *New Left Review* 117 (September-October 1978), pp. 69-89; William M. LeoGrande, "The Revolution in Nicaragua: Another Cuba?" *Foreign Affairs* 58, 1 (Fall 1979), pp. 28-50.

20. See, for example, Harold Jang, "Civil War in El Salvador," op. cit., pp. 3-25.

21. See "Guatemala: Labour Challenge," *Latin American Political Report,* XII, 34 (October 6, 1978), pp. 308-09; "Guatemala: Bus Fare Crisis," *Latin American Political Report* XII, 40 (October 13, 1978), pp. 314-15; "Growing Militancy Provokes Clampdown in Guatemala." *Latin American Economic Report* VI, 46 (November 24, 1978), p. 368.

22. For a well-documented and convincing study of this process in another context, see Maurice Zeitlin, *Revolutionary Politics and the Cuban Working Class* (Princeton, New Jersey: Princeton University Press, 1967).

23. International Labor Organization, *Yearbook of Labor Statistics 1979* (Geneva), p. 616.

24. Harold Jang, op. cit., p. 18; "Deepening Crisis Alarms Nicaraguan Private Sector," op. cit., p. 133; "Spotlight on Honduras," op. cit., p. 8.

25. Karen de Young, "Somoza Legacy: Plundered Economy," *Washington Post* (November 30, 1979), p. A30; "Common Market: Little to Spare in the CACM's Money Box." *Latin American Regional Reports: Mexico & Central America* RM-81-02 (February 13, 1981), p. 8.

26. See U.S. Agency for International Development, *Congressional Presentation. Fiscal Year 1982, Main Volume* (United States International Development Cooperation Agency), pp. 235, 243, 251.

26a. On the terror in Guatemala, see, for example, Jean-Pierre Clerc, "Bananas and Death Squads." Le Monde Supplement of the *Manchester Guardian Weekly* (August 10, 1980), pp. 12, 14, Clifford Kraus, op. cit., pp. 303-07.

27. See James Nelson Goodsell, "IMF Loans to Nicaragua Give Somoza Breathing Space." *Christian Science Monitor* (May 16, 1979), p. 7; Hobart Rowen, "Blumenthal Supports Loan to Nicaragua." *Washington Post* (June 14, 1979), p. D1; Institute for Policy Studies, *Update #2: Background Information on El Salvador and U.S. Military Assistance to Central America* (November 1980), p. 8.

28. See "El Salvador: U.S. Ready To Put Pressure on the Aid Donors," *Latin American Regional Reports: Mexico & Central America* RM-81-03 (March 20, 1981), p. 2.

29. Institute for Policy Studies, op. cit., p. 4.

30. "Problems From the Barrels of Israeli Guns," *Latin American Weekly Report* WR-80-19 (May 16, 1980), p. 9.

31. Institute for Policy Studies, *Update: Background Information on El Salvador and U.S. Military Assistance to Central America* (June 1980), pp. 6-7.

32. Ibid., p. 7.

33. Ibid., p. 8; Institute for Policy Studies, *Update #2 . . .* , op. cit., p. 2; Christopher Dickey, "Political Violence Spreads to Once-Peaceful Honduras, Costa Rica." *Washington Post* (March 29, 1981), p. A16.

34. Institute for Policy Studies, *Update #2 . . .* , op. cit., p. 4.

35. Socorro Jurídico (Legal Aid Office of the Archbishop of El Salvador), *El Salvador* (February 1981), p. 9.

36. Ibid., p. 22.

37. James Petras, op. cit., p. 17.

38. Office of the President-Elect, Washington, D.C., Memorandum to: Ambassador Robert Neumann. From: Pedro A. Sanjuan, State Department Transition Team. *Subject: Interim Report on the Bureau of Inter-American Affairs and Related Bureaus and Policy Areas*, Department of State.

39. Quoted in John M. Goshko, "Reagan State Department Aide Sees 'Nationalistic' Policy." *Washington Post* (December 18, 1980), p. A1.

40. Jeane Kirkpatrick, United Nations Ambassador-designate, quoted in Philip Geyelin, "Human Rights Turnaround." *Washington Post* (December 12, 1980), p. A23.

41. Roger Fontaine, quoted in Warren Hodge, "Reagan Aides, in South America, Say He Would Not Favor Dictators." *New York Times* (September 22, 1980), p. 12.

42. Juan de Onis, "Reagan Aides Promise Salvadoreans More Military Help to Fight Rebels," *New York Times* (November 29, 1980), p. 1.

43. Institute for Policy Studies, *Update #3: Background on U.S. Military Assistance to El Salvador* (January 1980).

44. John M. Goshko and Don Oberdorfer, "U.S. to Send More Aid, Advisers to El Salvador." *Washington Post* (March 3, 1981), pp. A1, A11.

45. Edward Walsh, "Policy on El Salvador Narrowly Survives First Hill Test, 8 to 7." *Washington Post* (March 25, 1981), p. A14.

46. See Edward Walsh, "El Salvador Protests Called 'Orchestrated' Communist Effort." *Washington Post* (March 24, 1981), p. A3. Also see Judith Miller, "15 U.S. Green Berets To Aid Salvadorans." *New York Times* (March 14, 1981), pp. 1, 8.

47. See Ibid.; "Reagan Seeks Big Rise in Military Aid to Latin America." *Latin American Weekly Report* WR-81-14 (April 3, 1981), p. 5.

48. Excerpts from Transcript of an interview with President Reagan by Lou Cannon and Lee Lescaze, *Washington Post* (March 29, 1981), p. A6.

49. Edward Walsh, "Policy on El Salvador Narrowly Survives First Hill Test, 8 to 7," op. cit., p. A14; "Reagan Seeks Big Rise in Military Aid to Latin America," op. cit., p. 5.

50. See "El Salvador: U.S. Ready To Put Pressure on the Aid Donors," op. cit., p. 2.

51. Alan Riding, "Ally of Honduran Army Expects U.S. Right-Face." *New York Times* (April 15, 1981), p. 2; "Reagan Seeks Big Rise in Military Aid to Latin America," op. cit., p. 5.

52. See "Guatemala: Army Steps Up Its Terror," *Latin American Regional Reports: Mexico & Central America* RM-81-03 (March 20, 1981), p. 3.

53. "Guatemala: A Government Program of Political Murder—The Amnesty Report (Extracts)." *The New York Review of Books* (March 19, 1981), p. 38.

54. Quoted in Alan Riding, "Nicaragua Seeking Accord in El Salvador." *New York Times* (February 12, 1981), p. 11.

55. See Juan de Onis, "U.S. Halts Nicaraguan Aid Over Help for Guerrillas." *New York Times* (January 23, 1981), p. 1.

56. Quoted in Juan de Onis, "Wheat Sale to Nicaragua Delayed." *New York Times* (February 11, 1981), p. 4.

57. See "U.S. Halts Economic Aid to Nicaragua." *New York Times* (April 2, 1981), p. 3, Edward Walsh, "U.S. Economic Aid to Nicaragua Suspended But May Be Resumed." *Washington Post* (April 2, 1981), p. A2.

58. See "Reagan Seeks Big Rise in Military Aid to Latin America," op. cit., p. 5.

59. See, for example, "Nicaraguans Prepare Themselves for the Gathering Storm." *Latin American Weekly Report* WR-81-15 (April 10, 1981), pp. 1-2.

The New Cold War and the Nicaraguan Revolution: The Case of U.S. "Aid" to Nicaragua

Susanne Jonas

In the first year and a half after the victory of the Frente Sandinista de Liberación Nacional in Nicaragua, an intense drama unfolded in the highest circles of the U.S. government. Both the Carter Administration (in its last 18 months in office) and Congress were locked in a fierce debate over U.S. policy toward Nicaragua, focusing on a proposed $75 million "aid" package. During the course of the debate, the House of Representatives twice went into secret session—for the first time in 149 years—to discuss Cuban influence and the possibility of "another Cuba" in Nicaragua. The highest officials of the Carter Administration and leading Congressmen testified during the debate, and, as a precondition for releasing the aid funds, the President himself was instructed to verify every three months that Nicaragua was not aiding revolutionary movements in other countries. Because of this debate, the aid to Nicaragua was held up for an entire year.

The Nicaragua aid debate, which pitted transnational bankers against right-wing militarists, was not an isolated phenomenon. It was a drama of the new Cold War which had been aggressively and deliberately revived by the U.S. ruling class in mid-1979. It was in many respects a compressed version of a larger debate in U.S. policy circles: how the United States should exercise its declining power in the world today— whether to continue pretending to wield unilateral power or to make certain pragmatic adjustments to the reality of eroded U.S. power—and how to pursue a Cold War interventionist stance in the hemisphere.

In historical perspective, particularly in the light of the more aggressive and adventurist policies of the Reagan Administration, it would seem that the Carter Administration was moderate in dealing with the Sandinista government. Nevertheless, the Carter policy toward Nicaragua must be seen in the broader context of the revival of a Cold War U.S. foreign policy in 1979-80, which was a foreign policy of the entire U.S. ruling class. To be sure, the U.S. ruling class is not monolithic; it is composed of different blocs or fractions, principally the trans-national interests represented by the Trilateral Commission and Carter, and a domestic fraction tied into the military-industrial complex (although all fractions rely on U.S. military power to achieve their goals). These fractions contend and cooperate in the formation of U.S. foreign policy. Although they diverge on a number of points, they appear to have been converging in 1979-80 in regard to the abandonment of detente, the revival of the Cold War and some form of interventionism abroad, combined with the imposition of austerity policies within the United States.

This apparent convergence was a most dangerous development for the people of the United States, as well as for Latin America. A majority of Americans opposed Cold War interventionism after Vietnam, and recognized that overall such policies harmed more than they benefited the American people and the American economy (except insofar as increased military spending means a bailout for military industries). There is no clearer example than the balance of payments crisis caused by the Vietnam War.

Therefore, if we use the term "U.S. imperialism" in reference to the Cold War policies of the U.S. government, we must be clear that this refers solely to the ability of the various fractions of the U.S. *ruling class* to set foreign and military policy. In fact, their anti-Soviet, Cold War rhetoric is an attempt by the ruling class to win over the American people to policies that do not benefit them (interventionism abroad, austerity at home), in order to justify *increased* military spending at a time of economic crisis, austerity, and *reduced* spending to meet domestic needs.

The Decline of U.S. Power and
The Consolidation of a New Cold War Policy

Let us begin by examining briefly the global situation of U.S. power.[1] The United States has seen its power seriously undermined since the late 1960's by internal and international capitalist crisis. By the 1980's, it is not the U.S. or any other *national* economy which is the principal locus of imperialism, but giant transnational corporations and banks. The dominant economic force is the drive for capital accu-mulation by these corporate giants that rule the capitalist world-economy. The ruling class within a particular nation and its military arsenal may be used to serve transnational interests, but these trans-nationals know no single national constituency; their interest lies in their own capital accumulation, and comes into frequent contradiction with the needs of the national economy.

Thus the "international capitalist crisis" is a crisis not for the transnational corporations or banks, but in the national economies of the Western capitalist powers, most notably the United States. The crisis, which began in the late 1960's and gave rise to a full-fledged recession in the United States by 1973-75, was manifested concretely as a profit squeeze for large domestic industries. In order to restore their profit margin, these industries have moved to transfer their accumulation crisis to the U.S. working class through the imposition of *austerity* policies (long pursued in the Third World). Austerity for U.S. workers has meant a deliberate campaign to reduce the social programs and benefits returned to the working class from the taxes they pay, and more specifically: no real controls on price inflation, reduction in real wages; layoffs and planned unemployment; and across-the-board cutbacks in necessary and basic social services.

The transnational corporations have responded to international capitalist crisis in their own way, by restructuring the international division of labor[2] (for example, relocating industrial production from the "core" capitalist countries to the underdeveloped countries of the periphery and semi-periphery where, above all, they have access to unlimited supplies of cheap labor). This shift gives rise to the proliferation of "runaway shops" and means rising unemployment, lower wages and living standards, and reduced political rights for the working classes in the core countries. Thus, the response of the transnationals further intensifies the crisis of the national core capitalist economies and the imposition of austerity upon the working classes in those countries.

Internal economic crisis has been matched by the decline of U.S. hegemony internationally, particularly since the U.S. defeat in Vietnam. This decline has meant, first, the intensification of inter-imperialist rivalry between the United States and the other Western capitalist powers (Western Europe and Japan). The fraction of the U.S. ruling class most deeply rooted in transnational capital has attempted to hold together the "Western alliance," for example through the Trilateral Commission. Over time, however, the Trilateral alliance has been subjected to increasing strains, as the U.S. ruling class is less able to coordinate international capitalist interests or to maintain hegemony over its counterparts in Europe and Japan (who have their own priorities, including preservation of *their* detente with the Soviet Union).

Second, the direct challenge to U.S. power worldwide has come from escalating resistance by oppressed and exploited peoples in the "Third World." The United States emerged from the Vietnam War drained, isolated and defeated. Yet the potential for "more Vietnams" existed in many parts of the world, including Central America.

International decline has meant that the U.S. ruling class no longer has the power to set the terms of its relations with other countries unilaterally. U.S. options are more limited, and the United States is less able to force its will unrestrainedly on other nations through instant military interventions, as it did, for example, in Guatemala in 1954, in the Congo in 1961, in the Dominican Republic in 1965. Beyond

Vietnam, the United States had to accept the overthrow of its long-standing puppet Somoza, and the victory of a progressive, nationalist, Marxist-led revolution in Nicaragua, a country long viewed as "our own backyard." In other parts of the world as well, the United States had to make concessions.

Particularly since the U.S. ruling class has always regarded Latin America as its natural sphere of domination, the response to defeats elsewhere was an intensified effort to preserve U.S. hegemony in Latin America. The brutal overthrow of the Allende government and installation of a right-wing regime in Chile was only the most extreme example. In numerous other countries, such as Guatemala and Argentina, U.S. imperialism has shown its shameless brutality in supporting, indeed instructing and training, the right-wing butchers.

After the U.S. defeat in Vietnam, with the lack of domestic support for foreign intervention, and with increasing isolation internationally, the U.S. ruling class had to make certain adjustments in its foreign policy. Tactically, in order to regain lost prestige internally and internationally, and in order to reconstitute its ability *long-range* to intervene in the Third World, the United States had to project a short-range policy of nonintervention and detente with the Soviet Union. At the same time, after 1976, Carter/Brzezinski went on the offensive against the Soviet Union by criticizing "human rights violations" there. But they could not call for "human rights" in the Soviet Union without making a show of advocating human rights elsewhere, hence, Carter's "human rights policy" in Latin America. In fact, this represented no real commitment to human rights; it was a tactical adjustment to new realities in the world— a short-range concession in order to preserve U.S. options long-range[3] —and a platform for attacking the Soviet Union.

This shift and the years of detente did create, for a short time, a less dangerous, less interventionist, international climate. In some sense, the Nicaraguan people benefited indirectly from this opening; they won their victory at a time when the United States was constrained from intervening militarily to stop the overthrow of Somoza. However, the ephemeral nature of this opening, and the fact that it was always tactical rather than long-range U.S. policy, became clear in the increasingly provocative policies of the U.S. government after mid-1979, the deliberate revival of the Cold War with the Soviet Union[4].

An early sign of Washington's increasingly aggressive posture was the drummed-up "crisis" over the "discovery" of Soviet troops in Cuba in mid-1979 — troops which, by Carter's own admission, had been there for at least several years. This became the pretext for an escalating program to reestablish U.S. military hegemony in the Caribbean and Central America. More broadly, it was an opening shot in the Carter Administration's global Cold War offensive. In October 1979, Carter provoked the crisis in Iran and used this opportunity to rattle the U.S.

saber (as well as to override domestic opposition to U.S. intervention abroad by whipping up "patriotic" fervor).

Subsequently, the Carter Administration continued its deliberate provocations of the Soviet Union (new nuclear missiles in Western Europe, shelving of the SALT II Treaty, a greatly increased military budget, etc.). In addition, the United States continued to solidify an anti-Soviet alliance and "encirclement" policy with the People's Republic of China. These provocations threatened to elicit a less moderate response from the Soviet Union, which had previously pursued a policy of detente; concretely, they set the stage for the Soviet intervention in Afghanistan, which in turn gave the U.S. ruling class a new opportunity to heat up the war machine and to fan the flames of anti-Soviet hysteria.

Thus, Carter's foreign policy in 1979-80 catapulted the United States from an era of detente into an era of Cold War, an era of increasing instability, unpredictability, and brinksmanship. The "Carter Doctrine" reflected the U.S. government's desire to undertake an anti-Soviet offensive, and to assert U.S. power, *precisely at a time when actual U.S. power worldwide is declining*. Because U.S. power is in fact limited and declining, this offensive has been more provocative, less controlled, less predictable. Once again, the U.S. ruling class has been willing to intervene abroad and literally to threaten world peace, using the Soviet Union as a scapegoat.

The Policy Debate Over U.S. "Aid" to Nicaragua

During the year and a half following the victory of the Sandinistas, U.S. policy toward Nicaragua was the subject of intense debate. After having their way for over 40 years, the advocates of overt U.S. military intervention to keep the right-wing Somoza dictatorship in power were temporarily silenced in the summer of 1979—not out of any change of heart by the U.S. ruling class, but rather out of necessity, a necessity imposed by the military victory of the revolutionary Frente Sandinista over the Somoza dictatorship. These circumstances forced a reappraisal in Washington, and presented the opportunity for a different breed of interventionists to be heard— the soft-line interventionists. These officials, represented most clearly by former Assistant Secretary of State for Inter-American Affairs Viron Vaky and his successor, William Bowdler, sought to prevent "another Cuba" in Nicaragua (and "another Nicaragua" in El Salvador) by giving conditioned U.S. economic aid. Elsewhere in Latin America, they advocated creating a "democratic opening" in the most repressive regimes. The goal of the soft-line interventionists was the same in all cases: to recoup or at least to minimize the losses of U.S. power. Their principal weapon was not the machine gun but the dollar.

The weapon of the dollar was particularly powerful because at the time of the Sandinista victory, the Nicaraguan economy was in ruins and required massive international aid. Somoza had maintained the country in a state of underdevelopment for years, and waged a brutal war against the Frente Sandinista which left a number of towns utterly destroyed and 70% of industry damaged or destroyed. Physical damage from the war was estimated at $600 million, with an additional $500 million or more in capital flight because of the war. When Somoza fled the country, he left barely $3.5 million in international reserves. Unemployment had reached 34% in Managua, higher elsewhere, with an additional 25% underemployment. Eight hundred thousand people, more than one-fourth of the population, needed daily food handouts.[5]

Clearly, the job of reconstructing a devastated country required massive international aid, and the Nicaraguan government sought $2.5 billion in aid from a wide variety of sources, including the United States.[6] The Carter Administration responded with various small loans and grants, and with a longer-range proposal of $75 million for Nicaragua as part of the overall foreign aid bill for Fiscal Year 1981. This sparked an intense, months-long debate within the Carter Administration and within the U.S. Congress.

Before tracing the details of this debate, let us see briefly who were the main players and what interests they represented. The Carter Administration was itself divided, with a number of State Department officials such as Vaky and Bowdler taking the "accommodationist" view toward Nicaragua, while others in the Pentagon and intelligence agencies took a "hard-line" approach. Behind the "accommodationists," on the one hand, was a significant chunk of transnational banking capital (which, as we shall see, had its own interests in controlling U.S. relations with Nicaragua) and the major Eastern newspapers (*New York Times, Washington Post*, etc., which carried numerous editorials supporting aid to Nicaragua). Aligned with the hard-liners, on the other hand, was a vocal right-wing bloc in Congress, whose goal was to stop U.S. aid to Nicaragua altogether—or to impose so many conditions as to make U.S. aid unacceptable to the Nicaraguan government. As we shall see, they were able to make great headway toward achieving that latter goal.

Lest the intensity of the debate obscure the underlying unity of objectives, let us be clear from the outset: all parties were in agreement that the United States must preserve maximum control over Nicaragua (within the context of declining U.S. power worldwide); the debate was merely about *how* best to achieve that objective. Because the stakes were high, the tactical debate was intense, but at no time was this underlying objective ever questioned.

From the very beginning, an underlying issue in U.S. policy circles was not simply Nicaragua, but Cuba (and, by extension, the Soviet Union): how to stop Cuban assistance to Nicaragua, how to prevent Nicaragua from following the "Cuban model," how to counter Cuban training of Frente leadership, "Cuban troops" on Nicaraguan soil, etc., etc. Or at least, so it seemed in the Congressional debate; in fact, the international bankers had other objectives as well.

Thus, when President Carter presented the aid request to Congress in late 1979, the right wing lost no time in launching a counteroffensive. In response to the dominant position within the Administration that the United States could only keep control over future developments in Nicaragua (and keep Nicaragua out of the Cuban/Soviet camp) by giving U.S. aid, the right wing argued that it was already too late for any real U.S. influence, and U.S. funds would only aid the consolidation of a pro-Cuban, Marxist regime; therefore, the United States must move directly to overthrow that regime, and certainly must send no aid.

After Carter submitted the request for $75 million in U.S. "aid" (of which $70 million was credits to buy U.S. goods, and only $5 million a grant),[7] the Senate Foreign Relations Committee approved the aid package, and the House Foreign Affairs Committee approved it after attaching a condition requiring Carter to cut off aid if Cuban or Soviet combat troops were found in Nicaragua.[8] The bill was approved on the floor of the Senate in January 1980. When it came to the floor of the House in February, the House convened a highly unusual two-hour secret session (for the second time since 1830—the first being in June 1979, also on Cuban influence in Nicaragua) to hear testimony on classified documents as to whether Nicaragua had become "Cuba-like." After this unprecedented session, the bill was passed in the House by a thin five-vote margin, and with several onerous conditions attached:[9]

First, the legislation itself contained a stipulation that 60% of the aid go to the private business sector—the idea being to strengthen the influence of the private sector in the new regime and in the economy. Those funds would not go to the public sector, which is controlled by the popular government, but rather to private businessmen.

Second, the House added a stipulation making the aid conditional on Nicaragua's "overall human rights performance," and on the holding of elections within a "reasonable period of time." This of course could become a ready-made justification for cutting off aid and possibly intervening in the future. This stipulation calls to mind the Marshall Plan in Western Europe after World War II, in which U.S. "aid" was tied to the purging of elected socialists from office. In fact, one U.S. businessman spoke of Nicaragua's need for a "Marshall Plan."[10]

A third condition placed on the $75 million package was that the funds could not be used in facilities with Cuban personnel. This meant that, at a time when the literacy campaign was a principal national priority, no U.S. funds could be used in schools or educational facilities where there were Cuban volunteers or technicians, as would be likely, given Cuba's extended experience with such campaigns.

A fourth condition prohibited Nicaraguan involvement with "international terrorism or attempts to subvert other governments," or the presence of Soviet or Cuban combat troops in Nicaragua.[11]

The Nicaraguan government and people reacted angrily to these conditions. On the one hand, they needed approval of the aid—not so much because of the amount (which, as many have pointed out, was almost insignificant compared with Nicaragua's needs)—but because international banking sources were holding up some $500 million in additional international funds for Nicaragua until passage of the aid bill as a "signal of U.S. confidence in the stability of Nicaragua."[12] On the other hand, the conditions imposed amounted to blackmail. Junta member Sergio Ramírez contrasted U.S. aid with that of other countries:

> We think of the revolutionary generosity of that poor but proud people [Grenada], who gave us what they had. [If the U.S. were to offer a per capita equivalent, it would mean] not $75 million, but $7.5 billion—and without conditions.[13]

Twenty thousand Nicaraguans marched in the streets to protest the conditions on the U.S. aid. The Nicaraguan government indicated that it would study the aid package in its final form before deciding whether to accept it—and meanwhile negotiated new trade and technical agreements with the Soviet Union[14] and Eastern European countries, as well as with Western Europe, all of which was "absolutely without conditions."

In April, the situation took a new turn, with the resignation of businessman and political "moderate" Alfonso Robelo from the government junta. Conservatives in Nicaragua, consulting with the U.S. Ambassador,[15] seized the opportunity to renew their clamor for "pluralism" and representation for the private sector in the government. Conservatives in Washington seized upon the Robelo resignation and the Nicaraguan government's agreements with the Soviet Union and Eastern Europe to continue their efforts to stall or kill the U.S. aid bill. Speaker of the U.S. House of Representatives, Tip O'Neill, stated publicly that there was concern about Nicaragua becoming a "Marxist state," and that Congress would not approve the Nicaragua aid bill "unless they have a bipartisan government down there"[16] (meaning, unless the private sector representatives were appointed to the government). The State Department declared that Nicaragua's agreements with the Soviet Union "clearly signalled" a Soviet move to expand its influence in Nicaragua. Others went further, pointing to the agreements as evidence of "a Soviet plan to communize Central America and use that land bridge as a dagger pointing north and south. . . ."[17]

These pressures were somewhat relieved when the Sandinista leadership, while denouncing U.S. "blackmail," appointed two new "moderates" to the Junta. In Washington, the Senate accepted the House version of the aid bill with all the new conditions. The House voted to approve the measure, after Carter had a top-level Congressional delegation visit Nicaragua; Speaker O'Neill, in his first foreign aid speech in 28 years, and Majority Leader Jim Wright pushed through the bill, after 9 hours of debate on the House floor.[18] The final version of the bill required President Carter to report every three months "on the state of Nicaraguan democracy" and to give assurances that Nicaragua was not aiding revolutionary movements in other countries.[19] In signing the authorization measure, Carter declared the U.S. intention to resist "interference" by Cuba "and others."[20]

However, only the first stage of the battle was over, for the funds still had to be appropriated by Congress. New pressures began building up for the Nicaraguan government to announce a date for "free elections." In July, the Republican Party platform directly attacked the "Marxist Sandinista takeover of Nicaragua," opposed the Carter aid program, and stated support for any movement to overthrow the Sandinista government.[21] In August, there were reports that conservative groups within the Carter Administration (the intelligence agencies and the Pentagon) were trying to stop appropriation and disbursement of the aid until after the November elections in the United States, when the whole aid package could be canceled by a Reagan Administration— and that these officials were deliberately leaking information (to the Evans and Novak column, published August 1, 1980), portraying Nicaragua as a "Soviet and Cuban puppet, supplying arms to Communist insurgents in neighboring El Salvador."[22] The Carter Administration complied with the Congressionally required investigation, and on September 12, 1980, reported that the Nicaraguan government was not supporting violence or terrorism in Central America (as opposed to right-wing allegations that Nicaragua was shipping Cuban arms to other countries.[23] The path was finally cleared for Congressional release of the $75 million, and the final agreement releasing the funds was signed with the Nicaraguan government in October. Thus ended, at least temporarily, the year-long Nicaragua aid debate.

The Hidden Actors: The Transnational Banks

What were the goals of the pro-aid forces, the soft-line interventionists? And who were they, really? Throughout the debate, the dominant force in the Carter Administration argued that U.S. aid must be given to keep Nicaragua out of the Cuban/Soviet camp, and that the long delay in Congressional approval of the aid was having a "radicalizing impact" on Nicaragua.[24] On the surface, the goals of the soft-line interventionists in the State Department were:

—to shore up the political role of Nicaragua's "moderates" and businessmen and to assure a future political role for non-Sandinistas;
—to preserve the role of the private sector in the economy and maintain a "mixed economy," rather than follow the "Cuban model" of socialism;
—to prevent Nicaragua from lining up internationally in the Soviet camp;
—to exert pressure to get Cuban technicians out of Nicaragua.

To be sure, these political goals were important. But there was another hidden force which provides the key to the Carter/Trilateral strategy:

> Pressure on the Administration to help Nicaragua has come from a consortium of U.S. banks, which recently negotiated a refinancing of $600 million of Nicaragua's debt.[25]

In fact, Carter released the U.S. aid only after Nicaragua reached an agreement with the private banks.[26]

Here, finally, we find the key to the mystery— the counterforce strong enough to resist the political/military right-wing forces. Just at the time that Carter was presenting the foreign aid bill to Congress, this consortium of the capitalist world's largest transnational banks was beginning a long series of negotiations with the Nicaraguan government to reschedule payment on the staggering foreign debt left by Somoza. All in all, this was a debt of over $1.6 billion. More than $618 million was due by the end of 1979 (more than the total value of Nicaraguan exports), of which $444 million or 70% was owed to private foreign banks;[27] 75% of the foreign debt was owed to U.S.-based banks.[28] According to the U.N. Economic Commission on Latin America, Somoza had deliberately designed this private debt so that most of it could be drained from Nicaragua, rather than being invested there![29]

Talks between the Nicaraguan government and a steering committee of 13 bankers representing 90 creditor banks began informally in the winter of 1979-80. The meetings continued in March, with the Nicaraguan government attempting a) to obtain a grace period for repayments; and b) as against the pressures of the international bankers, to keep the International Monetary Fund (IMF) out of the picture. As one official stated, "It is not for us to involve the IMF at this stage and to get involved in an austerity program"; in the words of another, ". . . we consider that the IMF has no role to play in the formation of economic policy."[30] Later in 1980, the issue of the IMF did block an agreement between the Nicaraguan government and the "Paris Club," which represented Western governments to which Nicaragua owed most of its $250 million bilateral debt: the United States insisted that Nicaragua open discussions with the IMF, and Nicaragua refused to do so under such pressure.[31] After nine months of talks (and a last-minute ploy by Citibank of New York, the largest creditor, to push for annual debt-service payments, beginning in 1980, of more than 30% of Nicaragua's 1980 export revenues!), an agreement was reached in September, rescheduling the $582 million due in 1980 for repayment at commercial rates over the next 12 years.[32] Nicaragua succeeded in keeping the IMF out of the agreement and gaining a five-year grace period, but the banks had Nicaragua's agreement to repay all of the Somoza regime's debts, at commercial (not concessionary) rates.[33]

Now it is clear why the banks pressured the Carter Administration not to bow to right-wing political pressure to delay U.S. aid until after the November election:[34] at the moment when they were successfully completing their own negotiations with Nicaragua, the banks had a great stake in not allowing the apple cart of U.S. aid to Nicaragua to be upset.

Why did the transnational banks care so much about their negotiations with Nicaragua? First, they saw the issue as much larger than Nicaragua itself, as a kind of test case: they wanted to establish a clear precedent of a revolutionary government not defaulting (in contrast to Cuba some years earlier), and of agreement to pay the debt at commercial rates, even under the outrageous circumstances of a staggering debt accumulated *by Somoza*, primarily for his own gain, and on which Somoza had defaulted after the fall of 1978. Such a precedent would serve them well in their negotiations with other countries ranging from Bolivia, Brazil and Jamaica to Poland, Sudan and Turkey. As one banker stated, the Nicaragua settlement "could make it more palatable for other countries to go the rescheduling route."[35]

Second, the banks and their political spokesmen had a strategy *for Nicaragua*. In a situation where the Nicaraguan government began with only $3.5 million total in international reserves, whatever paltry reserves could be accumulated through international aid would have to be used for paying off the international banks for loans made *to the Somoza regime*, rather than for meeting Nicaragua's domestic needs for the coming years—reconstruction of a devastated economy, creation of 90,000 new jobs, stimulation of economic growth, and reduction of inflation from 60% to 20%. The Nicaraguan government accepted this intolerable burden for one simple reason: without doing so, they would have faced closed doors for all short- and medium-term credit from international banks in the capitalist world. (In fact, the banks did refuse to extend any new credits to the Nicaraguan government until the rescheduling negotiations were concluded.)[36] This would have left no option other than massive aid from the Soviet bloc; and it is questionable whether the Soviet Union would have undertaken such a responsibility for a second time in the Western hemisphere.

This unspeakable situation had political ramifications as well: it meant that the Sandinista government was forced into the position of imposing austerity upon the Nicaraguan people as the price of their liberation, of asking the Nicaraguan people, who had fought and died for a better life, to suffer and sacrifice still more, so that the international banks could be paid off. As soon as the government made its first move in this direction, by limiting the end-of-year bonus for workers to $150 at the end of 1979, the middle class had its golden opportunity to begin its protest against the government. (Now we can see why the Nicaraguans so strongly opposed IMF involvement, which would have meant a *formal* austerity plan.)

More broadly, and over a longer range, this situation gave the international bankers a lever to exert pressure upon and squeeze the new government—and then to wait for the discontent bred by the necessary austerity measures to erupt into anti-government demonstrations (along the lines of the middle class women's "March of the Empty Pots" against Allende in Chile) and eventually perhaps a Chile-style counterrevolution.

Thus, transnational capital may be seen to have adopted a strategy which *appeared* less direct than the militarists', but which was every bit as hostile in attempting to undermine and destabilize (and eventually to "moderate" or get rid of) the Sandinista government. The new gnomes of international finance capital are indeed the *patient interventionists*, but not one whit less interventionist than the shrill right-wing Congressmen in Washington. Their concern (and it was clearly communicated to Carter, we may speculate via the Trilateral Commission) was above all to assure that U.S.-Nicaraguan relations were not interrupted too early, which might prompt the Nicaraguan government to pull out of the debt renegotiations and refuse to repay Somoza's loans.

This, then, was an important source of the policy of the "soft-liners" in Washington, who were arguing publicly that the U.S. must maintain good relations with Nicaragua, aid Nicaragua, etc. Underneath the Carter position lay the determination to get hard cash repayments, and politically, over the long range, to undermine and destabilize the Sandinista government through austerity policies which would turn the middle class against the government.

Thus the transnational banks presented Nicaragua with a serious political problem. In a situation where either compliance (paying off the huge Somoza debt) or resistance (resulting in no new credits or aid) would result in austerity for the Nicaraguan people, why did the Nicaraguan government play the game of the international bankers, and what other options did it have? As the Nicaraguan government knew only too well, there was no easy answer: this was the dilemma that Cuba had faced nearly 20 years earlier, this was the vise which ultimately brought the Allende government in Chile to its knees (the U.S./transnational bank credit blockade, which laid the groundwork for austerity and the 1973 coup). Other than transnational capital, there was only the Soviet bloc (the option chosen by Cuba), or a larger bloc of Central American/Caribbean/eventually Latin American nations, once they were liberated. The latter is, of course, the "domino" specter that haunts the U.S. ruling class—which is precisely the reason for the phobia about Nicaragua aiding revolutionary movements in other countries, and the reason why, even as he signed the Nicaragua aid measure, Carter also increased U.S. aid to El Salvador to $72 million, to prevent "another Nicaragua" there.[37] Clearly, the future options of the Nicaraguan Revolution would be profoundly affected by the struggles in other countries, especially in Central America.

Conclusion:
Prospects Under the Reagan Administration

While the Carter Administration was forced to permit the Sandinista victory in July 1979 — it was too late to do anything else — no wing of the U.S. ruling class necessarily accepted the Sandinista regime, long-range. Particularly if we remember the history of solid U.S. support for the Somoza dictatorship for nearly 45 years (primarily under Democratic administrations), and U.S. opposition to the Sandinista victory up to the very last minute (attempting to preserve the National Guard, to send an OAS "peacekeeping force," to form a "moderate government" and isolate the Frente), we must expect the U.S. government to make trouble in Nicaragua, secretly or openly, directly or indirectly. All the more so under an openly hostile Reagan Administration.

In the early months of the Reagan Administration, it is not yet clear exactly what the United States can or will do in Nicaragua, but there are some indications. It seems relatively clear that the Reagan Administration will not continue U.S. government aid to Nicaragua, also in question is future aid from U.S.-dominated multilateral agencies. The Republican Party platform in the summer of 1980 stated opposition to the Carter Administration's aid program to Nicaragua, and subsequently this position was maintained, with Reagan spokesmen stating that aid to Nicaragua would do the U.S. no good, as it would not really go to the private sector or diminish the dominant role of the "Marxist Sandinistas."[38]

In the last days of the transition from the Carter Administration to the Reagan Administration, using the pretext that Nicaragua was "supplying arms to the guerrillas in El Salvador," the U.S. government suspended aid payments and food shipments to Nicaragua and gave Nicaragua 30 days to stop the arms flow. On April 1, 1981, the Reagan Administration formally cut off U.S. aid, and left open for the future threats to demand immediate repayment of the $60 million already disbursed to Nicaragua and to pressure international aid agencies and international banks to decrease their lending to Nicaragua.

To justify these actions U.S. officials cited "intelligence reports" which supposedly showed the "entry of men and arms from Nicaragua [to El Salvador] as well as clandestine training camps and rebel radio stations in Nicaraguan territory."[39] In subsequent reports, however, senior U.S. officials indicated that they lacked hard information about the real situation in El Salvador, and had no proof of any official Nicaraguan involvement.[40] The Nicaraguan government categorically denied the U.S. allegations and maintained that the documents were a "CIA fabrication,"[41] and that the U.S. aid cutoff amounted to "economic warfare" and "economic aggression."[42]

In fact, the U.S. aid cutoff came shortly after State Department claims that Nicaragua had halted the flow of arms to El Salvador in response to U.S. pressure—claims, in effect, that the economic blackmail had worked. This raises serious questions as to U.S. intentions in its pressure games with Nicaragua. In the first place, the U.S. "evidence" that Nicaragua was *ever* involved in El Salvador was highly suspect. In the second place, even the U.S. acknowledged by April that Nicaragua was *no longer* involved in El Salvador. Thus we may conclude that the issue of shipping arms to El Salvador was sheer pretext all along, and that the real purpose of these pressures and of the aid cutoff was to bring greater hardship on the Sandinista government. In fact, according to reports in March, the real issue was "Nicaragua's close relationship with Cuba and the insistence of powerful U.S. foreign policy conservatives that the government is already too far to the left to merit assistance."[43] (Secretary of State Alexander Haig even went so far as to declare publicly that the Nicaraguan Revolution was the first phase of a Soviet plan ["hit list"] to dominate Central America.)[44]

A second, related aspect of the Reagan policies is political destabilization in Nicaragua. The 1980 Republican platform stated, "We will support the efforts of the Nicaraguan people to establish a free and independent government," (i.e., to overthrow the Sandinista government). Even before the 1980 U.S. election, Reagan representatives were reported to have held discussions with possible leaders of a movement to overthrow the Nicaraguan government. The U.S. aid cutoff in April "encouraged right-wing Nicaraguan exiles to step up attacks from inside Honduras and to start planning a full-scale invasion" of Nicaragua, and there was widespread belief that Washington will "soon provide covert aid to topple the Sandinistas."[45] Nicaraguan exiles (including former members of Somoza's National Guard) were also being trained in camps run by Cuban exiles outside Miami, possibly with CIA or Pentagon support.[46] According to the *New York Times*, "Some State Department officials are also known to favor a policy of first 'strangling' the Sandinista government economically and then . . . 'financing dissent groups'."[47] In the face of these indications of U.S. support for counter-revolutionary movements, the Nicaraguan government began training a popular militia of 200,000 to resist any invasion.

Third, simultaneously, the Reagan Administration greatly increased military aid to right-wing governments surrounding Nicaragua, in El Salvador, Guatemala and Honduras; and in the wake of the Reagan victory, right-wing forces throughout Central America have gone on an all-out offensive. Reagan advisers have talked openly of a regional "Truman Doctrine solution" for Central America, using as a model U.S. policy toward Greece after World War II (i.e., massive economic and military aid to Guatemala and El Salvador, combined with sending U.S. military advisers).[48] Exactly what this will mean for Nicaragua is not clear. At the very least, it means militarily strengthening the hostile neighboring governments to "contain" Nicaragua's influence. At worst, it could portend direct aid to Somocista exiles in neighboring countries,[49] and/or an overt move to overthrow the government, similar to the overthrow of the Arbenz government in Guatemala in 1954. In this regard, there is also the question of what would be the effect on Nicaragua of a possible U.S. intervention in a neighboring country (most likely El Salvador)—and whether Nicaragua might be the indirect target of such an intervention.

Despite these initial indications of Reagan policy, the Reagan Administration in office will have to deal with the real constraints on U.S. power, those same constraints that faced the Carter Administration. For one thing, a number of Western European governments, including the formerly staunch U.S. ally West Germany, have moved toward an open break with U.S. policies in Central America: the European-based social democratic movements had refused to go along with U.S. maneuvering to keep Somoza in power and aided the revolutionaries; and in 1979-80, they continued to pursue their own interests and policies in Central America, which did not coincide with those of the United States.[50] In addition, some Latin American governments, primarily the Mexican, went on record as warning the United States not to intervene in Central America.[51] Although this hardly constitutes a military deterrent to U.S. action, it does raise the political issues which are likely to become the subject of debate within the Reagan Administration: what would be the political costs of an isolated U.S. intervention in Central America?

In addition, there are political considerations stemming from the situation within Nicaragua. The Nicaraguan people are organized and armed; unlike Allende's Chile, the army is in the hands of the Revolution. If the United States were to send the Marines or attempt some other form of military intervention, the Nicaraguan people could and would defend their revolution. Moreover, the net result of such an intervention would most likely be to radicalize the Nicaraguan Revolution and to hasten the march toward socialism (similar to the overall effect of the U.S. Bay of Pigs invasion of Cuba in 1961). Indeed, even the talk of U.S. intervention as a possibility can only serve to further polarize an already unstable situation within Nicaragua.

Finally, Reagan faces problems of anti-interventionist sentiment within the United States. A June 1979 poll indicated that two-thirds of the American public opposed the Somoza regime; and an October 1980 poll showed that 60% of all men and 68% of all women "opposed the use of U.S. military force in trouble-spots in developing countries."[52] By the end of March 1981, polls showed that only one-third of the American people believed the U.S. should continue to support the Salvadorean government, and two-thirds of "informed Americans" feared another Vietnam in El Salvador.[53]

Thus, the Reagan Administration faces a complex situation in Nicaragua, with many of the same constraints that Carter faced still operative. And within the Reagan Administration, representatives of the Trilateral Commission (e.g., Vice President Bush) are jockeying for power with the more vociferous right-wing militarists. Certainly, the international bankers who worked so hard to get an agreement with Nicaragua on debt repayments are not likely to agree readily to adventurist policies, and can be expected to play some role in moderating Reagan policies. For all these reasons, it would be an oversimplification to draw a sharp line demarcating Carter policy from Reagan policy. The Carter Administration, as we have seen, was bitterly divided, with "hard-liners" playing a significant role at times. As a number of dissidents within the Carter foreign policy apparatus stated in their November 1980 "Dissent Paper" (they were speaking of El Salvador, but their words held true for all Central America):

> Should President Reagan choose to use military force in El Salvador, historians will be able to show that the setting for such actions had been prepared in the last year of the Carter Administration. . . .[54]

Nevertheless, whatever the continuities between Carter and Reagan, and despite the fact that Reagan policy will not be a "180-degree turn" from Carter policy, there are also important differences. Carter policy, with its rhetoric of human rights and its actual emphasis on regional security, was contradictory and hypocritical. However, the very contradiction of "human rights" policy boxed in the Carter Administration and forced the United States to denounce its allies (even Somoza, eventually) in Central America. The rhetoric of human rights became a fetter on the policies of hemispheric security. This is a fetter which will not bind the Reagan Administration. And with this political constraint removed, the Reagan Administration has at least several degrees more freedom to intervene directly or follow aggressive policies in Central America, including Nicaragua. Such a prospect is cause for serious concern on the part of the workers' movements and all progressives opposed to U.S. intervention abroad, both in the United States and in Central America.

NOTES

1. The following draws from the analysis developed by Marlene Dixon at the Institute for the Study of Labor and Economic Crisis in San Francisco. See, for example, "Responsibilities of the U.S. Working Class to Latin American Revolutionary Movements in a New Cold War Period," the Introduction to *Contemporary Marxism* No. 1: "Strategies for the Class Struggle in Latin America" (Spring 1980).

2. See Susanne Jonas and Marlene Dixon, "Proletarianization and Class Alliances in the Americas," in *Contradictions of Socialist Construction* (San Francisco: Synthesis Publications, 1980).

3. See, for example, James Petras, "U.S. Foreign Policy: The Revival of Interventionism." *Monthly Review* (February 1980).

4. For the following analysis, see *Rebel Worker News Journal* and insert, *Plain Speaking* 4, 1 (February 1980).

5. See *Miami Herald*, December 11, 1979, and *New York Times*, February 3, 1980. Note: these and most of the newspaper articles cited below were found in Information Services on Latin America (ISLA), a monthly clipping service which follows major English-language newspaper coverage of Latin America (ISLA, 464 19th St., Oakland, CA 94612).

6. *Financial Times*, December 5, 1979.

7. *Miami Herald*, December 14, 1979.

8. *New York Times*, December 12, 1979.

9. See *Wall Street Journal*, February 29, 1980.

10. *New York Times*, October 9, 1979.

11. *Miami Herald*, March 17, 1980.

12. *Wall Street Journal*, February 29, 1980.

13. *Miami Herald*, March 2, 1980.

14. *Miami Herald*, March 20, 1980.

15. *Miami Herald*, May 8, 1980.

16. *Washington Post*, May 21, 1980.

17. *Los Angeles Times*, May 17, 1980; *New York Times*, May 16, 1980.

18. *Washington Post*, June 6, 1980; *New York Times*, June 10, 1980.

19. *New York Times*, June 10, 1980; *Washington Post*, August 8, 1980.

20. *Miami Herald*, June 1, 1980.

21. *Washington Post*, August 8, 1980.

22. *Washington Post*, August 8, 1980; *Miami Herald*, September 6, 1980.

23. *New York Times*, September 13, 1980.

24. *Washington Post*, September 13, 1980.

25. *Financial Times*, September 16, 1980.

26. *New York Times*, September 13, 1980.

27. *New York Times*, November 27, 1979; *Miami Herald*, December 11, 1979.

28. *Financial Times*, December 18, 1979.

29. *Miami Herald*, September 5, 1979.

30. *Financial Times*, March 18, 1980; June 28, 1980.

31. *New York Times*, December 25, 1980; *Inforpress Centroamericana* (Guatemala), No. 421 (December 4, 1980).

32. *Latin America Regional Reports* (Mexico/Central America), August 15, 1980; *Latin America Weekly Report*, August 15, 1980; *Financial Times*, September 16, 1980.

33. *New York Times*, September 9, 1980; see also Terri Shaw in *Washington Post*, October 5, 1980; *Latin America Weekly Report*, September 12, 1980.

34. *Financial Times*, September 16, 1980.

35. *New York Times*, September 9, 1980.

36. *Journal of Commerce*, May 9, 1980.

37. *Washington Post*, September 13, 1980.

38. *Latin America Weekly Report*, July 18, 1980; *Miami Herald*, August 24, 1980.

39. *New York Times*, January 23, 1981; *Miami Herald*, February 1, 1981.

40. *Washington Post*, February 21, 1981.

41. *Washington Post*, March 15, 1981.

42. *Washington Post*, March 15, 1981; *San Francisco Examiner*, April 2, 1981.

43. *Washington Post*, March 16, 1981.

44. *New York Times*, April 5, 1981.

45. *New York Times*, April 5, 1981.

46. *New York Times*, March 17, 1981 and April 2, 1981.

47. *New York Times*, April 2, 1981.

48. See Susanne Jonas, "Reagan Policy for Guatemala" (manuscript: Institute for the Study of Labor and Economic Crisis, December 1980).

49. *Latin America Weekly Report*, September 26, 1980.

50. *San Francisco Chronicle*, September 17, 1980; *Latin America Weekly Report*, August 22 and August 29, 1980.

51. *Latin America Weekly Report*, November 14, 1980; *New York Times*, January 4, 1981.

52. "Dissent Paper on El Salvador and Central America," DOS November 6, 1980, pp. 19-20.

53. *Los Angeles Times*, March 25, 1981; *New York Times*, March 26, 1981.

54. "Dissent Paper," pp. 1-2.

U.S. Strategies in Central America

Philip E. Wheaton

Despite U.S. denials of a regional "Vietnamization" in Central America, it is increasingly becoming a reality. Already now, we see the indications of regionalization of the conflict in El Salvador and of "Vietnamization." First, at least two other countries, Guatemala and Honduras, are already involved in paramilitary and military operations in coordination with the U.S. government's counterinsurgency campaign in El Salvador. Second, preconditions for a Vietnam-style involvement of the U.S. exist—although as yet no combat troops have been sent.

Third, the U.S. government has been deeply involved in setting military and political strategy objectives in El Salvador and Honduras. Fourth, the Central American Defense Council (CONDECA) has been reconstituted since the fall of Somoza, and its headquarters moved from Nicaragua to Guatemala. Fifth, even the Costa Rican government is indirectly involved, for example through the arrest of exiles from the other Central American countries. All of these indications point to a region-wide struggle which could even expand into an attack against the revolutionary Nicaraguan government.

As an attempt to hide these developments and create a veneer of legitimacy, the U.S. has at the same time instituted or supported governments which appear to be "centrist"; but underneath the facade lies the reality of militarization and of repression directed even against the moderates.

This is the setting in which we can understand recent developments in Central America, particularly in El Salvador and Honduras.

Part I: El Salvador: "Reform" with Repression

Context

The underlying policy objective of the U.S. government in its strategy in El Salvador from October 15, 1979 through January 19, 1981 was to prevent "another Nicaragua" in Central America; that is, *to control or destroy the indigenous popular revolutionary movement which was uniting and expanding.* In order to accomplish this task and at the same time maintain a liberal image, the Carter Administration sought to create a "centrist" government of its own making, while it simultaneously allowed the military and paramilitary forces to take whatever steps necessary to keep the progressive forces in check.

During these 15 months, severe tensions developed as a result of this tightrope act between the so-called "center" and the right, because of a deep *antagonism* between the U.S. government and the Salvadorean oligarchy, on the one hand, and a close *collaboration* between the U.S. Embassy and the military-civilian juntas, on the other, over the question of policy. As a result, the United States had to acquiesce in the political repression from the right while it pretended that the juntas actually held power.

In both cases, the role of the U.S. government during this period was one of *foreign intervention— political, logistical and economic—in the internal affairs of El Salvador.* At the same time, the Carter Administration had to wage a sophisticated war of propaganda in which it justified its actions through the suppression and distortion of information to the international community, pretending to support a "centrist government" which was struggling to resist the "extremes of the right and the left."

The "proof" presented by the U.S. government and the media that this policy was both liberal and successful was the enactment of *an agrarian reform which became the cornerstone of what was in effect a counterinsurgency strategy.*

1. The Marginalization of the Younger Officers and Centrist Civilians Legitimized the Control of the Reactionary Military (First Junta, October 15 - January 3)

The primary argument used by the United States during the first junta was that it was supporting a "centrist" government.* In fact, as we will show, the Carter Administration systematically marginalized both the moderate military—the younger officers under Col. Adolfo

---

* The October 15, 1979 U.S.-supported coup overthrew General Carlos Humberto Romero and the Agrarian Front, representatives of the reactionary agrarian oligarchy. The coup came in the wake of popular protests, of Romero's resistance to U.S.-supported policies of industrialization and agrarian "reform," and of the desire of the U.S. to avoid "another Nicaragua" by giving aid to a regime which appeared to be centrist and moderate. The October coup initiated a period of rule by successive military juntas. Moderate members subsequently left the juntas and denounced their repressive character. The best known examples are: a) Enrique Alvarez Córdova, wealthy cattle rancher and political moderate who served as Minister of Agriculture

Majano—and the centrist civilians, led by Guillermo Ungo.

While the State Department enthusiastically welcomed the coup by the "younger officers," it is now public knowledge that by early December 1979, Col. Majano and his tendency were effectively marginalized from power. The evidence that the U.S. Embassy did not support the younger officers in terms of allowing them to control either the junta or the Supreme Command of the Armed Forces came in the first days of the coup, when these officers nominated Col. René Guerra y Guerra as their second representative on the junta. The U.S. Embassy opposed his selection and proposed instead Cols. José García and Jaime Gutiérrez. When the younger officers were asked why they acceded to this foreign pressure, they responded: "We needed American support, and we agreed to this."[1] This acquiescence to the State Department was decisive in the early weeks of the coup in terms of the younger officers' subsequent loss of power.

The U.S. strategy now appears to have been: support the conservative military in the Supreme Command of the Armed Forces while using the image of the younger officers in this media campaign. Significantly, the pro-U.S. choices—Cols. García and Gutiérrez—had connections with El Salvador's telephone and telegraph company, ANTEL, which in turn is closely linked to the International Telephone and Telegraph Company (ITT). (The role of ITT in the 1973 overthrow of the Salvador Allende regime in Chile has long since been documented in U.S. Congressional hearings.) Furthermore, García's second in command was Col. Nicolás Carranza, a former technical manager of ANTEL; and another member of the junta, Mario Antonio Andino, was associated with CONELCA, a major supplier of cable to ANTEL; these facts point to a pattern "providing a clue to the rationale for American support of García and Gutiérrez."[2] These two men were representatives of the technocratic military tendency which the United States has long supported as its alternative to the reactionary oligarchy.

Meanwhile, the reactionary military officers within the Armed Forces were strengthening their control. As the younger officers saw power slipping from their grasp, they created in desperation a suborganization within the military called the "Permanent Council of the Armed Forces" (COPEFA), through which they hoped to solidify their

in the first junta. He resigned in January 1980 and declared that the junta was controlled by right-wing militarists. He joined the Democratic Revolutionary Front and became its president, only to be murdered by government troops in November 1980. b) Guillermo Manuel Ungo, civilian member of the first junta, Secretary General of the social democratic Nationalist Revolutionary Movement. Since the murder of Córdova, Ungo has been in complete opposition to the junta, as president of the Democratic Revolutionary Front. c) Col. Adolfo Majano, one of the leaders of the October 1979 coup and generally regarded as the most liberal military officer in the junta. He was ousted on December 6, 1980. Since then he has joined the opposition, calling for the overthrow of the present government.—_Ed._

position in relation to the Supreme Command. Unfortunately, COPEFA was a last-ditch effort which came too late and underestimated the power and ruthlessness of the rightist officers.[3] Through officer transfers and substitutions, Col. Marenco—a nephew of "Chele" Medrano, head of ORDEN*—gradually reorganized COPEFA, taking complete control of the organization in December, in the process transferring its loyalty from Majano to García. Thus, by the time the "civilian centrists" resigned on January 3, 1980, although Col. Majano was still in the government, he was powerless, while real power lay in the hands of Cols. García and Gutiérrez, the U.S. choices.

In terms of centrist civilians, although the U.S. government affirmed and supported the October 15 coup, it maintained an indifferent attitude towards their critical struggle with the conservative civilians (over agrarian reform) and with the reactionary officers (over political repression). Indeed, the State Department operated behind the backs of the centrist civilians through its ongoing cooperation with the military:

> On November 9, 1979, the U.S. government sent a shipment of $205,541 worth of tear gas, gas masks, and protective vests as well as a six-man U.S. Mobile Training Team to train Salvadorean troops in riot control. Also in November, a U.S. Defense Survey Team visited El Salvador *without the knowledge or consent of civilian members of the junta, Guillermo Ungo or Román Mayorga.* (Emphasis added.)[4]

Nonetheless, the U.S. government maintained its pro-"centrist" argument from junta to junta, even though the political spectrum of the civilians in each moved increasingly to the right. Furthermore, the United States continued to argue that the Christian Democratic Party (PDC) was that "center," even though the PDC was rapidly losing its social base, and despite the fact that it divided— as a party—precisely over the issue of joining the third junta. Prominent Salvadoreans, such as Enrique Alvarez Córdova of the first junta, challenged the U.S. position, stating:

> There are really only two forces in El Salvador—the left that represents the great majority of the people and the alliance of the government with the right. . . . *The junta is being sustained exclusively by the United States.* (Emphasis added.)[5]

Reflecting on the process of fall 1979, Guillermo Ungo, leader of the centrists in the first junta, said that the demise of the junta was

---

* ORDEN is a right-wing paramilitary organization made up of about 150,000 members; its origins date back to the 1960's as a network of spies and government loyalists whose task it was to keep track of potential "subversives" within the community.—*Ed.*

"the crisis of a model imposed by the U.S. government that has failed and will continue to fail."[6]

2. The Implementation of an Agrarian Reform Was Made Acceptable to the Right Through the Institution of a State of Siege (Second Junta, January 3 - March 10)

The crisis of the first junta had become evident to everyone by mid-December 1979, which was precisely the moment when the U.S. government began to step up its military assistance to the Salvadorean armed forces:

> On December 14, 1979, the Defense Department informed Congress of its intent to reprogram $300,000 in International Military Education and Training grants from Fiscal Year 1980 funds (i.e., 1979-1980) for El Salvador. These funds, which are now available to be spent, would go primarily for the purchase of U.S. Mobile Training Teams, placing U.S. military personnel in El Salvador for training purposes. . . . In Fiscal Year 1981, the [Carter] Administration is asking for an additional $5 million in Foreign Military Sales credits and $498,000 in training grants, bringing total proposed assistance (reprogramming plus new funds) to a total of $11.5 million or 69% of all military assistance El Salvador has received since 1950. With no further authorizations of U.S. money, El Salvador still has $472,000 "in the pipeline" from authorizations from previous years.[7]

The argument ran: if the junta fails, the popular forces will be strengthened and the military will need more assistance in order to contain them.

When the first junta resigned on January 3, the U.S. government brought extreme pressure to bear on the Christian Democratic Party (PDC) between January 3 and 10 to join the second junta. In a private conversation with members of the PDC in January, James Cheek, acting interim Ambassador to El Salvador for the United States, told them of the need to implement a "clean war of counter-insurgency."[8] The term *"clean* counter-insurgency" apparently implied two things for the Carter Administration: a) the sending of "non-lethal" military equipment and b) the training of Salvadorean troops in large numbers in counter-insurgency tactics.

During the month of February, the U.S. Embassy, together with the Ministry of Agriculture (MAG), began to put together an agrarian reform plan it hoped to implement subsequently. The goal of its model of reform reflected its decade-old strategy of modernizing the rural economy of El Salvador by breaking the iron rule of the coffee barons. There were two aspects of the plan: first, to nationalize the largest plantations, offering to compensate the owners with 25% in cash and 75% in bonds, redeemable only through reinvestment in the commercial or industrial sectors of the economy. Presumably, this would modernize the feudal power of the large landholders. The second aspect was to nationalize the banks, which were largely controlled by the rural oligarchy, thus removing the financial domination of the country from their hands.

The agrarian reform aspect of this overall reform strategy dealt with how to distribute these large plantations once they were confiscated and subdivided. Based on the draft of a plan developed by Enrique Alvarez Córdova during the first junta, the agrarian reform plan was reworked and then sent to Washington, D.C., for approval by AID (U.S. Agency for International Development). There were two fundamental problems with the plan: first, as Jorge Alberto Villacorta, Assistant Minister of MAG, explained, there was no accompanying legislation to legalize the projected expropriations. Second, as AID officials admitted:

> Neither this Phase (I) nor any other phase of the Agrarian Reform was planned or directed in any way whatsoever by the *campesinos* [peasants]; a state of affairs contrary to the Agrarian Reform envisioned by certain *campesino* organizations and Agrarian Reform advocates in the past.[9]

And as Oxfam-America found in its study:

> The land reform program is a "top-down" model solution imposed on the government and people of El Salvador by agencies and advisers to the U.S. Government.[10]

Furthermore, the reform was implemented in response to a military coup set for February 26, which was well-organized and at the point of being implemented. As so many times in the past, this represented a move by the conservative Agrarian Front in collaboration with its reactionary military cohorts. Such a coup would have wrecked the counterinsurgency strategy of the Carter Administration and would have reestablished the extreme right in power as the official government. Therefore, James Cheek warned the coup leaders that the U.S. government was radically opposed to any such move and that it would result in the United States holding up its promised military aid.

The alternative offered by the Carter Administration was an agrarian reform *with assurances to the military that the left forces would be contained.* The companion legislation to the Agrarian Reform of March 6, 1980 was a law imposing upon El Salvador a State of Siege. This law—Decree No. 155—was enacted on March 7, the day after the Agrarian Reform was promulgated, the government justifying this action on the basis of a potential threat by certain persons who might try to create "a state of agitation or social unrest."[11] As a result of this State of Siege, all rights of free speech, freedom of press, right to public assembly, and the right of _habeas corpus_ were automatically suspended for the entire society.

> The army carried out the military occupation not only of the large _haciendas_ of 500 hectares (and larger) but of the whole national territory.... Since then until the present, this military occupation and suspension of guarantees has continued in effect terrorizing the Salvadorean population.[12]

It was this State of Siege, presented by the United States as an integral part of the agrarian reform "package," that convinced the reactionary military—who were opposed to the reform by itself—of the validity of the U.S. strategy from their perspective. It is instructive to recall that this is precisely the form and sequence of the U.S. model of rural pacification used in Vietnam and the Philippines: Reform with Repression. In the case of the Phoenix program in Vietnam, at least 35,000 Vietnamese peasants were systematically murdered.

3. Justifying U.S. Military Aid to El Salvador in the Name of Agrarian Reform (Third Junta, March 10 - December 12)

In light of the assassination of Archbishop Oscar Arnulfo Romero on March 26, 1980, and the rapidly escalating level of violence, especially in the countryside against unarmed peasants—including peasants involved in the agrarian reform— it is instructive that April 1980 became the month of stepped-up U.S. military assistance to the Salvadorean military:

> In April 1980, the House Appropriations Subcommittee on Foreign Operations voted 6-3 to approve the reprogramming of $5.7 million in Foreign Military Sales credits to El Salvador. The aid includes:
>
> $3.3 million for 2½ ton cargo trucks, ¾ ton cargo trailers, and ½ ton ambulances;
>
> $1.3 million for communications equipment, including radios, field telephones, cables, antennas, and batteries;
>
> $.3 million for night vision sights and image intensifiers;
>
> $.03 million for gasoline generators;
>
> $.3 million for riot control equipment, including tear gas, gas masks, and bullet proof vests;
>
> $.47 million for transportation and administrative costs.[13]

There was opposition in the U.S. Congress to this legislation and therefore the Carter Administration had to use sophisticated arguments in presenting its case. The argument was made by John A. Bushnell of the State Department to the same Subcommittee on Foreign Relations on March 25, 1980:

> The principal obstacle to the reform, however, is that the extremists both from the left and right are intent on dividing the Government and preventing the consolidation of a powerful coalition which it (the Agrarian Reform) will attract to its program if it is allowed to prosper. . . . I want to emphasize that contrary to a common misconception, our proposals for security assistance are not disconnected from nor contrary to our support for reform in El Salvador. The redistribution of land would not be possible if it wasn't for the *protection and security provided by the Salvadorean Army* to the new property holders and the civilian technicians and agents who are helping them. . . . Although these proposals are modest, they are also expenses that cannot be delayed for future years without losing unique opportunities *to change the political balance in our favor.* (Emphasis added.)

While the idea of an agrarian reform did not please the "hawks" in Congress, it fulfilled a far more important function: it immobilized the liberals, and this allowed the military appropriations bill to pass.

Innumerable reports from Salvadorean peasants have testified that almost all confiscations of large landholdings were carried out as *joint operations* of military and paramilitary forces, both of which were involved in acts of torture, pillaging, kidnappings and assassinations. Therefore, the so-called "security and protection" mentioned above by Bushnell did not mean protection for the peasants but for the troops and technicians. Furthermore, Bushnell's argument clearly linked the U.S. strategy of reform and counterinsurgency, and openly admitted that the purpose behind the strategy was *political advantage for the United States.* This political motivation was further underscored by AIFLD's special adviser on agrarian reform, Roy Prosterman, when he said: "If the reforms are successfully carried out here, the armed movement of the left will be effectively eliminated by the end of 1980."[14]*

Nor was the U.S. military assistance limited to El Salvador. Since the victory of the Nicaraguan revolution, U.S. policies toward El Salvador have increasingly been framed in a regional context. Not only were the operations of CONDECA (Central American Defense Council) transferred to Guatemala, but on May 20, 1980, William Bowdler of the State Department declared: "The development of any one country in

---

* AIFLD, the American Institute for Free Labor Development, was founded in 1962 as a virtual creation of the CIA; it has played an active role in subverting the labor movement throughout Latin America. — *Ed.*

the region is closely linked to the fate of the others. Our policy must take this into consideration."[15]

Thus, at the same time the Carter Administration requested $5.7 million in military assistance reprogramming for El Salvador, it also requested and obtained a reprogramming grant for Honduras, which shares a long border with El Salvador:

> The package (to Honduras) included $3.5 million in Foreign Military Sales credits, and an increase in International Military Education and Training (IMET) from the budgeted Fiscal Year 1980 level of $225,000 to the new level of $347,000. The FMS credits will be used to purchase such items as trucks and jeeps, communications equipment, M16 and M14 rifles, night vision sights, helicopter spare parts, spare aircraft engines, and patrol boats. In addition, Honduras will be permitted to lease U.S. Army HU-1H helicopters under special loan procedures.[16]

One need only reflect on the coordination of military activities between the Honduran and Salvadorean armies in the massacre of some 600 Salvadorean peasants at the Río Sumpul on May 14, 1980,[17] where trucks, jeeps, communications equipment and helicopters were used by the Honduran forces (who maintained ongoing communication with the Salvadorean armed forces via U.S.-made walkie-talkies during that day-long genocide) to see how a regional strategy of keeping the Salvadorean struggle confined within a *cordon sanitaire* involved, at the very least, material complicity by the U.S. government in this atrocity.

Guatemala's role in this regional strategy is even more shocking in terms of its present actions and promised assistance to the Salvadorean military in helping to put down the revolutionary struggle:

> Members of Guatemala's fiercely anti-communist National Liberation Movement, headed by Mario Sándoval Alarcón, have stated that their "troops" are ready to fight subversion in El Salvador. According to the *Washington Post*, "Western diplomats believe that Guatemalan rightists have already crossed into that country." In May, a high-ranking Guatemalan official admitted that training of members of Salvadorean para-military troops takes place on Guatemalan soil.[18]

4. Domestic Political Reversal and Leftist Offensive Bring Out the True Interventionist Character of Carter Administration Strategy

In addition to the Carter Administration's inability to resolve the Iranian crisis before the U.S. presidential election and the fact that Carter's election campaign was not going well, the fall of 1980 produced two other reversals related to El Salvador: first, the agrarian reform was failing; second, Carter's interventionist intentions were revealed by a group of dissident liberals from *within the U.S. government.*

First the much-heralded agrarian reform was under heavy attack. Not only did Salvadorean government officials from MAG and other agencies oppose Decree 207, the "Land-to-the-Tiller" concept, which was a policy added to the agrarian reform through pressure from AIFLD and the U.S. Embassy;[19] not only had 8 Executive Departmental Councils of the UCS (Unión Comunal Salvadoreña)* stated their opposition to the reform because of the assassination of 12 of their *campesino* members in Santa Ana;[20] not only had the links been established between the U.S. reform model and that of its rural pacification program in Vietnam;[21] but the ultimate cost of the reform in the long run was causing consternation in Washington:

> The costs of implementing the reform, both financial and from a foreign exchange point of view, are substantial, around one billion dollars over the next five years. There is no possibility of financing any significant part of the cost of the reform implementation with internal resources without driving the country into hyperinflation.[22]

Thus, the grand reform design was being rejected by both Salvadorean "beneficiaries" and technicians, and was becoming an intolerable economic burden that would have to be borne entirely by its sponsor, the United States.

Second, immediately after Carter's defeat at the polls, a group of liberals—claiming to be from the State Department, National Security Council, Department of Defense and CIA— published a critique of the interventionist intention of the Carter policy with regard to El Salvador. In a document released on November 6, 1980, entitled "Dissent Paper on El Salvador and Central America," the critics stated:

> Should President Reagan choose to use force in El Salvador, historians will be able to show that the setting for such actions had been prepared in the last year of the Carter Administration. . . . Various government agencies have taken preparatory steps to intervene militarily in El Salvador. Policy makers appear to have concluded that such a move could succeed in preventing the collapse of the current regime.[23]

While the State Department denies this Dissent Paper is legitimate because it did not pass through the regular "dissent channel," subsequent action by the Carter Administration to send in military aid and advisers confirmed the interventionist thesis.

---

* UCS, the Unión Comunal Salvadoreña, is a labor union of rural workers and peasants created by AIFLD in 1968; its purpose was to channel the militancy of the rural working class into reformist activities and prevent radical politicization. — *Ed.*

Reagan's defeat of Carter at the polls triggered even more explosive events in El Salvador. The first was the assassination of four North American religious women on December 2 simply because they were working with poor peasants in El Salvador. The repercussions of this atrocity were electrifying in the United States, as millions of Americans began to see the connections between the nuns' deaths and the assassination of 9,000 Salvadoreans during 1980. This produced such a national outcry, especially from the religious community, that President Carter was forced to suspend all aid to the Salvadorean government. But within a few days, on December 16, after unconvincingly declaring that there was "no proof" that Salvadorean security forces had committed the crime, Carter not only resumed $20 million in government economic aid to El Salvador but triggered an Inter-American Development Bank approval of an additional $40.4 million to the junta *on the same day*.

The second unexpected event involved the visit to Managua and San Salvador of one of President-elect Reagan's advisers on Latin American policy—Cleto DiGiovanni, a former CIA agent and analyst. DiGiovanni, meeting with reactionary leaders in each country, advised them not to pay attention to the old strategy of Carter's ambassadors Robert White in El Salvador and Lawrence Pezullo in Nicaragua, since they would soon be removed from their posts. Two months earlier, DiGiovanni had written a study released by the Heritage Foundation, a pro-Reagan think tank, in which he said:

> The best signal that the U.S. government could send to the Salvadorean military would be to supply it with the military equipment it needs for offensive warfare without human rights and other strings.[24]

The combination of the assassination of the religious women and DiGiovanni's revelations led to a reshuffling of Salvadorean leadership, virtually ending the third junta and establishing a so-called "executive government" headed by "President" José Napoleón Duarte* and Col. Gutiérrez, once again legitimized by U.S. mandate.

The third event in this series was the greatest shocker of all to the Carter Administration: at a late night meeting in the Hotel Sheraton in San Salvador on January 3, 1981, the peasant leader and president of ISTA (Salvadorean Agrarian Reform Institute), Rodolfo Viera, and two top AIFLD representatives dealing with agrarian reform, Michael Hammer and Mark Pearlman, were gunned down by persons who

---

* José Napoleón Duarte is one of the founders of the Christian Democratic Party; he was elected president of El Salvador in 1972, but was arrested and prevented from taking office. More recently he made a political comeback, and in March 1980 was named to the junta, after the resignation of another Christian Democrat who condemned the state of violence and repression. He became president of the junta in December 1980, following Majano's ouster.— *Ed.*

President Duarte admitted were "from the right." The close linkage between AIFLD and the CIA and between AIFLD and the agrarian reform could only be explained as a warning from the pro-oligarchic military forces, under orders from the Agrarian Front members now located in Miami, that they would no longer tolerate any U.S. government policies imposed upon El Salvador which were at variance with those of the oligarchy. In effect, these three murders represented the high point in the smoldering antagonism between the U.S. government and the Salvadorean ruling class over the issue of agrarian reform.

Subsequent events bear out the fact that the oligarchy won this struggle over policy formulation, and the Carter policy which had been covertly interventionist now came out in the open. On January 14, 1981—only five days before leaving the presidency—Carter resumed military aid "to the embattled Salvadorean government, in an indication of growing U.S. concern over the strength of guerrilla forces there."[25] The $5 million in military aid included money for "helicopter support, individual uniforms and equipment, armour-plated jeeps, commercial trucks and 10,000 smoke grenades."[26] In addition, helicopters were leased, mobile training teams were sent in, and President Duarte urged U.S. President-elect Ronald Reagan "to come to the aid of the embattled government."[27]

Soon after Ronald Reagan became President of the United States, alarmist but totally unconfirmed charges were made by the U.S. ambassador in El Salvador that Nicaraguan soldiers had landed on Salvadorean soil. This seems to be little more than a pretext for widening the Salvadorean struggle into a regional conflict. The thesis of this paper is that the nation primarily guilty of foreign intervention into El Salvador — covertly since 1961 and overtly since October 15, 1979—is the U.S. government and its several agencies. As U.S. Representative Barbara A. Mikulski, following a visit to the Honduras-El Salvador border with U.S. Representatives Gerry Studds and Robert Edgar in January 1981, said:

> Our weapons are being used to kill people, commit horrendous atrocities—burning crops and creating a very serious food shortage . . . in many ways, *we* are the threat in Central America.[28]

NOTES FOR PART 1

1. Carolyn Forche, "The Rainy Season" (unpublished, May 1980).
2. Carolyn Forche, "The Road to Reactionary El Salvador." *The Nation* (June 14, 1980), p. 713.
3. FAPU, *Polémica Internacional* (San Salvador, April-May 1980), p. 44: Before Romero's exit from power, the reactionary military set up a rightist structure called ANSESAL—an army within the army—"a double command, integrated and coordinated within the Armed Forces with control over the intelligence services,

G-2 and S-2," with power to make high-level decisions behind the backs of whoever was in the Supreme Command.

4. Institute for Policy Studies (IPS), Cynthia Arnson, "Background Information on El Salvador and U.S. Military Assistance to Central America." Update (June 1980), pp. 6-7.

5. Ibid., pp. 2-3.

6. Robert Armstrong, "El Salvador—A Revolution Brews." *NACLA Report* (July-August 1980), p. 11.

7. IPS, Cynthia Arnson op. cit., p. 9.

8. NACLA interview, Summer 1980, Ungo.

9. U.S. AID, *Agrarian Reform Organization*, Annex IIA, *A Social Analysis*, p. 30.

10. Oxfam-America, Simon and Stephens, "El Salvador Land Reform: 1980 - 1981," Impact Audit, General Findings, No. 3, p. 70.

11. *ECA*, San Salvador, March-April 1980, "State of Siege," Decree No. 155, p. 390.

12. Alberto Arene, EPICA interview, Washington, D.C., Fall 1980.

13. IPS, Cynthia Arnson, op. cit., p. 6.

14. *Overview Latin America* (Cambridge, Mass., July 25, 1980), citing a report from Inter Press Service.

15. Hearings, House Subcommittee on Inter-American Affairs.

16. IPS, Cynthia Arnson, op. cit., p. 8.

17. "Chronology of the Massacre of Río Sumpul," Mons. José Carranza y Chávez and all priests and clergy, Santa Rosa de Copán, Honduras, June 19, 1980.

18. IPS, Cynthia Arnson, op. cit., p. 9.

19. Oxfam America, op. cit., p. 52, citing Norman Chapin, AID/Washington.

20. Comunicado de la Unión Comunal Salvadorea al Pueblo Salvadoreño, June 5, 1980.

21. Inter Press Service, "El Salvador: Land Reform as a Counter-Insurgency Programme Like the CIA's Phoenix Operation in Vietnam" (July 25, 1980).

22. Oxfam America, op. cit., p. 64, citing AID/El Salvador *Strategy Paper*, p. 4.

23. "Dissent Paper on El Salvador and Central America," from the El Salvador-Central American Task Force (November 6, 1980), pp. 1 and 2.

24. The Heritage Foundation, "U.S. Policy and the Marxist Threat to Central America." *Backgrounder* (October 15, 1980), p. 12.

25. *Wall Street Journal* (January 15, 1981).

26. IPS, Addendum to Update, November 17, 1980.

27. *Washington Star* (January 12, 1981).

28. *Baltimore Sun* (January 21, 1981).

Part 2: The Iron Triangle: The Honduran Connection

Si vis pacem, para bellum. . . . If you want peace, prepare for war.
—Byword of the Roman Empire

A peace built upon the threat of a growing violence which is uncontainable, is not peace any more but purely and simply the preparation for war masked under the lying cloak of an empty set of values. . . . At this point, language no longer serves to communicate the truth, but to hide the interests of the few.

—Materiales de Reflección, No. 12
Honduras, January 20, 1981

Recently, the ex-Minister of Foreign Relations for Colombia and a prominent member of the Conservative Party, Alfredo Vásquez Carrizosa, pointed out the more significant aspects of a plan which called for the establishment of a "triangle of iron" in Central America. Recalling a ceremony held at Santa Marta, Colombia, on December 17, 1980, to formalize the U.S. decision to designate José Napoleón Duarte "President" of the Republic of El Salvador, Vásquez Carrizosa pointed to the origins of the plan:

> Some months ago, the United States and Venezuela advanced a "joint operation" with parallel, consistent objectives towards creating an absolutely artificial political regime under the leadership of the Christian Democrats, which is nothing more than the hyphenated title "financial oligarchy-armed forces." That proposal has gone from bad to worse. . . . No one at Santa Marta imagined that by promising their solidarity to president Duarte, a foreign military-type intervention, Venezuelan or Colombian, would be the beginning of the "Vietnamization" of the problem.[1]

As Gregorio Selser added in his article published in Mexico in which this information is cited, the consolidation of the "triangle of iron" coincided with the date of Ronald Reagan's ascendency to the presidency of the United States.[2]

The Iron Triangle refers to El Salvador, Guatemala and Honduras and to the coordinated activities of their respective military and paramilitary forces. The goal of this strategy is to suffocate the popular revolutionary movement in El Salvador through a combined operation of extermination: first, through the elimination of any potential base of support for the left among the Salvadorean peasantry; second, through the ultimate destruction of the FMLN (Farabundo Martí National Liberation Front) guerrilla forces.

The strategy was not, however, indigenous to the region; it was not even a Machiavellian invention of the fascist death squad commanders of these neighboring countries. It was the brainchild of U.S. imperialism, concocted in Washington upon critical reflection about the loss of Nicaragua by Somoza's National Guard to the Sandinistas. The victory of the FSLN (Sandinista National Liberation Front) had shown that a mere national military apparatus (even one as well-armed, ruthless and multi-faceted as that in El Salvador) might be no match for a guerrilla vanguard if it has the support of the people, and especially if the country's borders remain relatively open. The U.S. strategy for El Salvador responded to these weaknesses:

a) El Salvador had to be enclosed, placed within a *cordon sanitaire;*

b) The Salvadorean peasantry had to be destroyed, removed or frightened into submission;

c) The Salvadorean armed forces had to have the coordinated support of the military apparatus of its two neighbors.

Moreover, political alterations or adjustments in all three countries had to facilitate this military strategy since the fundamental goal— overriding all other concerns—was to prevent "another Nicaragua" in Central America. Thus the rationale for the creation of an Iron Triangle.

Historically, we first became aware of the Iron Triangle strategy— although not known by that title then—following the events of May 14, 1980: the massacre of 600 peasants at the Río Sumpul on the border between Honduras and El Salvador. That genocidal act was decided on at a secret meeting of high-level military officers from Honduras, El Salvador and Guatemala on May 5 at the frontier town of El Poy, 20 kilometers from the place of the massacre.[3] The day before the massacre, on May 13, some 250 strongly armed Honduran soldiers arrived from their bases in Santa Rosa de Copán and Santa Lucía at the Río Sumpul, where they immediately began to build stone barriers along the length of the Honduran shore of the river—to protect themselves from Salvadorean bullets. At 7 a.m., the massacre began and during that long, bloody, macabre day, the Salvadorean troops maintained ongoing communication with the Honduran forces, who would not allow the trapped Salvadorean peasants to cross the river, and then watched, stunned by the slaughter in which they were accomplices.

The second signal we received about the Iron Triangle involved a strange diplomatic development on October 31, 1980: in the midst of a civil conflict, El Salvador suddenly and unexpectedly sought a peace treaty with Honduras. After 10 years without resolution of the conflict, and at the very moment when El Salvador was diplomatically in its weakest position while Honduras was in its strongest position, a treaty was signed that is completely favorable to El Salvador! However, the treaty did not resolve either the border demarcation or any economic settlement; it did resolve the question of the *"bolsones"*—the use of the 3-mile-wide strip on either side of the border established by the OAS (Organization of American States) in 1969. That problem was resolved by allowing Salvadorean troops to cross the border on search-and-destroy missions in cooperation with the Honduran army, which was given "the task of policing the border area for political-military security purposes."[4]

The third signal came recently (December 1980-January 1981), with reports of rising violence against Salvadorean refugees who were often sent back across the border by Salvadorean soldiers to almost certain death; the pressure against and defamation of the Catholic priests in the border area, especially those carrying out *capacitación* (training) and *conscientización* (political consciousness raising) courses for Honduran peasants, such as in the case of the priests from Santa Barbara; and the systematic removal of refugees from the border area, and thus of the international relief agencies aiding the refugees— who might report on violence in the region.[5]

But these signals, which came to our attention only gradually during 1980, were recently woven into a wholistic pattern by Hondurans as having their origins in an overall "plan" developed much earlier, sometime in March 1980. Prior to the Honduran elections (April 20), General Policarpio Paz García* traveled to Washington, where he conferred at length with William Bowdler, a high-level State Department official. The result of those conversations was a U.S. offer to Paz García of economic and political support on the condition that the political reform process, then underway (free elections and a new constitution), would not be defrauded by the military. Apparently, Carter's new strategy for Honduras, as contrasted to the coup strategy in El Salvador, October 15, 1979, was to use the elections to legitimize the government while putting its main efforts toward building up the Honduran armed forces. In April, the United States Executive requested and obtained a reprogramming grant for Honduras of $3.5 million in Foreign Military Sales credits, and an increase in International Military Education and Training (IMET) grants from the budgeted Fiscal Year 1980 level of $225,000 to the new level of $347,000.[6]

General Paz García returned to Honduras and guaranteed the electoral process, which the Partido Liberal won overwhelmingly; this was taken by the Honduran press as an expression of anti-military sentiment, since the pro-military Partido Nacional lost decisively. But the Liberal Party's victory quickly turned sour: development projects underway in 1979 suddenly bogged down; the country became quickly and significantly indebted, as in 1980 Honduras absorbed 18% of all aid destined for Latin America from AID (U.S. Agency for International Development). Additional factors were the frustration of the reformist elements in the new constitutionalist effort, the rapid and massive beefing up of the military, and the flight of more than $500 million during the year 1980, at the same time as the cost of living index jumped from 12% to 20%.[7]

This past year can best be described as the "year of the militarization of Honduras," a period when the Honduran people went quickly from political hope to alienation. The absence of promised reforms, the

* President Policarpio Paz García, third general to rule Honduras in the past nine years, took power in 1978 and remained as of 1981. — *Ed.*

economic deterioration of the country, and the systematic weakening of the Liberal Party were matched by the rapid expansion of the military, the rise in repression by the hardening line of the military (without mentioning the clash between the Catholic Church and the military over the Sumpul massacre), and the consolidation of power under the leadership of Paz García. All these developments reinforce the argument that this was simply the carrying out of the Iron Triangle strategy. The thesis is further reinforced by the growing numbers of U.S. military advisers and trainers in El Salvador, the increased collaboration between Honduran and Salvadorean military and paramilitary forces along the border, and by the recent appearance of Honduras' first death squad, the Movimiento Anti-Comunista Hondureño (MACHO).

As the authors of "Materiales de Reflección" have so aptly put it:

> Summing up, it could be said that the present peace treaty is nothing more than an attempt to reinforce once again North American interests in Central America. In this sense, one may say that Honduras, by signing the peace treaty with a government which represents only a small minority of the Salvadorean people (although the best armed), has itself declared war on the revolutionary Cuscatlecos (Salvadorean people). The consequences of the treaty are yet to be seen, but it is clear that the treaty carries with it an implicit participation by Honduras in the internal affairs of El Salvador. And it is also evident that its declared support of the Military-Christian Democratic Junta will broaden the parameters of the conflict in which El Salvador is now engaged. Therefore, the peace which has been signed can easily convert itself into a wider war. Thus those advocating war have fabricated their own kind of peace. . . .[8]

Central America Is Already at War

We have focused only on the Honduran connection of the overall strategy of the "Iron Triangle." Obviously, the role of Guatemala is equally if not more important in the sense that the linkages between the paramilitary and military forces across that border and with the struggle in El Salvador have been much more continuous and integrated during 1980-81. The Honduran connection is important because it clearly shows an alteration in the internal policy of Honduras responding to U.S. initiative and support, whereas the Carter Administration had relatively kept its hands off Guatemala because of the fascist nature of the Lucas military regime, publicly contradicting the Carter human rights policy. But the U.S. role in Honduras is more cynical and dangerous because it attempts to hide the same kind of regional strategy under the guise of a (now) coopted democratic process and elected government.

There is considerable talk and press these days about the possibility of "another Vietnam" in Central America. Certainly, we should take that analogy seriously, given the Reagan Administration's call for overkill in El Salvador: $100 million in economic aid, $25 million in military aid, the sending of (at least) 54 military advisers and technicians into El Salvador. However, it would be an error to define "Vietnamization" of the region only in terms of the commitment of significant numbers of U.S. military troops, though—as we saw in Vietnam—this could in a short time easily happen. More importantly and more to the point is the fact that now, in these three countries comprising the Iron Triangle, war is already a reality with U.S. assistance, prodding and propaganda. The military, paramilitary and mercenary squads from all three countries—including, at least, mercenaries from Somoza's National Guard—are already coordinating and cooperating in actual armed operations against the progressive forces in El Salvador as well as against the unarmed Salvadorean peasantry.

Thus the form of this latest U.S. imperialist engagement has an important nuance: the use of these surrogate forces as its front line of defense to prevent at all cost "another Nicaragua" in El Salvador. Such a form of aggression and intervention (through the use of surrogate forces) is not quite like Vietnam because no U.S. troops have as yet been committed. This could lull some citizens of the United States into assuming that this is a "different" kind of conflict. But surely such an interpretation would be both naive and cynical given the massive and significant levels of participation of the U.S. political and military institutions already in El Salvador. The point is *that a significant portion of Central America is already at war, and that the Iron Triangle strategy was conceived and is being directed by the U.S. government.*

March 15, 1981

NOTES FOR PART 2

1. Signed editorial, published by *El Espectador* (Bogota, Colombia, January 2, 1981).

2. Gregorio Selser, "El Salvador como referencia, pero la DC apunta hacia toda América," *El Día Internacional* (Mexico City, February 11, 1981).

3. "Cronología De La Masacre Del Río Sumpul," *Sumpul: Una Masacre Contra Refugiados Salvadorenos*, Honduras, July 1980; published by Casa Salvador "Farabundo Martí" (San Francisco, Calif.), p. 28.

4. "Materiales De Reflección," No. 12, January 20, 1981, Honduras, p. 5.

5. Report by the Spanish investigating team for Investigaciones y Estudios Para Latinoamérica y Africa (IEPALA), Permanent People's Tribunal, Mexico, February 11, 1981.

6. Institute for Policy Studies, Cynthia Arnson, Update (Washington, D.C., June 1980), p. 8.

7. "Materiales de Reflección," No. 12, op. cit., p. 6.

8. "Materiales de Reflección," No. 10, November 10, 1980, p. 8.

U.S. Military Strategy in Central America: From Carter to Reagan

Antonio Cavalla Rojas

We propose to do the following in this article:

1) Describe the main steps in the decision-making process in U.S. national defense;

2) Present the strategic military objectives for Latin America as defined by the Carter Administration;

3) Analyze the military and non-military appraisals made by the U.S. establishment of the Central American region;*

4) Establish what Carter's Central American Policy was, up to the triumph of the Sandinista National Liberation Front in Nicaragua;

5) Analyze the strategic changes or readjustments that were implemented after the events in Nicaragua and Iran; and

6) Put forward some preliminary hypotheses regarding the military strategy that the Reagan Administration will apply toward Central America.

The Formal U.S. Decision-Making Process
With Respect to National Defense

We disagree with two approaches common in the social sciences and in analyses of Latin American political affairs to the problem of formal decision-making in U.S. national defense. For some, the following axioms would be sufficient: that imperialism is the expression of a phase of capitalism's development; that the imperialist state is con-

---

* We have excluded Panama from our analysis of the U.S.-Central American relations, as is usually done in Latin American social sciences. Regarding Panama, see: Xabier Gorostiaga, "Las relaciones de Estados Unidos-Panamá bajo la Administración Carter," in *Cuadernos Semestrales de Perspectiva Latinoamericana de Estados Unidos* (CIDE, Mexico), No. 6, Second Semester of 1979, and our article "Objetivos militares de EEUU en América Latina: el caso de los Tratados Canaleros," in *Plural* (Cultural magazine of Excélsior, Mexico, No. 83, 1979).

trolled by the hegemonic sectors of the empire's ruling classes; that the armed forces and defense policies of that state have the mission of guarding the interests of those classes. What one can expect, then, from the military, is permanent, coherent, uncontradictory action against the subordinate classes, particularly in the peripheral countries which are structurally dependent on the center of the empire. This view considers it to be fruitless, and even dangerous, to monitor and analyze the governmental processes by which a formal consensus is developed among U.S. interest groups regarding their strategic decisions.

For others, the evolution of post-industrial society has reached such a level of economic and political crisis of imperialism that efforts to find coherence between the superstructural decisions and economic tendencies become "dogmatic." They consider the degree of contradictions to be such that a line of decisions in national defense, for example, could well go against the vital (historic) interests of the hegemonic sectors of the ruling classes.

In contrast to both of the above, we believe that U.S. political and military decisions have a permanent historical thrust, which is none other than the defense of the imperialist "destiny" of the U.S. bourgeoisie. However, the form of articulation by the hegemonic sectors, the complexity of the system of reaching consensus and then imposing that consensus on the whole of civil society, allows for the expression of profound contradictions at various conjunctures, contradictions which at certain moments have even paralyzed the United States' capacity to respond. This reality compels us to learn about the system's most internal functioning and to draw conclusions regarding each point in the development of the imperial center/periphery relation. At the same time, we cannot lose sight of the fact that the errors and clashes among the sectors at the imperial center are conjunctural and that, sooner or later, efforts will be made to bring policy back in line with the historical purpose of defending the imperialist system as a whole.

Having made these clarifications, we view the study of the U.S. national defense decision-making process as a matter of studying the arena in which different U.S. interest groups attempt to articulate their positions concerning threats to the maintenance and development of the imperialist model, and in regard to global and localized actions which need to be implemented in order to avert and suppress these threats.

A kind of ideological reasoning exists to deal with these matters, which has been shared for many years by the military "establishment," the class of civilian policy-makers, the corporate world, U.S. researchers and academics, the mass media, and to a large degree, public opinion. U.S. strategic doctrine on "national security" is rooted in the geopolitics and idealist ideologies born of rationalism and positivism. Such reasoning starts from the premise that each nation-state has a national potential for growth and development which is inexorably opposed to the potentialities of other nation-states. Each nation-state itself—not its classes or sectors of classes—also has a vision of life and human development which must be defended and even imposed on other nations with different (and therefore, of course, erroneous) visions. From there, it follows that each nation-state has national goals that the society as a whole must pursue by any means. The attainment of these objectives will be blocked by internal as well as external threats, necessitating the deployment of economic, ideological, political and military forces (which constitute national power) capable of overcoming or at least neutralizing these threats.[1] U.S. "strategic doctrine" would then be, in the words of Henry Kissinger, that which "defines the objectives worth fighting for, and determines the degree of force appropriate to achieve them."[2] *

This conceptual agreement underlies, for the most part, the relatively harmonious development of the United States' national defense decision-making process. The principal actors in this are: the Armed Forces; the Executive (primarily the Secretaries of State and Defense and the President); and Congress. U.S. pressure (lobbying) groups direct themselves to each one of these sectors, and decisions regarding which interests will be imposed and what forms of defending them will be employed are determined by the totality of the process.

At the level of the Armed Forces, the Joint Chiefs of Staff is the body that expresses consensus out of the disputes among the different armed forces and agencies, and the pressure groups which act on them. The Joint Chiefs of Staff produces a series of documents which circulate, in a two-way dialogue, within the civilian sectors of the Defense Department. The position of the military is expressed annually in the document signed by the general who functions as President of the Joint Chiefs of Staff, entitled "Military Posture for Five Years."

The consensus reached in the Defense Department is reported to the Presidency, where for about two months it is analyzed by the agencies of the Executive Office of the President—primarily the National Security Council and the Budget Office—and by the President, all of whom are supposed to make the requirements of Defense compatible with the rest of the government departments and agencies and with the Administration's general strategy and policies.

After this phase, the Executive, through the intermediary of the Secretary of Defense, presents to Congress its "Annual Report for the Fiscal Year" which describes the basis for the defense policies and the budgetary requirements asked by the Executive.

The Senate and the House of Representatives begin a process of discussion in the committees and subcommittees which lasts approximately six months. Discussion then continues, first in the joint com-

* This is the first of numerous quotations of statements by U.S. officials, presented here as translated from the author's Spanish.—*Ed.*

mittees and later on the floor in full sessions of both Houses, where the Executive's proposals can be passed or amended. During the Congressional discussion, the committees, subcommittees and plenaries can hold hearings and inquiries on the whole of the defense program/ budget, or on particular sections of it. They can at the same time assign advisory staff or experts designated to research the subject, and they can ask for testimony from specialists, including civilian and military personnel from the Department of Defense and the Armed Forces.

To follow this process in Congress adequately, one should not focus only on the Armed Services Committees, but should look also at a series of committees, subcommittees, and full sessions of Congress which deal with defense problems, such as those dedicated to foreign affairs, government operations, budgetary appropriations and authorizations, etc. One must also consider that the President can veto Congressional amendments to legislation. In such a case, the discussion will be renewed in the Senate, which can override the Executive by a three-fourths majority vote.[3]

This process in Congress is particularly important in finding out the opinions of the government agencies (including the Armed Forces) as well as of the private groups that lobby the legislative bodies. The great majority of these debates are public, and are later published by the committee which conducts them, by the respective house, or by the Government Printing Office.

Military Strategy During The Carter Administration[4]

The Carter Administration took office at a time when the military and civilian establishment of the Pentagon had just finished an extended debate on the strategic, tactical and operational errors committed in the Indochinese war.[5] It is notable, first of all, that none of the positions taken in the debate excluded military intervention. All of them maintained that the Joint Chiefs of Staff should be able at the proper time to propose to the President and the National Security Council, as one logical measure, the deployment of troops to a foreign country whose government or whose opposition threatens the "vital interests" of the United States.

In the second place, it is clear that the strategy of flexible response, which was defined in essence in General Maxwell Taylor's time[6] and was sanctioned by the Kennedy-McNamara Administration, is considered fully applicable. Flexible response presupposes a field of action outside war in which there are varying degrees and combinations of covert actions on the psychosocial, economic and diplomatic-political levels. Action in the field of war itself continues to be flexible—ranging from military actions involving advisers and weapons, to the commitment of U.S. forces in growing numbers and quality, to the point of a nuclear confrontation with the Soviet Union. The following strategic concepts were to be readjusted and redefined in light of Vietnam:

1) The first error made was the gradualism with which U.S. military force was applied in Indochina in direct combat. Coercive pressures of various kinds should be applied against the enemy as directly as possible, with a decision to employ force as needed, with rapid deployment of sufficient forces to meet specific military objectives, consistent with specific political objectives.

2) The impression of weakness must be avoided. All available "national power" must be applied to achieve the political goal, and all military power must be applied to achieve the military goal that makes the political goal attainable. This relates both to the treatment of allies, neutrals and enemies in terms of their reactions to the intervention and to the internal situation. Measures must be taken to avoid having sectors inside the U.S. align themselves with "anti-U.S." forces in order to cause too much "noise" about decisions for and the execution of political-military intervention.

3) The previous points lead to a readjustment of the concept of intervention forces and their deployment both to U.S. bases and to war zones. From the point of view of force, it is best to gather the most mobile forces—preferably airborne for distant areas, and amphibious and airborne for nearby areas—in great enough density to be able to saturate the staging area and achieve military victory in the least amount of time. From the point of view of applying U.S. force, it is best to unleash it directly on the military enemy and its supplies or logistical lines (including resupply regions and faraway supply depots), totally leaving to the native allies the task of controlling the civilian population.

4) The political objective of intervention should be preceded as much as possible by the concept of "tactical termination of the conflict." That is, the result of the military confrontation should be such a victory over the enemy that there is no one left in the war zone with whom the U.S. can negotiate the end of the war.

Within this definitional framework already adopted by the military establishment, President Carter introduced his particular "trilateral" vision of international relations; he did so without replacing the readjusted military strategy, which was based on rivalry and not detente, with an alternative strategy coherent with his diplomatic proposals. An analysis of the main official documents seems to confirm this.[7]

The strategic plans of the Carter Administration affirmed in the first place that the basic goal of U.S. "national security" was to preserve the U.S. as a free nation, with its institutions and values intact. In order to achieve this, it was necessary to assure not only territorial integrity, but also an "international environment" in which U.S. interests were protected and freedom of action for the U.S. was guaranteed.

The main premise that governed this "international environment" was that the U.S. and the USSR were the major powers and that Europe was the area of their main direct confrontation. Because this environment was in constant flux, the Administration established seven fundamental objectives as the means to keep it favorable to the U.S. in the present conjuncture.

First: Strengthen ties with "true friends"[8] who shared U.S. values and were in a similar phase of industrial development. In other words, strengthen the trilateral relations with Western Europe and Japan.

Second: Broaden the scope of bilateral relations with friendly countries considered to be "emerging powers," such as Brazil, Venezuela, Iran, Saudi Arabia, India, Indonesia, etc.

Third: Build a North-South policy that would deal with the problems of extreme poverty and misery, considered to be seeds of instability.

Fourth: Establish relations with the USSR which would impede the growth of its influence and avoid nuclear confrontation.

Fifth: Resolve the most explosive regional problems in favor of U.S. interests. In this respect, the confrontations in the Middle East and the Southern Horn of Africa became priorities.

Sixth: Take charge of so-called "global problems," the main ones being the arms race and nuclear proliferation.

Seventh: Attempt to restore the legitimacy of the U.S. system by identifying the foreign policy and defense policy of the U.S. with its so-called "fundamental values": democracy and the defense of human rights.

There was an eighth goal which was embodied in several of the others but tended to become autonomous: the energy problem. As Senator Kennedy pointed out, "With the energy problem, the dangers to the security of the hemisphere have grown. The desire to reduce dependence on sources of fossil fuels has increased interest in non-fossil alternatives, the most important being nuclear energy. But, as has been demonstrated by the nuclear explosion in India in 1974, the expansion of nuclear energy raises the specter of nuclear arms proliferation." Or, in the more direct and less rhetorical words of the military, spoken by General George Brown, "The role of resources, especially energy resources, becomes crucial in foreign policy and national security. . . . Developing nations rich in oil exercise a coordinated control over resources vital for the development of the industrial nations."[9]

Military strategy for the five-year period 1979-1983 was defined within the context of these goals, i.e., the "basic strategy of the U.S. is to maintain a balance of military power (U.S./USSR), as much as possible; to restrain armed conflicts with a spectrum of actions from strategic nuclear war to minor crises; to prevent military coercion (which another military power might be able to exercise over the U.S.); to influence international affairs from a position of recognized U.S. strength; to fight if necessary; and to terminate external conflicts on terms favorable to the U.S."[10]

Latin America in U.S. Military Strategy

In the totality of both global and military strategic definitions, references to Latin America were few in relation to other regions. President Carter and his main collaborators, both during the presidential campaign and in the first foreign policy statements after he took office, made scarce mention of the subcontinent; and these few statements focused on "test cases" of the Canal Treaties, relations with Cuba, and the Chilean dictatorship. It was emphasized that there would not be one single policy towards Latin America, but bilateral relations with emerging countries, and subregional relations and policies (for example with respect to Central America and the Caribbean). In terms of the military, the President of the Joint Chiefs of Staff and General of the U.S. Air Force, George Brown (in spelling out the official North American military thinking regarding the 1979 Five Year Defense Program), dedicated three pages of a 110-page report to the policies which, in his judgment, the Carter Administration should apply to the subcontinent. He stated that Latin America plays a "significant role" in U.S. global strategy, and spelled out six main strategic objectives of the U.S. in the region:

1) Prevent control of Central America or the Caribbean by a power "hostile" to the U.S.

2) Maintain free passage through the Panama Canal for U.S. forces and logistical material, and if this passage were curtailed, then keep open lines of communication with the Southern Cone.

3) Maintain a "stable friendship" with Mexico.[11]

4) Maintain the supply of strategic raw materials provided in particular by Brazil, Mexico, Venezuela, Peru and Jamaica.

5) Insure the support of the Latin American armed forces in "hemispheric defense," which meant giving them the preferential mission of maintaining Latin America's political and economic stability, and containing "internal threats." The exceptions to this were the armed forces of Brazil and Argentina (due to their particular potential for becoming nuclear powers), and the armed forces of Panama (because of its function in assisting U.S. armed forces in defense of the Canal).

6) Prevent the USSR from realizing its strategic interest in Latin America, which is defined as "establishing bases near the U.S."

The Strategic Value of Central America to the U.S.

U.S. concern for the Central American region and the Caribbean dates back a long time. Nicholas Spykman, rightly considered the main North American geopolitician of the 1930's and 1940's, defined the strategic value of that region in the following manner:

> The strategic importance of the American Mediterranean[12]
> derives from the fact that its location is not only between

North and South America, but also between the Atlantic and Pacific Oceans, the latter's importance being accentuated by the construction of the Panama Canal—though it did not originate with the Canal. This is proven by the relations between Panama and the Philippines during the times of Spanish rule. The Canal, finished in 1914, enabled the U.S. to enjoy all the benefits of being geographically situated between the two oceans. Although the Canal is in an enclave far from our borders, it remains an important link in the chain of our coastal navigation, and it has reduced the distance between Atlantic and Pacific ports by more than eight thousand miles. More importantly, it shortened the route from the Pacific states to Europe, and from the Atlantic states to Asia, where there is demand for their respective products.[13]

Essentially, Spykman merely continued the tradition of U.S. geopoliticians. Alfred Thayer Mahan, who forged U.S. naval power strategy at the beginning of the century, proposed that his country should strive for absolute domination over the Gulf of Mexico and the Caribbean. Mahan stated that the U.S. should not tolerate a single foreign fueling station closer than 3,000 miles from San Francisco. This should be an inviolable rule in our foreign policy, he believed.[14]

This attitude has continued to be found in the U.S. military establishment and has increased since the triumph and consolidation of the Cuban Revolution and the periods of intensely nationalist posture in Panama, beginning with the military coup that put Omar Torrijos into power. This concern is markedly present in the strategic and military policies defined by Carter's Administration in the documents we are analyzing.

Central America is seen in terms of two U.S. strategic military goals: as a group of countries forming part of Latin America which must be "stable, friendly towards the U.S. and free from outside influences"; and as a geopolitical "border" area in which it is imperative to avoid the installation of a "hostile" government, especially because that would "permit a wide range of military actions" including strategic attacks on U.S. territory.

To achieve these military objectives, the Carter Administration pointed out that they "counted heavily on the indigenous armed forces to oppose internal threats; they maintain forces in the (Latin American) territory which, together with forces deployable from the U.S., could assure security and the functioning of the Canal and Canal Zone [and I would add: why not of other Latin American zones?]. They support regional alliances and treaty organizations [i.e., the Organization of American States, the so-called Interamerican Defense System and CONDECA]; they conduct joint maneuvers and training, and obtain and maintain the active participation of other countries in the defense of the Western Hemisphere." In this last respect, Central American armed forces were considered irrelevant.

An American self-criticism [which was transformed into Administration policy] applies to Central America as well as to the rest of Latin America. It stems from the following paragraph in General Brown's report, which was subsequently ratified and put into effect by the Secretary of Defense on behalf of the government:

> Although relations between representatives of the U.S. armed forces and the Latin American militaries are declining, they are still viable. The unique character of leadership exercised by the Latin American militaries makes it important to stimulate these traditional relations between the military of one country and another. These relations reinforce the understanding and acceptance of the need for basic human rights policies. By responding to the legitimate needs for modernizing the armed forces, the USA creates a more favorable atmosphere for achieving its political and economic goals, and 'its goals for hemispheric security. Arms limitations, sanctions against giving aid to certain countries, reductions in military groups, have been interpreted as a reduction in North American interest in the region.

Non-Military Evaluations of Central America

To analyze adequately the most important developments of the present conjuncture and their impact on U.S.-Central American relations, it is necessary to repeat that the final decisions which the imperialist center makes regarding a particular country are not based on purely military factors. Rather, they come out of a complex process ripe with diverse interests and considerations related to the country in question, as well as to the internal situation of the United States. We agree with Gorostiaga[15] that the fundamental variable is the level of class struggle in each Latin American country. When this struggle intensifies to the point that popular alternatives cannot be manipulated or neutralized, then the imperialist center has historically moved to make decisions tending towards a more or less dramatic intervention (Santo Domingo in 1965; Chile in 1973). There will always be a second evaluation, related to the importance of the country in the world capitalist economy. The evaluation will be different if, for example, the country has abundant energy resources (Mexico, Venezuela), or if it contains a substantial percentage of direct U.S. foreign investment (Brazil), than if its natural resources or economy is insignificant (Nicaragua, Paraguay). Another factor would be the level of commercial trade. On these terms, the Central American region is not economically important to the U.S. The internal market of the region as a whole is too small to have an impact on import demands—barely 9% of U.S. exports to Latin America in 1977[16]—and total direct U.S. investment in all the countries of the Central American Common Market (Costa Rica, Guatemala, Honduras, El Salvador and Nicaragua) was only 2.6% of the total investment in Latin America.

With the exception of Guatemala, there has not been a significant presence in the region of transnational corporations which are highly influential in the decision-making process within the United States. In 1974, there were 126 U.S. firms in Guatemala (62.4% of all firms); 77 of them were in the *Fortune* 1,000 of 1974, and 31 were among the top 100 of *Fortune*, representing the giants of the capitalist world from a variety of areas of production. Among the transnationals which operate there are Exxon (No. 2 in *Fortune*), Texaco (No. 6), IBM (No. 8), U.S. Steel (No. 13), ITT (No. 9) and Gulf (No. 10). The Bank of America, No. 1 in finance according to *Fortune*, is also in Guatemala, as is UAL, the main tourism corporation. To these can be added the investments of important clans from the U.S. sunbelt—most importantly investment capital since the late 1960's from Alabama, Florida, southern California, New Orleans and Texas.[17] Together with the infamous traditional banana companies—United Brands, Del Monte and Standard Fruit—there are now subsidiaries of 21 agribusiness firms that number among the 100 largest in the world. Standard Oil of California is yet another investor. In Guatemala, unlike other Latin American countries, it is not possible to identify one or two main business groups that control a large percentage of investments or concentrate in only one area of the economy.

Another factor is the existence of raw materials which the U.S. is dependent upon for running its modern industrial economy. Even though the official report of the U.S. Department of Defense excluded Guatemala as one of the six Latin American countries with strategic raw materials,[18] this country has important reserves of oil and nickel, both of which are key to U.S. industry and the U.S. war machine, and for which the U.S. must depend on foreign sources. Guatemalan agencies and the foreign companies which hold the rights to extract oil have been sparing in giving official statistics, but Basic Resources, one of the three companies that have wells in the Rebelsanto and Chinaje Oeste regions, has estimated that there are 80 million barrels in proven oil reserves.[19] And though present production is very small (in U.S. terms)—only 10,000 barrels per day in early July 1979—the investments being made by one of the three corporations make it possible to assume that production doubled by the end of 1980. The shipments of oil to the U.S. steadily increased in 1980, from 122,000 barrels in the first shipment, to 136,000 in the second, and 140,000 in the third.[20] It must also be remembered that since 1961 the first refinery in the region has been operating in Santo Tomás, Guatemala. It is owned by Breux Bridges Oil Refining Co.,[21] and has a capacity for producing 200,000 tons a year. Three years after its opening, Texaco was granted a concession.

The importance of Guatemalan oil becomes clearer when we remember that in 1978 four of the "seven sisters" operated in the country: *Gulf Oil*, with its affiliate Petróleos Gulf de Guatemala; *Exxon*, with three affiliates, Essochem de Centroamérica S.A., Esso Standard Guatemala Inc., and Esso Central America S.A.; *Standard Oil* of California with three affiliates: Refinería de Petróleo de Guatemala-California Inc. (Guatcal), Refinerías de Asfaltos Chevron Inc. and Cía. Petrolera Chevron Ltda.; and *Texaco* with its affiliates, Texaco Petroleum Co. and Texaco Guatemala Inc.

We find a similar situation with nickel, in terms of the inexistence of data. It is positively known that Guatemala has huge reserves of this strategic metal that is highly valued in the war industries and other branches of heavy industry. The president of the principal transnational corporation involved in nickel, International Nickel Company of Canada, Ltd. (INCO), told *Forbes* magazine in 1967 that "the most important potential sources of nickel in the free world outside of Canada are in New Caledonia, and we are there; those of Guatemala, and we are there, those of Indonesia, and I think we will be there too."[22] The other huge nickel mining company which also "is there" is the Hanna Mining Co., owner of the only nickel mine in U.S. territory. Along with INCO, Hanna owns a large part of a nickel mining concession in Guatemala, Exploraciones y Explotaciones Mineras Izabal, S.A. (EXMIBAL). Starting in 1971, the Guatemalan government gave its public approval to a $250 million project of EXMIBAL to produce 32,000 tons of refined nickel per year. In early 1974, the company announced that the investment had been reduced to $120 million to produce 12,500 tons of less refined metal. The results of the project, which finally got started in 1975, have never been published by either the companies or the government. We can see from this that the figures which list only $6.8 million of direct foreign investment in mines and quarries are doubtful indeed, as are the official figures for nickel exports which show only $4 million—about 0.3% of the total value of exports from the country.[23]

Central American Policies of the Carter Administration

When Carter became President of the United States, his advisers on Latin America had formulated a policy for this region that appeared to some as new and hopeful. Without attempting to offer here an analysis which has already been made elsewhere,[24] it is necessary to raise several key points that explain Carter's policies toward Central America and point toward the future. The principal ideas that the Carter Administration put forward were the so-called "human rights policy" and the abandonment of an approach that treated Latin America as a monolithic block which could be dealt with by a single U.S. policy. The human rights policy supposed that the U.S. government, returning "to the (liberal) roots of the nation," would guide its conduct towards other nations of the world based on their degree of respect or violation of the rights of individuals. The second part of the Carter policy proposed to establish policies from country to country or, in the case of Central America and the Caribbean, it established a subregional policy when there was real similarity in the economic, social and political conditions of the countries involved. The permanent bureaucrats of the State Department added a third idea: the necessity of fostering "viable democracies" in Latin America, according to the variables of each nation—that is, regimes halfway between dictatorships and the old liberal democracies like Chile, which had permitted the electoral victory of a Marxist candidate. The Carter team enthusiastically made this policy their own, so long as it coincided with one of the most important political documents of the Trilateral Commission, which laid out the limits (the "governability") of democracy in post-industrial society.[25]

For the Carter Administration, Guatemala appeared to be the first country where conditions favored the implementation of this policy. The elections announced for the first half of 1978 provided fertile ground in which to give incentives for the formation of a political "center" that would marginalize both the ultra-right MLN ("National Liberation Movement," the extremist right-wing party—Ed.) and the revolutionary organizations, and at the same time offer an image of acceptable democratic participation. On the other hand, the intensity of human rights violations made it possible to think that reprimands from Washington would be well received by a large spectrum of public opinion in the U.S. and throughout the centers of the capitalist world (to which they were directed, as a factor in restoring legitimacy). It was also hoped that the human rights policy would be well received by the regime that won the election, without damaging counterinsurgency efforts and without breaking U.S.-Guatemalan relations. Finally, Guatemala seemed to be the first link in a regional chain of "normalizations" that would be followed by Panama, Honduras and in 1981, at the end of the four years of Carter's Administration, by Nicaragua.

The U.S. plans, however, were disrupted by persistent developments. The electoral fraud that brought Fernando Romeo Lucas García to power, and the electoral muscle shown by the ultra-right led by Marco Sandoval Alarcón, left the "center"—represented in Lucas' formula by Vice Presidential candidate Francisco Villagrán Kramer and his Partido Revolucionario—reduced to minimal strength. Furthermore, the human rights policy that took the form of lukewarm proposals for reducing aid to the armed forces was strongly rejected by Guatemalan officialdom, which, following the path of the Southern Cone military regimes, chose to move even farther to the right. Intensified class struggle, especially at the level of the workers' movement and revolutionary groups with a military capacity, clinched the nonviability of a "limited democracy" formula for Guatemala.

Changes After Nicaragua and Iran

The U.S. government's view of Central America was substantially changed by the triumph of the mass insurrection in Nicaragua led by the Sandinista National Liberation Front. *For U.S. military and diplomatic strategy, this was, strictly speaking, a grave defeat. In the first place it demonstrated that the U.S. could no longer govern the political pillar of the so-called "Inter-American system."* In spite of the efforts of Washington diplomacy and pressures of all kinds, it was impossible for the Organization of American States, the OAS, to legitimize any kind of intervention aimed at sabotaging the Sandinista triumph. This time the correlation of forces in the region prevented the repetition of another Santo Domingo.

In the second place, it was demonstrated that in certain conjunctures, the regional military agreements are no longer operable. In spite of efforts by Somoza, the Pentagon, and friends of both within U.S. political circles, they could not invoke the Inter-American Treaty of Reciprocal Assistance to put together a "peace-keeping force." Furthermore, the subregional pact that was designed precisely for situations like the one in Nicaragua, the Central American Defense Council (CONDECA), could only offer weak undercover support to the pro-Yankee dynasty. And what is worse, CONDECA is now virtually destroyed by the withdrawal of the Nicaraguan National Government of Reconstruction and its Sandinista Army of the People.

Finally, the defeat of Somoza's National Guard *destroyed one of the pillars of U.S. military strategy for Latin America: that the "native armed forces" are capable of maintaining "stability" and "order" and control* over mass movements led by political forces that propose autonomous alternatives to dependence upon the United States. The National Guard, created, trained and sustained by imperialism, was incapable of militarily defeating the irregular FSLN forces and the rebelling masses. It then totally disintegrated when its political leadership fled the country, overwhelmed by internal and international pressures. Furthermore, it was shown that another armed force that has received preferential attention in the past, the National Guard of Panama, not only refused to support Somoza, but in fact was one of the basic factors in the military and diplomatic triumph of the Sandinistas.

Following a complete readjustment of the diplomatic corps in the Central American section of the State Department, the Carter Administration then played its cards in El Salvador. They attempted to take advantage of the existence of an "antifascist" section of the armed forces to help set up a civilian-military government that would be broad enough to effectively isolate the revolutionary left and the far right, the latter being, in Washington's judgment, the principal instigator of the brutal violations of human rights.

The civilian-military junta which emerged from the October 15,

1979 coup possessed many of the requisites laid out in the U.S. State Department's model for "viable democracies." The elements that came together to form the junta were the armed forces, cleansed of the most repressive elements linked to the former regime, according to the Carter Administration; the Christian Democrats; local social democrats; and people linked to the Communist Party and the progressive Catholic Church. The "radical left," defined as the principal enemy, was to be isolated and divided. The U.S. could thus support a broad-based government in which "moderates" predominated. However, the development of events tended to support those who believed that the lesson of Nicaragua was that "viable democracies" were incapable of defending U.S. interests in Latin America and therefore a return to military forms of control was necessary. The successive juntas isolated some of the armed forces, which were increasingly vexed by military and mass activities led by the revolutionary left, which for its part was uniting all progressive and democratic forces into one solid opposition front, the Frente Democrático Revolucionario (FDR). The "center" of Washington's dreams was reduced to the upper echelon of the armed forces, under the hegemony of the most repressive sector, along with some conspicuous, rightist Christian Democratic leaders headed by Napoleón Duarte and Antonio Morales. The rest of the Christian Democrats, including historical figures of the caliber of Héctor Dada and Rubén Zamora (formerly government ministers and members of the second and third juntas) formed the Popular Social Christian Movement and, along with the social democracy of Guillermo Ungo and broad centrist forces, joined the FDR.

While the failure of "viable" democracy was making itself evident in El Salvador, a new policy had already begun to be developed in Washington, emerging principally from the "national security" community, bureaucrats of the National Security Council, the CIA, the Defense Department and its intelligence and strategic analysis agencies. They were looking to redefine the picture of alliances and the composition and deployment of U.S. military forces—all against the background of lessons from revolutionary movements which had defeated Shah Pahlavi and Somoza.

The change from a policy of flexible response to the one we referred to above appeared clearly, and with the approval of the U.S. military, in a document entitled "Military Posture," which General George Brown presented to Congress when the 1979 budget year was discussed. The new policy was totally ratified during the first two years of the Carter Administration, both at the executive and legislative levels. The most notable proof of this was the founding of the Rapid Deployment Force (RDF). When the RDF was formed in August 1979, it was composed of two air transport divisions, two batallions of special Army land forces, and three divisions of Marines with their respective transports, accompanied by a flotilla of air transport planes from the Military Airlift Command (70 C-5 and 23 C-141). General Paul Kelly, commander of the force, has pointed out that since its founding they have had $5 billion at their disposal for a five-year period, with troop levels going from 80,000 at their founding to some 200,000 at the end of 1979. The Rapid Deployment Force was envisioned primarily— though not exclusively—as confronting regular armies that might invade countries where U.S. security is endangered, or allied armies which might deviate and thus seriously harm vital U.S. interests (Saudi Arabia, for example).

The new strategy is also oriented towards preparing battle forces for deployment in regions of high interest. These forces would be specialized in that region and situated near the hypothetical war zone. This is what is being negotiated with Egypt, Israel, Oman and Somalia for the Persian Gulf and Middle East; likewise, it is the Carter Administration's legacy to Reagan for Central America and the Caribbean. In Carter's own words of October 1, 1979, in effect a headquarters has been created exclusively for this region in Key West, Florida, to which "I will assign forces from all the military services for the expansion and carrying out of operations." Carter added, "This headquarters will use forces designed for action, if it is necessary." An official of a Latin American government told us that in the highest circles of his country it is estimated that the Joint Task Force on the Caribbean and Central America had nearly 15,000 soldiers mobilized by the end of 1980.

In addition to forming the Rapid Deployment Force especially for the "American Mediterranean," there has been a proposal to restructure the inter-hemispheric military alliance. Military relations, it is said, have become outdated and new bases of understanding must be developed to be able to tighten the links that join the supposedly common interests of all parties. It is suggested that greater responsibility be given to Latin American military leaders in defining military policy for the hemisphere; that a greater participation of the "regional powers" in continental defense be sought; and that there be increased participation of Latin American military leaders in evaluating the "threats" in the region and designing means of confronting them. The means that would accompany the proposals are: providing Latin American armed forces with modern and technologically sophisticated arms; stimulating the development of "more defense systems" in the region; advising the existing military in logistical support, operations planning, and other activities of the military high command; and inviting officials and cadets to participate in U.S. schools and academies on the same level as American participants. [26] In summary, they propose to elevate inter-American military relations at all levels, qualitatively and quantitatively, turning over to the southern armed forces some of the decisions on "continental defense" that before were made only by the United States.

The strategy of flexible response has been in effect for Central America and the Caribbean since even before the defeat of Anastasio

Somoza's National Guard in Nicaragua. For El Salvador, as for other countries, the native armed forces are the first line of defense. U.S. military assistance programs testify to this fact. Taking into consideration only four of the main programs—Foreign Military Sales Agreements, the Military Assistance Program, the International Military Education and Training Program and the Commercial Sales Program—we find that the armed forces of El Salvador received a total of $3,488,000 in 1976-78. This is a considerable amount for a tiny country the size of the state of Massachusetts, with a population of 4 million and a per capita gross national product of around $600. Between 1974 and 1978, the Salvadorean government bought 4 planes and 4 helicopters from the U.S.; 49 military planes, submachine guns, bombs and portable missiles from Israel; 12 planes from Brazil; and 12 tanks and 3 planes from France.[27]

After the military triumph of the Sandinistas in Nicaragua, reinforcement was accelerated. In November 1979, the first groups of U.S. advisers arrived in El Salvador to hand over equipment and provide training in riot control. In March 1980, $5.7 million was rerouted from the U.S. foreign aid program, including military ground transport, sophisticated communications equipment, precision guns and scopes, and abundant riot control materials.[28] Later, three more groups of advisers on intelligence operations and high command were sent. *The first stage of U.S. intervention had begun, with 36 U.S. military men in the war zone.*

Along with this military involvement, the Carter Administration tried to gain diplomatic support, with little success. Only a few Christian Democratic parties—including the ruling parties of Venezuela and Costa Rica—were willing to help the Christian Democratic military junta. Carter was successful, however, in arranging loans from the U.S., international agencies and other Western European countries to sustain the crisis-ridden economy and stave off the danger of a fiscal moratorium. Between March and September of 1980, they rounded up more than $400 million in loans from the Inter-American Development Bank, the World Bank, the International Monetary Fund, AID (U.S. Agency for International Development), the Central American Bank for Economic Integration and others. Some of these credits were used for military purposes, like the ambulances donated by AID (which prompted a formal complaint) or the funds for the so-called Salvadorean Institute for Agrarian Transformation to buy helicopters. The Catholic Church has denounced other forms of aid, but it is not possible to pinpoint them easily, since they do not require Congressional approval nor have they been publicized. To this list must be added the $10 million in parts for lethal arms that Carter decided to send a few days before leaving office, and the massive renewal in late 1980 of training in the Panama Canal Zone for 200 Salvadorean soldiers and officials.[29]

The second stage of intervention undertaken during the Carter

Administration was that of coordinating the armies of Honduras, Guatemala and El Salvador under the direction of the Southern Command of U.S. Armed Forces, based in the Canal Zone. Not only has the U.S. coordinated the actions of these armies, but in March 1980 it provided Honduras with $5 million in planes, helicopters and other equipment. The U.S. also authorized the sale of Israeli and French planes, rifles and other arms to both countries and did not oppose military aid offered by the armed forces of Chile, Venezuela and Argentina. This stage involves border protection operations and limited border incursions—incursions which have included massacres of civilians, denounced time and time again by the Archbishop of San Salvador, Arturo Rivera y Damas.

In the event that the first two stages of intervention might not be sufficient, the Carter Administration, prepared for a third stage: the use of U.S. armed forces. It seems clear that the Joint Task Force based in Key West would be involved in an action of this nature. According to official documents from the Pentagon, a war with Central America would also involve the Norfolk and Charleston bases on the Atlantic coast, and the San Diego base on the Pacific. Proof of this can be found in the latest maneuvers, called Rivers 2-80 and Rivers 2-81, that were carried out in the Caribbean basin and included 30 warships from Brazil, Venezuela, England and the U.S.— including 14 ships from Norfolk. The U.S. could make use of the 9,000 troops in the Canal Zone, but it does not seem likely that U.S. officials would overlook the possibility of internal conflict in Panama that would endanger the Isthmus passage. Finally, in case the above-mentioned troops were insufficient, the Rapid Deployment Force was already 70% constituted in nearby Tampa, Florida—again as a result of the Democratic Administration of Jimmy Carter.

The New Administration: Neoconservatives in Power

The knowledge that Latin American revolutionaries have about a U.S. administration has in the past usually been based on shaky foundations and generally ideologized. This time, however, the rise of an aggressive, anticommunist Republican leader like Reagan, plus the existence of a larger nucleus of academics from our subcontinent who are dedicated to studying the United States, have made it possible for more scientific, political attention to be given to the issues raised in the presidential election. One's own reading, and the collective analysis made in Mexico of current research projects on the neoconservative program of Reagan, have made it possible to advance more coherent hypotheses about the policies that the new administration will be implementing in Latin America.[30]

Our first hypothesis is that the neoconservative group which surrounds the new U.S. President is trying to represent for neoconservatism what the political philosophy and strategy of the New Deal and

Keynesian economics represented for the neoliberalism initiated by Franklin D. Roosevelt. Their refusal to contaminate their proposals with reactionary content of a "feudal" or rural type, and their presentation of these, instead, as typically bourgeois thinking; the degree of internal logic in their statements, despite the very different ideological backgrounds of their principal representatives; the intensity with which their proposals were disseminated throughout academia and the mass media; the solid linkage they have established with the ruling class, which perceives that a renovated program is necessary if it is to continue as the "ruling" class; their insistence that they possess an all-encompassing cosmic vision whose content is strategic, not tactical; and their rise following the failures of the liberal pragmatic regime of Johnson, the conservative pragmatic regime of Nixon-Ford, and Carter's trilateralism; all this tends to prove that we are witnessing a new group that will attempt nothing more and nothing less than burying one epoch and inaugurating a new one.

The second hypothesis, which comes out of reviewing the writings of the neoconservatives and the speeches and documents of candidate Reagan,[31] is that the neoconservatives diagnose a grave crisis in U.S. society centered on moral and cultural factors (authority, individual incentives, etc.). From their position in government they propose to attack the "enemy counterculture" throughout the whole of American society and, indeed, the world. Their strategy for the government and their strategy for the outside world are marked by this decision to regain the "collective will" and the "intellectual and moral leadership" of the United States and of the Western Christian world.

The third hypothesis, which tends to prove itself, is that even though Reagan has had to negotiate certain marginal aspects of his proposals, the basic ideas of the neoconservatives are those which have been implemented in government programs and in the principal appointments up to this time (March 4, 1981). Economic policies are an obvious demonstration of this.

With these evaluations in mind, we can better analyze the fundamental lines of strategy, foreign policy and defense that will guide U.S.-Central American relations during the Reagan Administration.

In our judgment, there are five basic lines of policy that we must keep in mind:

1) The new administration understands foreign policy as inextricably tied to defense policy. Strictly speaking, foreign policy is defense policy, or it is no policy at all.

2) The most important challenge facing the United States is the reestablishment of military might. This involves not simply going from supposed lost parity to parity, but from parity to superiority in all areas of war and in every corner of the globe.

3) "Foreign-defense" policy, when this involves areas or countries, must always be seen through the prism of the balance of power between

the U.S. and the Soviet Union. To put it another way, it is not possible to conceive of national or regional situations, or national struggles, or regional or national analysis, because whatever occurs in whatever part of the world is seen in relationship to the confrontation with the USSR. This leads, among other things, to the negation of the North-South axis and its replacement—in rhetoric and in deeds—by the East-West axis.

4) The United States must regain its leadership of the Christian and Western world. Allies must certainly be consulted about the decisions that directly involve them, but the only power with global capabilities is and should continue to be the U.S.—which thus becomes the *factotum* of the defense of Western civilization.

5) The neo-Clausewitzian paradigm of the legitimacy of the ends vs. the legitimacy of the means must be reestablished. The capitalist world must be convinced that war is legitimate and that it is not true that it is uncontrollable. In this way, flexible response, the strategic matrix for "containing communism," is brought back to life, and—with the lessons of Vietnam supposedly well learned—new levels of flexibility are added to the responses. A new nuclear step must be created—limited nuclear war—and better-armed Joint Rapid Deployment Forces must be diversified and extended to all parts of the globe. The allies as well should be armed and trained so they are able to defend themselves from the enemy on their own territory.

These central lines of policy have their correlaries for Latin America, but they are exaggerated by the kind of Latin Americanists who were part of the Reagan candidacy team, and are now beginning to occupy the key positions in decision-making about the subcontinent. For the most part they come from the so-called "geopolitical school" of the Center of Strategic Studies at Georgetown University. They began their work of making contacts with the most authoritarian governments and most right-wing reactionaries of Latin America as soon as they began their association with Ronald Reagan. Their willingness to impose their views upon bureaucracies that do not share the same perspective has already been demonstrated by the removal of ex-Ambassador to El Salvador Robert White, and ex-Assistant Secretary of State for Inter-American Affairs William Bowdler.

The new team happily accepts the idea—even more so because they played an important role in its formulation—that Latin American policies should be subordinated to the global, geopolitical confrontation with the Soviet Union. They believe that the "ill-omened" style of the Carter Administration, with its proclivity for statements and rhetoric, must be abandoned. They, in contrast, will take *action*, because of its "surprise value." They are firmly convinced that Latin America and the Caribbean are the geopolitical zones in which they can achieve their results most effectively, quickly and with the least costs—to demonstrate new U.S. strength and resolve to both the Soviet Union and under-developed nations. It is an area where sufficient friends can be found; it is too far from the USSR (which has already recognized that this is a zone of influence reserved to the U.S.), and, in the case of crises, the only countries involved are economically, politically and militarily weak. They believe it their duty to connect foreign and defense policy to the private U.S. interests that are spread throughout Latin America. And finally, they believe it is more beneficial to establish bilateral relations than to permit regional and subregional treaties which increase the negotiating power of their Latin American counterparts.

The Reagan Administration Faces Central America

With this analytical arsenal — much more sophisticated than space permits us to describe — the formulators of Reagan's Latin American policy believe they see three kinds of countries in terms of U.S. interests in Latin America.

1) Medium-sized countries — those which Brzezinski's rhetoric called "emerging powers," because they have military or economic power (due to their industrial base or strategic raw materials) that makes them fundamental to U.S. "vital interests." Mexico and Brazil constitute the first line in this category, Venezuela and Argentina the second. U.S. power must be focused on them by means of preferential negotiations so that they line up as much as possible with the U.S. in the global confrontation.

2) Loyal allies which are not medium-sized powers. This includes the rest of the countries except the critical cases. They range on a scale from the "very loyal" at one end (Jamaica and Chile) to the disobedient at the other (Ecuador and Panama), with the quantity and quality of U.S. economic, military and diplomatic aid being in direct relation to their degree of loyalty.

3) "Critical cases" where there are openly enemy governments (Cuba, Grenada and Nicaragua), or friendly governments that are besieged by "communist insurgency supported by the USSR and Cuba" (El Salvador and Guatemala).

In the eyes of the new administration, Central America has become a critical case, since three countries in the region are classified in this category and one is an ally that must be disciplined. Furthermore, the weakness of the El Salvador government and the strength of the political-military opposition in El Salvador makes this country, and the region as a whole, the most important and urgent of all world problems to be resolved.

To confront this threat, the administration has applied the rejuvenated strategy of flexible response. In the cases of Cuba and Grenada, the administration creates conditions to justify intensification of the blockade, with an eye towards exacerbating existing problems in both countries and laying the bases for possible future action against weakened regimes. In the case of Nicaragua, at the moment there is a barrage of every form of non-military destabilization: covert action, psychological warfare, economic blockade, use of the food weapon, diplomatic struggles, open support of the pro-U.S opposition, etc. In Guatemala and Honduras, the indigenous defense network is being fortified and the establishment of regional coordination of all armed forces loyal to the U.S. is being hastened. Panama is under increased pressure to fall in line with U.S. policies. In El Salvador, the stakes are being raised by massive aid to the native military forces, greater coordination at the level of a regional battle zone, and preparations are intensifying for the eventual use of U.S. forces already built up by the Carter Administration under the strategy of the "rapid deployment strike force." The need to point to "communist intervention" in order to justify use of U.S. troops has already been met by the fabrication of the "White Paper" which the State Department has circulated since February of this year. The weakness of this incredibly shabby "evidence" simply points to the firmness of the U.S. decision to prevent, by all possible means, the establishment of another "hostile government" in the area.

Conclusions

1) The study of the formal decision-making process of U.S. foreign policy provides useful and valid tools for grasping the policies that will be applied to Latin America and for predicting changes, even within a given presidential regime. It is true that part of the process is secret, and its instrument or its product not accessible to the researcher (the National Security Council and the CIA, for example). However, the need for Congressional review of some of the decisions, before or after they are taken, and the publicity that others require, make it possible to know the strategic and political consensus that exists concerning the subcontinent and the central lines that will be implemented to defend "national interests" at a given time and place.

2) Even though Latin America has not received priority attention in the overall U.S. political system—as many believed *a priori* —strategic and military considerations make it a high priority, particularly in the Central American and Caribbean region (including Mexico). Economist interpretations that understand U.S.-Latin American relations from the sole perspective of what role a country or region plays in the U.S. economy will make a grave error if they look only at trade levels and direct investment. Indeed, an adequate analysis of this factor (the role in the U.S. economy) requires finding out which U.S. corporations are involved in each country and how important a role they play in the U.S. political process. This explains, for example, why Guatemala is considered more important than other countries in the area, and how private banking is supporting the El Salvador junta because of its interests located mainly in Guatemala.

3) The Central American policies of the Carter Administration can be divided into two periods, separated by the triumph of the Frente

Sandinista de Liberación Nacional in Nicaragua. During the first period, preference was given to implementing the model of "viable democracies." During the second, the "military solution" and alliances with armed forces of the region were given preference, except during a brief interval in El Salvador prior to the collapse of the October 1979 junta. (The collapse came in January of 1980, at least in political terms.) The application of this policy was facilitated by the Pentagon's strategy of re-accommodating U.S.-Latin American military relations, similar to what was done after the triumph of the Cuban Revolution.

4) In this context, the "solution" to the Salvadorean crisis became the cornerstone of the new policy. Once it was diagnosed as a critical "test case," the Establishment acted without the vacillations it showed during the Sandinista insurrection and gave unqualified support to the Duarte military junta. It not only provided arms and training, but also mobilized a huge amount of credits, "aid" and economic gifts. The latter, in addition to being aimed at preventing the total collapse of the government, were designed to give the government greater ability to repress and control the population and the "insurgents" (by offering a few jobs, organizing the peasants in strategic hamlets as was done in Vietnam, coopting the urban poor, etc.).

5) The rise of Ronald Reagan to the U.S. Presidency represents a profound change in the conception of international relations that will have profound repercussions in U.S. policies toward Latin America. In essence, as Roger Fontaine, U.S. adviser for Latin American affairs to the National Security Council, said without mincing words, the "Truman Doctrine" will once again be carried out in Latin America. The ideas of the new administration coincide with and strengthen the strategic definitions already formulated by the U.S. military establishment. There is no longer a voice in the civilian sectors of the Executive branch to speak out against the danger of military intervention. Only the force of popular and progressive U.S. organizations and the actions of governments and peoples of other continents can stop this decision from being made—can prevent the youth of the United States from being hurled once again into another dirty war that, like Vietnam, will end in another defeat. Progressive and democratically minded people from the United States and Latin America must organize a broad, active solidarity movement that acts *now* so as to dissuade the U.S. generals and politicians at the moment when they would come to such a decision. And if open intervention does occur, our peoples must initiate a bold struggle at all levels and wage it—for the sake of all the Latin American countries and their national autonomy, and for the sake of the future of the North American people—until the final defeat of the invaders and the triumph of Central America's democratic movements.

Mexico—March 4, 1981

NOTES

1. Abundant literature exists on "National Security" and on strategy related to the U.S. conception of national security; a good summary of the most accepted concepts will be found in Stephen B. Jones, "The Power Inventory and National Security." In *World Politics*, Vol. VI (United States, 1954), pp. 421-52.

For a broader bibliography, see the one included in our book, *Fuerzas Armadas y Defensa Nacional* (University of Sinaloa, Mexico, 1980). Researchers familiar with the focus given to the decision-making process by official U.S. political science will readily note that this school would be of the "classic model" of Graham T. Allison, *Essence of Decision* (Boston, Little Brown, 1971) and what other authors have called "of the rational actor." The class content of these is obvious, which is why we avoid using them in this work.

2. Henry Kissinger, "Armas nucleares y Política Internacional," Edit. Rialp (translation by R. Cremades, Madrid, Spain, 1962).

3. For a more detailed description of this process, see our research abstract: "El Proceso formal de decisiones de la Defensa Nacional de Estados Unidos," *Cuadernos CELA* (Facultad de Ciencias Políticas y sociales, UNAM, 1979).

4. The principal documents that we use in our analysis are:
— "United States Military Posture for FY 1979," by the Chairman of the Joint Chiefs of Staff, General George S. Brown, edited by the Joint Chiefs.
— "Informe Anual para el Año Fiscal de 1979," by Harold Brown, Secretary of Defense, edited by the Department of Defense. We use the translation in *Cuadernos Semestrales de Estados Unidos, Perspectiva Latinoamericana*, Second Semester of 1978, No. 4, edited by CIDE, Mexico.
— Comments and press interviews of President Jimmy Carter and his principal foreign policy advisers (Secretary of State Cyrus Vance; National Security Adviser Zbigniew Brzezinski).
— Publications of the U.S. Congress and the Government Printing Office from the respective Congressional committees on this topic.

5. The debate can be followed by consulting the magazines of the military establishment, especially issues from 1975, 1976 and 1977, and books published by its primary spokesmen. In our opinion, the following works are particularly relevant:
— Major Marc B. Powe, "The U.S. Army After the Fall of Vietnam: A Contemporary Disjuncture." *Military Review* (February 1976).
— Brigadier General Edward B. Atkeson, "International Crises and the Evolution of Strategy and Forces." *Military Review* (October 1975 [Part I] and November 1975 [Part II]).
— William V. O'Brien, *The Conduct of Just and Limited War* (Washington, D.C., American Enterprise Institute, 1978).
— General William C. Westmoreland, "Vietnam in Perspective." *Military Review* (January 1979).
— Colonel Charles J. Bauer, "Military Planning in National Crises." *Military Review* (August 1975).
— Major Wesley K. Clark, "Gradualism and U.S. Military Strategy." *Military Review* (September 1975).

6. To understand the "strategy of flexible response" and its history, see:
— Robert Osgood, "The Reappraisal of Limited War." *Adelphi Papers* No. 54 (London).
— Maxwell D. Taylor, *The Uncertain Trumpet* (New York, Harper and Row, 1960).
— Theodore Sorensen, *The Counterinsurgency Era* (New York, Free Press, 1977).

7. We have reviewed the annual "Military Posture" of the Chairman of the Joint Chiefs, the "Annual Report" of the Secretary of Defense, and the principal published interviews granted to the press on the subject by President Carter and his National Security Adviser, Zbigniew Brzezinski.

8. Interview with Carter by national U.S. editors. Published in the "Documentos" section of *Cuadernos Semestrales de Estados Unidos, Perspectiva Latinoamericana,*" First Semester 1979, CIDE, Mexico.

9. Speech by Senator Edward Kennedy before the 34th General Assembly by the Inter-American Press Association.

10. See "Military Posture," op. cit.

11. Ibid. p. 5.

12. Spykman understood the "American Mediterranean" as the waters between the Atlantic coast of southern Mexico, Central America, Colombia, Venezuela and the chain of islands that extends from eastern Venezuela up through Cuba and ends with the Bahamas; he divided this "Mediterranean" into a western sector (the Gulf of Mexico) and an eastern sector (the Caribbean Sea).

13. R. Antonio Cavalla, "Geopolítica y Seguridad Nacional en América," edited by the Universidad Autónoma de Mexico (UNAM), *Colección Lecturas Universitarias* No. 30 (1978).

14. Cited by J.B. Durosell, *Política Exterior de los Estados Unidos: De Wilson a Roosevelt (1913-1945)* (Fondo de Cultura Económica, Mexico, 1965). The works of Mahan— four books and 150 articles—strongly influenced American strategic thinking in the first three decades of this century.

15. Xabier Gorostiaga, "Las relaciones Estados Unidos— Panamá bajo la Administración Carter," study presented to the CIDE Seminar on "Los Impactos nacionales de la política de Carter en América Latina" (Mexico, January 1979).

16. From *Estados Unidos, perspectiva latinoamericana* 4, 9 (September 1979). The issue is dedicated to analyzing U.S. reactions to the Sandinista triumph in Nicaragua.

17. From S. Jonas and D. Tobis, *Guatemala, una historia inmediata*, Siglo XXI (Mexico, 1976). This book is indispensable to the study of our present topic.

18. See the "Military Posture" of the Chairman of the Joint Chiefs of Staff of the U.S. Armed Forces, presented annually to the U.S. Congress.

19. Declarations of Julio Mathew, executive of the BRC, given to reporter Rafael Cribari of *Inter Press Service*, August 10, 1980, in Panama City.

20. *Time* (August 18, 1980) reported that the U.S. has received 258,000 barrels as of that year.

21. Gerard Pierre-Charles, *Dominación y Dependencia*. From Mario Monteforte, *Centroamérica*, IIS (UNAM, 1972), p. 348.

22. Cited in S. Jonas and D. Tobis, *Guatemala, una historia inmediata*, Siglo XXI (Mexico, 1976).

23. In *Los rasgos fundamentales de la formación social guatemalteca*, presentation by the IIES of the Universidad de San Carlos of Guatemala to the I Congreso Científico Universitario, on "La problemática de la Niñez Guatemalteca" (Guatemala City, 1980).

24. See: Luis Maira, "Estados Unidos-América Latina: Perspectivas de cambio bajo la Administración Carter?" in *Cuadernos Semestrales del CIDE*, No. 6 (1979). By the same author, "Fracaso y reacomodo de la política de Estados Unidos hacia Centroamérica," in *Foro Internacional* XX, 4 (April-June 1980). See also our work, "Centroamérica y la Defensa 'nacional' norteamericana," in *Análisis* (March 1980, Santiago de Chile).

25. The report on the "Governability of Democracy" was prepared by Harvard professor Samuel Huntington, in collaboration with Michel Croizier of France and Joji Watanki of Japan. For an excellent interpretation of this and other aspects of the Trilateral Commission, see the article by Carlos Rico, " 'Interdependencia' y trilateralismo: orígines de una estrategia." In *Cuadernos Semestrales del CIDE* No. 2-3 (1977-78).

26. See, for example, the series of declarations by representatives of the

"national security community" published in *U.S. News and World Report* and articles in such magazines as *International Security Military Review*, and others tied to the Department of Defense. See the article by M.D. Hayes, "Security to the South: U.S. Interest in L.A." in *International Security* (Summer 1980).

27. Cynthia Arnson, several works published by the Institute for Policy Studies during 1980.

28. Statement of Franklin D. Kramer, Principal Deputy Assistant Secretary of Defense—International Security Affairs, before the Subcommittee on Foreign Operations—Committee on Appropriations, mimeo (March 25, 1980), pp. 3-4. For a similar focus see John Bushnell, Acting Assistant Secretary of State for Inter-American Affairs, in *Arms Trade in the Western Hemisphere*, hearings before the Subcommittee on Inter-American Affairs, doc. H 461-9, Washington, D.C., GPO, 1980).

29. See Tommie S. Montgomery and Antonio Cavalla, "Interés Nacional Norteamericano e intervención en El Salvador," in *El Día* (Mexico, February 3, 1981); and our work "Centroamérica en la estrategia militar norteamericana durante la Administración Carter," in *Iztapalapa*, Año 2, No. 3 (July-December 1980).

30. We refer to the works of researchers Atilio Borón and John Saxe-Fernández of the Facultad de Ciencias Políticas de la UNAM; and of Luis Maira, Roberto Bouza and the team from the Instituto de Estados Unidos of CIDE in Mexico. Since we have seen all these works in the form of manuscripts for discussions and conferences, we will omit the references to them, pointing out that the greater part of the ideas contained here come from the works of the above-mentioned researchers.

31. Among the principal resources that we have reviewed are:

— Data Center, Files on Reagan's Campaign. Data Center, Oakland, CA, 1981.

— Richard Fagen (ed.), *Resurgent Cold War Ideology: The Case of the Committee on the Present Danger* (Stanford University Press, 1979).

— Roger W. Fontaine, *On Negotiating With Cuba* (Washington, D.C., American Enterprise Institute for Public Policy Research, 1975).

— Roger W. Fontaine, *Brazil and the U.S.: Toward a Maturing Relationship* (Washington, D.C., American Enterprise Institute for Public Policy Research, 1978).

— R. Fontaine, C. DiGiovanni, Jr., and A. Kruger, "Castro's Specter." *The Washington Quarterly* (Autumn 1980).

— Roger W. Fontaine, and James D. Theberge (eds.), *Latin America's New Internationalism: The End of Hemispheric Isolation* (New York, Praeger Publishers, in cooperation with the Center for Strategic and International Studies, Georgetown University, 1976).

— James L. George, *Problems of Sea Power as We Approach the Twenty-First Century* (Washington, D.C., American Enterprise Institute for Public Policy Research, 1978).

— Nathan Glazer, *The American Commonwealth* (New York, Basic Books, 1976).

— Alexander M. Haig, Jr., "Judging SALT II." *Strategic Review* (Winter 1980).

— Charles D. Hobbs, *Ronald Reagan's Call to Action* (New York, Prentice Hall, 1976).

— Kenneth P. Jameson, "Supply Side Economics: Growth Versus Income Distribution." *Challenge*, (November-December 1980).

— Lewis Coser and Irving Howe, *The New Conservatives: A Critique From the Left* (New York, Meridian Books, 1977).

— Jeane Kirkpatrick, "Dictatorship and Double Standards." *Commentary* (November 1979).

— Jeane Kirkpatrick, "The Hobbes Problem: Order, Authority and Legitimacy in Central America" (Paper presented at the December 1980 Public Policy Week of the American Enterprise Institute for Public Policy Research), Washington, D.C., 1980.

— Jeane Kirkpatrick, "U.S. Security and Latin America." *Commentary* (January 1981).

— Irving Kristol, *On the Democratic Idea in America* (New York, Harper and Row, Torchbooks, 1972).

— Ronald Reagan, "Presentation to the Joint Session of the U.S. Congress on his Economic Program," February 18, 1981 (various sources).

— James Theberge, *Presencia soviética en América Latina*. Editorial Gabriela Mistral, Santiago de Chile, 1974.

— James Theberge and Roger W. Fontaine, *Latin America: Struggle for Progress*. (Commission on Critical Choices for Americans, Vol. XIV, Massachusetts, Lexington Books, 1977).

Contradictions of Revolution and Intervention in Central America in the Transnational Era: The Case of Guatemala

Susanne Jonas

The author wishes to acknowledge and thank her colleagues at the Institute for the Study of Labor and Economic Crisis, and in particular its Research Director, Marlene Dixon, for significant assistance and theoretical orientation in the writing of this chapter. It was originally prepared as a paper for the conference, "Central America and the Caribbean: Crisis and Revolt," April 22-23, 1983, State University of New York at Albany. Portions of this work were presented by Institute representatives at the Permanent People's Tribunal session on Guatemala, held in Madrid, Spain, in January 1983.

Introduction

The realities of the transnational era have radically altered the relations between Central American revolutionary movements and the forces of U.S. intervention. Although the fundamental changes are obscured by the daily news headlines, they are very material and very materially affect the prospects for the future of the hemisphere. In this chapter, we shall focus on Guatemala, keeping in mind, however, the broader regional picture in Central America. The contradictions of revolution and intervention in the transnational era which we shall examine here are an outgrowth of basic changes in the capitalist world-economy and in the world balance of forces over the last two to three decades, which have altered the forms and options of U.S. Cold War politics.

Nearly 30 years ago, in 1954, the U.S. government, in direct and active collaboration with U.S. corporate interests, intervened directly and militarily in Guatemala to oust the progressive, nationalist, and anti-imperialist, bourgeois democratic government of Jacobo Arbenz, the second government of the 1944-54 Guatemalan "Revolution." At the time, U.S. interests were able to act with a free hand to achieve their objectives, unfettered by any significant opposition either internally from within the U.S. or internationally, for reasons which we shall indicate below.

Today, the Reagan Administration is no less determined to follow a Cold War policy in Guatemala (and in Central America generally), and indeed has deliberately made Central America a theater of Cold War politics. However, the world and the position of the United States within the world have changed sufficiently that it is no longer possible to view U.S. policy in Central America simply in terms of the interests of the U.S. government, nor the conflict there as a simple conflict in the "backyard" of the United States. Today there are new forces which substantially affect the international arena and the Central American region.

Marlene Dixon has analyzed the most important of these new forces as the transnational capitalist enterprises, and the most basic structural changes in the capitalist world-economy in terms of a *dual power* relationship that has evolved between the ruling elites of the bourgeois national governments and the bourgeois transnational corporate enterprises.[1] Since the end of World War II, nation-states have increasingly been compelled to *share power* with world-spanning transnational enterprises, which owe allegiance to no single nation-state, and elude governmental regulations of any one nation as a result of their ability to maneuver globally and to manipulate a broad network of the world's nation-states to their own advantage.

As a consequence of the above, whatever the objectives of the Reagan Administration (i.e., the current government of one national capitalist power), they are not fully determinative, as transnational capital is able to operate independently, although in coordination with the U.S. government. This may seem a technical distinction at a time when the Reagan Administration appears to be acting in concert with corporate interests. However, even today, if we look beneath the surface, we can begin to see the practical manifestations of this distinction; and if we project into the future, the implications become even clearer, as we shall suggest below.

Furthermore, since the late 1960s, the rise of transnational capitalist enterprises which are ultimately ungovernable by *any* single nation-state has occurred simultaneously with, and has been directly linked to, the decline of the United States as the single hegemonic power in the international capitalist arena.[2] As we shall see, this is another crucial factor in reshaping and limiting the options of the Reagan Administration in Central America and specifically in Guatemala.

There are additional reasons why the Reagan Administration has been unable to impose a simple defeat upon the revolutionary forces in Guatemala. The Reagan government is using the apparatus of the Guatemalan counterinsurgency state, constructed and maintained over the years by the U.S., and now epitomized by the Ríos Montt regime, in an attempt to destroy the resistance movement. However, it has not succeeded in that attempt, both because of the growing strength of the resistance and because of the fragility and internal contradictions of the counterinsurgency state.

Of course, the Reagan Administration has the military power to intervene directly, Vietnam-style, an option which has by no means been definitively discarded. But even this kind of intervention could achieve its objectives only by literally exterminating entire sectors of the Guatemalan population and literally destroying the country. In fact, such a process has already begun in recent years and is a crucial component of U.S. policy; it is for this reason that one government after another in Guatemala, essentially since 1954, has been identified as among the world's most vicious violators of human rights, with the U.S. government identified as the chief accomplice. But even these systematic policies of destruction, now approaching genocide, have not succeeded in destroying the resistance movement; moreover, aiding and abetting these policies, as will be detailed below, has left the Reagan Administration isolated both internationally and domestically.

Meanwhile, it is important to keep in mind another fundamental change: the Reagan Administration, far from representing U.S. "national interests" (the interests of the American people), does not even represent the totality of U.S. ruling class interests. In fact, the very term "U.S. ruling class" is a shorthand term, a gross oversimplification of a very complex reality. "The U.S. ruling class" is not one entity, but an extremely complex combination of fractions of the bourgeoisie representing transnational capital and national capital, and their respective political agents who run the state apparatus.[3] When necessary to meet a common threat, these various fractions and strata of the ruling class can and do unite. In the case of Guatemala, we may define that unity as the shared determination not to "lose" Guatemala, i.e., not to permit there the permanent institutionalization of an independent, revolutionary, anti-capitalist government. However, even within that unity, we shall argue that important tactical differences are developing over what it really means to "lose" Guatemala, and how to prevent such a loss, in the short and long range. The debates within ruling circles over U.S. policy toward the Sandinista government in Nicaragua may be, as we shall see, an indication of present and future debates over Guatemala.

The profound changes in the structure of the world-economy and polity and in the global balance of forces also have serious implications for the Guatemalan revolutionary movement. Its immediate objective — to overthrow the counterinsurgency state which has dominated Guatemala for 20 to 30 years — remains unchanged. But the situation which a postrevolutionary Guatemalan government will face is far from easy, for the tremendous power of transnational capital (which is not subject even to the pressures of public opinion that affect the U.S. government or any national government) intensifies greatly the contradictions of socialist construction for newly liberated countries. Contemporary Nicaragua is a case in point. In this sense, the struggle of the Guatemalan people will not be over with the revolutionary seizure of state power, but will enter a new phase. The contradictions of the Guatemalan Revolution in a transnational era are no less real than the contradictions of U.S. intervention today.

In this paper, then, we shall address ourselves to analysis at two levels. First, we shall trace the development of the Guatemalan counter-insurgency state and the U.S. policies designed to create and maintain such a state as a counterrevolutionary instrument. This is the basis for understanding the stark realities of the current Guatemalan situation, and it remains the determinative factor in the lives of millions of people on a daily basis. Second, going a step farther, we shall also attempt to address the less obvious, more complex issues facing both the forces of intervention and a postrevolutionary state in Guatemala in the future.

I. The Imposition of the Guatemalan Counterinsurgency State by the U.S. Government

For many years, successive regimes in Guatemala have been identified as among the world's most vicious violators of human rights. If we define human rights in the strict sense, Guatemala has sustained one of the highest rates in the world of right-wing/official assassinations, "disappearances," executions, and torture, directed against individuals and against groups. According to conservative estimates, 80,000 people have been the victims of right-wing/official violence since 1954,[4] over 5,000 under the Lucas García regime (1978-82),[5] and more than 8,000 from May to November of 1982, under the present regime of General Efraín Ríos Montt.[6]

This pattern of systematic human rights atrocities against individuals must be understood in its broader context, to include the social and economic rights of the Guatemalan people as a whole. From this perspective, we can only explain the level of oppression by going back to the 1954 U.S. intervention which overthrew the Arbenz government, the second government of the progressive, nationalist, reformist Guatemalan Revolution of 1944-54, and instituted a counterrevolutionary government designed to protect U.S. interests; the Counterrevolution was subsequently institutionalized in the form of a U.S.-maintained counterinsurgency state. The stark realities of human rights violations and the steady deterioration of the social existence of the vast majority of the people that have become constant, unchanging features of Guatemalan life are the necessities of the U.S.-imposed Counterrevolution and counterinsurgency state.

The Guatemalan Revolution of 1944-54 was the object of the first major U.S. intervention in Latin America after World War II—the first application in the hemisphere of the Truman Doctrine (developed to justify the 1947 U.S. intervention in Greece)—and the test case and model for this policy in Latin America. Without repeating here the details of the CIA intervention to oust the Arbenz government in 1954, which are now public knowledge and have been well chronicled elsewhere,[7] we must ask: Given that the Guatemalan Revolution was explicitly not socialist, but progressive, democratic, nationalist, and anti-imperialist in character, why was the U.S. ruling class united in its determination not to tolerate such a revolution?

First, the national capitalist Arbenz government imposed regulations on existing U.S. monopoly investments there, and threatened future prospects for maintaining the area as a "safe" preserve for expanding U.S. monopolistic corporations. The U.S. ruling class would not tolerate any regime which might make trouble for U.S. capital. In this regard, the cardinal sin of the Arbenz government had been its implementation of an agrarian reform law in 1952 which affected the (unused) holdings of the United Fruit Co., the largest landowner in Guatemala. Second, U.S. private investors and the U.S. government became concerned over the increasing radicalization of the Guatemalan Revolution under Arbenz—defining "radicalization" as that government's policies of permitting the operation of opposition political parties (including the Communist Party), and of guaranteeing the right of workers and peasants to organize to defend their interests— in other words, basic bourgeois democratic freedoms. From the point of view of the U.S. ruling class, the situation could well get "out of control."

Third, the Arbenz government refused to submit blindly to the dictates of Washington in its foreign policy—an unpardonable challenge, at the height of the Cold War. Finally, the U.S. was afraid that the *example* of a progressive and democratic and anti-imperialist government in Guatemala would cause the spread of such "revolutions" to other countries in Latin America.[8] As will be seen below, the U.S. ruling class defines a "threat to its strategic interests" in Guatemala today for many of the same reasons as in 1954.

As the U.S. moved immediately to reverse the progress made during 10 years of the Revolution, the 1954 intervention established the basic pattern of human rights violations which has prevailed since that time. It began with a suspension of all constitutional guarantees and a sweeping witch-hunt against political and labor leaders. Thousands of workers and peasants were jailed, tortured, exiled, or killed. The political parties supporting the Revolution were dissolved, and the labor unions were disbanded. Teachers were fired, books were burned. All of the progressive laws of the Revolutionary era—the land reform, the nationalistic laws regulating foreign investors, the labor code—were wiped off the books. All of the land distributed to peasants under the 1952 agrarian reform was returned to the former owners. The doors of the country were opened wide to U.S. private investors.[9]

The ouster of Arbenz was the first or preliminary step in U.S.

Cold War policy in Guatemala; once having intervened, the U.S. had to fashion an effective counterrevolutionary alternative by installing a puppet regime and pouring in massive amounts of U.S. aid ($80-90 million in economic aid alone, in the first 3 years).[10] Longer-range, it meant that the U.S. was committed to a continuing intervention in Guatemalan political life, in order to repress popular movements, to maintain a pro-U.S. client bourgeoisie in power, to open up Guatemala (and the Central American region as a whole) to new foreign investment, and to create there a "stable" climate for such investment.

By the end of the 1950s, it became clear that simply overwhelming Guatemala with U.S. economic aid and political control would not work. After the initial shock of the counterrevolutionary intervention wore off, political unrest increased, particularly among students and workers, and paved the way for the rise of an armed guerrilla movement by 1962. This movement was able to grow throughout the 1960s because, in spite of much rhetoric during the era of the Alliance for Progress, the U.S. government proved completely unwilling to make or support any serious reforms in Guatemala (or elsewhere in Central or Latin America). In fact, the U.S. government was committed to policies designed to stabilize Central America for "security" reasons and in order to protect the interests of foreign capital; it could not at the same time be seriously committed to making land or tax reforms—or any of the reforms which would have been necessary to alleviate the growing social contradictions in the country and the region.[11]

Since social conditions actually worsened during the 1960s, and since the dominant political reality was not democracy but repression and military dictatorship, it is not surprising that the incipient guerrilla movement formed in the early 1960s grew. By 1966-68 it was strong enough to require a major U.S.-sponsored counterinsurgency offensive using Vietnam-tested technology. This offensive succeeded temporarily in containing the insurgency, through widespread repression directed against entire sections of the population as well as against the guerrillas.

It was during this first serious armed confrontation that we may see the beginnings of what is being today consolidated as the *counterinsurgency state*. Such a state, as spelled out by Ruy Mauro Marini, is a particular form of counterrevolutionary government, based on counterinsurgency doctrine,

> ...which establishe[s] the line of confrontation with revolutionary movements on three levels: annihilation, winning over social bases, and institutionalization.... [Counterinsurgency] sees the opponent as the enemy that not only must be defeated, but also must be annihilated, destroyed. This implies seeing the class struggle as war, and leads to the adoption of military tactics and methods of struggle.... Its general characteristic [is] the

recourse to state terrorism by the victorious fraction in order to defeat both its rival fractions and most especially the working class.[12]

The counterinsurgency *state*, in this conception, is:

... the corporate state of the monopoly bourgeoisie and the armed forces, independent of whatever form the state might adopt, that is to say, independent of the prevailing political regime.[13]

The key to the basic continuity of Guatemalan politics from the 1960s to the present lies in the shaping, imposition, and institutionalization of the counterinsurgency state as a mechanism for controlling the population. The role of the U.S. government in creating and maintaining this state is documented in the Tables 1 through 4 and in the following section.

II. The Generalization of the Counterinsurgency State as an Apparatus of Repression Against the Population

Why has a counterinsurgency operation — presumably designed to wipe out the several thousand active guerrilla fighters — today become a war of extermination approaching genocide, directed against entire sectors of the population? In order to fully understand the scale of the war taking place in Guatemala and its toll in human rights terms, we must trace its evolution and deepening as a class war, and the elaboration of the counterinsurgency state in the context of this war.

The early protests against the Counterrevolution in the late 1950s and early 1960s were staged primarily by labor unions (such as were left after the decimation of the labor movement in 1954) and by radicalized sectors of the petty bourgeoisie. The demands of the students, workers, and teachers at this point were directed primarily against economic hardship and political repression, culminating in widespread street demonstrations in the spring of 1962. Simultaneously, disaffected army officers who were radicalized by the peasants among whom they sought refuge after an abortive uprising in 1960 joined forces with elements of the Communist Party to form the first guerrilla movement in 1962.

The U.S. took preliminary steps to fight the insurgency by establishing in 1962 a secret counterinsurgency training base directed by U.S. Special Forces.[14] Meanwhile, the Guatemalan military responded to these early signs of unrest with the 1963 coup led by Col. Peralta Azurdia (to prevent the electoral victory of reformist Juan José Arévalo, who had headed the first Revolutionary government, from 1945 to 1950). The Peralta regime imposed a state of siege, repressed the legal opposition movements, and established the system of army agents/informers (*comisionados militares*) in the countryside as a means of identifying and eliminating guerrilla sympathizers.[15] In general, however, Peralta's repressive apparatus could not stop the growth of the guerrilla movement. U.S. officials viewed Peralta as an inefficient and insufficiently active counterinsurgent, who furthermore could not be counted on to listen to U.S. advisers.[16] With the accession to power of the supposedly "reformist" civilian Méndez Montenegro government in 1966, the army undertook its first major counterinsurgency offensive — this time (and subsequently) securely under the direction of the United States and with massive U.S. aid. (See Table 3.) Méndez Montenegro is said to have given the army and the U.S. counterinsurgency strategists a free hand, in exchange for increased U.S. aid.[17]

The full-scale 1966-68 counterinsurgency offensive, which bore a serious resemblance to the early days of U.S. involvement in Vietnam (and which has been fully detailed elsewhere)[18] was advised, equipped, and run directly by the U.S. The ratio of U.S. military advisers to local army forces was higher for Guatemala than for any other Latin American country. In many respects, Guatemala became a kind of laboratory for counterinsurgency in Latin America. In a macabre "transfer of technology" from Vietnam, napalm, radar detection devices, and other sophisticated hardware were used in the 1966-68 campaign. Green Berets and other advisers and combat forces trained in Vietnam were sent to Guatemala (and vice versa); even Guatemalan police officials confirmed the presence and combat role of Green Berets — an estimated 1,000 of them, according to a number of observers and reporters.[19] Torture methods strikingly similar to those used by Green Berets in Vietnam were applied by the Guatemalan security forces.[20]

This period also saw the development of the right-wing death squads, financed by large property-owners and composed largely of off-duty army officers and police forces. There is substantial evidence of the direct role of U.S. military advisers in the formation of these death squads, and the U.S. military attaché during this period publicly claimed credit for instigating their formation.[21] By extending the war (called "pacification") to the population in the guerrilla areas, the U.S. and the Guatemalan army temporarily defeated the guerrilla movement militarily in the late 1960s. The death toll of the 1966-68 "pacification" has been estimated at 6,000-8,000 lives.[22]

Simultaneously, the U.S. government revamped the Guatemalan police system. As early as 1957, the U.S. had begun training the Guatemalan police under the "Public Safety" Program (technically under the U.S. Agency for International Development), and this continued until the OPS program was abolished in 1974 (under U.S. public pressure). From 1966 to 1970, the national police grew from 3,000 to an estimated 11,000-12,000 and funding for U.S. police assistance doubled.[23] The U.S. set up a police training center, organized the rural police (the Policía Militar Ambulante—the unit linked to the death squads), and organized the secret police (judiciales), whose function was to investigate and harass political opposition forces, and who were publicly acknowledged to be engaging in torture.[24] U.S. police training programs were tailored to meet counterinsurgency needs, focusing on communications mobility, training (of more police), and intelligence; as in the case of military advisers, many of the U.S. police advisers sent to Guatemala had previously served in Vietnam.[25]

It was in 1970 that the counterinsurgency state itself was institutionalized, with the ascension to power of Col. Carlos Arana Osorio, head of the 1966-68 counterinsurgency campaign, for which he became known as the "butcher of Zacapa." With the army terrorists directly in state power, and under cover of a prolonged state of siege, the right-wing death squads were given free rein to eliminate virtually all opposition forces. Beginning with the Arana presidency (1970-74) and throughout the 1970s, opposition party leaders, professors and student activists, professionals, and journalists who spoke out were assassinated in broad daylight. In 1972 the entire top leadership of the Guatemalan Communist Party was kidnapped, "disappeared," and is generally thought to have been disposed of in the Pacific Ocean by government forces.[26] Meanwhile, in the countryside it became part of the daily reality to find tens, sometimes hundreds, of peasants tortured and murdered. Although for public relations purposes these acts were attributed to "uncontrollable" right-wing death squads run by landowners, the involvement of official army and police forces has been documented, and was even acknowledged openly in 1981 by a leading Guatemalan businessman and adviser to the Lucas García regime: "The death squads were organized under the patronage and the approval of the government and the Army because it was the only way to fight guerrillas."[27]

By the mid-1970s, other factors aggravated an already potentially explosive situation, particularly within the urban working class: economic crisis and the 1976 earthquake. Inflation on an unprecedented scale and increased living costs, unalleviated by adequate wage increases, combined with rising unemployment, led to a series of consumer protests and strikes by teachers and public service workers in 1973-74, and threatened to spread to the private sector. A large May Day demonstration in 1974 was violently repressed. The deteriorating economic situation was brought to a head by the earthquake of 1976 which left 25,000 dead, 70,000 injured, and 1.25 million (20% of the population) homeless. Coming on top of the pre-existing economic crisis and the 1974 electoral fraud, the class-quake (so-termed because of its devastating impact on Guatemala's working class and poor), revealed the incapacity of the government to deal with the staggering social problems of dislocation and unemployment by any nonrepressive means.

In the cities, this combination of factors sparked a series of strikes and contributed to the revival of a militancy by organized labor not seen since 1954. In April 1976, a unified labor confederation was formed, bringing together unions of different political tendencies. Once again, all visible leadership, both national and local, became the targets of government/right-wing assassination campaigns, forcing those labor leaders who were not killed to go into exile or underground.

Simultaneously, two other political realities intensified the class war. First, there was no longer any doubt that electoral politics, or legal politics in any form, were impossible: electoral fraud had become the norm; all forms of legal political organization had been smashed; the political arena had been totally pre-empted by the military and a handful of corrupt, compromised politicians; a new wave of political assassinations physically eliminated the possibility of an opposition victory (or even of opposition politics). In Guatemala, quite literally, there was no "middle ground." By the late 1970s, all legal channels of political activity had been closed to any and all oppositional movements, be they peasant, trade union, electoral, professional, university, or Church-based.

Second, and directly related to the above, the mid-1970s had seen the re-emergence of several revolutionary (political/military) organizations, strengthened by having learned from the mistakes of the 1960s (insufficient mass base) and by their ability to operate in the midst of counterinsurgency. In the words of one analyst,

> Today these organizations are born in the very heart of counterinsurgency itself; they have learned to organize and work under the strictest clandestine conditions, with cadres trained in the art of operating under the most brutal repression.[28]

By the end of the 1970s, "politics" had been transformed into class war, and the main internal actors were, on the one hand, the counterinsurgency state and, on the other hand, the revolutionary organizations which had been forged in the counterinsurgency context. To give only one example of the latter: a clandestine peasant organization led a major strike by sugar workers (Indian and ladino, seasonal and permanent) in February 1980.

The most significant advance in the revolutionary process in the late 1970s and early 1980s has been its extension to large sections of the countryside, particularly the Indian highlands, and the progressive incorporation of the Indian population into (or as a base for) the revolutionary organizations. At the military level this forced the army to expand and generalize the war against the rural population, particularly in the Indian highlands; hence the bloody record of the Lucas García regime (1978-82). This in turn created a political problem: effective prosecution of the war militarily required a full and open resumption of U.S. military aid (cut off in 1977), which in turn had to be approved by the U.S. Congress. But by this time, as will be seen below, Guatemala's human rights atrocities were so blatant that even a massive lobby campaign by the Reagan Administration in 1981-82 failed to convince Congress.

Politically Washington responded to the necessity of maintaining the counterinsurgency state by attempting to give it a new image. Thus we have the Ríos Montt coup of March 1982, which Washington knew about for months, if it did not directly engineer.[29] Even before the Ríos Montt regime asked for it, the U.S. was pushing for a renewal of U.S. military aid.[30] U.S. Assistant Secretary of State Thomas Enders himself has stated the link between political and military considerations: "In Guatemala a coup has installed a new leader who has improved the human rights situation and has opened the way for a more effective counterinsurgency. . . ."[31]

Initially the U.S. mass media played up Ríos Montt as a "born again Christian," leaving the implication that his "humane religious values" would somehow alter or "humanize" the existing pattern of Guatemalan military rule. In fact, however, the most salient aspects of Ríos Montt's background are not his new-found fundamentalist commitments (which in any case, as will be seen, are much more reactionary than progressive, and if anything, an attempt to respond politically to the growing identification of progressive Church forces with the resistance), but the following:

• He is part of a "modernized," technified sector of the Guatemalan army, trained in "special warfare," using the techniques of civic action, psychological warfare, etc., that are essential components of counterinsurgency.

• In the early 1970s, under the brutal Arana regime, he was Chief of Staff of the Guatemalan army, in which capacity he presided over at least one peasant massacre, calling out 1,000 troops to respond to a land invasion by Indian peasants.[32]

• In 1973 he became the head of the Department of Studies of the Interamerican Defense College in Washington, D.C., developing close ties with the U.S. counterinsurgency establishment.

• After being denied victory as presidential candidate in 1974 by electoral fraud (from which stems his reputation as a relative "progressive"), he became the military attaché in Spain, in representation of the very government that had canceled his electoral victory — without a word of protest. He subsequently returned to Guatemala to become chief of the National Military Reserves.

In short, the most significant factors shaping Ríos Montt are his army career and in particular his counterinsurgency training, and it is this more than anything else that brands his government today. As a consequence, it is not surprising that the Ríos Montt facelift has changed nothing, and in his first year in power, the reports of massive human rights violations in the countryside have become an avalanche. In prosecuting the war against the Indian base of the guerrilla movement the government has resorted once again — but this time more intensively — to techniques which are best known to the world from the U.S. war in Vietnam: "scorched earth" policies (burning crops, forests, and entire villages in order to "pacify" areas out of control — one is reminded of the U.S. forces using cigarette lighters to torch entire villages in Vietnam); indiscriminate, village-wide massacres of children, women, and men; forced relocation of populations into controllable towns (parallel to Vietnam's "strategic hamlets") in order to clear out guerrilla areas; creation of massive refugee populations internally and in neighboring countries; extrajudicial executions carried out under the auspices of secret tribunals, within the legal framework of a state of siege since July 1982; and so on.[33] (Even after the state of siege was technically lifted in March 1983, the tribunals were maintained and the executions continued.)

The appearance of Vietnam-type techniques in the Ríos Montt pacification campaign is no coincidence. In fact, it corresponds to a specific U.S. plan, developed in the mid-1970s, "Program of Pacification and Eradication of Communism," according to direct testimony by Elías Barahona, who read the project while press secretary for the Interior Ministry from 1976 to 1980. (The credibility of Barahona's revelations was confirmed by a high official of the Lucas García regime, who acknowledged to a U.S. journalist that the Minister had taken Barahona into his confidence.)[34] According to Barahona, the Lucas regime was unable to implement the plan effectively (and in general to unify the various factions within the army or to win the war against the guerrillas),[35] and this was a major reason for the coup that brought Ríos Montt to power. The current regime is applying this plan, which details lessons and tactics from the Vietnam War,

> ... combin[ing] psychological warfare with regular and irregular military tactics. The main point is to confuse and to create the belief, both internally and internationally, that in Guatemala there is a civil war between the peasants and the revolutionary forces; meanwhile the military junta launches a propaganda campaign with reforms and spectacular measures.[36]

This explains a number of the new pacification techniques which have been introduced under Ríos Montt:

a) Forced recruitment of thousands of Indians and peasants in the guerrilla areas into pro-government "civil defense" (paramilitary) units designed to perform the functions of right-wing death squads against guerrilla sympathizers. The army is forcing villagers to take sides: according to one army officer, "If you are with us, we'll feed you; if not, we'll kill you."[37]

b) Stepped-up psychological warfare, sending in official forces dressed as guerrillas in order to blame the guerrillas for army massacres, combined with a U.S.-advised propaganda offensive about guerrilla "abuses";[38]

c) The use of fundamentalist preachers doubling as counterinsurgency aides to the army in mobilizing villagers into the anti-guerrilla militias. These preachers (and Ríos Montt himself) are members of a U.S.-based organization of the new religious Right, Gospel Outreach, which has the backing of powerful right-wing religious interests in the U.S. and of their leaders (Jerry Falwell, Pat Robertson, Billy Graham, etc.), and the cooperation of the State Department in going into Guatemala.[39] Gospel Outreach has been expanding its operations in Guatemala since the 1976 earthquake, and now claims to have 1,200 members in Guatemala.[40] They arrive at small villages in army helicopters, and work together with the army to organize the "civil defense patrols."[41] Aside from its counterinsurgency functions, *politically* this operation serves as a counter to the significant contingent of priests who have been radicalized by liberation theology and/or by the evolution of the struggle in Guatemala, and who are viewed by the government as "subversives."[42] A number of them have become targets of right-wing/government threats and assassinations in recent years.

Refugees from the terror in Guatemala who have fled over the border to southern Mexico have remained targets of the Guatemalan army, which is reported on numerous occasions to have crossed the border to raid the refugee camps. In October 1982, Amnesty International charged that the Guatemalan army had massacred more than 2,600 Indian peasants under the Ríos Montt regime. In the urban areas, the government has prosecuted its war with the aid of sophisticated computerized technology and the centralization of all counterinsurgency functions. In the summer of 1982, the government moved once again against political opponents, with massive detentions, kidnappings, "disappearances," and assassinations[43] — meanwhile supressing all criticism and suspending all constitutional rights under the state of siege regulations. Ríos Montt is said to have acknowledged that the state of siege was declared "so we could kill legally."[44]

Whether or not the Ríos Montt version of the counterinsurgency state will be able to demonstrate enough temporary "success" in its pacification program to last is irrelevant; if it fails, there are numerous other factions of the army and the civilian right wing (principally the Movimiento de Liberación Nacional, the ultra-right political movement created in 1954 as a local artifact of the U.S. intervention — or even conceivably a right-wing sector of the Christian Democratic Party) which could pick up the ball if it is dropped by Ríos Montt. From Washington's viewpoint, it is simply a question of the most effective counterinsurgency state.

Clearly, the maintenance of the counterinsurgency state, in whatever particular form, implies the massive violation of the most basic rights of the Guatemalan people—the right to life—as well as of all broader political, economic, and social rights. This inescapable reality was given expression by Wayne Smith, who recently resigned as chief of the U.S. Interests Section in Cuba, writing in the *New York*

Table 1: U.S. Construction of the Counterinsurgency State

Dates (in Fiscal Years)	Program	Personnel Trained	Cost (in millions of $)
FY 1961-1973	Office of Public Safety (OPS) (police training)	377[b]	$ 4.855m[a]
FY 1950-1980	International Military Education and Training (IMET) (military training)	3,360	$ 7.5m[c]
FY 1950-1980	Military Assistance Program (MAP) (direct military grants)	—	$16.25m[a]
FY 1950-1980	Foreign Military Sales (FMS)	—	$31.998m[a]
FY 1950-1982	Direct Commercial Sales (DCS)	—	$ 5.848m

a. For these programs, the U.S. spent far more in Guatemala than in any other Central American country through FY 1980, when the "cut-off" of U.S. military aid took effect.

b. Additionally, in 1957 (not included in this table) OPS trained 435 Guatemalan police in the U.S. and Panama: *OPS, Termination Phase-Out Study of the Public Safety Project: Guatemala* (Washington, U.S. AID, July 1974), p. 38.

c. This figure from Institute for Policy Studies, "Background Information on Military Sales to Guatemala" (July 1980).

Sources

This table was compiled from tables in *Dollars and Dictators: A Guide to Central America*, pp. 66-73. The sources include: Michael Klare and Cynthia Arnson, *Supplying Repression* (Washington: Institute for Policy Studies, 1981). Department of Defense, *Foreign Military Sales, Foreign Military Assistance Facts as of September 1981*. Hearings before the Subcommittee on Foreign Operations and Related Agencies of the Committee on Appropriations, U.S. House of Representatives, *Foreign Assistance and Related Programs Appropriations for 1983*, Part 6 (Washington: GPO, 1982).

Times on October 12, 1982: "Indeed the [Guatemalan] Government's atrocities make the Sabra and Shatila massacres in Beirut pale by comparison. Guatemala may be the most dangerous powder keg in the region."

From the foregoing, it becomes clear that the ferocity of human rights violations in Guatemala is the product of a war that began with

Table 2: Major U.S. Security Assistance to Guatemala
Fiscal Year 1950-Fiscal Year 1981 (in thousands of $)

Year	FMS	MAP	Commercial Sales	IMET	No. Students Trained Under IMET
1950-69	2,542[a]	14,801	n.a.	4,217	2,192
1970-75	15,275	8,040	1,891[b]	2,308	881
1976[c]	3,499	156	345	487	134
1977	6,484	7	1,020	449	127
1978	2,789	1	550	—	—
1979	1,802	6	1,103	—	—
1980 (est.)	1,000	3	750	—	—
1981 (est.)	2,000	—	750	—	—
TOTAL	35,391	23,014	6,409	7,461	3,334

Key:
   FMS = Foreign Military Sales
   MAP = Military Assistance Program (includes Excess Defense Articles Program)
   IMET = International Military Education and Training Program

Notes:
   a. Figure is for FY 1955-69.
   b. Figure is for FY 1971-75.
   c. FY 1976 includes transition quarter (July-September 1976).

Sources

U.S. Department of Defense, Defense Security Assistance Agency, *Foreign Military Sales and Military Assistance Facts* (Washington, D.C., 1979). U.S. Department of Defense, *Congressional Presentation Document: Security Assistance Fiscal Year 1981.*

   This table from: Institute for Policy Studies, "Background Information on Military Sales to Guatemala" (prepared by Cynthia Arnson and Delia Miller) (Washington: Institute for Policy Studies, July 1980), p. 4.

the 1954 U.S. intervention. From the side of the Guatemalan people, the war is rooted in centuries of underdevelopment and exploitation, leaving a people deprived of the most basic necessitites of life; quite literally, entire sectors of the population are fighting for their survival. This is why, despite every measure brought to bear against it, what began as a political opposition movement with a limited class base has been generalized into a mass political-military resistance movement,

Table 3: The Counterinsurgency Build-Up, 1964-72

U.S. Military and Police Aid to Guatemala
1950-72
(By Fiscal Year; dollars in thousands)

Year	MAP Grants	FMS Weapons Sales	AID Public Safety Funds[b]
1950-63	6,401	787	562[c]
1964	1,837	261	128
1965	1,292	444	270
1966	1,280	478	249
1967	2,072	101	644
1968	1,030	329	218
1969	1,857	580	411
1970	1,224	99	1,129
1971	1,824	815	413
1972	1,592	1,464	456
1950-72	20,409	15,358	4,480[c]

a. Source: U.S. Congress, House Committee on Foreign Affairs, *Mutual Development and Cooperation Act of 1973*, 93rd Cong., 1st Sess., 1973, pp. 127-38.
b. Source: *USAID Operations Report*, 1962-72 editions.
c. Excludes data for 1950-60.

This table from: "The Vietnamization of Guatemala," in Jonas and Tobis (eds.), Guatemala, *(Berkeley: NACLA, 1974), p. 196.*

which Guatemala's counterinsurgency army and repressive apparatus has been unable to destroy. In the words of one foreign journalist,

> It is one thing to ask an army to honor human rights when its main problem is distinguishing between the guerrillas and the people, but it is something else again when the guerrillas have so many civilian collaborators, old men, women and children among them, that in entire towns and districts, for all intents and purposes, the guerrillas *are* the people. . . ."The problem is not human rights," one [Guatemalan army colonel] says. "The problem is leftist humans."[45]

The counterinsurgency state itself has given birth to one of the strongest, most developed and organized resistance movements in Latin

Table 4: U.S. and International Economic Aid to Guatemala

	1953-61	1962-69	1970-79	Total 1953-79
U.S. Bilateral (including Export-Import Bank)	$134.7m (million)	$170.8m	$220.5m	$526m
International Financial Institutions	$ 21.6m	$ 76.1m	$495.2m	$593m

Sources

U.S. Agency for International Development, Statistics and Research Division, Office of Program and Information Analysis Services, *U.S. Overseas Loans and Grants and Assistance From International Organizations* (July 1, 1945 - September 30, 1976), pp. 43, 47-48, 53-55, 183-85; U.S. Agency for International Development, Office of Planning and Budgeting, Bureau for Program and Policy Coordination, *U.S. Overseas Loans and Grants and Assistance From International Organizations* (July 1, 1945 - September 30, 1979), pp. 45, 49-50, 53, 55-57, 218-22.

Compiled from: James Petras and Morris Morley, "Economic Expansion, Political Crisis, and U.S. Policy in Central America," in this volume.

	FY 1981	FY 1982	FY 1983 — proposed
U.S. Bilateral (excluding Export-Import Bank)[a]	$18.735m	$23.878m ($10m Economic Support Fund)	$15.36m
International Financial Institutions[b]	$223.9m (June 81 - Sept. 82)		over $188m

Sources

a. House of Representatives, *Foreign Assistance and Related Programs Appropriations for 1983, Part 6* (February 1982); Congressional Quarterly, *Weekly Report* (August 21, 1982); cited in *Dollars and Dictators*, p. 243.
b. Center for International Policy, *Aid Memo* (October 1, 1982).

America — one whose origins and growth are clearly domestic. While official U.S. propaganda will undoubtedly persist in attempting to demonstrate that it is "fomented" or "instigated" from abroad (at various times naming the Soviet Union, Cuba, or Nicaragua as the responsible agent), the history of Guatemala since 1954 makes clear that the real causes are oppression and exploitation, sustained by a counterrevolutionary regime, institutionalized as a counterinsurgency state designed, imposed, and sustained by the U.S.

III. The Continuity of U.S. Policy Since 1954

Since the 1950s, every U.S. administration has adopted, with slight variations, essentially the same stance toward Guatemala. Put simply, the principal fractions of the U.S. ruling class have been united in the view that Guatemala should not be permitted to have an independent government, responsible to the needs of its own people — that, in a very profound sense, Guatemala should not be a sovereign nation. This was the reality underlying the decision (which was supported by all sectors of the U.S. ruling class) to intervene directly and militarily in 1954 against Arbenz.

Since that time, the thrust of U.S. policy in Guatemala has not changed in any fundamental way because the dominant sectors of the U.S. ruling class are not prepared to live with independent, nonaligned, progressive governments in Central America and define any such project as a "threat" to "U.S. vital interests." This is reflected in the Reagan Administration's maneuverings today to overturn the Nicaraguan Revolution, and its stance of "drawing the line" in El Salvador (because if El Salvador "falls," according to this logic, Guatemala will surely be next). To accept an independent, sovereign state would be, in the U.S. view, to "lose" it to the "Soviet camp," and the U.S. is not prepared to permit another such "loss" as has occurred in Cuba and Nicaragua.

To assert that this stance, which the Reagan Administration has enunciated clearly and in Cold War terms, has been the basic position of *all* U.S. administrations since 1954 may sound extreme: the two "exceptions" which some might raise are the Kennedy Administration with its Alliance for Progress, and the Carter Administration with its "human rights" policy. But for all its reformist rhetoric, the Alliance for Progress was part of a larger strategy which, as has been seen, was in essence a counterinsurgency strategy with a civic action component, and a buttress of U.S. private investors (see below).

The Carter "human rights" policy which has created an unpleasant and contradictory political situation for U.S. policymakers today, nevertheless brought no basic change and in fact presided over a clear worsening of the human rights situation in Guatemala, as well as an intensification of Cold War policies globally. In fact, the Carter "human rights" policy was *primarily* a justification for anti-Soviet policies, and secondarily an attempt to improve the U.S. image in the Third World.[46] After supposedly cutting off military aid to Guatemala in 1977 (when Guatemala rejected such aid because of U.S. human rights criticisms), the Carter Administration in fact delivered $8.5 million in military assistance during fiscal years 1978-80;[47] and in 1980, the U.S. was reported by sources within the Guatemalan government to have given assurances of "discreetly" resuming arms supplies to Guatemala if the situation in El Salvador became critical.[48]

Under Reagan, however, there is no ambiguity as to U.S. intentions. Even before taking office, Reagan's New Right advisers were in direct contact with the Lucas García regime in Guatemala as well as with leading members of right-wing organizations linked to Guatemala's death squads; in addition they were promising to restore U.S. military aid to the regime, and generally spelling out a Truman Doctrine approach to the entire region – that is, everything short of sending U.S. combat troops.[49] Once in power, the Reagan Administration has deliberately made Central America including Guatemala an issue of the Cold War. Witness its declarations soon after taking office about taking a stand against "international communism" there and its incessant efforts to "demonstrate" that the struggles in Central America are being fomented by Nicaragua, Cuba, and ultimately the Soviet Union. Furthermore, the Reagan Administration (and, before it, the Carter Administration[50]) has openly stated that direct intervention in Central America is an option that cannot be discarded; increasingly the Reagan Administration has made threats and taken provocative measures in the region, particularly against Nicaragua. The Administration got the Senate to legalize this aggressive, threatening posture, with the August 1982 Symms Amendment (called the "Caribbean version of the Tonkin Gulf Resolution") committing the U.S. to prevent by any means "including the use of arms" the extension of Cuban influence in the hemisphere.[51]

IV. Strategic Importance of Guatemala to U.S. Interests: U.S. Capital as the Invisible Accomplice in Human Rights Violations

The constancy of U.S. policy over 30 years, and the determination not to "lose" Guatemala, i.e., not to permit an independent and sovereign state there, raises the broader issue: Why is Guatemala so important to the United States? What is the U.S. government protecting there? Given that the U.S. has defined as a "threat to U.S. interests" any government in the Western Hemisphere, and certainly in Central America, that it cannot control and dominate – a "given" which we consider absolutely without legitimacy, but which must be accepted for the purpose of analysis –there are several respects in which an independent Guatemala would "threaten" the interests of dominant sectors of the U.S. ruling class.

Guatemala is the largest of the Central American countries, the most populous, and economically the most important. It has sizable U. S. private investments in industry, oil, and nickel – $226 million as of 1980, more than double the amount in El Salvador;[52] the nickel and oil deposits, even if not being fully exploited now, are undoubtedly viewed as resources for the future. Guatemala is on the southern border of Mexico, so that any significant change there could only reinforce the currents of change in an increasingly volatile Mexico.

Moreover, it was one thing for the Carter Administration and one wing of the U.S. ruling class (after they had supported Somoza up to the last minute) to accept as a fait accompli an isolated revolutionary government in Nicaragua – a government they could continue to threaten with aggression and attempt to manipulate through aid loans, debt obligations, etc.[53] However, the prospect of a revolutionary or even an independent bloc in Central America and the Caribbean, including Guatemala as well as El Salvador, is viewed as intolerable. This is the reality underlying the vehement statements from the dominant sectors of the U.S. ruling class about "drawing the line" in El Salvador (though there is considerable disagreement as to *how* to accomplish that objective). The particular importance of Guatemala was stated explicitly by Lt. Gen. Wallace Nutting, head of the Panama-based U.S. Southern Command, in arguing that it is "imperative" to resume U.S. military aid to Guatemala:

> The population is larger, the economy is stronger, the geographical position is more critically located in a strategic sense. The implications of a Marxist takeover in Guatemala are a lot more serious than in El Salvador.[54]

But if we were simply to accept at face value the statements of officials like Nutting (echoing earlier statements by then-Secretary of State Haig[55]), we would be accepting a very distorted and incomplete picture – one which in essence justifies the imposition of the counter-insurgency state (and the attendant human rights violations) as the necessity of protecting U.S. "national interests." In fact, what the U.S. government has been protecting all these years is not the U.S. national interest, much less the interests of the American people. Rather, it has been providing cover for the operations of the less visible U.S.-based actors and interests: the corporations, many of them giant monopolies, which have seen in Guatemala not a people with human rights, but a variety of opportunities for profit. From this corporate perspective, the Guatemalan economy is a market; the Guatemalan territory is a source of necessary raw materials; the Guatemalan people are, alternatively, prospective consumers, or a reserve of exploitable cheap labor for enterprises producing for the world market – and certainly, when organized, a negative factor in the "investment climate." Let us trace very briefly the expansion of U.S.-based capital in Guatemala since 1954.

At the time of U.S. intervention in 1954, the main U.S. investments in Guatemala were three monopolistic corporations: United Fruit Co., International Railroads of Central America (a virtual subsidiary of United Fruit), and Electric Bond and Share. Certainly the U.S. intervention was in part a response to regulations imposed upon the operations of these corporations. But the unanimity within U.S. ruling circles in favor of the intervention reflected the fact that other corporate interests, in the heyday of their expansion, were looking at Guatemala (and Central America) as a region for new investments in the future.

It was for this reason that one of the first measures of the U.S.-directed Counterrevolution was to remove from the books all legislation regulating foreign investment or in any other way detracting from a "favorable investment climate" (e.g., the progressive Labor Code). Under the very close supervision of the U.S. government (through predecessors of the U.S. Agency for International Development) and of the private U.S. consulting firm Klein and Saks, the nationalist laws were replaced by new laws and incentives designed to make Guatemala "attractive" to foreign investors (e.g., low tax rates, repressive labor legislation, specific subsidies, repeal of laws taxing profits and limiting profit remittances). After the counterrevolutionary government adopted an oil code which literally gave away Guatemala's rights to its oil resources to foreign companies, to take only one example, U.S. corporations solicited concessions totaling more than half the entire area of Guatemala.[56]

During the 1960s, foreign investment in Guatemala increased dramatically, largely through the acquisition of local firms by U.S.-based multinationals.[57] So massive was the penetration by U.S. capital that by 1969, 86% of all foreign private investment was U.S.-based.[58] The first wave of U.S. investments was oriented toward production for the untapped consumer market in Guatemala: this was the strategy of the Alliance for Progress, which took the form of the Central American Common Market in the region. However, profit maximization for U.S. investors emerged clearly as the overriding consideration. One Central American government after another (and their U.S. advisers) refused to make any redistributive reforms. The U.S. government refused to push for an integration and investment strategy which would have made possible the expansion of the consumer market in Central America. To the contrary, the U.S. government, through its aid agencies, pressured against any form of planning, and for free trade, unrestricted operation of the "free market," and absolute freedom from regulation on foreign capital.[59] Such policies proved incompatible with the development of a broader Central American consumer market.

Subsequently, the investment strategies of the 1970s and 1980s adopted by both U.S. corporations and the U.S. government aid agencies were based on the assumption that the working class in Guatemala and Central America would be kept at a bare subsistence level, and that no redistributive reforms would be made. After the late 1960s, the major corporate investors used Guatemala as a base for operations oriented toward world market production: agribusiness in the form of "non-traditional" agricultural exports, tourism, extractive mining, and cheap-labor industrial operations (runaway and subcontracting shops).[60] They discarded any thought that living standards should be raised to the point where local producers could become consumers, and instead they used the local population as a cheap labor reserve. This strategy corresponded in particular to the interests of a sector of U.S. capital which was interested in using cheap labor to make overnight profits (in alliance with local partners, largely from the Guatemalan military). The fact that this was the strategy not only of U.S. corporations but also of the U.S. government becomes clear from an examination of U.S. aid loans, which were oriented toward stimulating exports from Central America.[61] The view of Central America as a cheap labor haven was taken to its ultimate extreme in El Salvador, where there were ambitious plans (until disrupted by the war) to promote the development of "free zones." What is currently being articulated in terms of the "Caribbean Basin" strategy is a view of the entire Central American/Caribbean region as a cheap labor haven for transnational capital, kept in line by subservient, anti-labor, right-wing regimes.

Most recently, in Guatemala the major new investments have corresponded to the discovery of valuable raw materials in extractive mining and oil. The International Nickel Company's $120 million investment is the largest private investment in Central America. For reasons corresponding to the needs of the U.S.-based parent companies and to conditions in Guatemala, however, these oil and mining projects have thus far been only partially developed — but they significantly raise the stakes of foreign capital in the country. The Guatemalan economy overall is in serious trouble as a result of the counterinsurgency war, with business feeling the effects (for example, 100 companies connected with the previously booming tourist trade have been forced to fold since 1980[62]), and with even traditionally enthusiastic multinational corporations now considering Guatemala the most dangerous place to operate[63]. Consequently, the Ríos Montt regime is going out of its way to attract foreign investment — with plans to remove restrictions on oil investments, to give greater incentives to runaway industrial investments, and to loosen foreign exchange controls.[64]

None of the above foreign investments have brought the supposed great "benefit" for the Guatemalan people—significant employment— and in fact, since 1979 unemployment has ranged from 25% to 35%, according to official figures.[65] Nevertheless, the cumulative impact of U.S.-based private investment, which by 1980 was worth $226 million (over 300 firms with U.S. interest[66]), has created a considerable vested interest in Guatemala — and this is an unspoken part of the reality of Guatemala as a "vital interest" of the U.S. These investments have been promoted, subsidized, and protected by the U.S. government, primarily through its economic aid agencies, and a symbiotic relationship based on a coincidence of interests has developed between the U.S. government and private investors in maintaining the status quo — the counterinsurgency state — in Guatemala.

For this reason, it is not surprising to find an active collaboration, in word and deed, between U.S.-based corporate investors and the

U.S.-created Guatemalan counterinsurgency state itself, as well as with the right-wing death squads. We shall cite here only some of the more blatant examples.

• Typical of the attitudes of U.S.-based investors in Guatemala was the April 1980 speech by Thomas Mooney, President of the American Chamber of Commerce in Guatemala, to corporate executives in New York. Mooney criticized the Carter State Department's opposition to the "non-official exercises of violence," i.e., the right-wing death squads, and counterposed his own view:

> There is another point of view that contends that the only feasible way to stop Communism is to destroy it quickly. Argentina and Chile are demonstrated as nations which used this approach with considerable effectiveness and have gone on to become among Latin America's most stable and successful countries.[67]

• A long-standing investor in Guatemala, Fred Sherwood, who had participated in the 1954 U.S. intervention operation, today justifies the death squads: "Why should we be worried about the death squads? They're bumping off the commies, our enemies. . . .I'm all for it." In the first half of 1980, six union organizers were killed at Sherwood's kenaf factory.[68]

• In the late 1960s, the most brutal part of the "pacification" campaign was carried out in the Izabal and Zacapa region, where International Nickel was planning its massive investment with Hanna Mining Co. In the early 1970s, while negotiating the terms of the nickel investment, the Guatemalan government imposed a state of siege, accompanied by an unprecedented wave of terror and blanket censorship, to silence criticism of the give-away terms of the contract. During this period, several prominent critics of the contract were assassinated.[69]

• During the course of a prolonged effort to organize at the Coca-Cola bottling plant in the late 1970s, workers were repressed by military raids, assassinations, and mass firings; the American manager of the franchise, John Trotter, was a leading member of the Freedom Federation, a right-wing corporate interest group with ties to the military and the death squads.[70]

• The Bank of America (whose spokesman has stated publicly, "If you use human rights in a country with guerrillas, you're not going to get anywhere.") has been actively involved in the lobby to resume U.S. military aid to Guatemala, and has made loans to numerous Guatemalan businesses headed by well-known leaders of the death squads.[71]

Despite the efforts of other investors to maintain the image of being in Guatemala strictly to do business and of staying out of politics, the pattern of capital's complicity in maintaining the counterinsurgency state (which, after all, exists in good measure to protect its interests) is too consistent over the years to sustain this myth.

V. Changes in the International Context

From the above, it is clear that the U.S. government has been intervening in Guatemala for the past 30 years to prevent the establishment of an independent, democratic government, and to protect the interests of foreign, mainly U.S.-based corporations. This is the meaning of the U.S.-established and -maintained counterinsurgency state. But today, with the generalization of the Guatemalan resistance to entire sectors of the population and the real possibility of a victory by the resistance movement, the options for and forms of U.S. intervention have been redefined.

In 1954, the U.S. ruling class intervened directly in Guatemala to oust the Arbenz government, very much as it had intervened in the name of "containing communism" in Greece in 1947. At that time, the U.S. ruling class was able to achieve its objective with a virtually free hand, for several reasons. At the international level, in the era of unchallenged U.S. hegemony in the capitalist world and at the height of the Cold War, U.S. allies exerted no serious counterpressure. At the same time, the socialist bloc could not risk a confrontation with the U.S. in an area accepted as a U.S. sphere of influence. Within the U.S., a fierce propaganda campaign beginning in the late 1940s to manipulate U.S. public opinion and construct the so-called "Cold War consensus" had silenced all criticism of U.S. foreign policy. Any organizations of the U.S. working class which might have opposed the intervention had been emasculated or destroyed (the unions through the Taft Hartley Act of 1947, systematic redbaiting, and the imposition of a class collaborationist leadership; the Communist Party through the Red Hunts of the late 1940s and the 1950s). The application of the Cold War to the working class and its organizations within the U.S. was a necessary condition for the triumph of U.S. Cold War and interventionist foreign policy.[72]

Today, officials of the Reagan Administration like Lt. General Nutting or former Secretary of State Haig speak as though the U.S. can still operate with a free hand in Guatemala and in Central America generally. But 1982 is not 1954, and during the intervening years new international and domestic forces have been unleashed. As a result of profound changes in the international economy and polity, Guatemala — and Central America as a region — is no longer simply the backyard of the United States as it was in 1954, and some of the international and internal conditions which permitted the U.S. a free hand in 1954 have altered. The U.S. economy today is in crisis, and U.S. power in the world has declined; and the Reagan Administration must act in a world shaped by forces beyond its control, which leave it in virtual political isolation.

These new realities have altered the terms of and options for U.S. intervention in Guatemala. As will be seen, however, this does not lessen the danger for Guatemala. Because even as the U.S. government is no longer able to intervene openly as in 1954, and even as it has already lost the political battle to legitimate any form of intervention, it is resorting to indirect, covert, and even illegal means to maintain the Guatemalan counterinsurgency state militarily.

What are the principal changes in the international context? First, having emerged from the Vietnam War drained, isolated, and defeated, the U.S. no longer has the power to set the terms of its relations with other nations unilaterally. In general, the U.S. must negotiate its positions and in many parts of the world has had to make concessions.

Moreover, while remaining the most powerful capitalist nation, the U.S. has suffered a progressive decline as the single hegemonic center within the capitalist world. The balance of power among the capitalist nations has been altered to the degree that the U.S. is no longer able to speak for or even to coordinate international capitalist interests, or to maintain hegemony over such powers as West Germany and Japan. The U.S. has been unable to stop the erosion of the NATO Alliance and the long-term emerging realignment of Western Europe economically and potentially politically with Eastern Europe and the Soviet Union.[73] Moreover, in the last few years, progressive social democratic governments have come to power in France, Greece, Sweden, and Spain.

In regard to Central America, this has meant that, despite intense U.S. pressures, a number of traditional U.S. allies in Western Europe and Latin America are no longer willing to follow dictates from Washington. Since the Ríos Montt coup, both the European Economic Community and Canada have decided to stop all economic aid to the Guatemalan government.[74] Moreover, an independent stance has been adopted by the Europe-based Socialist International (which has been supporting a negotiated settlement in El Salvador and opposing U.S. destabilization of the Nicaraguan government). In the case of Guatemala, the SI stated in April 1982 its support for its fraternal party, the Democratic Socialist Party of Guatemala,[75] whose leader, Carlos Gallardo Flores, is a vice-president of the Guatemalan Patriotic Unity Committee, the broad-based political opposition front formed in February 1982. In November, the Bureau of the SI adopted a resolution,

> ... to condemn and denounce the policy of systematic extermination of the Indian population by the military regime in Guatemala which has taken the form of genocide. Equally, we condemn the state's sanctioning of the murder of political leaders.[76]

There exist some divisions within the SI (particularly since some of its

Latin American members are under the influence of U.S. social democracy, which has always been strongly anticommunist). Nevertheless, many of the member parties are influenced by pressures from the working class sectors of their base, in this case coinciding with the interests of transnational capital and several Western European governments in pursuing a course independent of Washington. These factors contribute significantly to the political isolation of the Reagan Administration.

In Latin America, too, the U.S. is increasingly isolated (relative to the 1950s and 1960s). First, by defining a fundamentally progressive stance toward the struggles in Central America, Mexico has denied the U.S. what it would have most needed in the region: a powerful, stable, local subimperial agent for repressing revolutionary movements in Central America. So long as its own contradictions with Washington persist and increase, and so long as it perceives an interventionist U.S. stance as a future threat to Mexico, the Mexican government can be expected to play a role to one degree or another independent of the U.S.[77]

Other Latin American powers, including Brazil and now possibly even Venezuela, also have their own interests and policies to pursue in Central America, and therefore are not the old reliable allies of the U.S. as they were in the past. Furthermore, in 1982, Washington's stance during the Falklands crisis severely damaged the OAS, the Rio Treaty, and the entire apparatus of U.S.-dominated "Inter-American cooperation" and "mutual defense." This was further compounded by the loss of Argentina as a dependable subimperialist proxy in Central America. In fact, the Argentine military (U.S.-trained) had supplied advisers and intelligence technology in the counterinsurgency campaign in Guatemala and throughout Central America in 1981[78] — much of which Argentina reportedly withdrew when the U.S. supported England in the Falklands crisis.

Within Central America and more broadly in the area of the Caribbean Basin, there no longer exists a solid wall of anticommunist puppet regimes subservient to Washington. The Cuban Revolution has been institutionalized and, like it or not, the U.S. must live with it, having been unsuccessful in all its efforts over the years to overthrow it. Revolutionary governments in Nicaragua and Grenada, while playing no active role in Guatemala and El Salvador, stand as more recent examples of the possibilities for social change in the region. The U.S. still has client regimes in Central America and is able to fortify its position (and may well intervene indirectly in the region) through these proxies. In this regard, the U.S. military build-up in Honduras is particularly alarming, as will be seen. But Honduras and Costa Rica, while not facing full-blown insurgencies such as exist in Guatemala and El Salvador, are by no means stable, and are increasingly vulnerable to the pressures stemming from the same economic and social contradictions internally.

Another set of considerations concerns U.S. relations with the Soviet Union and the socialist bloc generally. In 1954 the U.S. moved into Guatemala with a virtually free hand, in part because the Soviet Union would not risk a confrontation with the U.S. in what was defined as a U.S. sphere of influence. Today, adventurist right-wing policies on the part of the U.S. could provoke a more activist role in support of the revolutionary movements by Cuba (which until now has acted with great caution, emphasizing that the outcome of the struggle in Guatemala will depend upon the efforts of the Guatemalan people) and risk a larger confrontation in Central America or elsewhere in the world. Certainly, if the Reagan Administration acts on its verbal threats of a naval blockade against Cuba (to "punish" Cuba for supposedly supplying arms to the Salvadoran guerrillas), the conflict will be internationalized. No longer in a position of absolute hegemony, the U.S. today cannot warn the Soviet Union not to move into Poland while simultaneously intervening directly and overtly in Central America.

Internationally, then, the Reagan Administration is increasingly isolated except for a few solid imperialist allies like Israel — allies whose role cannot be discounted militarily, as will be seen, but which in no way can ameliorate the political isolation of U.S. interventionism. A concrete expression of this fact was the December 17, 1982, Resolution overwhelmingly approved in the U.N. General Assembly, condemning the Ríos Montt regime for its massive human rights violations. Joining the U.S. in opposing the Resolution were only such regimes as Argentina, Chile, El Salvador, Israel, the Philippines, and Haiti. Even the Pope denounced the Ríos Montt regime for its human rights atrocities in early 1983.

The other factor which has constrained the Reagan Administration from acting on its most aggressive desires is public opinion within the United States. This is a time of economic crisis in the national economies of the leading capitalist countries, most notably the U.S. Certainly, the easiest "solution" for the U.S. bourgeoisie is to transfer this crisis onto the U.S. working class; hence, the austerity policies, which are being greatly intensified under Reagan (e.g., deliberately engineered unemployment, cutbacks at all levels). Yet at the same time, Reagan is calling for a vastly expanded defense budget; and certainly, any direct military intervention in Central America would be costly, since the revolutionary struggles there are too far advanced to be contained without a major U.S. effort. No major intervention abroad can be undertaken without consideration of the domestic consequences in the age of austerity; promises of "guns and butter" are no longer believed or believable.

The vast majority of the American people, particularly the working class, are experiencing the effects of the crisis in the U.S. economy. Their concern is not to "stop communism" in the Western Hemisphere, but to stop rising unemployment, inflation, and social service cutbacks within the U.S. Furthermore, it is too late to pretend that the war in

Vietnam never happened or that the U.S. was not decisively defeated there. One of the preconditions for direct U.S. interventionism abroad no longer exists; the so-called "Cold War consensus" has been shattered. Thus, there is within the U.S. growing sentiment opposed to intervention in Central America, despite the massive propaganda effort to gain support for U.S. policy (and despite even such maneuvers as the 1982 U.S.-staged "elections" in El Salvador, which were designed largely to win over U.S. and Congressional opinion). Since mid-1979, opinion polls have consistently shown that over two-thirds of the American people oppose U.S. intervention abroad, particularly in Central America; and this sentiment has been steadily increasing in 1981-82. A March 1982 poll published in *Newsweek* showed 90% of those polled in opposition to sending U.S. troops to El Salvador, and 75% fearing another Vietnam there.[79]

An additional factor is the increasing involvement of progressive religious organizations in anti-interventionist activities — not unrelated to the vicious persecution of priests and Church officials identified as sympathetic to the Left in Guatemala. In November 1982, the President of the National Conference of Catholic Bishops reiterated the Bishops' opposition to U.S. military assistance as stated a year earlier, and called upon the Administration to withhold such aid until "substantial and verifiable" proof is given of the cessation of systematic human rights violations in Guatemala.[80] In November 1982, over 300 religious leaders of various denominations denounced Reagan Administration policy in Central America.[81]

On another front, in response to the savage repression unleashed against the Guatemalan labor movement, a number of international and U.S. unions — including the International Union of Food and Allied Workers (whose Guatemalan affiliate is the Coca-Cola union), the National Education Association, and the International Federation of Unions of Hotel Workers — have organized pro-human rights campaigns and boycotts against the Guatemalan government.[82] These currents in U.S. public opinion represent an important broadening of the traditional anti-intervention movement and increased working class participation in that movement.

Moreover, the above currents are strong enough to have produced visible (if small) effects upon two traditional allies of the State Department: the corporate mass media, and Congress. By 1982, some of the leading newspapers in the U.S. (including the *New York Times* and the *Miami Herald*[83]) published strong editorials opposing resumption of U.S. military aid to Guatemala. One of the major television networks reported extensively on the growing U.S. combat presence in Guatemala — a fact which hitherto has been hidden from the American public and will necessarily intensify the debate and opposition within the U.S. And in the U.S. Congress, questions are being raised not only by liberals who themselves oppose another Vietnam in Central America (see below), but even by self-defined "hawks," who personally would not oppose a U.S intervention, but who are being pressured by their constituents to oppose it.[84]

Finally, all of the above factors have fed into debates even within the inner circles of the Reagan Administration, as to *how* to maintain control in Central America. Top Pentagon officials are on record as opposing direct military intervention, on the grounds that 1) there is no guarantee that the U.S. could win a land war in Central America; 2) involvement in an unpopular, losing venture in Central America would jeopardize the things they really care about — strategic areas like the Persian Gulf or Europe, and bigger bomb and missile systems; and 3) they cannot discount the possibility of a Soviet response to U.S. provocations, especially to a U.S. move against Cuba. In August 1982, Assistant Secretary of State Thomas Enders stated that "the use of U.S. combat forces would be counterproductive (and unacceptable) [in Central America].[85]

What emerges clearly from the above is not by any means a guarantee that the most reckless forces within the Reagan Administration will not prevail, in spite of all the anti-interventionist domestic pressures. Indeed, as the actual power of the U.S. in the world declines, the temptation to assert and use power recklessly and perilously could easily grow — particularly given the reality that nothing short of a direct U.S. intervention has been effective in stopping the spread of the resistance movement in Guatemala.

However, given the isolation of the U.S. government internationally and at home, and given the fact that the U.S. has lost *political* legitimacy for a direct intervention on all fronts, the Reagan Administration has been playing out other options for covert and indirect military intervention in Guatemala. These are as dangerous for Guatemala as sending the Marines, and therefore must be fully exposed and denounced by the peoples of the world.

VI. Forms of U.S. Intervention Today

Given the constraints on direct military intervention, as outlined above, the issue for the Reagan Administration is how to intervene through maintenance of the counterinsurgency state in Guatemala. Even in 1966-68, there was no widespread challenge to Washington's authority to sustain the counterinsurgency efforts of the Guatemalan government. But in the early 1980s, the American people recognize this as the first stage of another Vietnam in the making. Moreover, as a result of the Carter Administration's announced (though never fully implemented) cutoff of direct military aid to Guatemala in 1977, and as a result of public furor over the U.S. role in El Salvador and U.S. destabilization of the Nicaraguan Revolution, U.S. military aid to Guatemala has become an issue of intense debate in the U.S. Congress. On the one hand, the Administration has made every effort, through intense lobbying and direct pressure, to gain Congressional approval for the resumption of the aid. On the other hand, evidence is mounting every day that, failing to win this battle politically, the Administration is already sending military aid, indirectly, covertly, and in some instances illegally (i.e., in violation of U.S. law), through a series of mechanisms described below.

To the extent that it is operating in the political arena at all, the Reagan Administration has pulled out all the stops to gain Congressional authorization for the resumption of military aid—particularly the spare parts for U.S.-made helicopters, which are truly essential for the prosecution of the counterinsurgency/extermination campaign. Without entering into all the details of this political battle, it suffices to say that the continuing atrocities of the counterinsurgency state under the regimes of Lucas García and Ríos Montt have made it impossible to gain such authorization. The Administration has been working with a combination of special interests, both Guatemalan- and U.S.-based, to lobby for the resumption of military aid.

"New Right" organizations such as the American Security Council, which were advising Reagan even before he took office, developed close ties with the Lucas government and the most right-wing private sector organizations in Guatemala, Amigos del País and the Guatemalan Freedom Foundation— those same private sector forces that finance and run the right-wing death squads. At the time, those Guatemalan groups hired a public relations firm headed by close Reagan advisers, who had already begun their campaign against U.S. criticism of death squad assassinations; and Reagan himself met with leading spokesmen of these Guatemalan groups. [86]

Under the Reagan Administration, these same groups in the Guatemalan and the U.S. right wing—and indirectly, U.S. corporate interests—have continued to lobby actively for the resumption of U.S. military aid. MacKenzie, McCheyne, Inc., one of Washington's traditional public relations firms representing the interests of right-wing Latin American dictators (a previous client was Nicaragua's Somoza), is one of several such firms hired by the Guatemalan Freedom Foundation[87] (whose board includes John Trotter, former manager of the Coca-Cola franchise at the time of the violent attempts to break the union there). The "cosmopolitan" Bank of America, which is the largest private creditor in Guatemala, and second only to the government in financing the agro-export sector,[88] is also part of this network, with some of its executives being members of Amigos del País.[89] A spokesman for Caribbean/Central American Action, which represents major U.S. corporate interests, publicly endorsed resuming U.S. military aid.[90]

Since the Ríos Montt regime has taken power, the religious New Right has played a notably active role (although the Moral Majority has been part of the Guatemala lobby since 1980). The counterinsurgency fundamentalists who have become so active in Guatemala are also well-connected in Washington. Top officials of the Reagan Administration (including presidential adviser Ed Meese, Interior Secretary James Watt, U.S. Ambassador to the Organization of American States William Middendorf) are reported to have met in Washington with Ríos Montt's spiritual and political adviser, Francisco Bianchi and U.S. religious Right leaders Pat Robertson and Jerry Falwell[91] —and this was only the most important of several such meetings. Apparently their efforts have borne fruit: Congressman Jack Kemp (himself long identified with the lobby to resume military aid to Guatemala) sent a letter to constituents, "strongly endors[ing] and support[ing] Christian efforts to give support" to the Ríos Montt regime.[92] While Falwell, Robertson, Billy Graham, and others have made lavish promises of raising millions of dollars to aid the Ríos Montt regime through their own networks, their lobby efforts for the restoration of military aid are much more tangible and much more effective as a vehicle for the maintenance of the counterinsurgency state.

There is another role which the fundamentalists may well come to play in the U.S. with regard to Guatemala. It is quite likely that the fundamentalists will be used in the U.S. to neutralize the active role of leading Catholic organizations and officials (as well as progressive Protestant organizations, such as the National Council of Churches) in opposing U.S. support for the Guatemalan government and intervention in Guatemala. We may project that, just as the shock troops for counterdemonstrations in the case of El Salvador have come from the right-wing church of Rev. Sun Myung Moon, New Right fundamentalist youth could be mobilized to perform a similar function in opposing anti-intervention efforts with respect to Guatemala.

The underside of the lobby to restore military aid to Guatemala is a campaign by the White House and the State Department to discredit human rights organizations, such as Amnesty International, which have played a crucial role in denouncing one regime after another in Guatemala. Some Congressional offices have received (presumably from the State Department) a report from the U.S. Embassy in Guatemala not only refuting documentation of human rights violations made by Amnesty International and numerous other human rights organizations, but also attacking the credibility of those organizations, and concluding, "Embassy believes that what is being planned and successfully carried out is [a] Communist-backed disinformation plan. . . . "[93] Assistant Secretary of State Thomas Enders took a similar line publicly (using weaker language) in contesting a recent Amnesty International report.[94]

The importance of the Administration's lobbying efforts should not be underestimated if it is recalled that a similar lobbying effort was an integral part of both the U.S. intervention in Guatemala in 1954 and the U.S.-financed Counterrevolution imposed in the aftermath of the intervention.[95]

While working on the political front through its lobby to gain

Congressional authorization for the restoration of military aid, the Reagan Administration has actually been sending such aid through a series of mechanisms, ranging from indirect and disguised to covert and illegal (i.e., in defiance of a Congressional ban).

1. **Indirect military aid, through U.S. allies** (mainly Israel), proxies in Central America (mainly Honduras), and regional military alliances.

a) Israel: Although Israeli involvement did not begin with the Carter "military aid cutoff," it was fully developed after that time, to the extent that by 1982, Israel had become Guatemala's major source of arms.[96] Both Lucas García and Ríos Montt have attested to the importance of Israeli aid, and Ríos Montt attributed the success of his coup to the Israeli training of his soldiers.[97] The scope of Israeli military assistance includes

> . . . arms, training, and military advisers in the field, together with sophisticated computerized systems for keeping files on suspected guerrillas and a computerized system that detects electricity consumption in suspicious locations across the capital city. . . . [98]

All of the Israeli assistance is specifically designed for counterinsurgency operations—from the transport planes to the Israeli-funded and technologically equipped Escuela de Transmisiones y Electrónica servicing Guatemala's military intelligence.[99]

It remains to be investigated whether Israel is actually *channeling* part of its own military aid allocation from the U.S. to Guatemala, as is documented in the case of El Salvador.[100] What *is* clear is that Israel has been developing its own arms industry through sales to dictatorships like Guatemala, and sending its own advisers; in this regard, Israel is functioning as a U.S. surrogate (as Israeli officials openly admit) by providing to the Guatemalan military what the U.S. has been formally prohibited from directly providing since 1977. In sum, particularly since the rift between the U.S. and Argentina in the wake of the Falklands War, Israel has fulfilled a vital function on behalf of the U.S. government in maintaining the Guatemalan counterinsurgency state. Over the protests of labor and political opposition parties internally,[101] Israel has become an accomplice in the violation of human rights in Guatemala.

b) Regional aid to Central America and the role of Honduras: Since the 1960s the U.S. has given great importance to regional alliances and coordination among the Central American armies. The first such alliance formed at the initiative of the U.S., CONDECA, was so centered around Nicaraguan dictator Somoza and his National Guard that it fell apart after his overthrow. Now a similar project has been revived in the form of the "Central American Democratic Community," founded in January 1982, which includes all of the Central American military dictatorships and excludes the Sandinista government in Nicaragua. While the CDC is not explicitly a military alliance, military collaboration is one of its two stated objectives.[102] The Council on Hemispheric Affairs has suggested that the CDC may well be:

> ...designed to enable the Reagan Administration to ask Congress for what it perceives as a more palatable military aid request for 'regional security,' rather than having to ask for bilateral weapons grants to such controversial regimes as those now exercising power in El Salvador, Honduras, and Guatemala.[103]

Since 1980, the U.S. has attempted to consolidate an "Iron Triangle" in the region (El Salvador-Guatemala-Honduras).[104] The linchpin in current U.S. "regional security assistance" is Honduras. The Reagan Administration mounted a greatly increased military assistance program to Honduras in 1982, upgrading airfields and roads, sending in 104 U.S. military advisers during one 3-month period in 1982, scheduling joint U.S.-Honduran military exercises, and so on.[105] In addition, the U.S. has launched a massive covert (CIA) operation in Honduras.[106] Given that Honduras itself does not yet face an advanced insurgency, this build-up can only be seen in regional terms. First and foremost, it is clearly part of the U.S. offensive against the Nicaraguan revolutionary government (as is well documented elsewhere);[107] but in addition, it must be seen as part of the contingency planning for indirect U.S. intervention in El Salvador and Guatemala. The involvement of Honduran troops against the Salvadoran resistance has already begun; and such a role will no doubt emerge as needed with respect to Guatemala— particularly if it is kept in mind that Honduras was the staging ground for the U.S. operation to overthrow Arbenz in 1954. Reagan chose Honduras as the site for the meeting with Ríos Montt on Dec. 4, 1982.

c) International financial institutions: There has developed a pattern of U.S. military aid which is not only *indirect* (i.e., avoiding Congressionally scrutinized and approved bilateral aid from the U.S. to Guatemala) but also *disguised*—military aid in the form of economic assistance. Such aid is channeled in part through the international financial agencies such as the Inter-American Development Bank and the World Bank, which presumably exist to finance economic development. But in the case of Guatemala, recent loans have virtually nothing to do with "economic development," and are clearly military in orientation. As a legacy of Carter's "human rights" policy, the U.S. government was supposed to vote against loans through the international banks to governments identified as consistent human rights violators, unless those loans fulfilled "basic human needs." However, this stipulation was honored more in the breach than in the fulfillment, and in late 1982, it was formally abandoned.

The clearest example is the Inter-American Development Bank (IDB) loan for funding a rural telecommunications system, which under no interpretation is oriented toward meeting "basic human needs." According to Amnesty International,

> The selection of targets for torture and murder and the deployment of security forces to carry out these acts is coordinated from an annex of the National Palace of Guatemala under the direct control of the President of the Republic. . . . The presidential agency which runs the governmental program of murder was known until recently as the Regional Telecommunications Center.[108]

This telecommunications facility was built by the U.S. in 1964. At this late date, it is absurd to deny that "telecommunications" is part of the military infrastructure. Over public and Congressional protests that U.S. support for this IDB loan is "flat-out illegal," the Reagan Administration on September 29, 1982 announced its decision to resume support for non-basic needs loans to Guatemala in the IDB and the World Bank. That decision will affect not only the particular IDB loan described here and a related pending World Bank loan also for "telecommunications," but a number of other loans totaling hundreds of millions of dollars.[109]

2. **Direct (bilateral) U.S. aid**, through government-licensed commercial military sales, and through official government aid by way of loopholes and reclassifications in which military aid is disguised in nonmilitary terms:

a) Commercial sales: The most obvious way to get around the Congressional prohibition on official U.S. military aid to Guatemala has been through private (but State Department-licensed) commercial sales of military hardware, including police weapons. To take one example: Guatemala purchased $750,000 worth of police arms and equipment in this manner in 1982.[110]

b) The Foreign Military Sales Program, including official U.S. government sales and credits was partially covered by the 1977 Congressional ban; nevertheless, the deliveries of military aid under this program never ceased (even under the Carter Administration).[111]

c) Morever, military equipment has flowed into Guatemala under various loopholes and technical reclassifications which amount to bending legal restrictions. For example: paratroop carriers were sold as "nonmilitary" items in 1980;[112] in 1980 and 1981, the Guatemalan government bought $10 million in helicopters sold through the Commerce Department as "nonmilitary" items, but the helicopters were subsequently fitted with machine guns for counterinsurgency use;[113] in 1981, the Commerce Department issued a license for the export of $3.2 million worth of trucks, jeeps, and spare parts to Guatemala by reclassifying these obviously military items from "Crime Control and Detection" (under which category they would have been subject to the Congressional ban) to "Regional Stability Controls."[114] One source estimates that through the above mechanisms the U.S. has permitted the flow of more than $35 million in military equipment to Guatemala from 1978 through 1981.[115]

d) Direct military aid to Guatemala has also been continued under the disguise of various economic assistance programs. In fiscal year 1981, the U.S. spent $18.7 million in direct economic aid to Guatemala. In fiscal year 1982, U.S. AID provided Guatemala with $5.7 million in "development assistance" and $6 million in food aid.[116] More recently, the Reagan Administration was able to get Congress to approve $10 million in "economic aid" under the Caribbean Basin aid program, and for Fiscal Year 1983 is asking for $15 million more in "economic and development assistance" to Guatemala.[117] But this aid, like the aid through the international financial institutions, is a disguised form of military aid. In fact, the Economic Support Fund, through which the $10 million is going to Guatemala, comes under the security assistance budget, and is only administered by AID—reflecting the broader reality that the Reagan Caribbean Basin program was primarily designed to meet U.S. security objectives.[118] As one Congressman put it bluntly, "You know that economic supporting assistance is simply a device to say to a country: 'Look, take your money and buy weapons, and we will cover your exchange problems with it!'"[119]

3. Covert and illegal aid: As emerges clearly from the above, the Reagan Administration (and the Carter Administration before it) has bent every regulation which would have really stopped the flow of U.S. military assistance to Guatemala. The above is an accepted part of the political jockeying in Washington. In the last few months of 1982, however, evidence began to emerge that the U.S. is engaged in far more dangerous forms of aid—dangerous not only to Guatemala but also to whatever exists of "democracy" in the U.S., in that it is clearly unauthorized, covert, and in essence illegal.

a) Green Berets: Under the Congressional ban in effect since 1977, U.S. military training and U.S. advisers in Guatemala have been flatly prohibited. On the public front the Reagan Administration has never stopped pressuring Congress to approve military training funds for Guatemala, and in the summer of 1982 finally gained qualified approval for a $250,000 allocation from the principal Congressional committees. Meanwhile, however, the Administration had already proceeded covertly to send military advisers. As was revealed in October 1982, at least one Green Beret, Jesse García, is functioning in Guatemala as a counterinsurgency adviser, both in the Guatemalan army officers' training school and in the field: he is authorized, in his own words in an interview, to teach "anything [the U.S. Army] has."[120] Furthermore, he replaced another Green Beret who was serving in the same function. Even after the presence of these Green Berets in Guatemala was discovered and exposed by a free-lance journalist, the U.S. Defense Department maintained the blatant lie that they were in Guatemala as "English teachers," and denied what García himself had revealed about his mission. García predicted that within one to two years, up to 1,000 U.S. combat troops would be needed to wipe out the insurgency in Guatemala;[121] but in the meantime, despite official assurances to the contrary, there is no guarantee that more Green Berets have not already been sent covertly to Guatemala.

b) Helicopter spare parts and communications equipment: Simultaneously, the focus of public debate has been the authorization of spare parts for U.S.-bought helicopters and communications equipment, which are truly essential for the Guatemalan government's prosecution of the counterinsurgency war. Only a few of the 15-20 military helicopters are in working order,[122] in a country where government troops need helicopters to gain access and to bomb villages in guerrilla areas. In García's words,

> [With more helicopters] they'd have more control over the population, much more. . . . Their quick reaction forces would go out there to meet any kind of challenge. . . . A helicopter just gets up and goes, drops some bombs.[123]

To circumvent the Congressional ban, the Reagan Administration sold Guatemala civilian helicopters, which were then equipped for military use. In addition, after threatening throughout 1982 to send helicopter spare parts to Guatemala with or without Congressional assent, in January 1983, the Administration acted unilaterally to lift the arms embargo, and sold Guatemala $6.3 million in military equipment. Moreover, evidence was found in a helicopter shot down by one of the organizations of the resistance, showing that essential aircraft communications equipment had already been shipped to Guatemala covertly.[124]

The fact that the Reagan Administration has already proceeded so far down the path of covert military intervention in Guatemala is an indication of how dangerous the situation is—not only for the Guatemalan people, but also for the American people and the peoples of the world. In his determination to maintain the counterinsurgency state in Guatemala, Reagan is in fact engaged in the early stages of another Vietnam—but this time without Congressional authorization, and over massive public opposition. This open defiance of the will of the American people exposes the contradictions and the sham of political democracy within the U.S. that goes hand in hand with the Administration's lies about "improvements in human rights" in Guatemala. The question of the Guatemalan counterinsurgency state and its human rights violations becomes an issue directly affecting the American polity. The above is even more ominous, when coupled with evidence of a general renewal of emphasis on counterinsurgency in the upper echelons of the U.S. government—as indicated by the creation of a new unified command for counterinsurgency warfare at Ft. Bragg[125] and by an ideological purge in the State Department and Foreign Service under Haig, "with counterinsurgency and covert action credentials at a premium."[126]

More generally, this perilous situation is of concern to progressive peoples throughout the world. If the U.S. government—despite all the considerations to the contrary—should continue upon a course of direct intervention in Guatemala, introduced gradually (as in Vietnam), which is the logical course of its current policy, the consequences will be not only national for Guatemala (untold destruction) and regional for Central America, but international. The Reagan Administration has, in word and deed, defined the conflict in Guatemala as a focal point of global U.S. Cold War policy. In today's transnational world, such an interventionist posture, if continued (whether directly or indirectly), will have international repercussions that are not predictable or necessarily controllable. In this respect, ending the 30-year history of bestial violations of human rights in Guatemala and securing the sovereignty and independence of the Guatemalan people are imperatives of world peace.

In order to emphasize this imperative, we have included in this volume the *"Sentencia"* or "Judgment" rendered by the jurors of the Permanent People's Tribunal session on Guatemala, held in Madrid, in January 1983.

VII. Contradictions of Revolution and Intervention In the Transnational Era

Thus far we have addressed the actual policies of successive U.S. administrations, all of which have been premised upon the maintenance of the counterinsurgency state as the instrument of counterrevolution in Guatemala. There are no visible or public signs that the Reagan Administration has any intention of abandoning this strategy. Moreover, for all visible purposes, all fractions of the U.S. bourgeoisie explicitly or implicitly support this strategy, insofar as they have *done* nothing to advocate dismantling the counterinsurgency state in Guatemala. At most there have been a few scattered protests against its most brutal excesses from organs which we may suppose to represent certain corporate interests.

However, the absence of serious visible divisions within the ruling circles in the U.S. over Guatemala should not be taken as proof that the Reagan Administration speaks for all fractions of the U.S. bourgeoisie. In fact, as we have seen above, there are signs—in the corporate media, in the Congress, and even within the Administration—that the consensus on Central America has been breaking down. There are signs that within the inner circles of the bourgeoisie and its political agents, some serious questions are being raised about current U.S. policy in Guatemala and in Central America generally: *What if the strategy of the counterinsurgency state does not work?* What if the counterinsurgency state, for all the millions of dollars poured into it by the U.S., is so weakened by the basic contradiction that it has no popular base, that it cannot defeat the revolutionary movement—as happened in Nicaragua? What if the only way to prevent the victory of the resistance forces is a Vietnam-style massive military U.S. intervention—for which there is absolutely no support, and in fact massively expressed opposition, domestically within the U.S.? Moreover, what if even such an intervention cannot stop a revolutionary victory—as was the case in Vietnam?

To the extent that such questions are being debated (privately, for the bourgeoisie makes a point of shrouding its internal debates from public view for as long as possible), we must ask: What is the basis and the extent of the breakdown of consensus on Central America, and of the reluctance to being locked into the policies of the Reagan Administration exclusively?

It is our hypothesis that, broadly speaking, the impatience with Reagan Administration policy as the *only* policy toward Central America comes in general from transnational capital and, within U.S. ruling circles, from those sectors most closely tied to transnational capital. In order to substantiate this hypothesis we shall first refer to our analytical frame of reference, and then examine briefly some concrete evidence from recent experience in Central America.

Analytically, we refer back to Marlene Dixon's analysis of the dual power situation which exists in the world today, in which the nation-states of the world share power with world-spanning transnational enterprises. In regard to the latter, we are referring to:

> . . . the "new" transnational corporations . . . whose interests, holdings, and power [are] not invested in any single state; whose locus [can] not be and has not remained limited to a failing colossus, politically or economically. . . . A transnational corporation is not linked to any one state, nor is it dependent upon any one state, but must have relations and dependencies with and upon a network of states. . . .[127]

These world-spanning transnational enterprises owe allegiance to no single nation-state, and elude governmental regulations of any one nation, as a result of their ability to maneuver globally and to manipulate a broad network of the world's nation-states to their own advantage. The development of transnational corporations as genuine transnational institutions effectively controlling significant chunks of the world market is the product of the progressive "denationalization" of their capitals (with the consequent freedom of these capitals from national controls and interference), as well as of the progressive decline of the United States as a single hegemonic power.

In short, within the capitalist world, transnational capital operates with great autonomy, using the territories and the populations of the nation-states, but not responsible to these populations—or to their governments. Free of the constraints operative upon national governments, transnational capital can use various of these governments to serve its interests and play out its policies, including different policies simultaneously.

In regard to the bourgeoisie of any one nation-state, we are dealing with an enormously complex configuration of fractions which compete, contend, and unite with each other in specific situations. Any one categorization for so complex an entity is of necessity partial and therefore misleading if rigidified, since "the bourgeoisie is a class with many elements and characterized by endless turmoil, as each individual, group, or sector of the bourgeoisie competes with the others for advantage."[128] Nevertheless, even keeping in mind this caveat, we suggest that for the purposes of understanding the contradictions within the interventionist forces with regard to Central America, it is useful to distinguish between the national and the transnational fractions of the U.S. bourgeoisie, the national fractions being those most directly linked to domestically based enterprises, to the domestic economy and polity, and the transnational fractions most directly linked to transnational capital.

Turning now to concrete evidence or indications to support our hypothesis that this distinction provides a key to understanding the current discussion and debate over Central America policy, let us begin with the case of Nicaragua, documented in earlier chapters of this volume. The victory of the revolutionary forces and the military defeat of Somoza in 1979 occasioned a serious debate within U.S. ruling circles over whether or not to extend aid to the new Nicaraguan government for reconstruction of its devastated economy. The larger issue was not whether, but how best, to keep the Nicaraguan Revolution out of the socialist camp—and ultimately, how most effectively to destabilize the Nicaraguan Revolution. The question was whether to move immediately and exclusively for intervention by directly aiding *Somocista* exile groups and withholding all U.S. aid, or whether to extend minimal U.S. aid, in order to force the revolutionary government into the intolerable situation of requiring austerity from the Nicaraguan people while paying off Somoza's debts to the transnational banks (as the quid pro quo for minimal U.S. "aid").

Within the Carter Administration, this debate pitted Trilateralists (representatives of transnational monopoly/banking capital), who advocated extending minimal U.S. aid as a mechanism for controlling the situation in Nicaragua, against representatives of nationally based competitive industrial capital, e.g., the military-industrial complex, who advocated no aid except to the *Somocista* counterrevolutionaries—as we have documented elsewhere in this book.[129] Under Carter, the transnational bankers won the day temporarily; with the advent of the Reagan Administration, the emphasis has shifted to a more openly aggressive and interventionist destabilization policy.

The Nicaraguan case is useful in indicating likely sources of dissent over U.S. Central America policy and U.S. policy in Guatemala today. Certainly we can make no cut-and-dried statements about the interests of nationally based enterprises and transnational corporate interests within U.S. ruling circles; for we have seen that such enterprises as the Bank of America which have an investment stake in Guatemala are on record as supporting current U.S. policy and the Ríos Montt regime (and its predecessors and presumably its successors). Nevertheless, if we look beyond those enterprises which have investments in Guatemala, as has already been noted, there are voices of disagreement with current Reagan policy in the corporate media and in some of the most established organs of the corporate/ruling class intellectuals (*Foreign Affairs, Washington Quarterly*, etc.).[130] The basic critique made of Reagan is that his intransigence on negotiations and his narrow insistence on tying the U.S. to delegitimized regimes are counterproductive in terms of the long-range and strategic interests of capital. In April 1983, a group of U.S. and Latin American businessmen and ex-officials (including such Trilateralists as David Rockefeller and other individuals identified with transnational capital) issued a report urging "dialogue" to settle the Central American conflicts, and implicitly criticizing Reagan Administration policy in the region.[131]

Furthermore, there are pressures from within Congress and divisions within the Reagan Administration over Central America policy, as noted above. From within the Administration there are even leaks (officially denied) of proposals in regard to El Salvador for a "two-track" strategy, with the U.S. seeking negotiations with the resistance while continuing military support for the government.[132] Finally, as we have seen, both the Socialist International and several Western European governments have openly criticized Reagan Administration policies. In so doing they are influenced not only by a progressive and profoundly anti-interventionist working class base, but also by transnational capitalist interests, which use these governments to leave open their options for the future[133]—just as they have used the U.S. government to pursue their interventionist objectives.

How do we interpret the above indications of disagreements and pressures upon the Reagan Administration, coming particularly, we would suggest, from transnational capital and the "transnationalists" within U.S. ruling circles? In general, we may postulate that transnational capital and those sectors of the U.S. ruling class most closely linked to transnational capital are following or will eventually follow a three-pronged strategy, which, in the long run, is far more dangerous than Reagan's no-win strategy. It is far more dangerous because it is not subject to the public opinion pressures that limit the U.S. government, and because it addresses itself not only to the present situation (how to prevent a revolutionary victory for as long as possible), but also to the postrevolutionary situation: how to create the kinds of contradictions for a postrevolutionary Guatemalan government that it has already created for the Sandinistas in Nicaragua (and in many other situations).

We suggest that the three principal aspects of this strategy are the following:

1) Acquiescence in (i.e., support for) the Reagan counterinsurgency strategy *precisely because* of its destructiveness in terms of productive structure and in terms of human lives. As James Petras and others have shown,[134] destruction of the means of production is a deliberate counterrevolutionary strategy of capital, one which not only affects the struggle for liberation, but also imposes untold burdens on the post-revolutionary society. Nicaragua and Vietnam today are only two of the most obvious cases of what it has meant that even those sectors of capital in the advanced capitalist countries that "saw the handwriting on the wall" *deliberately* encouraged the prolongation of the liberation struggle. (A case in point is the Carter policy toward Nicaragua, Carter representing the Trilateral or more "transnational" wing of the U.S. bourgeoisie. Long after it must have been crystal clear to Carter and to the fractions of capital he represented that Somoza was going to be defeated, they allowed/encouraged the war to go on as long as possible and to be as bloody as possible, in order to ensure as difficult a recon-struction process as possible.) Extrapolating from this experience, we may postulate that those same interests are pursuing a similar line of reasoning in El Salvador and Guatemala today.

Similarly, we may postulate that the genocidal policies being practiced by the Guatemalan government, aided by the Reagan Admin-istration, are not antagonistic to, but incorporated within, the strategy of the transnational corporate interests. The difference between them and the Reagan Administration is that while some in the Reagan camp may actually believe that this is a strategy for preventing a revolutionary victory in Guatemala, the transnationalists know full well that it is ineffective in terms of stopping the revolution; but they are prepared to make the revolutionary victory as costly as possible.

2) Opportunist sniping at the Reagan policy from time to time, doing nothing real to change the Reagan policies, but allowing Reagan to be the hatchet man, the man who will go down in history (and who is being tarred in international circles already) as the benefactor of the butcher Ríos Montt. In this sense, there is a method to the strategy of the transnational capitalists: they are indeed the *invisible accomplices* of the Reagan Administration, and part of their method is to remain as invisible as possible, preserving for themselves what Reagan has totally lost — legitimacy in the international community (and domestically).

3) Simultaneously, we would argue, the transnationalist sectors within U.S. ruling circles have a real difference of strategy from the Reagan Administration, a kind of contingency plan. As they did in Nicaragua, they in fact may be prepared to cut their ties to whatever General heads up the Guatemalan counterinsurgency state when it is

clear that the game is over. At that point, unlike the Reagan forces which might very well argue for a massive Vietnam-style intervention, the transnationalists are likely to oppose such a move (as they did in Nicaragua), knowing full well that there is much to be lost and nothing to be gained. At that point, not having their hands tied (as Reagan does) to the butchers in power, they could begin their maneuvering to ensure as moderate a government as possible. Meanwhile, they would pursue their plotting against the new government through the more sophisticated mechanisms such as international credit negotiations (for reconstruction), manipulation of credit and basic necessities (in order to foment middle class discontent), strengthening of vacillating petty bourgeois elements, and so on. In short, their strategy would be to follow the Nicaragua model: wage counterrevolution within the post-revolutionary situation, using all the leverage they have as a result of not having tied themselves down by openly and vociferously supporting the counterrevolutionary butchers before the victory.

All the above is, of course, nearly impossible to document. We are dealing here not with military aid appropriations, which are a matter of public record, but with the *logic* of a position that is an alternative to the Reagan strategy. Having seen it operative in Nicaragua, we have no reason to doubt that something like this is operative in Guatemala and Central America generally. It is important to understand, because it allows us to look beyond the daily headlines and to project some of the concrete implications for Central American revolution in a transnational era.

From the point of view of the revolutionary movement in Guatemala, the implications of the above are profound, redefining both the dilemmas and the possibilities facing a postrevolutionary government in the transnational era. The present structure of the capitalist world-economy could be said to favor national liberation struggles, *in the sense that* transnational capital is not *necessarily* tied to the immediate interests of the U.S. government (i.e., of an administration like that of Reagan), and that the U.S. government generally no longer has the absolute freedom that it once had to intervene directly to *successfully* prevent the rise of revolutionary governments in a situation like that of Guatemala. But within the context of the capitalist world-system, the tremendous power of transnational capital intensifies greatly the contradictions of socialist construction for newly liberated countries. As has become evident in Nicaragua, the Nicaraguan Revolution is out of the grasp of U.S. imperialism, strictly speaking, but in no way free of the pressures from transnational capital. Indeed, like Poland and other socialist countries, Nicaragua remains vulnerable through its debts, and this has placed real constraints upon the transition to socialism, as transnational capital, and transnational banks in particular, have attempted to use their leverage by dictating austerity measures, thus fomenting discontent. A revolutionary government in Guatemala would face some of these same constraints; for even by taking the most obvious basic measures to raise wages for the working class, it would immediately be challenging transnational capital and would be subject to the pressures currently operative in Nicaragua. In short, the revolutionary seizure of state power in the transnational era is not the end but the first step toward the full realization of sovereignty and people's rights—of true popular sovereignty.

However, the prospects for a revolutionary government in Guatemala are also affected by the fact that socialist states which operate within the world-economy as "national-transnational enterprises"[135] have the power to concentrate resources, to allocate surplus for social programs, and to set progressive social policies. Such a government has vastly more autonomy and self-determination in the most profound sense than the counterinsurgency state currently operative in Guatemala today, because the degree to which it responds to a popular/majoritarian constituency is the measure of its sovereignty and its ability to defy the impositions and manipulations of transnational capital. (Here too, Nicaragua serves as an example: the ability of the Sandinista government to defy the austerity demands which the transnational banks and the International Monetary Fund have attempted to impose is directly a product of that government's base of popular support and ability to mobilize the majority of the population.)

Thus, the revolutionary seizure of state power does not *in and of itself* guarantee sovereignty and independence, much less socialism; rather, the postcapitalist state in large measure defines its degrees of freedom by the policy choices it makes. This is the challenge that will face the new Guatemala. But this is also the hope, for the new Guatemala, unlike the present counterinsurgency state, *can* choose to reject austerity and to adopt policies which maximize the welfare of the Guatemalan people. All the more so because, unlike Nicaragua in relative isolation, the Guatemalan Revolution will be part of a revolutionary bloc in Central America and the Caribbean. Indeed, is this not precisely the nightmare of the capitalists, both national and transnational? Such a bloc, if it chooses to act as a bloc, has a vastly greater potential for defying the interests of transnational capital.

Taking an even longer-range view, the prospects for full independence and for socialist construction in Guatemala and in Central America generally will depend to a significant degree on the development of a revolutionary working class movement in the United States and in the other advanced capitalist countries—movements that would be capable of threatening and ultimately dethroning *all* fractions of capital, national and transnational. As the Latin American theorist and activist Ruy Mauro Marini writes earlier in this book:

> It is for this reason that, along with the liberating forces on
> the move in Nicaragua, El Salvador and Guatemala, and

arising along the length and breadth of Latin America, it is up to the North American people—*la palabra la tiene el pueblo norteamericano*—and the forces that can best express their historical interests.[136]

NOTES

1. The conceptual framework for these formulations comes directly from, and cannot be understood without referring to Marlene Dixon, "Dual Power: The Rise of the Transnational Corporation and the Nation-State," in *Contemporary Marxism* (Journal of the Institute for the Study of Labor and Economic Crisis) 5 (Summer 1982).

2. Idem.

3. Idem.

4. Because of the extent of the violence, an exact figure is almost impossible to obtain; the Latin American Association for Human Rights gives the range of 60,000-100,000 (*Excelsior*, March 8, 1982).

5. Amnesty International gave the figure of 5,000 in a 1981 study, *Guatemala: A Government Program of Political Murder* (London, 1981), p. 5. This does not include figures for part of 1981 and early 1982.

6. "Sentencia" (Judgment) of the Permanent People's Tribunal session on Guatemala, January 27-31, 1983, reprinted at the end of this chapter. The proceedings of the Tribunal session on Guatemala will be published in English by Synthesis Publications.

7. See, for example, Stephen Schlesinger and Stephen Kinzer, *Bitter Fruit* (Garden City: Doubleday, 1982); Blanche Wiesen Cook, *The Declassified Eisenhower* (Garden City: Doubleday, 1981); Susanne Jonas and David Tobis (eds.), *Guatemala* (Berkeley: NACLA, 1974), "Anatomy of an Intervention," pp. 57ff.

8. For a fuller interpretation, see the "Overview" in this volume and "The Democracy Which Gave Way," in Jonas and Tobis (eds.), op. cit., p. 44ff.

9. See "Showcase for Counterrevolution," in Jonas and Tobis (eds.), op. cit., pp. 74-75, and Susanne Jonas, *Guatemala: Plan Piloto para el Continente* (San José: EDUCA, 1981).

10. Sources for this figure include U.S. General Accounting Office, Comptroller General, *Report: Examination of Economic and Technical Assistance Program for Guatemala*, International Cooperation Administration, Dept. of State, 1955-1960 (Washington, D.C.: GPO, 1960), p. 19; also *New York Times* (July 16, 1957), interviews and other sources cited in "Showcase for Counterrevolution," footnote 21.

11. "Masterminding the Mini-Market," and "The New Hard Line," in Jonas and Tobis (eds.), op. cit., p. 86ff.

12. Ruy Mauro Marini, "The Question of the State in the Latin American Class Struggle," in *Contemporary Marxism* 1, "Strategies for the Class Struggle in Latin America" (Spring 1980), pp. 2-3.

13. Ibid., p. 4. Three excellent expositions of the functioning in Guatemala of what is called here the "counterinsurgency state" are: "Vida y Muerte en Guatemala" and other essays in Edelberto Torres Rivas, *Crisis del Poder en Centroamérica* (San José: EDUCA, 1981); Gabriel Aguilera Peralta, Jorge Romero Imery, et al., *Dialéctica del Terror en Guatemala* (San José: EDUCA, 1981); and Guerrilla Army of the Poor, "International Declaration," in *Contemporary Marxism* 1 (Spring, 1980).

14. "The Vietnamization of Guatemala," in Jonas and Tobis (eds.), op. cit., p. 194.

15. Idem.

16. Ibid., pp. 195-96, and "The New Hard Line," in Jonas and Tobis (eds.), op. cit., p. 105, 117; see also Edwin Lieuwen, _Generals vs. Presidents_ (New York: Praeger, 1964), p. 38.

17. Idem; see also Thomas and Marjorie Melville, _Guatemala: The Politics of Land Ownership_ (New York: Free Press, 1971), pp. 192, 196; Jerome Levinson and Juan de Onis, _The Alliance That Lost Its Way_ (Chicago: Quadrangle, 1970), p. 85.

18. "The Vietnamization of Guatemala."

19. Georgie Ann Geyer, _Chicago Daily News_ (Dec. 12, 1966); _Washington Post_ (Dec. 13, 1967); Eduardo Galeano, _Guatemala: Occupied Country_ (New York: Monthly Review Press, 1969), p. 79.

20. See "Guatemala: The Politics of Violence," NACLA's _Latin America and Empire Report_ (Feb. 1972), p. 26; see also Geyer series in _Chicago Daily News_ (Dec. 1966), and Donn Munson, "America's Top-Secret Jungle War," _Saga_ (Nov. 1967); Galeano, op. cit.

21. This claim was made by military attaché Col. John Webber in an interview in _Time_ (Jan. 26, 1968), p. 23; see also Latin American Studies Association, Ad-Hoc Committee on Guatemala, _Report_ (April 15, 1973), p. 4; "The Vietnamization of Guatemala," p. 202.

22. Although estimates vary from 3,000 to 8,000 this is the generally accepted figure; see LASA, op. cit., p. 8, "The Vietnamization of Guatemala," p. 202.

23. David Wood, "Armed Forces in Central and South America," _Adelphi Papers_ (London: Institute for Strategic Studies, 1967); Melville and Melville, op. cit., p. 275; "The Vietnamization of Guatemala," p. 199.

24. See "The Vietnamization of Guatemala," p. 199; _El Imparcial_ (July 4, 1966) (admission by Pres. Méndez Montenegro), cited in Washington Office on Latin America (WOLA), _Special Update_, "Guatemala: The Roots of Revolution" (October 1982), p. 7.

25. See table in "The Vietnamization of Guatemala," p. 201.

26. Amnesty International Statement, Nov. 10, 1972; _Latin America_ (London), March 2, 1973, and other press sources cited in LASA, op. cit., p. 9.

27. September 1980 interview with García Granados, quoted in WOLA, op. cit., p. 8; see also Amnesty International (AI), _Guatemala: A Government Program. . ._, pp. 7-9.

28. Ruy Mauro Marini, "The Nicaraguan Revolution and the Central American Revolutionary Process," in this volume.

29. _Latin America Weekly Report_ (April 22, 1982).

30. _The Nation_ (June 26, 1982).

31. Quoted in _Latin America Weekly Report_ (LAWR) (August 27, 1982).

32. See American Friends of Guatemala, _Guatemala Report_ 3 (July 1973), pp. 5-6.

33. These atrocities have been reported in the major news media internationally and in the U.S., as well as in all recent reports from U.S. Congressional delegations and fact-finding missions by Amnesty International, National Council of Churches, Americas Watch, OXFAM-America, American Friends Service Committee and other groups.

34. Allan Nairn, press release of Council on Hemispheric Affairs (COHA) (October 30, 1980), p. 5.

35. The fact that the war was going badly under Lucas is confirmed in other reports, e.g., _Latin America Regional Report_ for Mexico and Central America (_LARR_) (June 4, 1982).

36. Barahona interview, reprinted in _Guatemala News and Information Bulletin_ (_GNIB_) (September-October 1982), pp. 6-7.

37. _New York Times_ (July 18, 1982 and September 12, 1982).

38. *New York Times* (September 12, 1982 and September 15, 1982); Jack Anderson column in *Washington Post* (September 29, 1982); *Washington Post* (October 12, 1982).

39. *National Catholic Reporter* (August 27, 1982); *Baltimore Sun* (July 11, 1982); *Bay Guardian* (July 21, 1982); *The Forerunner* (no date) (published by Marantha Campus Ministries, in Gainesville, Florida).

40. *Baltimore Sun* (July 11, 1982).

41. Idem; *National Catholic Reporter* (August 27, 1982); *Washington Post* (July 19, 1982).

42. In regard to this general phenomenon, see Marlise Simons, "Latin America's New Gospel," *New York Times Magazine* (November 7, 1982); also *New York Times* (July 18, 1982).

43. *Inforpress Centroamericana* (September 9, 1982), *Central America Report* (Guatemala) (October 29, 1982).

44. *New York Times* (September 12, 1982).

45. Allan Nairn, *New York Times* (July 20, 1982).

46. For an analysis of Carter policies, see Marlene Dixon, "Responsibilities of the U.S. Working Class to Latin American Revolutionary Movements in a New Cold War Period," *Contemporary Marxism* 1 (Spring 1980); and Susanne Jonas, "The Political Economy of Human Rights," *Our Socialism* (Democratic Workers Party, San Francisco, March 1-15, 1982).

47. Lars Schoultz statement in "Human Rights in Guatemala," Hearing Before Subcommittees on Human Rights and International Organizations and on Inter-American Affairs, Committee on Foreign Affairs, U.S. House of Representatives, July 30, 1981 (Washington: GPO, 1981), pp. 98, 114; Institute for Policy Studies (IPS), *Background Information on El Salvador and U.S. Military Assistance to Central America* (November 1980), p. 4.

48. *LAWR* (September 12, 1980); IPS (Cynthia Arnson and Delia Miller), *Background Information on Military Sales to Guatemala* (July 1980), p. 2; the inside information came from Elías Barahona.

49. *LAWR* (July 18, 1980 and September 26, 1980); *Central America Update* (August 1980); *Miami Herald* (August 24, 1980); *Washington Post* (July 12, 1980); COHA press release (October 30, 1980); *New York Times* (August 4, 1980); *Journal of Commerce* (August 6, 1980); Roger Fontaine et al., "Castro's Specter," *Washington Quarterly* (Autumn 1980), p. 2.

50. *Central America Update* (August 1980); "Dissent Paper on El Salvador and Central America," DOS (November 6, 1980).

51. *New York Times* (August 12, 1980).

52. U.S. Department of Commerce figures, cited in Resource Center, *Dollars and Dictators: A Guide to Central America* (Albuquerque: Resource Center, 1982), p. 40.

53. In regard to the debates in the Carter Administration over U.S. policy toward Nicaragua, see Susanne Jonas, "The New Cold War and the Nicaraguan Revolution," in this volume.

54. *New York Times* (August 22, 1982).

55. *Washington Post* (April 18, 1982).

56. "Showcase for Counterrevolution," p. 79.

57. "The U.S. Investment Bubble in Guatemala," in Jonas and Tobis (eds.), op. cit., pp. 132ff, 144, and chart on p. 134.

58. Banco de Guatemala figures, cited in Ibid., p. 132.

59. See "Masterminding the Mini-Market," pp. 86ff.

60. *Dollars and Dictators*, pp. 22ff. and 37ff., "The New Hard Line," pp.110ff.

61. "The New Hard Line," pp. 109ff.

62. *LAWR* (August 20, 1982).

63. *Business Latin America (BLA)* (April 14, 1982), *LAWR* (November 6, 1981).

64. *LAWR* (July 2, 1982 and August 27, 1982); *Inforpress Centroamericana* (October 7, 1982); *BLA* (July 7, 1982).

65. Figures from *La Nación* (Guatemala), June 9, 1980, cited in WOLA, op. cit., p. 3; another source (*Inforpress Centroamericana*, October 7, 1982) puts the level of under- and unemployment at around 1/3 of the economically active population (without taking into account the massive number of refugees).

66. *Dollars and Dictators*, pp. 40, 125, 232.

67. American Chamber of Commerce in Guatemala, *Monthly Bulletin* No. 162 (May 23, 1980), quoted in John Purcell, "The Perceptions and Interests of U.S. Business in Relation to the Political Crisis in Central America," in Richard Feinberg (ed.), *Central America* (New York: Holmes & Meier, 1982) pp. 118-19.

68. Interview with Sherwood, September 1980, quoted in WOLA, op. cit., p. 3.

69. "EXIMBAL: Take Another Nickel Out," in Jonas and Tobis (eds.), op. cit., p. 160.

70. Purcell, op. cit., p. 118, *Dollars and Dictators*, p. 128; *LARR* (July 11, 1980).

71. See articles on Bank of America in *Multinational Monitor* (May 1981, March 1982, and October 1982); COHA materials reprinted in *Congressional Record* (June 16, 1982 and June 24, 1982).

72. For a more detailed analysis of the Cold War context for the 1954 intervention in Guatemala, see "Overview," in this volume; for a broader interpretation of the Cold War history, see the following works by Marlene Dixon: "An Outline of Working Class History, 1917-1979," in *Our Socialism* (Theoretical Journal of the Democratic Workers Party) 2, 2 (May 1, 1981); "Rethinking 50 Years of American History: From Roosevelt to Reagan," *Plain Speaking* (News Journal of the Democratic Workers Party) 5, 7 and 5, 8 (May 15-31, 1981 and June 1-15, 1981); "Responsibilities of the U.S. Working Class to Latin American Revolutionary Movements in a New Cold War Period" and "On the Situation in the USA Today," *Our Socialism* (October 1981).

73. See for example, Immanuel Wallerstein, "The USA in Today's World," in Marlene Dixon et al. (eds.), *World Capitalist Crisis and the Rise of the Right* (San Francisco: Synthesis Publications, 1982); and Wallerstein, "Friends as Foes," *Foreign Policy* 40 (Fall 1980).

74. *Guardian* (September 29, 1982); see also *Washington Post* (February 20, 1982).

75. *Central America Update* (June 1982).

76. Resolution of the Bureau of the Socialist International (Basel), November 3-4, 1982.

77. See "Deciphering Mexico's Foreign Policy," *Plain Speaking* 6, 7 (April 1-15, 1982); see also R.H. Zuniga and M. Ojeda, "Mexican Foreign Policy and Central America," in Feinberg (ed.), op. cit., and Olga Pellicer, "Mexico's Position," *Foreign Policy* 43 (Summer 1981).

78. *LAWR* (November 6, 1981).

79. "The Fire Next Door," *Newsweek* (March 1, 1982); see also "Dissent Paper," pp. 19-20.

80. Press Release of U.S. Catholic Conference, November 5, 1982.

81. *New York Times* (November 28, 1982).

82. COHA press releases of October 11, 1979, September 29, 1980, March 19, 1981; also *LARR* (July 11, 1980).

83. *New York Times* (October 17, 1982), "The Dirtiest War"; *Miami Herald* (August 26, 1982) "Evil in Guatemala".

84. See, for example, the case of Representative Don Bailey, reported in *Washington Post* (March 8, 1982).

85. Enders, cited in *LAWR* (August 27, 1982); in regard to the Pentagon views see *New York Times* (November 5, 1981), *Washington Post* (November 7, 1981, *Boston Globe* (November 22, 1981), *San Francisco Examiner* (December 6, 1981 and February 14, 1982); Mary McGrory column in *San Francisco Examiner* (November 14, 1981); and ISLEC interviews with close observers in Washington.

86. See full details in COHA press release, October 30, 1980; *Wall Street Journal* (October 31, 1980).

87. *CBS Reports* transcript, p. 12; COHA press release, March 19, 1981; American Friends Service Committee, "Militarizing Central America" (AFSC, 1981).

88. *Dollars and Dictators*, p. 245.

89. There was a big controversy when the Bank of America was first charged with being a corporate member of Amigos. This led to a challenge by stockholders and leading religious organizations in the U.S., at which the Bank denied a series of charges (including its corporate membership in Amigos and its loans to military government officials), through a series of public relations legalisms. See Nairn article in *Multinational Monitor* (May 1981); COHA memorandum of February 8, 1982; press release by Northern California Interfaith Committee on Corporate Responsibility, April 26, 1982; the Bank's replies appeared in a statement to shareholders, "Implementation of Bank America's International Policies in Guatemala" (1982).

90. "Caribbean Investment: Following the Flag?," *Multinational Monitor* (November 1981).

91. *CBS Reports* transcript, p. 9.

92. Kemp letter to constituents, July 30, 1982; in regard to his previous interest in Guatemala, see *Central America Update* (December 1980).

93. Document received by Congressional offices, written by U.S. Embassy in the fall of 1982.

94. *Washington Post* (October 12, 1982).

95. Jonas, *Guatemala: Plan Piloto*, pp. 46ff. and pp. 156ff.; "The Best Lobby in Washington," in Jonas and Tobis (eds.), pp. 59ff. and pp. 82ff.

96. International Institute for the Investigation of Peace, cited in "News from Guatemala" (Toronto, October 1981); Report carried on Israel Television System on January 25, 1982, cited in unpublished research by Benjamin Beit-Hallahmi.

97. *LAWR* (August 6, 1982).

98. Unpublished research by Benjamin Beit-Hallahmi.

99. *Excelsior* (Mexico, November 15, 1981); Agencia Latino Americana de Información (Canada), "Ingerencia de Israel en Guatemala" (October 9, 1981).

100. *Manchester Guardian* (September 5, 1982), cited in *Central America Update* (November 1982);

101. *LAWR* (August 6, 1982).

102. COHA press release, in *Congressional Record* (August 3, 1982); *Dollars and Dictators*, p. 69; *Inforpress Centroamericana* (July 15, 1982).

103. COHA press release in *Congressional Record* (August 3, 1982).

104. See Philip Wheaton, "U.S. Strategies in Central America," in this volume; and Wheaton, "The Iron Triangle: The Honduran Connection" (Washington: EPICA, 1981).

105. For details, see Institute for Policy Studies, Update No. 17, "Background Information on U.S. Military Personnel and U.S. Assistance to Central America" (prepared by Cynthia Arnson and Flora Montealegre) (November 1982).

106. *Newsweek* (November 8, 1982).

107. Idem.

108. Cited in "Human Rights in Guatemala," U.S. House of Representatives hearing, op. cit., p. 8; see also Amnesty International, *Guatemala: A Government Program. . .*, pp. 7-8, which makes reference to this center from declassified U.S. AID documents; this was also confirmed by Elías Barahona, according to COHA press release, October 30, 1980, p. 5.

109. Center for International Policy, *Aid Memo* (October 1, 1982); *New York Times* (October 10, 1982).

110. *Dollars and Dictators*, p. 73.

111. Lars Schoultz testimony, in "Human Rights in Guatemala," U.S. House of Representatives hearing, op. cit., pp. 113-14.

112. Research by George Black, forthcoming in NACLA *Report on the Americas*.

113. *Washington Post* (January 23, 1981).

114. U.S. State Department Testimony, in "Human Rights in Guatemala," U.S. House of Representatives hearing, op. cit., p. 11.

115. Research by George Black.

116. Idem.

117. *New York Times* (October 10, 1982).

118. Numerous analysts have drawn this conclusion; see M.D. Hayes, "U.S. Security Interests in Central America in Global Perspective," in Feinberg (ed.), op. cit., pp. 85ff.

119. Hearings before the Subcommittee on Foreign Operations and Related Agencies of the Committee on Appropriations, House of Representatives, *Supplemental Appropriations for 1982*, Part 2 (Washington: Government Printing Office, 1982), p. 43; see also *LAWR* (April 3, 1981).

120. Allan Nairn, in *Washington Post* (October 21, 1982); *CBS Evening News* (November 9, 1982).

121. Nairn, in *In These Times* (November 17-23, 1982).

122. Idem.

123. Idem.

124. *New York Times* (November 15, 1982).

125. *Inforpress Centroamericana* (September 30, 1982).

126. George Black, "Central America: Crisis in the Backyard," *New Left Review* 135 (September-October 1982), p. 28.

127. Dixon, "Dual Power," op. cit., p. 132.

128. Ibid., p. 140.

129. See Susanne Jonas, "The New Cold War and the Nicaraguan Revolution," in this volume.

130. See, for example, Robert Pastor, "Sinking in the Caribbean Basin," *Foreign Affairs* (Summer 1982); Pastor, "Our Real Interests in Central America," *Atlantic Monthly* (July 1982); Robert Leiken, "Reconstructing Central American Policy," *The Washington Quarterly* (Winter 1982).

131. *New York Times* (April 6, 1983).

132. *New York Times* (March 10, 1983); see also *Central America Update* (February 1983).

133. For several detailed analyses of European interests, see Latin America Bureau, *The European Challenge: Europe's New Role in Latin America* (London: Latin America Bureau, 1982).

134. James Petras, "Marxism and World-Historical Transformations" (manuscript) forthcoming in *Contemporary Marxism*.

135. For a fuller explanation of this concept, see Dixon, "Dual Power," pp. 143-44.

136. Ruy Mauro Marini, "The Nicaraguan Revolution and the Central American Revolutionary Process," in this volume.

Judgment Against the Government of Guatemala

Permanent People's Tribunal

In January, 1983, the Permanent People's Tribunal (a successor to the Bertrand Russell Tribunal) met in Madrid, Spain, to consider the situation of human rights in Guatemala. For three days, Tribunal jurors (including prominent writers, experts in international law, theologians, and scholars from Latin America, Western Europe, and the United States) heard testimony from Guatemalan witnesses and experts on various aspects of Guatemalan society.

The following "Judgment" is the summary of the Tribunal's 70-page verdict establishing the criminality of the present Ríos Montt regime in Guatemala (and all governments in Guatemala since 1954), the criminal complicity of the U.S. government, and the right of the Guatemalan people to exercise all forms of resistance to the government.

JUDGMENT

In consequence, the Tribunal

DECLARES that the successive Guatemalan governments since 1954, including the General Ríos Montt regime, are guilty of serious, repeated, and systematic violations of human rights, and thus of infringing the Universal Declaration of Human Rights, and the American Convention of Human Rights;

DECLARES that the successive Guatemalan governments since 1954, including the General Ríos Montt regime, are guilty, due to the totality of those violations, of attacking the inalienable right of the Guatemalan people to political and economic self-determination and the right of that people to exercise sovereignty over its own natural resources, such as is established in the United Nations Charter and in numerous resolutions of the General Assembly of the United Nations;

DECLARES that the successive Guatemalan governments since 1954, including the General Ríos Montt regime, are guilty, in the armed conflict against the forces now grouped in the URNG (Guatemalan National Revolutionary Unity) of serious, repeated, and systematic violations of the provisions of the 1949 Geneva Conventions, and of the Additional Protocols of 1977, with these violations constituting war crimes;

DECLARES that because of their breadth and extent, the tortures, killings, and forced disappearances of people constitute crimes against humanity in the sense of the Statute of the Nüremburg Tribunal;

DECLARES that the massacres and the terror unleashed against the indigenous peoples with the demonstrated purpose of partially destroying them, constitute genocide in the sense of the 1948 International Convention;

DECLARES that the heads of the successive governments in Guatemala since 1954, including General Ríos Montt, are personally responsible for the international crimes specified above, without excluding the responsibility of the other main members of those governments as well as the principal higher officials and upper functionaries implicated in the above-mentioned crimes;

DECLARES that the authors of these crimes cannot invoke as an excuse the orders they received, except in the case of junior officers who can cite extenuating circumstances;

DECLARES that the government of the United States of America is guilty of the crimes listed above, because of its decisive interference in the affairs of Guatemala, and that the Israeli, Argentine, and Chilean governments are guilty of complicity because of aid and assistance.

In Conclusion

The Tribunal declares that, in the face of the perpetration of the above-mentioned crimes by the public powers of the Guatemalan government, the Guatemalan people have the right to exercise all forms of resistance, including that of armed force, through their representative organizations, against tyrannical government powers; and that the use of armed force by the Guatemalan government to repress the resistance is illegitimate.

The New Nicaragua Critics: Social Democrats With Queasy Stomachs

The Editors

As the final chapters of this book have thoroughly documented, the counterrevolutionary apparatus mounted by the U.S. government against the revolutionary movements of Central America is massive and brutal. There are yet other forces—certainly less visible and powerful, but no less insidious—which must be addressed with particular concern by progressive North Americans.

Specifically, we are referring to the stand taken by some U.S. liberals toward the revolutionary government of Nicaragua. We are speaking of people who supported the Frente Sandinista when it was leading the struggle to overthrow the Somoza dictatorship. But today, with the Sandinista government in power and faced with resolving the difficult problems of reconstruction and eventual socialist construction in a completely hostile external environment, these liberals are turning their backs on the Nicaraguan government and people. In so doing they *objectively* side with the counterrevolution.

Let us take a very concrete example. In the January 13, 1982 issue of the newspaper *In These Times*, a member of the Democratic Socialist Organizing Committee (DSOC) wrote an article on Nicaragua entitled "Facing the 'Vanguard' Trap." It is worth quoting excerpts. The article begins:

> Democratic socialists have an unhappy and difficult responsibility: telling the Sandinistas that their conception of a "vanguard" role is almost certain to lead them into a Stalinist-type dictatorship. . . .
>
> Historically, two main paths have been traversed: a forced march under the dictatorship of a messianic elite, or the slower effort to create structural change through democratic processes. For the Sandinistas to believe that they will be able to avoid this choice is utopian.

The Bolsheviks too made efforts to live with coalitions. But they always ended up demanding subservience from their partners. The sharing of power was never genuine, because maintenance of their "vanguard" role remained the core of Bolshevik policy. The collision between sharing and the assertion of vanguard bedevilled Soviet politics until it was settled for once and for all by naked one-party rule. It is difficult to see how the Sandinistas if they persist in asserting their vanguard status can avoid a similar dénouement.

We cite this article because it does us at least the service of defining clearly the liberal position we are addressing. But the issue is *not* whether the Sandinistas are headed toward Stalinism. It is, rather, the issue of whether typewriter liberals or self-styled "democratic socialists" within the U.S. can possibly lay any claim to supporting or advancing the cause of the Central American revolutionary movements by setting themselves up as judges of the political choices which the Sandinista government has been forced to make. The issue is not just Nicaragua (or Cuba) today; it is also El Salvador and Guatemala tomorrow, because as soon as the revolutionary movements in those countries take state power, they will be faced with precisely the same choices—perhaps even more marked, because the social contradictions in those countries are even greater than in Nicaragua. And the sense of historic mission expressed by the DSOC writer when he speaks of the "unhappy and difficult responsibility" of democratic socialists to *"tell"* the Sandinistas that they are headed for a Stalinist-type dictatorship is not so different from the compulsion of U.S. government officials (under Carter as well as Reagan) to *tell* the top leadership of the Nicaraguan government what they like and don't like about the Nicaraguan Revolution.

What is it really that these liberals are calling into question? We refer here not only to members of DSOC or its successor, DSA, whose members raised the very same criticisms when they visited Nicaragua in January 1983. We refer also to a number of journalists, writers, Congressmen and others who cannot accept the closing of the opposition newspaper, *La Prensa*, for three days at a time, much less the declaration of a state of emergency provoked by escalating CIA covert operations against Nicaragua. *What they cannot accept is, in essence, the right of the Sandinistas to exert the strong centralized leadership that is essential to confront the much stronger, much more centralized government of the United States and transnational capital, which are determined to reverse the Nicaraguan Revolution.*

Let us be clear about the present situation. On the one hand, the Nicaraguan government faces three gargantuan tasks: first, reconstructing a country and an economy half-destroyed by Somoza's barbarity in the last years of the insurrection; second, overcoming decades and centuries of oppression and exploitation, which left a legacy of under-development and poverty—and overcoming them within years, not decades or centuries; and third, beginning a genuine socialist construction which can ultimately guarantee the Nicaraguan people not just food on the table and schools for their children, but full equality and an opportunity to develop their fullest potential as individual human beings and as a society.

On the other hand, the context in which these tasks are undertaken poses nothing but the most difficult obstacles. The Reagan administration is waging a full-scale war designed to overthrow the Nicaraguan Revolution. The CIA is funding, training and directing counterrevolutionary forces of former Somoza National Guardsmen to carry out daily armed aggression against the Sandinista government. At the same time, the U.S. has also waged a ceaseless propaganda war, including campaigns about violations of human rights by the Sandinistas. These include supposed human rights violations of the Miskito Indians, when in fact the CIA is using Miskitos as counterrevolutionary shock troops, and at the same time other indigenous people who have visited Nicaragua report no such violations to be taking place. Even if this were not so, we must ask: does the Reagan administration have *any* grounds for criticizing human rights violations by any other government in the world? The duplicity of the Reagan administration becomes clear from the fact that they are openly directing *Somocista* exiles in an invasion of Nicaragua, and then denouncing the Nicaraguan government for "militarizing" the country (referring to the building of a civilian militia in Nicaragua, to resist such an invasion).

Meanwhile, international capital and specifically the transnational banks are putting their own squeeze on Nicaragua by forcing repayment of the billions of dollars of *Somoza's* international debts—funds which are being diverted from the Nicaraguan people to the coffers of the transnational banks.

In sum, the Reagan administration and other sectors of the U.S. ruling class are determined to overturn the Nicaraguan Revolution—just as previous U.S. governments have tried to do or succeeded in doing so many times historically, from the Bolshevik Revolution in the Soviet Union to the Allende government in Chile. And here we come to the point: the only kind of government that has historically been able to survive against such pressures from hostile capitalist powers has been a strong, unified, centralized government. Allende made his concessions to the Chilean version of *La Prensa* and the capitalist class, and we have seen the results. It is for this reason that the current agonies of the so-called "democratic socialists" in the U.S., who are in reality bourgeois liberals, about the unified Sandinista response to Reagan's threats *objectively* serve the interests of the international ruling class and not the interests of the popular forces either in Nicaragua or in Central America generally.

This situation also has historical precedent. Indeed, it is reminiscent of the massive defection of U.S. liberals, led by Joan Baez, from support of the revolution in Vietnam, once the Vietnamese had defeated U.S. imperialism. This is not to deny the very real contradictions of socialist construction that we have all observed in Vietnam, including the intolerable role of the Vietnamese in Kampuchea and the equally intolerable invasion of Vietnam by the People's Republic of China. But none of this gives us in the United States the license to decide that we must suddenly abandon our support for the Vietnamese Revolution.

There is an even older example: the Arbenz government in Guatemala in 1954—a government that was explicitly not socialist, but was an embattled nationalist and progressive government that dared to defy U.S. interests at the height of the Cold War. Where were our fine liberals when the U.S./CIA actually intervened to overthrow that government? Many of them actively *supported* the U.S. actions. Perhaps they didn't like the fact that the Arbenz government permitted all political parties, including the Communist Party, to operate legally. Their excuse then, as now in Nicaragua, was that the Revolution was moving toward the Soviet model.

What, then, is an alternative to the stance described above? It is to recognize that the issue is not and cannot be defined as one of a revolution moving toward a Stalinist-type dictatorship. Rather, it is a question of understanding revolutionary necessity in a hostile capitalist world-economy and world order. In essence, we would maintain that this has been the issue since 1917. Understanding revolutionary necessity does not mean agreeing with or supporting every decision made by every socialist government; certainly there have been wrong decisions, i.e., decisions which did not overall maintain the integrity of the revolution or advance the process of socialist construction. But to understand these decisions and to analyze them within their historical context, and within the context of the hostile capitalist world-system, is a far cry from abandoning support of those governments once they are in power and forced to make difficult decisions.

Let us be clear that we are speaking of revolutions which overall maintain their integrity and advance the process of socialist construction. To pose it in these terms means that there are revolutions which do not maintain their integrity, and for which, therefore, at a certain point we must abandon our support. Such a case, we would submit, is the case of Iran: essentially, by promoting the slaughter of the Marxists in Iran, the CIA left no options but the creation of a new theocracy such as we see in the Khomeini government today. In such a case, we do not, of course, take the same attitude that we have indicated for Nicaragua.

A Call for Respect and Noninterference

The Editors of *Contemporary Marxism* believe strongly that the Nicaraguan Revolution is not "in danger of following the Stalinist road," as is being maintained by bourgeois liberal forces (regardless of what they call themselves) in the U.S. today. We believe that the issue in the Nicaraguan case is the right of the Nicaraguan government to mobilize its population to defend what they have won through sacrifice and struggle, to defend the integrity and the very survival of the revolution in the face of forces which are clearly determined to destroy it. For this reason, we believe that it is our obligation to speak out against the voices of defecting liberals. For this reason too, we believe that it is our obligation to strengthen the voice of a genuine proletarian internationalism, based on the respect of people in the U.S. for the right of the Nicaraguan people to resolve their own problems, without interference from the likes of the Reagan administration, and without interference from liberal ex-supporters of the Nicaraguan Revolution.

In the end, the issue is broader than Nicaragua: it involves the definition of the stance of American liberals toward events in today's world and in the U.S. more generally. In recent years, we have seen the spectacle of Susan Sontag declaring her "passionate support" for the struggle in El Salvador (before the Salvadoran resistance has taken power), while simultaneously denouncing *all* governments in which a Leninist party has taken power (*Nation*, Feb. 27, 1982), and urging the Salvadorean movement not to sing the "Internationale" in order not to contaminate itself with the history of the communist movement—that is, the history of revolutionary movements in the modern world. Such hypocrisies smack of the politics of the good liberals in the 1950s, who collaborated with the CIA abroad and abandoned the workers' movement within the U.S. The issue is, then, one of *American* politics as much as of support for Nicaragua and El Salvador.

Contributors

C. Martínez F. is the pen name of a Guatemalan sociologist, specializing in contemporary political affairs, and a leading spokesman for the struggles in Guatemala and Central America for liberty and social justice.

Edelberto Torres-Rivas, who was born in Guatemala, was the organizer and first director of the Social Sciences Program of CSUCA (Consejo Superior Universitario Centroamericano) and of the journal *Estudios Sociales Centroamericanos*. He has directed research programs in Argentina, Mexico and Chile, and is currently in Costa Rica doing research on the formation of the national state in Central America. He is the author of various works on political development, the Central American Common Market and other topics.

Ruy Mauro Marini, who is Brazilian and worked for a number of years in Chile, is currently in Mexico directing the work of the Centro de Información, Documentación y Análisis sobre el Movimiento Obrero Latinoamericano (CIDAMO). He is the author of numerous works on Latin America, including *Subdesarrollo y Revolución* and *Dialéctica de la Dependencia*.

Pablo González Casanova, ex-rector of the Universidad Nacional Autónoma de México (UNAM) and a leading Mexican sociologist, is currently at the Instituto de Investigaciones Sociales of UNAM. He is the author of *La democracia en México, Sociología de la explotación, Imperialismo y liberación en América Latina* and works on the state and political parties in Mexico.

James F. Petras, Professor of Sociology at the State University of New York, Binghamton, is a renowned expert on Latin America and international affairs. His books include *Class, State and Power in the Third World* (Allan, Heald, Osmun, 1981).

Morris H. Morley holds a doctorate in sociology from the State University of New York at Binghamton. He is the co-author of *The U.S. and Chile* and *The Nationalization of Venezuelan Oil*, and has written extensively on Third World development and U.S. foreign policy towards Latin America.

Philip E. Wheaton is the Director of EPICA (Ecumenical Program for Interamerican Communications and Action). EPICA serves as an advisory group to the Committee on the Caribbean and Latin America of the National Council of Churches. Wheaton, who has 12 years of experience in the Caribbean and Central America, is also a member of the National Advisory Committee of CISPES (Committee in Solidarity With the People of El Salvador).

Antonio Cavalla Rojas, a Chilean, is now a professor and researcher at the Universidad Autónoma de México (UNAM); President of the Latin American Research Council for Peace (Latin American Affiliate of the International Peace Research Association Council—IPRA); a leader of the Izquierda Cristiana of Chile. His recent books include *E.E.U.U., Fuerzas Armadas y Defensa Nacional* and *Cristianismo y Política en América Latina.*

ABOUT THE EDITORS

Marlene Dixon, noted author and organizer, is editor of the journal *Contemporary Marxism* and director of the Institute for the Study of Militarism and Economic Crisis. *Susanne Jonas* has written extensively on Central America and is a staff member of the Institute.

Index

Peasants
  in Guatemalan Revolution, 9
People's Leagues (LP-28), (El Salvador),
  42, 44, 167
People's Revolutionary Army – Party of the
  Salvadorean Revolution (ERP – PRS),
  43, 44
Peralta Azurdia, Colonel, 287
Permanent Committee of Intellectuals for
  Sovereignty of the Peoples of Our
  America, 117
Permanent Council of the Armed Forces
  (COPEFA), (El Salvador), 239
Permanent People's Tribunal, 68, 281, 317
Peru
  and El Salvador, 61
Petras, James, 180, 321
Petty bourgeoisie, 177, 229
  and Guatemalan union leadership, 10
  and guerrilla movements, 25
  in counterrevolutionary strategy, 322
  urban, and Guatemalan Revolution, 9
Pezullo, Lawrence, 247
Policía Militar Ambulante (Guatemala), 288
Political-Military Coordinating Council
  (El Salvador), 42-43
Popular Armed Forces of Liberation
  (FAPL), (El Salvador), 47-48
Popular Liberation Forces – Farabundo
  Martí (FPL), (El Salvador), 42, 44,
  47-48, 167
Popular Revolutionary Bloc (BPR), (El
  Salvador), 40, 42-43, 167
Popular Social Christian Movement (El
  Salvador), 61, 268
Private Enterprise Council (COSEP),
  (Nicaragua), 113
Proceso, 56
Proletarianization, 21, 24, 144, 198
Prosterman, Roy, 244 (quoted)
"Public Safety Program" (OPS), 288
Punto Final, 69

Radio Venceremos, 81, 83, 98-100
Ramírez Mercado, Sergio, 106, 226
  (quoted)
Rapid Deployment Force, 268-69
Reagan Administration, 28, 37-39, 65, 173,
  210-13
  and transnationalists, 321
  on Guatemala, 130, 152-53, 299, 309,
  317
  policy on Latin America, 271-75,
  282-84, 313
  pressures on Germany, France, and
  England, 60
Rebel Armed Forces (FAR), (Guatemala),
  128, 153, 167
Refugees, 55
Regional security assistance
  See Iron Triangle

Regional Telecommunications Center
  (Guatemala), 314
Republican Party
  platform on Sandinista government, 27,
  227, 232
Revolutionary Coordinating Council of the
  Masses (CRM), (El Salvador), 42-44, 71,
  166
  and Municipal Committees, 42
  and People's Committees, 42
  and Precinct Committees, 42
Revolutionary Federation of Unions (FSR),
  (El Salvador), 45
Revolutionary Party (Guatemala), 266
Revolutionary People's Army (ERP), 69
Ríos Montt, General Efraín, 126, 171, 284,
  291-92, 313, 320
Robelo, Alfonso, 112, 226
Rockefeller, David, 320
Romero, General Carlos Humberto, 50, 207,
  238
Roosevelt, Franklin Delano, 3, 4
Runaway industries, 18, 221
  and free trade zones, 19, 21, 302
Rural Workers Association (ATC),
  (Nicaragua), 115

Salazar, Jorge, 114
Salvadorean Agrarian Reform Institute
  (ISTA), 247
Salvadorean Federation of Unions of
  Workers in Food, Clothing, Textile and
  Related Industries (FESTIAVTCES), 45
Salvadorean Institute for Agrarian
  Transformation, 270
Salvadorean Revolution, 56
Sanders, Jerry, 11 (cited)
Sandinismo, 106, 107
Sandinista Defense Committees, 113, 115
Sandinista National Liberation Front
  (FSLN), 1, 3, 23, 112, 155, 166-68, 177,
  219, 250
  support of by German Social
  Democracy, 28
  third force strategy of, 173
Sandinista People's Army, 112, 121
Sandinista Workers Central (CST), 115
Sandino, Augusto César, 2, 3, 107
Sandoval Alarcón, Mario, 162, 245, 266
Sherwood, Fred, 303 (quoted)
Smith, Wayne, 293-94 (quoted)
Social Christian Party (Nicaragua), 114
Socialism
  constraints on socialist construction, 32,
  332-36
  in Central American revolutionary
  movements, 31
  in postrevolutionary Guatemala, 322-23
  of Sandinista Front, 110
Socialist International, 61, 65, 69, 305-06
  (quoted)